90-01-16

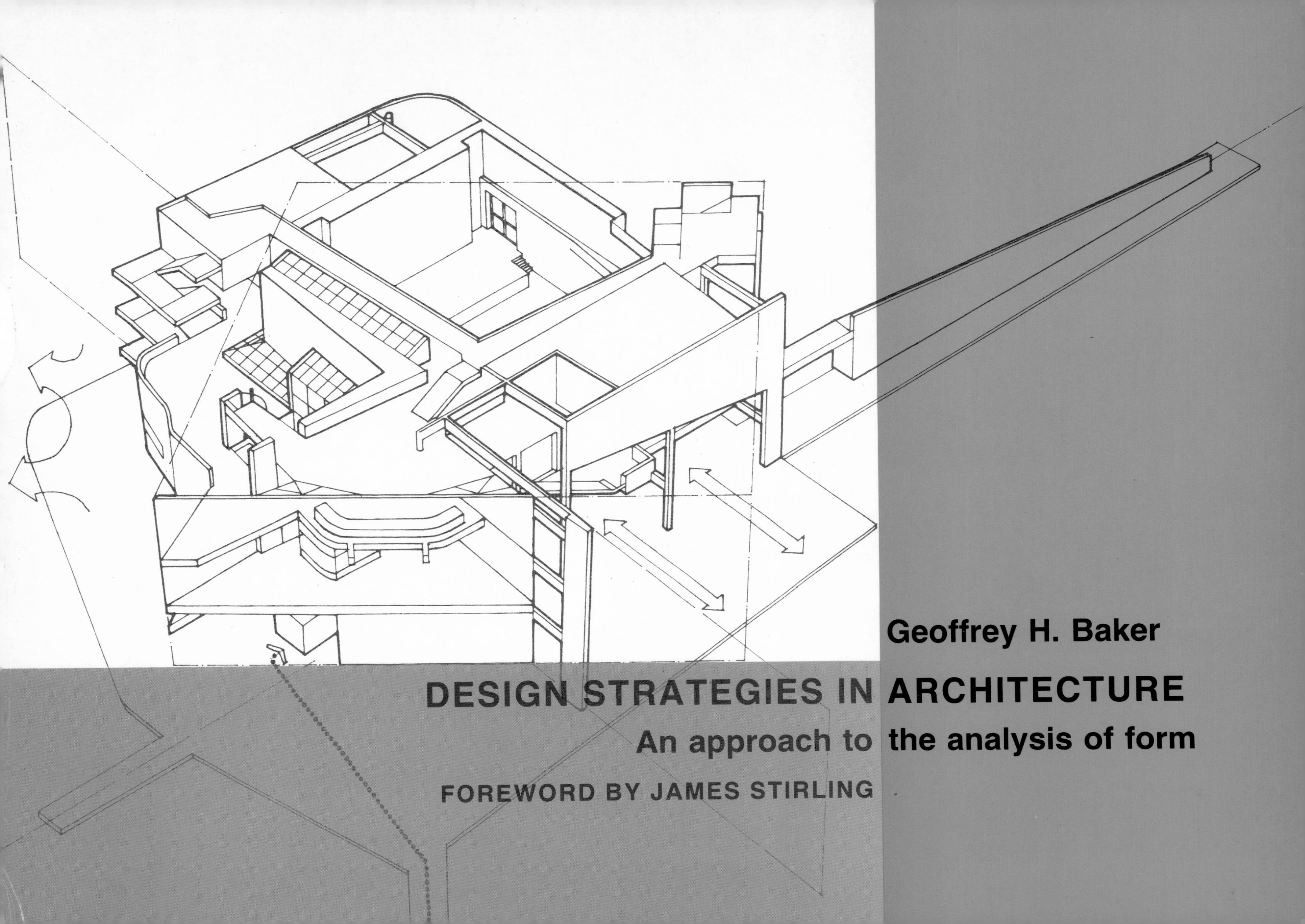

Geoffrey H. Baker

DESIGN STRATEGIES IN ARCHITECTURE

An approach to the analysis of form

FOREWORD BY JAMES STIRLING

DESIGN STRATEGIES IN ARCHITECTURE

DESIGN STRATEGIES IN ARCHITECTURE

an approach to the analysis of form

Geoffrey H. Baker
School of Architecture,
Tulane University, New Orleans

Van Nostrand Reinhold (International)

First published in 1989 by
Van Nostrand Reinhold (International) Co. Ltd
11 New Fetter Lane, London EC4P 4EE

Printed in Hong Kong

ISBN 0 7476 0041 4

British Library Cataloguing in Publication Data

Baker, Geoffrey H. (Geoffrey Howard)
Design strategies in architecture : an approach to the analysis of form.
1. Architecture
I. Title
720

ISBN 0-7476-0041-4

Illustrations and text which form part of the analysis of James Stirling's proposal for the extension to the National Gallery have previously appeared in the January and February 1987 editions of Architectural Design Magazine, and appear here by kind permission of Academy Editions.

To Kieran, for all your encouragement and enthusiasm

CONTENTS

ACKNOWLEDGEMENTS

This book draws together a selection of analytical material produced over two decades by myself and by students under my direction. I must give special mention to Simon Buckley, whose perceptive analyses of Warkworth, Siena and Assisi[1] have formed the basis of these studies in part two.

I am also indebted to Jeremy Blake, who has made an important contribution to the analysis of the Town Hall at Säynätsalo, and to students of the School of Architecture at the University of Arkansas who produced useful analytical work during my period of teaching at Fayetteville. All these studies have informed my research.

I must also thank Gordon Brooks for his coordination of the computer modelling which helped me to draw the diagrams of Richard Meier's Atheneum, and Beth Ledford and Chad Edby who generated the computer images.[2]

Although their work is not discussed in this book, and analyses of their buildings were done without consultation, I must thank Peter Ahrends, Richard Burton and Paul Koralek for invaluable feedback which has influenced the development of the analytical methodology.

Thanks are due to Ellen Weiss for help with the manuscript, and Margaret Hudson, Christine Hilker and Jean Middleton, librarians at the Universities of Newcastle-upon-Tyne, the University of Arkansas and Brighton Polytechnic, for all their help.

[1] 'Symbolism, situation and architecture: shifting emphases in making places.' Dissertation by Simon Buckley at the University of Newcastle-upon-Tyne, 1971.

[2] Atheneum : Analysis of Form, video, written and presented by Geoffrey Baker and produced by Gordon Brooks at the University of Arkansas, 1988.

PREFACE

T. S. Eliot has asserted that 'comparison and analysis are the chief tools of the critic,'[1] pointing out that for the author, the creative act is composed of critical labour, 'the labour of sifting, combining, constructing, expressing, correcting, testing: this frightful toil is as much critical as creative.'[2] He goes on to point out 'that some creative writers are superior to others because their critical faculty is superior.'[3]

This is true for all the arts. Composition, whether in music, literature or the visual arts demands opposite poles – the extension of ideas by the imagination, and selection from such ideas by an informed critical faculty. In linking analysis with criticism, Eliot underscores a key issue in creativity, namely the way analysis extends the critical frame of reference by giving the creator an enhanced awareness of attainable standards within his discipline. When Le Corbusier laid the foundations for his life's work by meticulously charting compositional techniques in Florentine frescos and Romanesque facades, he was simultaneously developing his range of ideas and sharpening his critical faculty.

With his influential publication Vers une Architecture, Le Corbusier propounded his philosophy by a series of observations based on analysis. Four decades later, a no less important book, again based largely on analysis, appeared in the form of Robert Venturi's Complexity and Contradiction in Architecture. Each book demonstrates the link between analysis and creativity in the resultant work of their authors and in each case there is an affirmation of Eliot's position regarding the relationship of the present to the past. Eliot explains how the poet 'must inevitably be judged by the standards of the past,'[4] and how 'the whole of the literature of his own country has a simultaneous existence and comprises a simultaneous order. This historical sense, which is a sense of the timeless as well as the temporal and of the timeless and the temporal together, is what makes a writer traditional.'[5]

Christian Norberg-Schulz has explained how 'architecture has a particular ability to

[1] T. S. Eliot: Selected Essays 1917-32, New York, 1932, p. 21
[2] Ibid., p. 18 [3] Ibid., p. 18 [4] Ibid., p. 5 [5] Ibid., p. 4

show how our values, how our cultural traditions determine our daily life. Only through cultural symbolization can architecture show that daily life has a meaning which transcends the immediate situation, that it forms part of a cultural and historic continuity. The other arts are not able to fulfil this task in the same way, because they do not so directly participate in our daily existence.'[1]

In supporting Eliot's position regarding analysis, I also share both his and Norberg Schulz' view of the significance of the historical dimension. I believe that architecture has a unique cultural role and that its practicality, symbolic content and relationship with its context make considerable demands on both architect and analyst. The situation is further complicated by the intuitive nature of the design process, this denying a scientific approach to the analysis of design.

It is for this reason that the approach to analysis outlined in this book focuses not on process but on the outcome of the process. The creative act is mysterious, a mixture of logic and instincts that may extend over short or long periods of time. This is a worthy area of study, but if the task is seen as the discovery of design strategies and tactics, I have always preferred to examine the completed work, in which the cul-de-sacs have been eliminated, along with the client's changes of mind and revisions to the budget. I have always found that the final work most clearly reveals the direction and purpose of the designer.

The analytical approach, therefore, seeks to investigate design principles by means of dissection, intending thereby to discuss design in an ordered way. The form of presentation may be thought of as showing how a design evolves in the mind of the designer; this however is not the case. Generally speaking I believe analysis is best done as an independent study without contact or collaboration with the architect concerned.

[1] Christian Norberg Schulz: Intentions in Architecture, Cambridge, Mass., 1965, p. 126.

As a form of interpretation, analysis must be subjective and, to an extent, speculative. The subjective element is as intuitive as the act of designing, to which it can be compared. But whereas in designing, the final outcome is in view in the distance as an unformulated concept, taking its shape by exploration and experiment, analysis starts with the whole, and, by dissection, gradually reveals relationships within the work.

The approach to analysis outlined in these pages takes as its starting point the generic form on which subsequent developments are based.[1] In so doing, the analysis attempts to show how various factors concerning the site and programme have led to a series of transformations of the form. This, as explained, is for reasons of clarity and does not intend to show how the design came into being. Elemental relationships are discussed in terms of their context, paying special attention to movement towards and through spaces.

Many different kinds of architectural analysis are possible. Each interpretation will be coloured by the analyst's view of his subject. As a clarification of my own position, and as an introduction to the analytical studies, part one summarises the philosophical background which has informed the analytical approach. In part two, case studies demonstrate how the technique may be applied to aspects of the city and to individual buildings.

In most books diagrams support the text. In the analytical section this is reversed and diagrams become the main means of communication. I have drawn all the diagrams myself, because, as an architect I see the analytical process almost as design in reverse. These three-dimensional explorations chart the inherent energy in a design, identifying those strategies and tactics used by the designer. Like design itself, this is a process of discovery which involves to-ing and fro-ing from the whole to the parts and back again. By such means the deeper structures and hidden relationships are revealed.

With diagrams as the basis of the analyses, it seems consistent to handwrite the text

[1] Generic is seen as primary form in its original state; this fundamental form is usually square, cubic or rectilinear.

so as to achieve the closest possible connection between text and imagery. One should belong to the other. The double page horizontal format enables a point to be made by several means simultaneously. Sometimes it is necessary to use a plan, axonometric and a diagram to explain relationships fully and clearly. 'Headlining' forms part of the same strategy, intended as an aid to clarity and comprehension.

Geoffrey H. Baker.

FOREWORD

I was surprised and delighted when Geoffrey Baker's analysis of our design for the National Gallery extension appeared in Architectural Design (January and February editions, 1987), and I am pleased he has included it in this publication.

I felt he had 'understood' most of the formal design moves we made in evolving the scheme — indeed he interpreted several design subtleties which I only felt intuitively, and until his exposition had not fully perceived. It seems he is able to clarify and describe a work of Modern Architecture in ways that others such as Wittkower have been able to do for historic buildings.

Surely his method and skill in explaining the design intentions which lead to the appearance of a new building is of more value to the public than the gratuitous jottings of the architectural journalists, who seem always (in the U.K.) to be writing from predetermined and irrelevant viewpoints. An exception (in the U.S.) is Ada Louise Huxtable who is able to visit a building without dragging behind her a sackful of prejudices.

Dr. Baker's article on the National Gallery project was like a breeze of fresh air, and I believe his ability to analyse and explain an architect's formal ambitions en route to a building form should be a basic credential and a responsibility for architectural writers, and should form a foundation for their criticism.

So I hope that Dr. Baker's skill will be appreciated by a new generation of architectural critics, that they will have a deeper and more sophisticated understanding of the design process related to a particular building, and that they will be able to communicate this to the intelligent reader who is surely striving to understand Modern Architecture.

For architectural students this publication is, of course, essential study matter.

James Stirling.

Salzburg : view of the city and castle

PROLOGUE

Unlike painting music or literature, architecture is of the earth. It belongs to the ground as a container for the activities of man and as such is part of his very existence. This intrinsic link is evident in the basic need for shelter— buildings give shelter and in so doing engage architecture in man's survival against the hostile forces of nature.

Architecture therefore becomes involved in emotional and practical needs that are quite different to the needs that are met by technology. A car, a radio, a TV, are not necessary in the way that buildings are, so architecture has a different role and can represent significant areas of life. Although concerned with space, form and the satisfaction of functional demands, arguably architecture's primary role is symbolic. Alone among the arts it can express the idea of government, the church or the monarchy — it can also symbolize home.

So architecture is quite distinct from the other arts, which can all be dispensed with. We can remove a painting, choose when to listen to music, leave a book on a shelf. Architecture is not like that because it creates not only the framework for personal or family life, it creates the framework for national life and thereby represents the prime characteristics of a culture.

A civilization can best be understood by its architecture because of the way buildings show the interests of a society, its organizational skills, affluence or poverty, the kind of climate and the attitude towards technology and the arts. In towns and cities the general structure of society can be understood through the medium of architecture, so it becomes the most pervasive mirror of man's presence.

Importantly, and again unlike the other arts, architecture exists in relation to two sets of conditions; on the one hand buildings must respond to fundamental issues such as the need for shelter and for ideas to be symbolized, whilst on the other they must relate to a region, to a specific location, to topography, to the path of the sun, to variations of temperature, to the movement of people.

How then can architecture be understood? How can it be examined? To what, primarily does it respond? Broadly speaking, there are three key factors which affect architecture; buildings must respond to site conditions, functional requirements and to the culture in which they find themselves. Regarding the latter, the state of advancement of the culture will affect the kind of structure and materials used. To understand buildings, all three of these factors must be taken into account and this becomes possible by analysis.

In any analysis of architecture it is convenient to consider the various factors as forces, and to begin with, because buildings are set on the ground, the topography should be examined. Here the forces are clearly apparent — a river is a force, a road is a force, a hill is a force, trees are a force, the climate is a force — and there are many subtle gradings of these forces.

Similarly, taking the second key factor outlined above, in satisfying functional needs, the organization of a building may also be considered in terms of its force characteristics. Form may be either linear or centroidal, static or dynamic. A tower for example may be thought of as a dynamic vertical force or a bridge as a static horizontal force, a castle may be seen as a centroidal defensive force.

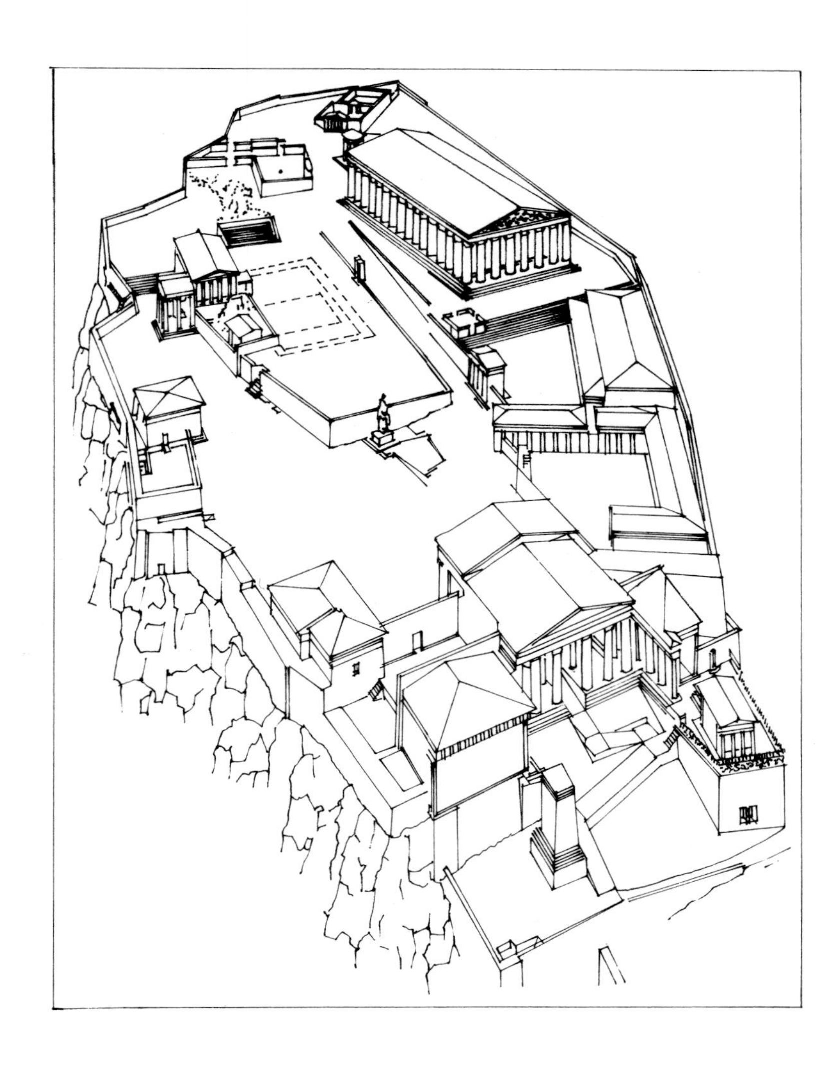

The third important factor which affects architecture is the force exerted by a culture. In Ancient Greece a particular culture evolved in relation to a special set of circumstances at a particular time. Attitudes developed in the areas of religion, philosophy, science, mathematics technology and art which led to an architecture which represented the main ideas of the culture.

Although we can understand the Greek civilization through the combined media of say art, philosophy and literature, architecture, by its special role draws these together so that they become embodied in buildings. The cultural forces are encapsulated in the architecture and it is not coincidental that this architecture and the cultural values which it represents have endured to the present day.

This crystalization of cultural forces in buildings has happened throughout history and in our own time the glass skyscraper represents vital features of the twentieth century, symbolizing our technological capacity and key concerns much as did the pyramids, the Greek temple or Gothic cathedral.

Athens : The Acropolis
A reconstruction according to G.P. Stevens

As a designer . . . I believe that what was, what is, and what will always be has always been. And from this position I see no discontinuity in architecture through the ages, from Greece, to Rome, to Romanesque, to Gothic, to the Renaissance . . . These periods have the quality of a great continuum although the circumstances which led to each period with its different characteristics were not the same at the specific time of these styles.

Louis I. Kahn, Architect's Challenge: Find Continuity: Kahn, Poet, Artist, Planner speaks of T.V. The Times Picayune, March 3, 1972, p. 8.

PART ONE

PRINCIPLES OF ANALYSIS

1

THE ROLE OF ARCHITECTURE

FORCES

In his study of place, Genius Loci, Towards a Phenomenology of Architecture, Christian Norberg Schulz explains the basic act of architecture as being 'to understand the vocation of the place.'[1] He describes the need 'to concretise the genius loci ... by means of buildings which gather the properties of the place and bring them close to man.'[2] Throughout the book Norberg Schulz draws out those features of topography and landscape which give a special character to places and shows how architecture can respond by creating a meaningful environment.

In his discussion Norberg Schulz constantly refers to man-made and natural forces as when he describes the siting of Prague as comprising 'all the main natural forces, undulating plain, rocky hills and water,'[3] explaining how the architecture in the city manages to embody this.

In the study, Norberg Schulz first identifies the characteristics of the region, showing how the city became a nodal point where a road from Ucrania and Poland which crossed the Vltava into Germany met the road from Austria in the south to Saxony and Prussia. He describes how Prague is situated on an extended hill which rises at the curve of the river; the hill and the river being 'opposed but complimentary forces.'[4]

[1] C. Norberg Schulz Genius Loci, Towards a Phenomenology of Architecture New York 1980 p. 23 [2] Ibid. p. 23 [3] Ibid. p. 99 [4] Ibid. p. 83.

Rome is seen as being at 'the centre of a landscape which contains everything,'[5] with the Piazza Navona demonstrating that the ideal equilibrium between nature and the culture has been achieved:

> At Piazza Navona we are really 'inside,' close to the earth, close to the palpable things of everyday existence, at the same time as we feel part of a comprehensive cultural totality. No wonder it has become the popular place of Rome _par excellence_. The synthesis of nature is condensed and visualized in Bernini's great fountain, where natural elements such as water and rocks are combined with human figures and religious symbols, as well as the _axis mundi_ of the obelisk. In front of the church of S. Agnese, finally, we find another characteristic Roman element, a broad flight of stairs. In Rome, stairs are not used to create a distance between different existential realms; rather they represent the articulation of the ground itself. The great Roman stairs bring us close to the earth and increase our sense of belonging to the place.

Rome: Piazza Navona

[5] C. Norberg Schulz, _Genius Loci, Towards a Phenomenology of Architecture_, New York, 1980. p. 164.

NATURE

In an essay discussing the relationship between art and nature, art and the world, John Berger argues that 'Nature is energy and struggle. It is what exists without any promise ... as an arena, a setting, it has to be thought of as one which lends itself as much to evil as to good. Its energy is fearsomely indifferent.'[1] He goes on to argue that we sense beauty because it is such a contrast to our struggle against nature.

> It is within this bleak natural context that beauty is encountered, and the encounter is by its nature sudden and unpredictable. The gale blows itself out ... Under the fallen boulder of an avalanche a flower grows ... beauty is always an exception, always despite of. This is why it moves us.

Berger asserts that the kind of aesthetic emotion we feel before a man-made object derives from the emotion we feel before nature :

> All the languages of art have been developed as an attempt to transform the instantaneous into the permanent. Art supposes that beauty is not an exception — is not despite of — but is the basis for an order.
> Art is an organized response to what nature allows us to glimpse occaisionally. Art sets out to transform the potential recognition into an increasing one.[2]

[1] John Berger. An article in The Guardian, December 30th 1985, p. 9

In his discussion Berger relates his argument to a white wooden bird, hung by peasants in their kitchens in certain regions of Czechoslovakia, Russia and the Baltic countries. These birds somehow manage to act as 'mediators' between man and nature.

As Berger explains, their figurative form, that of a dove, makes a direct reference to the world of nature. Being located indoors (where birds are not usually found) renders the object symbolic. Then there is respect for the way the material, wood, has been fashioned. There is also unity and economy in the object, a richness resulting from its design. Finally there is wonder as to how the object is made. This sense of mystery, the fine craftsmanship, provoke an aesthetic 'emotion.' Thus does man 'transform' nature into a work of art.

In a discussion of the cave paintings in Spain and southern France, Dr. Jacob Bronowski suggests that these works by early man 'act as a kind of telescope tube of the imagination; they direct the mind from what has been seen to what can be inferred or conjectured.' [1]

He explains how art and science are both human actions deriving from the ability to visualise the future, playing a vital part in cultural evolution, which he describes as 'a constant growing and widening of the human imagination.' [2]

[1] J. Bronowski, The Ascent of Man, London, 1973, p. 54. [2] Ibid., p 56.

ART AS SYMBOL

The link between art and man's emotions has been pursued by Susanne K. Langer, who has given her own definition of art: 'Art is the creation of forms symbolic of human feeling.'[1] She explains the importance of the term 'creation' because it is the creative act that produces the work of art. Merely to produce something is not enough; to erect a house is a mechanical act which is not the same as creating a work of architecture.

Discussing the content of forms Langer argues that what matters is their import so that they become 'logically expressive or significant forms. They are symbols for the articulation of feeling and convey the elusive and yet familiar pattern of sentience.'[2] The symbolic element is of the greatest importance because Langer asserts that art is always a symbol. 'In an articulate symbol, the symbolic import permeates the whole structure, because every articulation of that structure is an articulation of the idea it conveys.'[3]

Langer insists that in order to create significant form with an appropriate symbolic content an intellectual dimension is necessary. 'Works of art are made of sensuous elements, but not all sensuous elements will do.'[4] They must be capable of assemblage in the right kind of combinations; as symbols, works of art must communicate directly and immediately. 'An articulate form must be clearly given and understood before it can convey any import,' and 'the congruence of the symbolic form and the form of some vital experience must be directly perceived by the force of the Gestalt alone. Hence the paramount importance of abstracting the form, banning all irrelevancies that might obscure its logic, and especially divesting it of its usual meanings so it may be open to new ones.'[5]

1 S. K. Langer, Feeling and Form, A Theory of Art, London 1953, p. 40 2 Ibid., p 52 3 Ibid., p 52
4 Ibid., p. 56 5 Ibid., p 59.

Pagoda, Yasaka 1618

POETRY

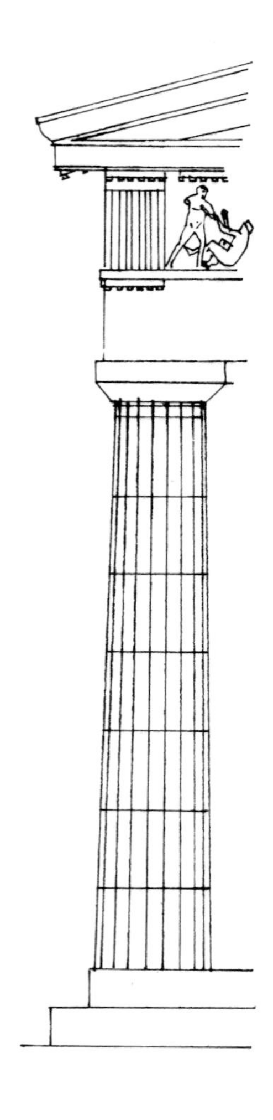

This discussion of art may be compared to Norberg Schulz's assertion that 'the fundamental function of art is to gather the contradictions and complexities of the life world.' Quoting Heidegger he goes on to explain how man must dwell on this earth 'poetically'. 'Only poetry in all its forms (also as in the art of living) makes human existence meaningful, and meaning is the fundamental human need.' [1]

To Christian Norberg Schulz 'architecture belongs to poetry' [2] and attains a poetic dimension when 'buildings gather the properties of the place and bring them close to man.' [3] As such architecture is also art, responding, as Berger insists, to man's desire to prolong the instantaneous into the permanent and to create order out of the chaos of nature.

It was in Ancient Greece, where the landscape is such that it became possible to identify the different characteristics of places, that man personified particular places as gods. Open air altars were formed so that man could contemplate a sacred landscape. Temples later gave form to this by extending the personification of the gods into an appropriate symbolic dimension.

Doric order column and entablature The Thesion Athens. 449-444 B.C.

[1] Norberg Schulz *Op. Cit.*, p. 23. [2] Ibid., p. 23. [3] Ibid., p. 23.

The Parthenon crystallizes the cultural intentions of the Greeks by its siting, its presence, its precision and order. The frieze and pediments portray important aspects of Greek life.

As an art work the Parthenon demonstrates Berger's mystery and permanence, realising Norberg Schulz's 'vocation' of place whilst also manifesting Heidegger's poetic dimension. Like the Egyptian pyramid and Gothic cathedral it gives meaning through form to a central idea shared by a culture.

The Parthenon Athens 449-444 B.C.
architects Ictinus and Callicrates

Through its dedication to gods and goddesses, personified in human form, Greek architecture embraces human characteristics, with the masculinity of Doric and feminine associations with Ionic. Moreover, the Greek temple in its articulation presents a unified whole in which every part relates to a central idea, being linked to each other by a proportional system. The Greek temple therefore brings together man, nature and the gods in a comprehensive representation of the values of a culture.

MEANINGS IN USE

The Greek temple exemplifies the important distinction between a work of art for its own sake such as a painting or a piece of sculpture, and a work of architecture, which must serve a purpose.

Colin St. John Wilson quotes Alberti to emphasize that architecture 'is born of necessity'[1] and explains the unique nature of architecture as being that it is

> a special form of art — the transformation of utility into icon . . . It is, however, a condition of this transformation that its origins lie in use, are humble, always some need to shelter or enframe some action or object special to its culture, and that if it loses its roots in that necessity it loses its status as a transforming agent.[2]

Wilson insists that the meaning of architecture lies in use, and that buildings only come into being to serve the needs of a culture. He asserts that

> the limits of an architecture are the limits of the culture that it serves. It is the embodiment of values that have been worked out before by a culture in all its levels of awareness (religious, political, economic). The cathedral did not invent religion![3]

[1] L. B. Alberti: Ten Books on Architecture; bk I ch IX.
[2] Colin St John Wilson 'The Play of Use and the Use of Play' Architectural Review July 1986, p. 17. [3] Ibid. p. 18

Wilson points out that architecture must serve the needs of society in two ways, first

> to set up a spatial order that makes possible the fulfilment of manifold operations in an <u>effective way</u>. This is the base of common use.
>
> Second, to bring to life an order of representation that embodies those occaisions so that they can be recognised in an <u>intelligible</u> way. [1]

If we consider either the great monuments of civilisation or the humblest dwellings, we may relate them to Wilson's assertion that architecture 'transforms utility to a level above that of necessity and thereby invents forms that truly celebrate a "way of life."' [2] He concludes this argument by quoting Wittgenstein's proclamation:

> Where there is nothing to glorify there can be no architecture [3]

ARCH OF TITUS ROME A.D. 82

1 St John Wilson, Op. Cit., p. 18 2 Ibid., p. 18 3 Ibid., p. 18 (taken from L. Wittgenstein, <u>Culture and Value</u>, p. 69).

PRIMITIVE ARCHITECTURE

Banani a cliff debris-type village of the Dogon
Timbuktu Africa

Discussing the way house forms evolve, Amos Rapoport explains how in Primitive societies everyone is capable of building his own dwelling, with the average family having all the technical knowledge that is needed.[1]

This also means that the needs of the dwelling are understood perfectly with certain ways of doing or not doing things. Rapoport points out how

> Certain forms are taken for granted and strongly resist change, since societies like these tend to be very tradition oriented. This explains the close relationship between the forms and the culture in which they are embedded, and also the fact that some of these forms persist for very long periods of time.[2]

The Dogon live in a series of compact villages on ledges and rocky slopes at the foot of cliffs near Timbuktu. The villages are formed of houses and granaries, crops being stored in the granaries. Each man and woman has at least one personal granary. Houses and granaries are built by the men assisted by male members of his family and those of his neighborhood.[3]

[1] Amos Rapoport, House form and culture, New Jersey, 1969. p. 3 [2] Ibid., p 4.

[3] For a full discussion of this see Aldo van Eyck's essays 'The Interior of Time' and 'A Miracle of Moderation', Meaning In Architecture edited by Charles Jencks and George Baird, London 1969 p.p. 171, 173.

VERNACULAR ARCHITECTURE

In Vernacular architecture the process of evolution using a model continues with adjustments and variations. The dwelling is now built by tradesmen. Vernacular architecture does not have theoretical or aesthetic pretensions and models develop in accordance with regional, climatic and economic factors.

Although in some ways limited, Vernacular models can be easily modified. This adaptability and the widely understood meanings inherent in such stereotypes ensures their authoritative role in society. In Britain and other derivative cultures the popularity and acceptance given to the neo-Georgian and neo-Tudor models indicate a strong preference for tradition. Such models have stood the test of time and are effective in both a practical and symbolic sense, far more so than the work of individual designers.

Rapoport explains the nature of folk architecture:

> The folk tradition... is the direct and unselfconscious translation into physical form of a culture, its needs and values — as well as the needs dreams and passions of a people... The folk tradition is more closely related to the culture of the majority and life as it is really lived than is the grand design tradition which represents the culture of the elite.[1]

Terrace housing in Brighton

[1] Rapoport Op. Cit., p. 2.

MONUMENTAL ARCHITECTURE

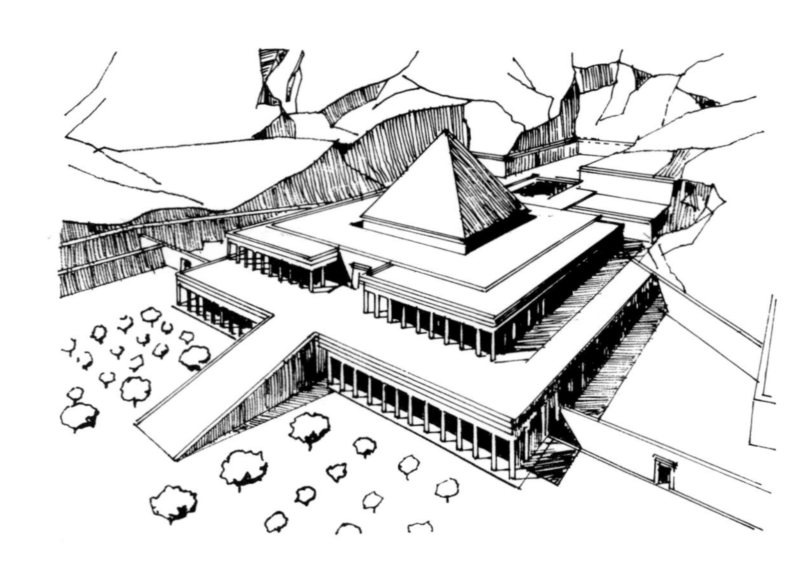

Funerary temple of Mentuhetep Dêr el Bahari 2065 B.C.

Historically, monumental architecture has given form to the collective ideals of a culture and has designated the hierarchical structure of society. Buildings such as the pyramid or temple acquired their symbolic role and conviction as a result of a long period of evolution.

This monumental architecture was concerned far more with its symbolic content than with utilitarian function, and in drawing upon greater resources and skills than ordinary buildings its course of development has been materially different.

The Egyptian Temple and Pyramids clearly demonstrate the principle which governs the development of monumental architecture. Such buildings tend to be wasteful in human resources, requiring a very considerable input of labour. They were built to impress rather than to inhabit and came into being as a result of the organizational skills that can only be supplied by a specialist, the designer or architect.

Because the role of monumental architecture has been primarily to communicate meanings of a very specific kind the forms are arranged in ways that give a high priority to aesthetic effects.

Whereas traditionally dwellings for the mass of the population assume meaning by fulfilling functional requirements related to protection and survival, it has been the function of monumental architecture to convey meanings concerned with ideals and status. Amos Rapoport has explained the phenomenon as:

> Monuments — buildings of the grand design tradition — are built to impress either the populace with the power of the patron, or the peer group of designers and cognoscenti with the cleverness of the designer and good taste of the patron. [1]

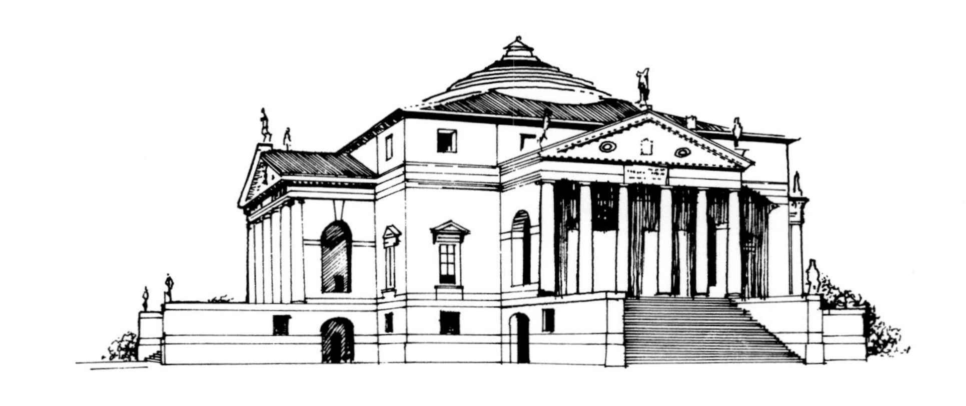

Villa Capra : Vicenza 1549 architect Andrea Palladio

Buildings such as the Villa Capra may be regarded as High Art. Such buildings demonstrate compositional principles based on theoretical propositions. A symmetrical arrangement ensures order, a system of proportional relationships ensures harmony, and the deployment of the classical language communicates meanings associated with elegance and enduring quality. There is a high degree of abstraction inherent in such works compared with the more practical concerns of the ordinary dwelling.

[1] Rapoport Op. Cit. p. 2.

CULTURE

In a discussion of the relationship between the individual and society, C. Norberg Schulz explains how satisfactory cultural integration depends on the existence of common symbol-systems :

> From birth we try to orientate ourselves in the environment and establish a certain order. A common order is called culture. The development of culture is based on information and education and therefore depends on the existence of common symbol-systems. The culture integrates the single personality into an ordered world based on meaningful interactions. [1]

From the earliest times man has used language as his basic form of communication, a system whereby words have a meaning understood by all within an ordered grammatical framework. The inadequacy of words to express certain meanings has led to the development of non-verbal communication systems whose purpose is to assist and extend comprehension of aspects of experience. Science, the arts and music each extend our understanding of the world by means of constructions not possible within language alone, and architecture gives meaning to aspects of life that cannot adequately be conveyed by words.

[1] C. Norberg Schulz 'Meaning in Architecture,' Meaning in Architecture (edited by C Jencks and G. Baird) London, 1969. p. 220

STATUS

Honington Hall Warwickshire England c. 1685

Architecture has always played a leading role in the way an individual may be identified within a culture and certain styles evolved during the later middle ages which were concerned with status within the social hierarchy.

Status may depend on different things in the various strata of society but for the landowners and aristocracy of seventeenth century England it was important to demonstrate a subtle combination of wealth, power and good taste.

This need was met perfectly with the introduction of Italian Renaissance architecture into the country by Inigo Jones. The style was based on the work of Andrea Palladio in and near Vicenza, and the classical principles embodied in his villas were interpreted in a manner appropriate to the English landscape and climate.

Classical proportions, symmetry and the use of certain kinds of ornament and sculpture led to an architectural style whose meaning was shared by a social group. So effective was this particular symbol-system that it still pervades the English-speaking cultures as the neo-Georgian style.

PROGRAMME AND SITE

Sydney Opera House 1973 architect Jorn Utzon

In his seminal work, Complexity and contradiction in architecture Robert Venturi explains that architecture occurs at the meeting of interior and exterior forces of use and space.' This interaction is one of the basic generators of architectural form as demonstrated in Jorn Utzon's Sydney Opera House in which the particular function and location inspired an extravagently picturesque solution. Two sets of forces determine the concept, those of the program and those of the site, using a constructional technology available to our twentieth century culture.

ORIENTATION AND IDENTITY

As Kevin Lynch has pointed out, it is necessary for man to locate himself in relation to his environment. He builds up a mental picture of recognizable features that mean 'home'.

A good environmental image gives its possessor a sense of emotional security.[1] He explains that it is by means of nodes, paths and districts that he can orientate himself... 'The world may be organised around a set of focal points or be broken into named regions or be linked by remembered routes.[2]

IDENTITY SPATIAL CONTEXT MEANING

Lynch cites identity, the spatial context and meaning as the three components of an environmental image. He explains how a door has a clear identity in that it can be recognized as such, how it is part of a general space pattern which enables the observer to locate it in relation to everything else, and also has 'some meaning for the observer whether practical or emotional.'[3]

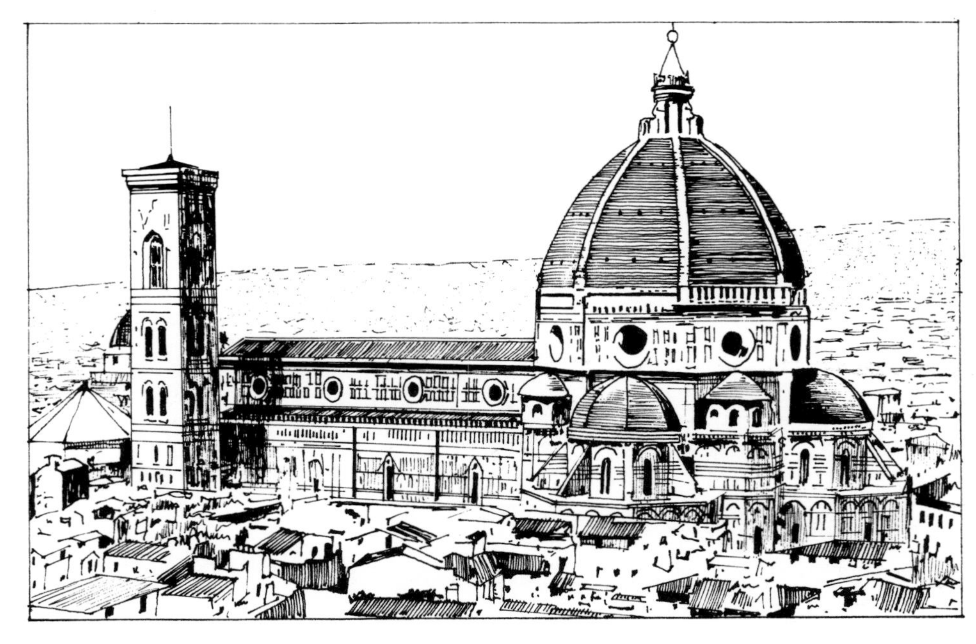

Florence Cathedral 1296-1462 architect Arnolfo di Cambio.

To illustrate this on a completely different level, the cathedral at Florence has a clear identity, can easily be located in the street pattern and has unambiguous meaning as a religious centre.

[1] Kevin Lynch, The image of the city Cambridge Mass. 1960 p. 4 [2] Ibid, p 7. [3] Ibid. p. 8

MOVEMENT

The mobility of man has led to the creation of routes. These have their own energy and as such constitute forces.

As with differences in natural forces (a river is not the same as a stream) so too are there differences in the force characteristics of routes. A major highway differs from a suburban street, a railway has a particular kind of limited and concentrated movement potential.

Viaducts and bridges are similarly concentrated vectors of movement and as with all routes they establish a special kind of relationship with the landscape. Heidegger explains how bridges do not merely connect two banks but 'brings stream and bank and land into each others' neighbourhood. The bridge gathers the earth as landscape around the stream.' [1]

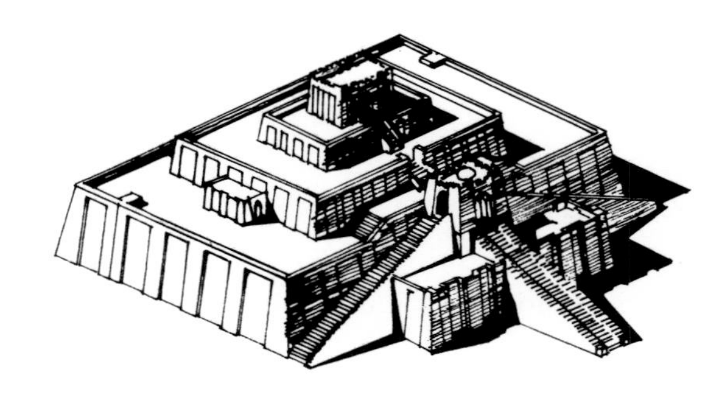

The Ziggurat of Urnammu Ur B.C. 2125

[1] Heidegger. Poetry, Language, Thought, New York, 1971. p. 152

Roman bridge across the Tagus, Alcantara Spain. A.D. 105-16.

Movement can be an important design generator and stairs, ramps, escalators and elevators also may be regarded as forces of different intensity.

As with Heidegger's bridge, each kind of movement has its own characteristics and a particular relationship potential with its immediate surroundings. Each of these devices has been fully explored architecturally at different periods in history, from the ramped approach to Babylonian Ziggurats to the twentieth century celebration of escalators and lifts.

The serene static quality of the arched Roman bridge in stone contrasts with the soaring drama of the lifts in the Hyatt Regency Hotel in Dallas. The vertical thrust is intensified by making the lifts visible and by juxtaposing their shafts so that they cut through the horizontal layers of balconies which look onto the atrium space.

This contemporary exploitation of movement as a significant design opportunity belongs to a tradition which includes such fine examples as the Scala Regia in the Vatican and Michelangelo's staircase to the Biblioteca Laurenziana in Florence.

Hyatt Regency Hotel Dallas Texas 1976-78
architects Welton Becket and associates.

Theatre Epidauros Greece c. 350 B.C.

If a route is a force resulting from man's mobility, a view also has force characteristics in terms of his ability to see.

Vincent Scully refers to the importance of views in the creation of special places in ancient Greece. He explains how Greek theatres were 'the primary device for attempting to bring city and landscape together' by pointing out how theatres at Megalopolis, Ephesos, Sikyon and the Piraeus in each case looked towards a distant view with conical hills.[1]

At Megalopolis all the holiest places of the city were laid out along the general axis of the view between the theatre and mountain cone. Scully reminds us that 'The importance of the theatre in creating sweeping views for Hellenistic cities can therefore not be overestimated.'[2]

He also mentions how some Hellenistic cities 'were like great theatres themselves, tipped forward on a height in order to achieve a dramatic view across the landscape.'[3] He describes how at Cassope the city is shaped like a theatre and how 'A mighty panorama opens out before it, while the savage mountains press up close behind its northern walls... the whole effect is of the city's command over an entire world of plain, mountains and the sea.'

1 Vincent Scully, The Earth The Temple and the Gods, New Haven and London 1962 (revised edition Yale University 1979) 2 Ibid., p. 194 3 Ibid p 194.

STRUCTURE

Although structure may be seen as a means towards an end, structural devices in buildings can be an opportunity for expression. This was the case in the earliest civilizations and the Greek column became an expression of refinement which also was interpreted in different ways to have different meanings.

Similarly Roman and Romanesque architecture exploited the arch and vault in ways that were appropriately meaningful for their period. The use of the arch and vault enabled the Romans to span greater distances than the Greeks and Roman buildings exemplify the advanced technology of their culture.

The use of columns, arches and vaults in Romanesque architecture led to the soaring naves of the great cathedrals.

In the Gothic period the column became part of the vaulted system so that column and vault merge in a celebration of structural audacity and technical skills. The intention was to glorify God with a structural 'miracle' in which the heavy ground based characteristic of stone was transformed into apparent weightlessness.

St. Philibert Tournus France 950-1120
after Francis D. K. Ching.

Beauvais Cathedral original choir 1272
after a sketch by R. Branner

If structure can be thought of as conveying meaning it may also be read as having force characteristics. These relate to the way structure has to withstand such phenomena as gravity, wind pressure, and soil characteristics.

The response, as in nature, produces geometrical solutions, with rhythmic linkages to give strength and a sense of elasticity or tension attributable to the way materials are handled.

These characteristics are admirably described by John Ruskin:

> Egyptian and Greek buildings stand, for the most part by their own weight and mass, one stone passively incumbent on another; but in the Gothic vaults and traceries there is a stiffness analogous to that of the bones of a limb, or fibres of a tree; an elastic tension and communication of force from part to part, and also a studious expression of this throughout every visible line of the building.

As D'Arcy Wentworth Thompson has explained [1] there are limits to the size/strength ratio of materials and the 150' high Gothic choir vaults at Beauvais collapsed in 1284. No structure as tall was attempted again by the medieval cathedral builders.

[1] D'Arcy Wentworth Thompson, On Growth and Form, Abridged edition edited by John Tyler Bonner, Cambridge University Press, Cambridge, 1961 p. 19.

STRUCTURE

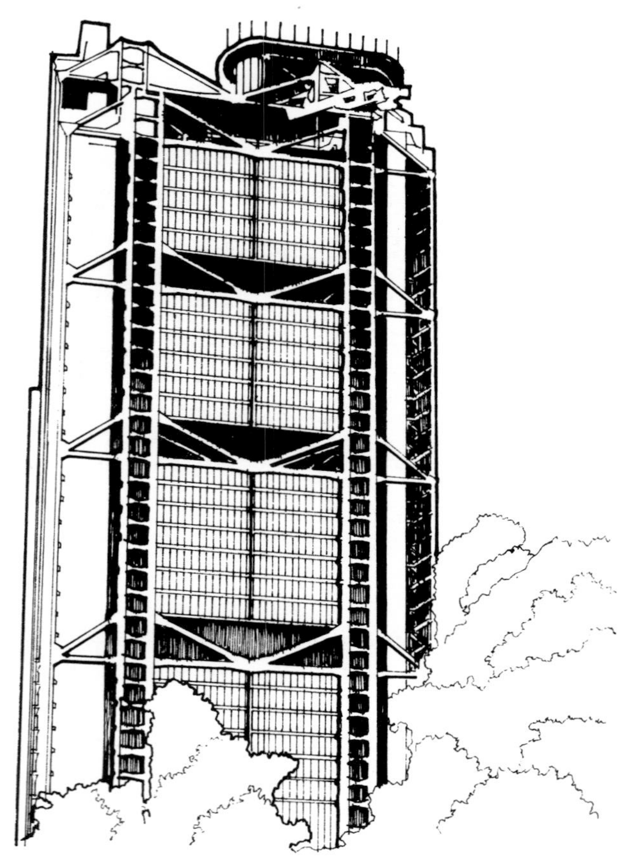

Headquarters Building
HongKong and Shanghai Banking Corporation
Architects Norman Foster and Associates

In the twentieth century Le Corbusier saw the column as a symbol of freedom. Using a reinforced concrete slab supported by columns and beams, he could eliminate the need for closely spaced supports whether these be walls or columns.

This use of columns enabled great latitude with planning and using the term 'pilotis' Le Corbusier saw the column as a way of lifting buildings above the landscape to enjoy 'sun space and greenery.'

More recently the High Tech. movement has used the expression of structure and service ducts to demonstrate not only a command of technology in building, but also the position of technology in the later twentieth century. Richard Rogers has exploited this in several buildings including the Pompidou Centre in Paris whilst Norman Foster's Headquarters of the HongKong and Shanghai Banking Corporation exemplifies the role of structure as an aesthetic device in a manner not dissimilar to that of the Gothic flying buttress.

Electronics Factory Swindon England 1965
Architects Norman and Wendy Foster and Richard Rogers.

The tensile qualities of steel have enabled architects and engineers to provide often dramatic structural statements in which Ruskin's 'elastic tension' is clearly evident. Tubular steel, used in space frames or as support struts has given architects considerable flexibility in articulating the 'skin' of buildings

The external expression of structure induces a sense of dynamism and vitality widely accepted as characteristics of twentieth century life.

GEOMETRY

St. Peters, Riga.

Geometry is the organizing discipline of architecture. It is necessary for the arrangement of structure so that geometrical constructs are as inevitable as they are in nature. Geometry is also a means of relating all the parts of a building to one another.

Throughout history it has been realized that a proportional system can assist both the ordering and the perception of buildings. Mathematical proportional systems were used by the Greeks in their temples and they evolved a proportion relationship known as the Golden Section.

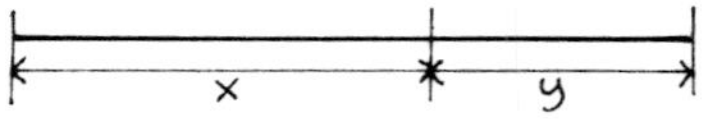

The Golden Section is based on a subdivision in which the lesser portion of a line is to the greater as the greater is to the whole or $\frac{x}{y} = \frac{y}{x+y}$. If a square be drawn within a Golden Section rectangle the remaining rectangle also has Golden Section proportions. The Golden Section was also used during the Renaissance and the medieval masons used a variety of sophisticated proportional systems to ensure harmonic relationships in churches and cathedrals.

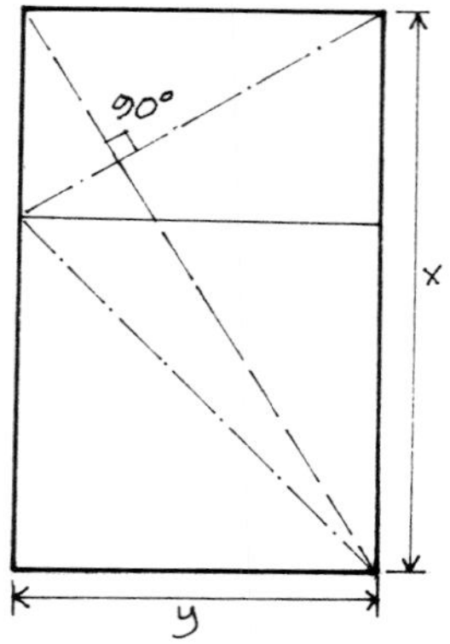

GOLDEN SECTION RECTANGLE

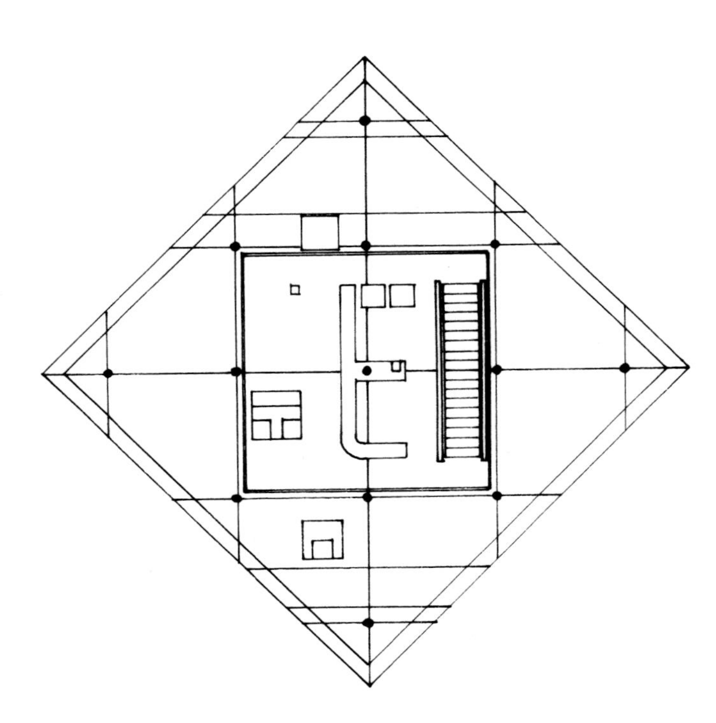

Diamond Series Project House 8 1962-66
entry level plan and projection.
architect John Hejduk.

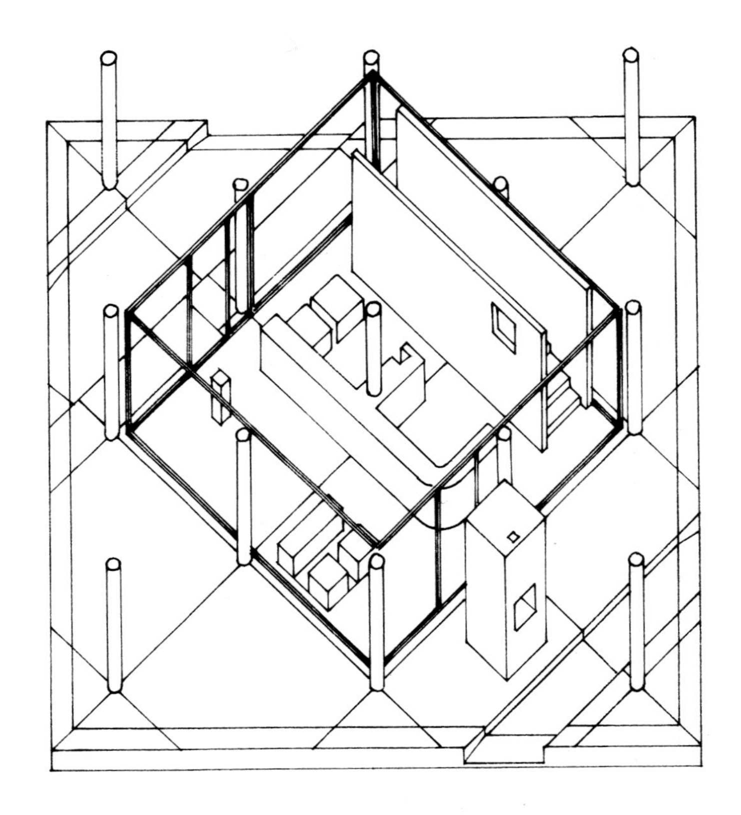

In the twentieth century Le Corbusier's geometric solutions of the twenties have been emulated and extended by a group of architects sometimes called The Five.[1] Of their work Peter Eisenman's geometry is the most complex whilst John Hejduk uses primary forms in powerful juxtapositions.

1 Richard Meier, John Hejduk, Charles Gwathmey, Michael Graves and Peter Eisenman. (The Five published a book illustrating their work in 1972).

SUMMARY

FORCES

Natural phenomena and buildings can each be understood in terms of 'forces'. These differ in magnitude and intensity as with the difference between a mountain and a hill, a swift flowing river and a gently meandering stream. Architecture may be seen as an interaction between three sets of forces, those of the site, those of the program and those of the prevailing culture.

GENIUS LOCI

The term 'Genius Loci' refers to the spirit of places, those frequently elusive characteristics which make them unique. The finest examples of architecture capture this spirit and bring together qualities inherent in the landscape and the culture.

NATURE AND ART

John Berger argues that 'Art is an organised response to what nature allows us to glimpse occaisionally. When Spring and Summer follow Winter we sense the contrast as beauty, our emotions are aroused. Art is therefore an attempt to make such transient aesthetic experiences permanent.'

POETRY

Poetry can be explained as an 'elevated expression of thought or feeling in metrical form.'[1] A poetic description differs from prose in that a subject is illuminated in ways that are imaginative and expressive. In architecture this poetic dimension transforms the ordinary into the significant so that as a container for living or working, the work of architecture may enrich life rather than merely sustain it.

[1] The Pocket Oxford Dictionary, Oxford, 1978, p. 682 (Edited by J.B. Sykes)

MEANING IN USE

Colin St John Wilson insists that architecture must 'transform utility into icon'. It must serve a useful purpose within a culture and must be effective in so doing. Buildings must not only demonstrate their purpose but must be intelligible, they must communicate their purpose clearly.

MATERIALS AND MEANING

The materials used in buildings have profound psychological implications. The extensive use of stone in various periods has increased the sense of monumentality in civic buildings and as a natural material stone also blends well into the landscape. Brick gives a more human scale to buildings and because of its cheapness and ease of manufacture has been used since Babylonian times for both domestic and public building. Brick is a friendly material unlike reinforced concrete which can appear hostile unless given a smooth finish. This hostility can be present in the use of steel and glass; mirror glass and sometimes tinted glass can create a sense of impenetrability which may be unsuitable for certain design tasks. Glass has become an important symbol in the twentieth century, matching the use of stone in previous civilizations. The failure of glass and steel to achieve a satisfactory rapport with users when forming office blocks or other public buildings has resulted in a shift back towards more solidity and a more 'friendly' surface treatment of many buildings.

Palazzo Pubblico Siena 1298

SUMMARY

PRIMITIVE ARCHITECTURE

In primitive societies everyone is capable of building his own house and certain forms evolve in response to people's needs, climate and available craft skills. These models become established and are resistant to change. The same form will be used for long periods of time partly because such forms embody meanings that are important to the society and are understood by everyone.

VERNACULAR ARCHITECTURE

In vernacular architecture, although the houses are built by tradesmen, models evolve which have shared meanings. These models respond to prevailing economic circumstances and also take account of regional climatic characteristics. Vernacular architecture is therefore an architecture of consensus, drawing together those issues of importance to society. In its twentieth century form, vernacular architecture takes account of the desire to conform, identification of social role, traditional associations and market forces.

Timber framed house Egerton Kent c. 1500.

Semi-detached houses Brighton England 1930s.

MONUMENTAL ARCHITECTURE

Unlike primitive and vernacular architecture, monumental architecture is built to impress and is largely concerned with aesthetic effects. Monumental architecture represents abstract theories and idealistic principles rather than practical issues but because of the need to communicate meanings shared by all, models evolve as they do in primitive and vernacular architecture. Such models as the Greek temple, the Medieval cathedral or Palladian country house emerge as much from a desire to communicate shared meanings as from a common technology. Monumental architecture may be regarded as High Art and may also be termed 'symphonic' in that it usually contains an elaborate composition of several contrasted but related parts.

CULTURE AND MEANING

For a culture to exist it is necessary for the individual to become integrated in 'an ordered world based on meaningful interactions.'[1] Non-verbal forms of communication are used to clarify certain intangible phenomena and architecture gives meaning to aspects of life that cannot adequately be conveyed by words. In particular architecture can identify the various stratifications within society, from church and government, the expression of the role of the arts, sport or technology, to the position of the individual in society.

PROGRAMME AND SITE

Architecture responds to three sets of forces, those of the site, the programme and the prevailing culture. The technology used will be that available within the culture.

1. C. Norberg Schulz 'Meaning in Architecture' Meaning in Architecture (edited by Jencks and Baird) London 1969 p. 220.

SUMMARY

ORIENTATION AND IDENTITY

In order to comprehend his environment man needs a clear image of his surroundings. These can be understood by man relating himself to nodes paths and districts.[1] Kevin Lynch lists the three components of an environmental image as being 'identity, spatial context and meaning.'

MOVEMENT

As a component of architecture movement may be thought of as a force having different kinds of intensity. A sports stadium or auditorium is concerned on the one hand with providing the best possible view for spectators and on the other with ensuring their swift and convenient access and egress. An arterial road is a major force in the landscape or city, a force comparable with that of a swift flowing river. The route towards, into and around a building is frequently a starting point for a design.

VIEWS

Similarly views constitute an important force to the architect, who may exploit their presence in his organization of either buildings or cities.

STRUCTURE AND GEOMETRY

Structure may be understood either in terms of the cultural meanings it expresses (as with different interpretations of the column historically) or as a means of creating a sense of the static or dynamic in a building. As an expression of dynamism structure may suggest tautness or elasticity and will often have a rhythmic component as part of its geometry. Geometry is inevitable in architectural organization as the means of ordering a design and relating the parts to one another.

[1] K. Lynch, Op., Cit., p. 7.

2

ASPECTS OF FORM

ARCHITECTURE AND CULTURE

Susanne K. Langer explains how the architect presents an image of a culture:

A culture is made up, factually, of the activities of human being; it is a system of interlocking and intersecting actions, a continuous functional pattern. As such it is, of course, intangible and invisible. It has physical ingredients — artefacts; also physical symptoms — the ethnic effects that are stamped on the human face, known as its 'expression,' and the influence of social conditions on the development, posture and movement of the human body. But all such items are fragments that 'mean' the total pattern of life only to those who are aquainted with it and may be reminded of it. They are ingredients in a culture, not its image.

The architect creates its image: a physically present human environment that expresses the characteristic rhythmic functional patterns which constitute a culture. Such patterns are the alternation of sleep and waking, venture and safety, emotion and calm, austerity and abandon; the tempo, and the smoothness or abruptness of life; the simple forms of childhood and the complexities of full moral stature, the sacramental and the capricious moods that mark a social order, and that are repeated, though with characteristic selection, by every personal life springing from that order.

Susanne K. Langer, Feeling and Form A Theory of Art, London, 1953. p. 96

ETHNIC DOMAIN

Langer continues this argument by asserting that an environment, 'the created space of architecture, is a symbol of functional existence'.[1] She explains that this has nothing to do with convenient arrangement or provident planning. To Langer, the work of architecture.

> does not suggest things to do but embodies the feeling, the rhythm. the passion or sobriety, frivolity or fear with which things at all are done. That is the image of life which is created in buildings; it is the visible semblance of an 'ethnic domain,' the symbol of humanity to be found in the strength and interplay of forms.[2]

Langer goes on to explain how, because we are organisms, our actions and feelings are organic. Our lives have a metabolic pattern consisting of 'Systole, diastole; making unmaking; crescendo, diminuendo.'[3] There is, as Langer points out, a close parallel between the organic pattern of our lives and the nature of art. 'It is perception moulded by imagination that gives us the outward world we know.'[4] This is how we react to the world and in consequence 'by virtue of our thought and imagination we have not only feelings, but a life of feeling.'[5]

Langer explains how our life of feeling is a 'stream of tensions and resolutions'.[6] In fact, our lives are an interplay of tensions — 'actual nervous and muscular tensions taking place in the human organism.'[7] It is because 'art is a symbolic presentation and not a copy of feeling that there can be as much knowledge of feeling projected into the timeless articulated form of a painting, or a stained glass window, or a subtly proportioned Greek temple, as into the flowing forms of music, dance or recitation.'[8]

[1] Ibid., p. 98. [2] Ibid., p. 99. [3] Ibid., p. 99. [4] Ibid., p. 372. [5] Ibid., p. 372. [6] Ibid., p. 372. [7] Ibid., p. 372. [8] Ibid., p. 373.

TENSION AND HARMONY

The emotions we experience throughout our 'life of feeling' are translated by the artist to harness the energy of the life situation. As such, the dynamic aspects of life, its drama and excitement combine with those other experiences of peace, sadness, suffering or exhilaration to become part of the artist's expressive palette.

The fact that life does indeed consist largely of Langer's 'tensions and resolutions' means that this is central to existence. The pattern of life has much to do with striving to attain goals or accomplish tasks resulting in a feeling of satisfaction and fulfilment. The desire and conditions which are created in order to reach such goals produce a certain tension. Once achieved there is a feeling of contentment.

These energies receive artistic expression in the major themes of tension and harmony. If tension and harmony are major forces in life and art they are supported by secondary forces also everpresent in each, the rhythms of night and day, the rhythmic flow of blood as it is pumped around the body, the rhythm of the seasons. Such rhythms are also interpreted by the artist or composer in ways appropriate to whatever medium is employed.

VIEW FROM THE SOUTH WEST

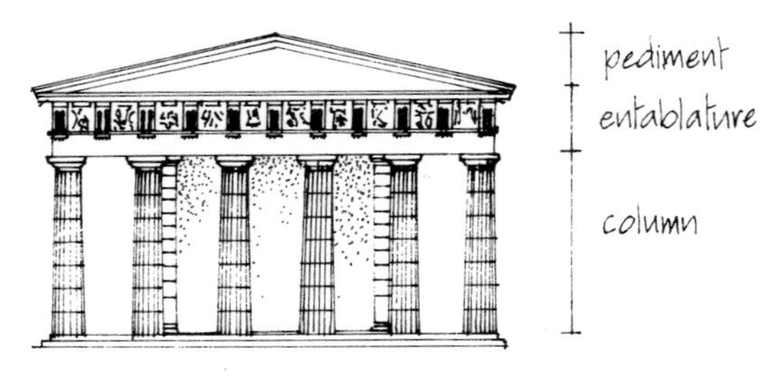

EAST ELEVATION

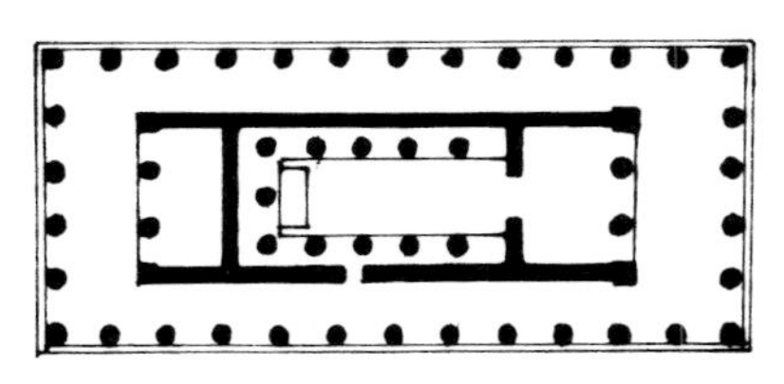

PLAN

The Thesion Athens 449-444 B.C.

If the overall statement of the Greek temple is one of harmony and unity, this is achieved primarily in the balance inherent in the bi-laterally symmetrical plan.

This unity has within it the opposing tension between the vertical column and horizontal entablature. The composition relies on a powerful rhythmic component with the major columnar rhythm supported by the secondary rhythms of triglyphs and metopes.

The inclined planes of the roof conclude at each end with the pediments, whose oblique planes and triangular formation suggest another kind of energy. As Maurice de Sausmarez has explained, 'diagonals introduce powerful directional impulses, a dynamism which is the outcome of unresolved tendencies towards vertical and horizontal which are held in balanced suspension.'[1] Although somewhat muted in the shallow angle of the temple pediment, this form is as necessary to terminate the composition at its upper extremity as is the stepped base at ground level.

1 Maurice de Sausmarez, Basic Design: The Dynamics of Visual Form, London, 1964, p.p. 20-22.

PERMANENCE AND HARMONY

Tempietto at S. Pietro in Montorio, Rome. 1502-10.
architect Bramante.

With its circular plan the Tempietto is a centroidal configuration, maintaining a balance of forces. Centroidal bodies suggest repose and stability whereas linear forms imply activity.

The permanence of architecture gives it a special role as the embodiment of 'the rhythmic functional patterns which constitute a culture.' This permanence makes a special demand on the architect to ensure that the work symbolizes the essence of its particular role in such a way that this can be sustained over a period of time.

The theme of harmony, with its implications of order and unity, is of particular importance to architecture, partly because these issues are preferred symbols culturally but also because the permanence of architecture denies a discordant statement. In this, architecture in general separates itself from the other arts, in which a greater degree of imaginative freedom is possible and in which the strident and discordant note may be acceptable.

The harmonic theme has been expressed in different ways during the various periods in different parts of the world. The Italian Renaissance displays a concern for harmony in a broad philosophical sense, and the compositions of Bramante and Raphael gave symbolic expression to belief in a harmonious universe. The centralized plan, used by Leonardo and Michelangelo, gave architectural conviction to this idea, whilst the gentle rhythm of the arcade became another manifestation of the serene tranquility of the period.

Although the circular plan is the most obvious architectural device to depict harmony, other centroidal configurations such as the square or polygon may also convey this theme.

One of the most complete statements of serenity based on a harmonious geometric arrangement is that of the garden courts and mausoleum of the Taj Mahal at Agra. Four large square courts subdivided into smaller squares front the mausoleum which is positioned centrally on a platform at one end of the main axis of the ensemble.

At the other end of this axis is the great gateway with its own entrance court flanked by two more courts. The secondary axes are terminated by appropriate incidents in an almost totally consistent application of bi-lateral symmetry.

Within the overall symmetry there are subtle contrasts of surface treatment. The hard white marble and rich decoration of the main platform and mausoleum contrasts with the softness of the garden courts, themselves defined axially by the water of the canals. Minarets give vertical punctuation and establish the main space zones.

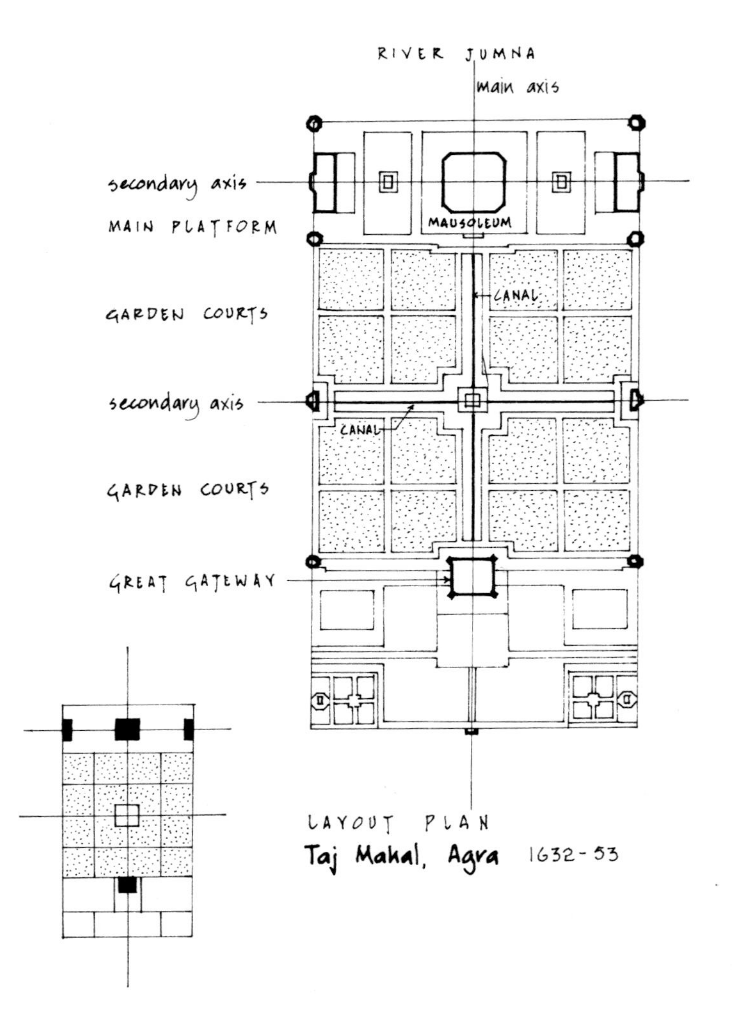

LAYOUT PLAN
Taj Mahal, Agra 1632-53

HARMONY BY GEOMETRY

The design principles used in the design of the Taj Mahal are concerned with mass, surface, geometry and the fact that the plan determines the entire arrangement.

We can relate the design of the mausoleum to a series of design maxims set out by Le Corbusier in his theoretical survey Vers une Architecture.

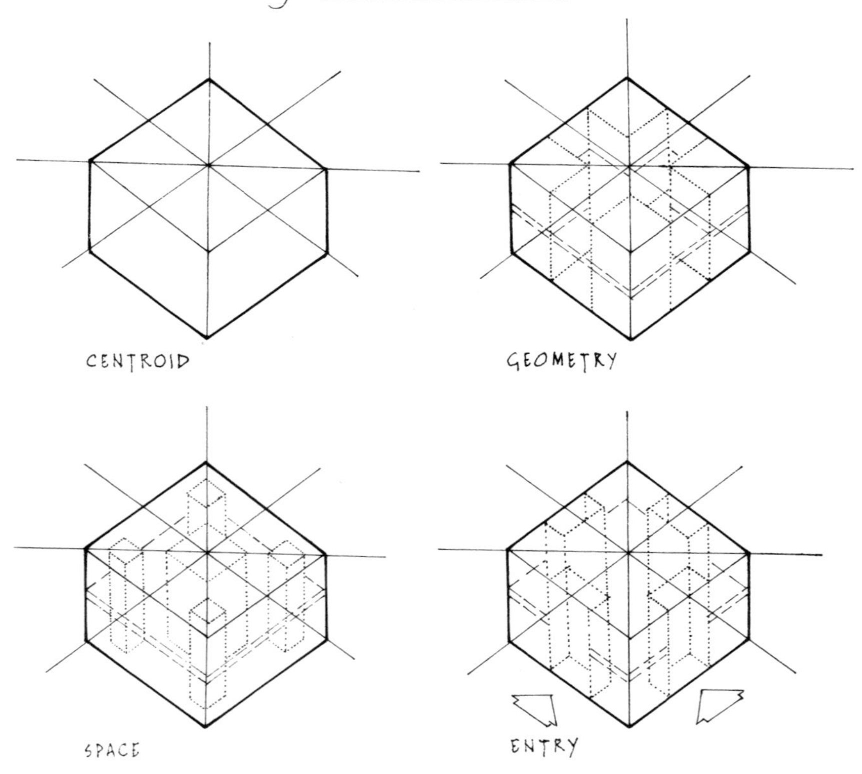

MASS

'Architecture is the masterly' (stress on the importance of technique) 'correct' (appropriateness of means, method and solution) 'and magnificent play of masses brought together in light.' Forms seen in light because 'Our eyes are made to see forms in light, light and shade reveal these forms; cubes, cones, spheres, cylinders or pyramids are the great primary forms which light reveals to advantage.' [1]

THE PLAN

'The whole structure rises from its base and is developed in accordance with a rule which is written on the ground in the plan...
The plan is at its basis. Without the plan there can be neither grandeur of aim and expression, nor rhythm, nor mass nor coherence. Without plan we have the sensation, so insupportable to man, of shaplessness, of poverty, of disorder, of wilfulness' [2]

GEOMETRY

'But in deciding the form of the enclosure... he has had by instinct recourse to right angles — axes, the square, the circle... For all these things — axes, circles, right angles — are geometrical truths... Geometry is the language of man.' [3]

1 Le Corbusier Vers une Architecture (translated into English as Towards a new Architecture by Frederick Etchells, London, 1946, p. 31
2 Ibid., p. 46. 3 Ibid., p. 68

In his discussion of form, Le Corbusier is at pains to point out that the geometric laws of any particular form should be the basis for subsequent action. Once these geometric laws are understood the various axes can be traced, the properties of forms depending on whether they are linear or centroidal, static or dynamic can be charted. Le Corbusier calls these the 'generating lines' of the form.

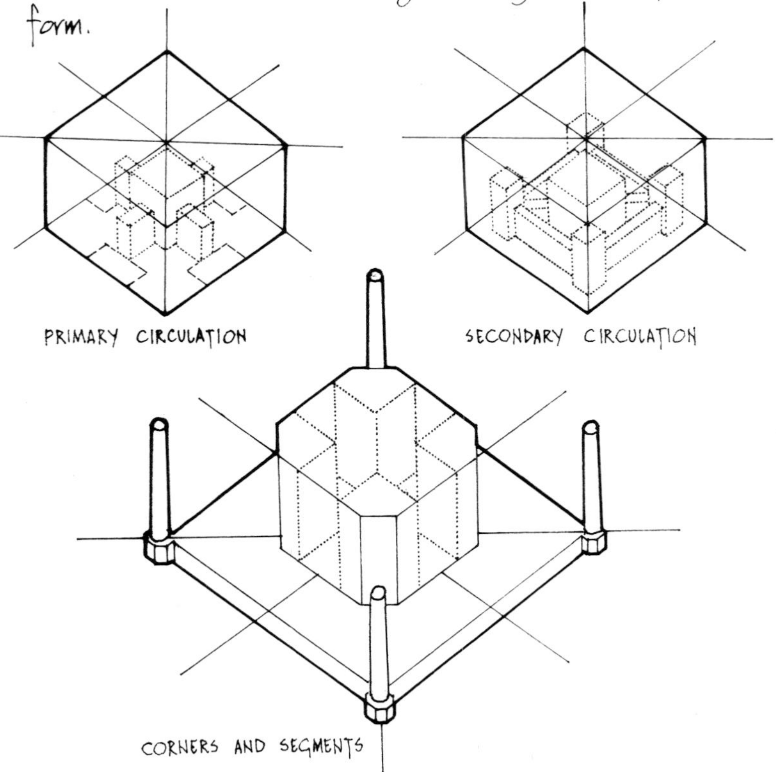

GENERATING LINES

'If the essentials of architecture lie in spheres, cones and cylinders, the generating and accusing lines of these forms are on a basis of pure geometry.'[1]

SURFACE

'To leave a mass intact in the splendour of its form in light, but, on the other hand, to appropriate its surface for needs which are often utilitarian, is to force oneself to discover in this unavoidable dividing up of the surface the accusing and generating lines of the form.'[2]

RHYTHM

'Arrangement is an appreciable rhythm which reacts on every human being in the same way.
The plan bears within itself a primary and predetermined rhythm: . .
Rhythm is a state of equilibrium which proceeds either from symmetries, simple or complex, or from delicate balancings.'[3]

HARMONY

'A profound projection of harmony: this is architecture.'[4]

1 Ibid., pp. 39, 40. 2 Ibid., p.p. 37, 39. 3 Ibid., pp 47, 48.
4 Ibid., p. 46.

GEOMETRICAL DESIGN

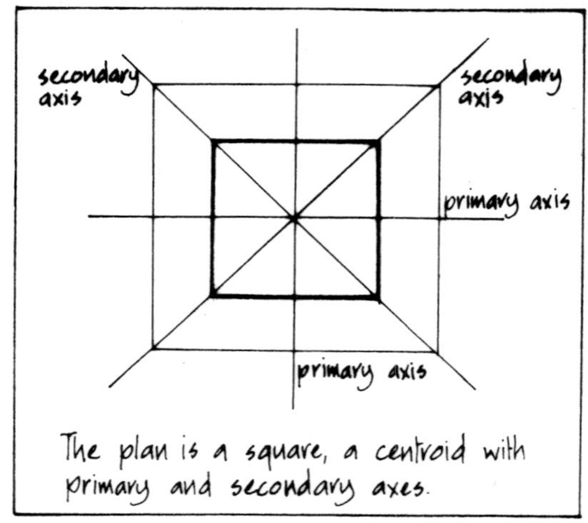

The plan is a square, a centroid with primary and secondary axes.

1 CENTROID

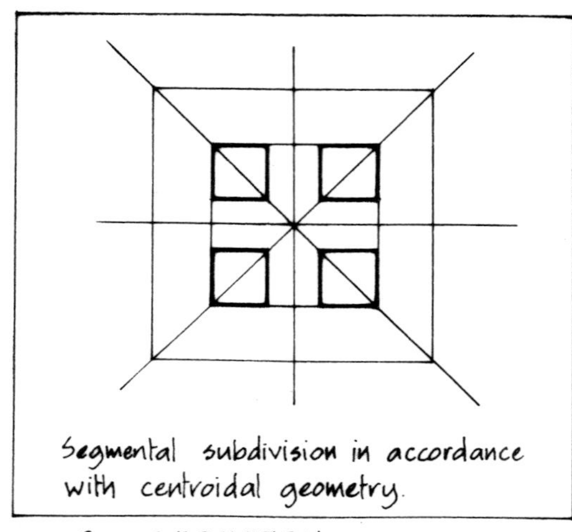
Segmental subdivision in accordance with centroidal geometry.

2 GEOMETRY

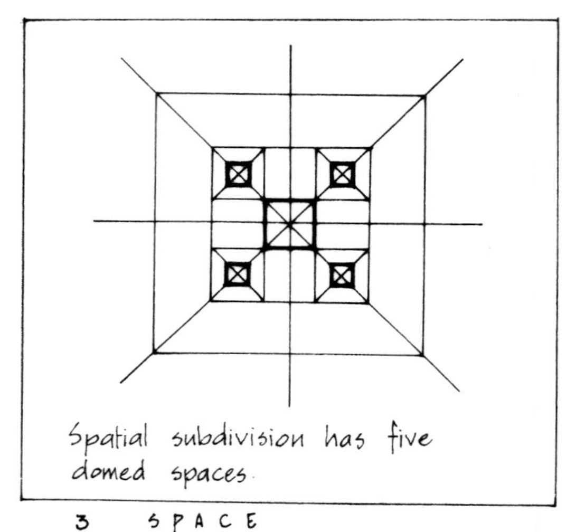
Spatial subdivision has five domed spaces.

3 SPACE

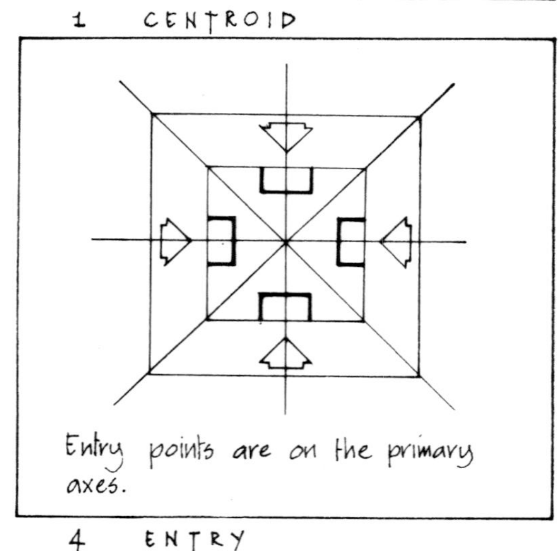
Entry points are on the primary axes.

4 ENTRY

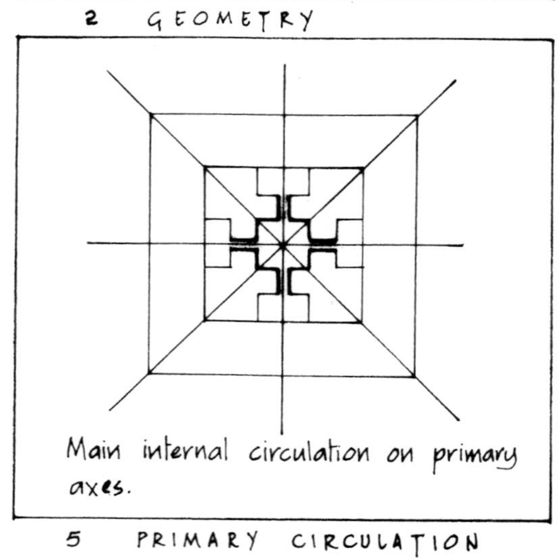
Main internal circulation on primary axes.

5 PRIMARY CIRCULATION

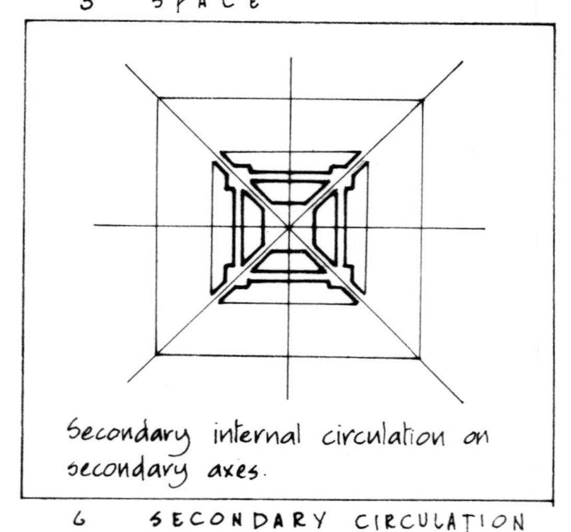
Secondary internal circulation on secondary axes.

6 SECONDARY CIRCULATION

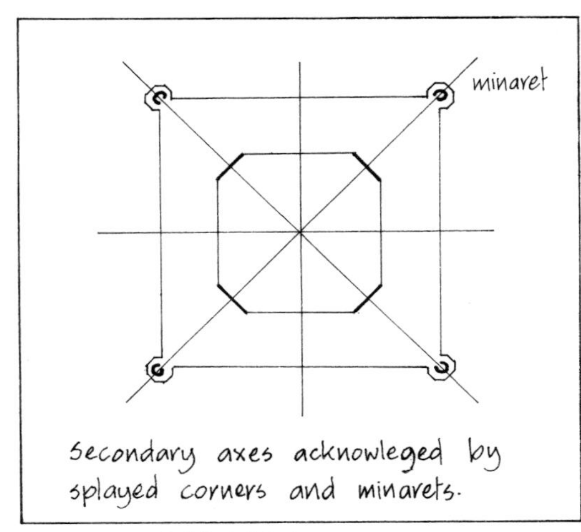

Secondary axes acknowleged by splayed corners and minarets.

7 CORNERS

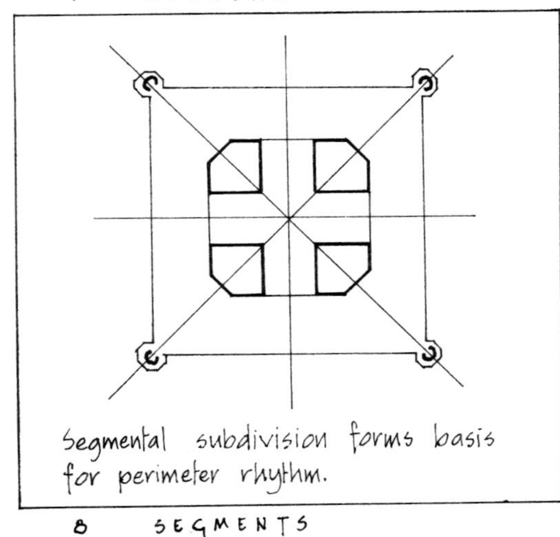

Segmental subdivision forms basis for perimeter rhythm.

8 SEGMENTS

Taj Mahal, Agra 1632–53

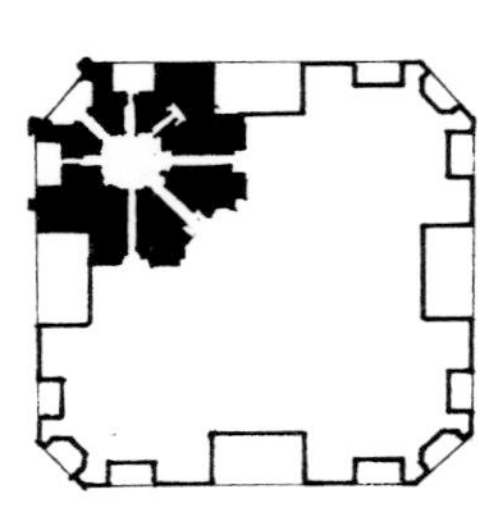

Primary and secondary perimeter rhythms.

9 RHYTHMS

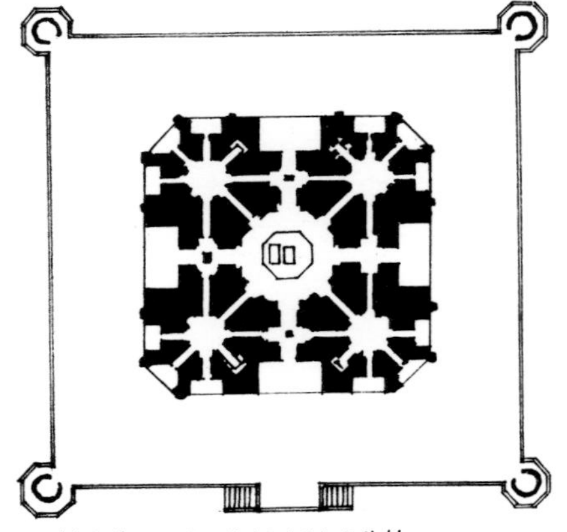

PLAN OF MAUSOLEUM

CENTROIDAL STATIC

The Selimiye Mosque Edirne 1568-74 architect Sinan.

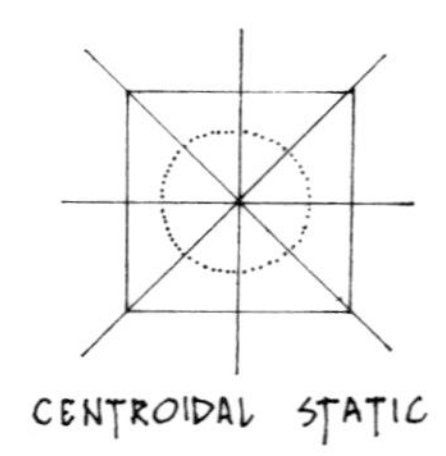

The Taj Mahal, built in the Moghul dynasty, uses the traditional motifs and elements of Islamic architecture. Expressed particularly in the mosques, the architectural language of Islam gives physical expression to the Muslim faith by creating a mood of dignity contemplation and tranquility.

The centralized plan becomes a favourite device, along with the courtyard, domes, arcades and elaborately decorated gateways. It is an architecture of form, space, light and surface decoration which relies on a well established code of authoritative symbols in order to ensure that the buildings are culturally meaningful.

In terms of technique this is an architecture of symmetry controlled by axes. Although the emphasis is on serenity and equilibrium the contrast between the 'soft' domes and rocket-like minarets becomes a powerful device. The silhouette assumes great importance as does rhythmic repetition, whether this be arches in an arcade, a rhythm of windows or of abstract decoration.

LINEAR DYNAMIC

The western equivalent of this serene architecture of the east is that of the Gothic period as demonstrated in the great medieval cathedrals. In some respects the religious requirements are similar in demanding a contemplative and reverential mood, but the western tradition is infused with dynamism; processional needs change the centroidal into a linear response and soaring verticality charges the interior with a majestic and awe-inspiring statement of the power and glory of God.

The structural audacity of the high nave vaults with 'curtain' walls of stained glass supported by flying buttresses creates a feeling of tension and energy, sustained by the vigorous repetition of elements both within and without.

Again axes control the design; again the overall composition resolves its tensions in a state of equilibrium. No less rich or mysterious than their eastern counterpart the cathedrals also rely on a well established architectural language in which form, space, light and decoration convey a range of symbolic intentions.

Chartres Cathedral (rebuilt 1194-1260)

LINEAR DYNAMIC

CHARTRES

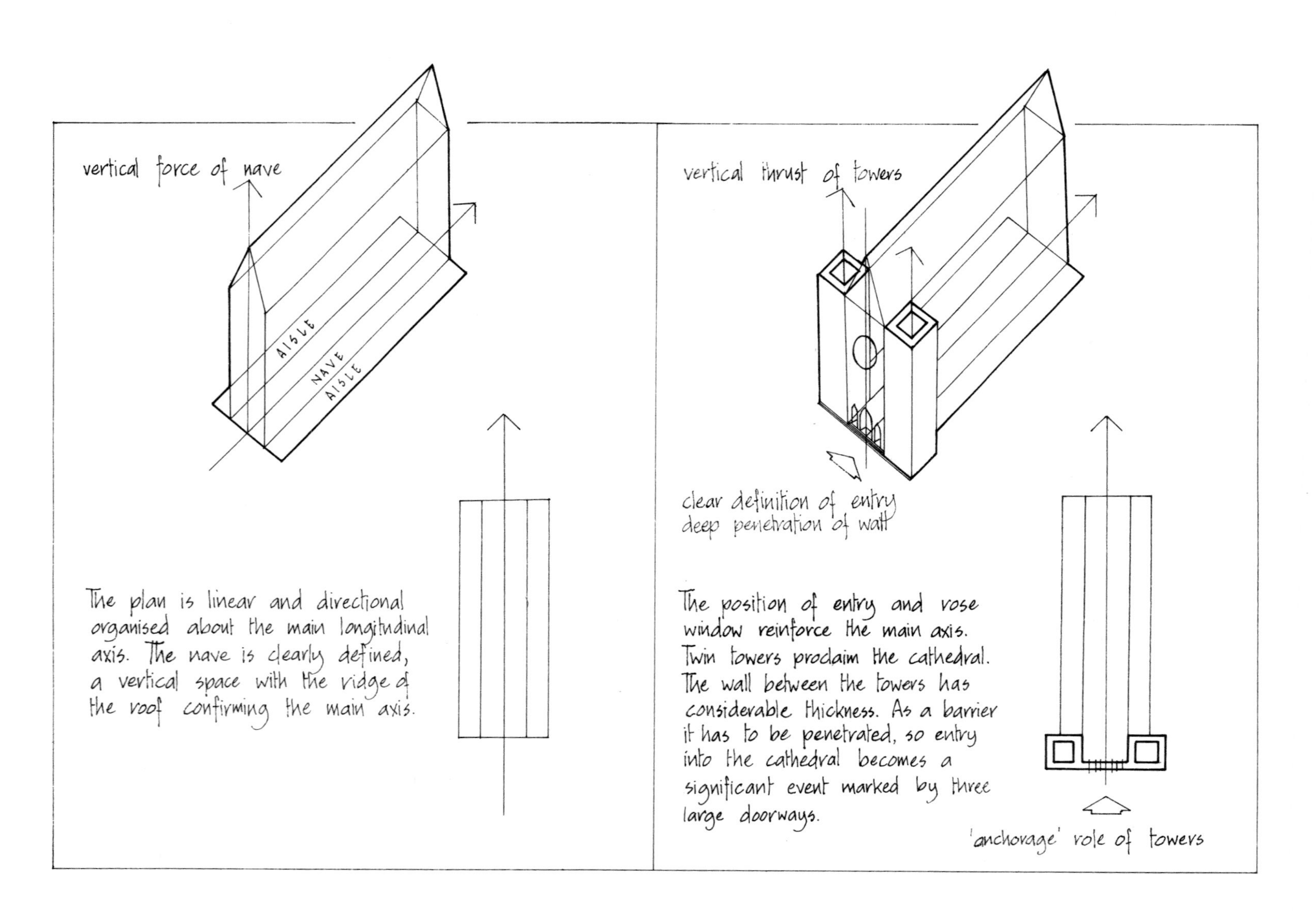
vertical force of nave
AISLE
NAVE
AISLE
The plan is linear and directional organised about the main longitudinal axis. The nave is clearly defined, a vertical space with the ridge of the roof confirming the main axis.
vertical thrust of towers
clear definition of entry
deep penetration of wall
The position of entry and rose window reinforce the main axis. Twin towers proclaim the cathedral. The wall between the towers has considerable thickness. As a barrier it has to be penetrated, so entry into the cathedral becomes a significant event marked by three large doorways.
'anchorage' role of towers

DYNAMISM

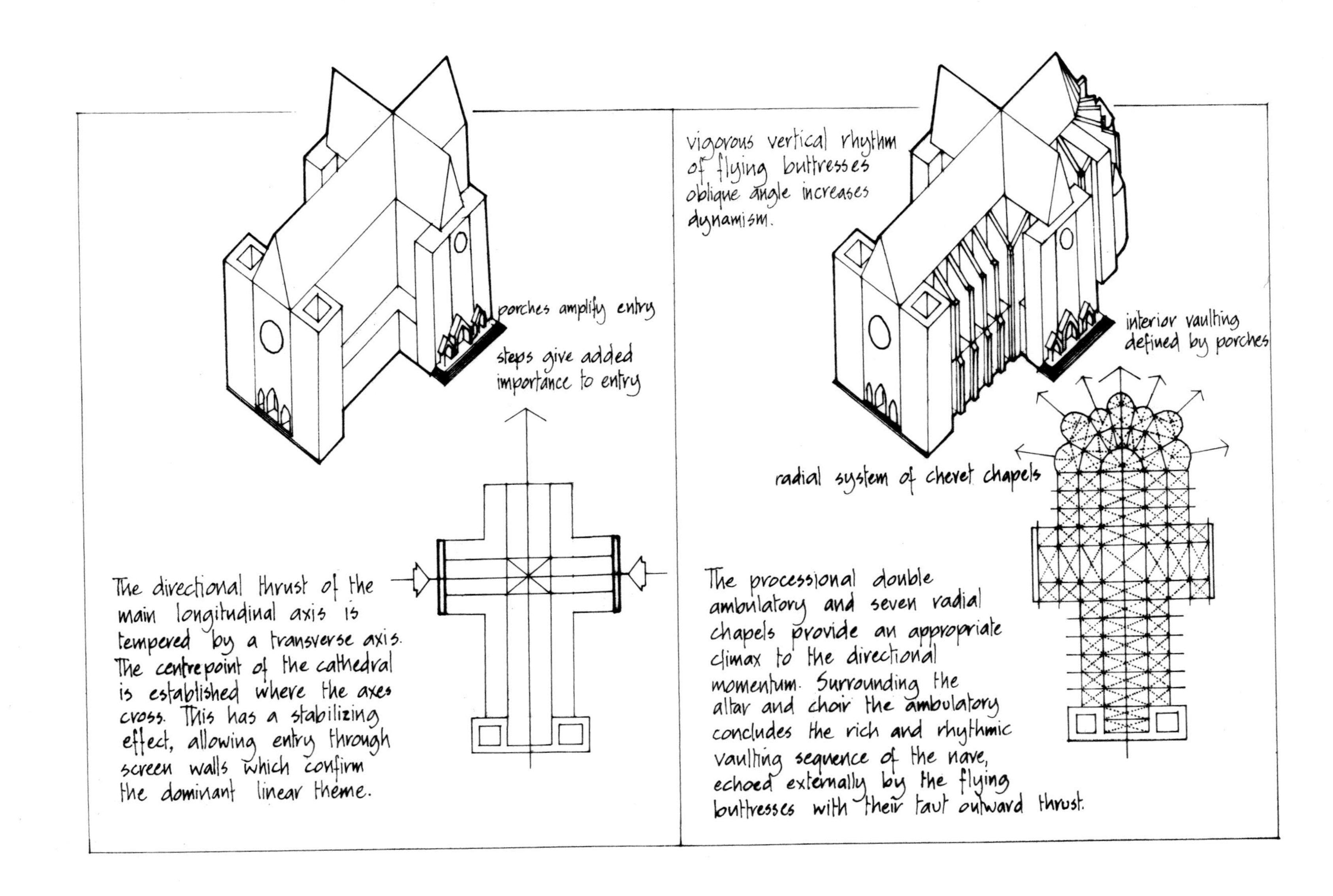
porches amplify entry
steps give added importance to entry
The directional thrust of the main longitudinal axis is tempered by a transverse axis. The centrepoint of the cathedral is established where the axes cross. This has a stabilizing effect, allowing entry through screen walls which confirm the dominant linear theme.
vigorous vertical rhythm of flying buttresses oblique angle increases dynamism.
interior vaulting defined by porches
radial system of chevet chapels
The processional double ambulatory and seven radial chapels provide an appropriate climax to the directional momentum. Surrounding the altar and choir the ambulatory concludes the rich and rhythmic vaulting sequence of the nave, echoed externally by the flying buttresses with their taut outward thrust.

FORCES

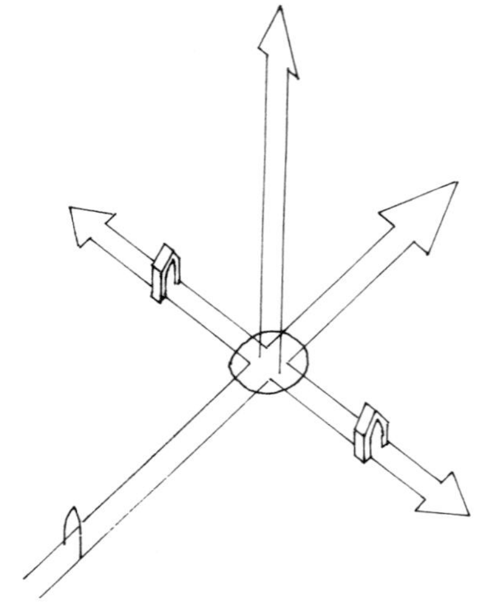

THREE POWERFUL DIRECTIONAL THRUSTS
LONGITUDINAL, LATERAL, VERTICAL.

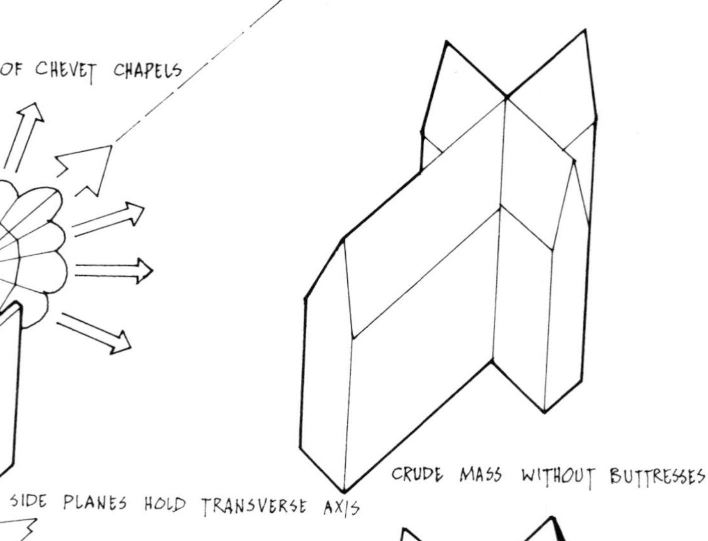

RADIAL RHYTHM OF CHEVET CHAPELS

TOWERS HOLD ENTRY

SIDE PLANES HOLD TRANSVERSE AXIS

CRUDE MASS WITHOUT BUTTRESSES

The Gothic cathedral takes the essential structural forces of wall vault and buttress and by a process of elimination reduces these to maximum visible effectiveness and drama. This is achieved by an accentuation of each potential force opportunity whether these concern the horizontal, vertical or oblique. The resultant total recognition of forces assumes equilibrium within a harmonic plan configuration compacted to maximize the dynamic tension.

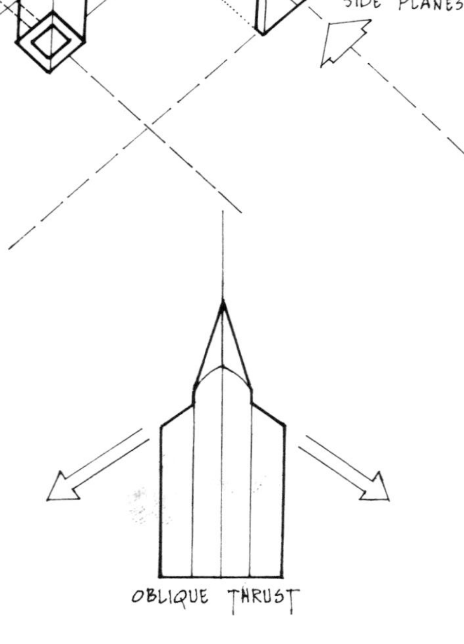

OBLIQUE THRUST

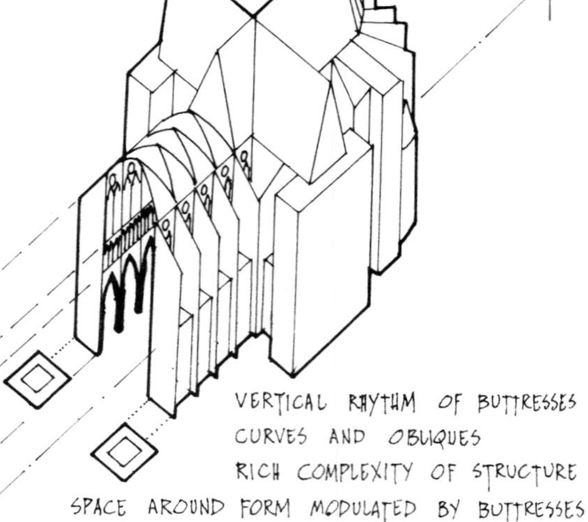

VERTICAL RHYTHM OF BUTTRESSES
CURVES AND OBLIQUES
RICH COMPLEXITY OF STRUCTURE
SPACE AROUND FORM MODULATED BY BUTTRESSES
CLOSE COMPACTION INCREASES DYNAMIC TENSION

ORGANIZATION

Erwin Panofski[1] has described how the High Gothic style of the great French cathedrals runs parallel to the development of High Scholasticism, and how these two important events in Western culture emanated during the twelfth century from an area less than a hundred miles around Paris.[2]

Panofski explains how scholars in the twelfth and thirteenth centuries saught to establish the unity of truth.[3] Elucidation or clarification was the controlling principle and for the first time Scholasticism established a logical sequence of division and subdivision in writing so that the reader is led 'step by step from one proposition to the other and is always kept informed of the process.' As Panofski points out, this does not mean that Scholastics were more orderly in their thinking than their predecessors but that they 'felt compelled to make the orderliness and logic of their thought palpably explicit.'[4]

This process of clarification and articulation of thought expressed through the written word can also be observed during this period in the organization of pictorial space and in musical notation. It was, however, architecture, with its hierarchy of functional needs, which provided the best opportunity for clear articulation. The Gothic cathedral had an unambiguous zonal distribution of space, with the nave taking precedence over the transcepts and aisles, and the choir and chevet chapels acting as the climax to the nave. Processional requirements ensured that axes controlled the arrangement, and structural needs ensured clarity in the rhythmic repetition of vaults and buttresses.

[1] Erwin Panofski, Gothic architecture and scholasticism. New York, 1957,
[2] Ibid., pp. 4,5. [3] Ibid., p. 28. [4] Ibid., p. 34.

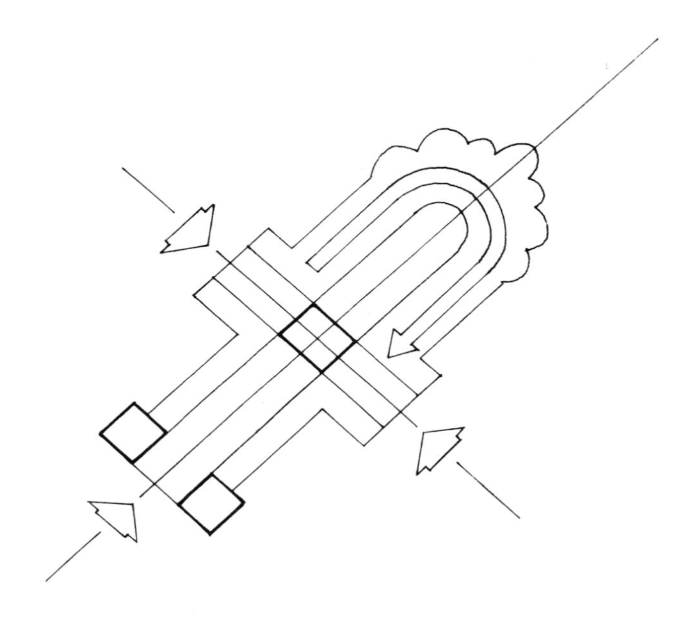

ZONAL ORGANIZATION OF THE GOTHIC CATHEDRAL

COMPLEXITY AND CONTRADICTION

The explicit clarity of the Gothic style may be compared to that of the Modern Movement in architecture, although the modernists, by substituting abstraction for applied decoration, produced far simpler shapes. This approach emerged from a desire to eliminate 'unnecessary' ornament and to rationalize and 'purify' architecture in terms of new technology and the twentieth century zeitgeist.

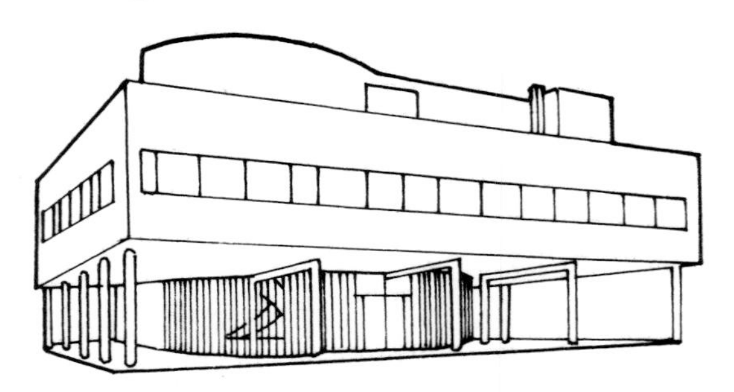

Villa Savoye Poissy 1929-31
architect Le Corbusier

Typical of this approach is the work of Le Corbusier, whose output during the twenties proved so influential in propagating the modernist credo. Although Le Corbusier relied heavily on an extensive knowledge of the architecture of the past, he became convinced (partly through this knowledge) that to communicate effectively on an emotional level it was necessary to use primary forms.

However, Le Corbusier's influential book Towards a New Architecture (1923) was followed four decades later by an alternative point of view put by Robert Venturi, who argued against the puritanically moral language of orthodox Modern architecture in postulating an argument for Complexity and Contradiction in Architecture (the title of his seminal study). In an attack on the limited reductionist position adopted by many modernists Venturi explains that he likes 'elements which are hybrid rather than "pure," compromising rather than "clean," distorted rather than "straightforward," ambiguous rather than "articulated," perverse as well as impersonal, boring as well as "interesting," conventional rather than "designed," accommodating rather than excluding, redundant rather than simple, vestigial as well as innovating, inconsistent and equivocal rather than direct and clear. I am for messy vitality over obvious unity. I include the non sequitur and proclaim the duality.' [1]

Porta Pia Rome 1561-64
architect Michelangelo

[1] R. Venturi, Complexity and Contradiction in Architecture, New York, 1966, p. 16.

This tirade, directed at the all too evident sterility of modern architecture, is supported by an extensive discussion in which Venturi draws perceptively on examples from all periods, explaining that both Le Corbusier and Alvar Aalto explored complexity and contradiction in their work.

But it is the architecture of the Baroque and Rococo styles which provide Venturi with some of his best evidence. He contrasts the Modern Movement tendency to prefer consistency between internal arrangement and external expression with the difference between inside and out in certain styles of the past. He explains that such contradictions between inside and out result in a tension between inner and outer form: 'Designing from the outside in, as well as the inside out, creates necessary tensions, which help make architecture. Since the inside is different from the outside, the wall – the point of change – becomes an architectural event. Architecture occurs at the meeting of interior and exterior forces of use and space. These interior and environmental forces are both general and particular, generic and circumstantial. Architecture as the wall between the inside and the outside becomes the spatial resolution of this drama.'[1]

Venturi demonstrates this maxim convincingly in his entrance treatment of the Extension to the National Gallery in London.

[1] Ibid. p. 86.

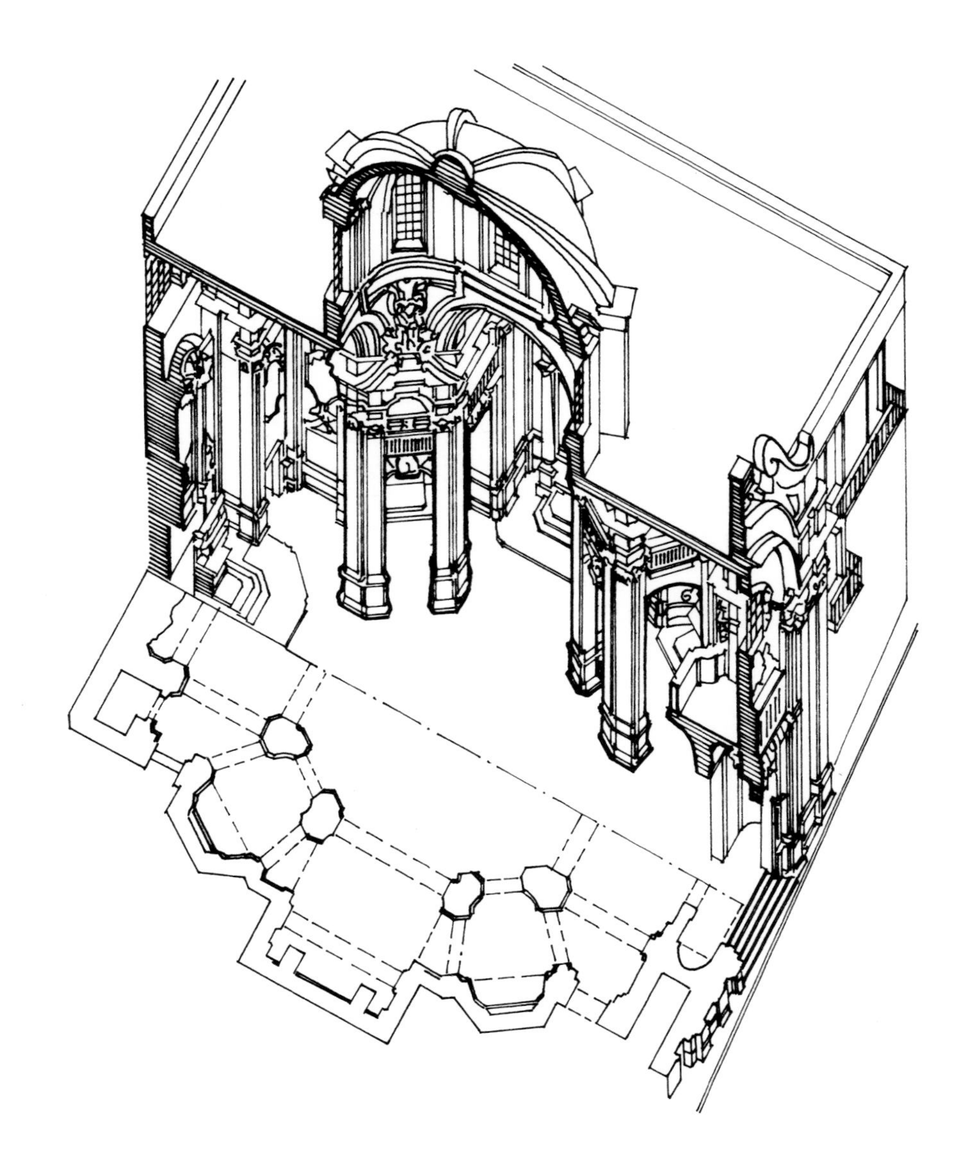

Church of the Concezione at Montecalvario 1718-24
architect Domenico Antonio Vaccaro

THE DYNAMIC ENERGY OF FORM

The vigorous handling of form evident in the Baroque and Rococo styles demonstrates the kind of energy that can be generated in works of architecture. Michelangelo's Porta Pia is but one example from his output to display the dynamism evident in his buildings. The expression of muscularity and power is closely related to these tendencies in his sculpture and painting.

This energy is not however confined to earlier periods and twentieth century architecture has often displayed a dynamic treatment of form, as for example in the work of the Futurists, Constructivists and Expressionists. It is nevertheless the work of certain important architects which most clearly illustrates the tendency, including Luigi Morretti, Hans Scharoun, Alvar Aalto and Le Corbusier. Each distributes this energy in different ways and Aalto frequently uses variations on radial themes as a means by which to induce dynamism.

In Aalto's work the energy is carefully controlled, with forms modulated so as to distribute the energy and at the same time contain it. In the Rovaniemi Libary, a typical Aalto format, the linear elements act as a holding baseline, pulling the form out sideways to house administrative accommodation and the lecture hall and ancillary facilities. In contrast, the reading room fans out beyond this, breaking free of the holding boundaries of the form. Functionally this distinction acknowledges the importance of the reading room as the heart of the library and creates a tension between the prosaic linear form and its radial offshoot.

The points where radial and linear conjoin are treated differently at each end, with an echelon at one side and an abrupt stop at the other. This gives the form directionality so that it can be read as pointing like a pistol.

Within the main shapes Aalto creates supporting shapes so that banks of offices become rhythmic sequencies and circulation in the long section reinforces the linearity of the plan, modulating differences between the parts as it meanders alongside them.

The reception desk to the reading room establishes the difference between the two zones by responding to both in its angled shape on plan. This fluency in planning is taken through into the third dimension as the section provides sunken levels, giving greater intimacy in the reading room whilst helping to articulate the radial segments.

Further definition is given by angled light sources which modify the spatial, functional and symbolic role of the reading room.

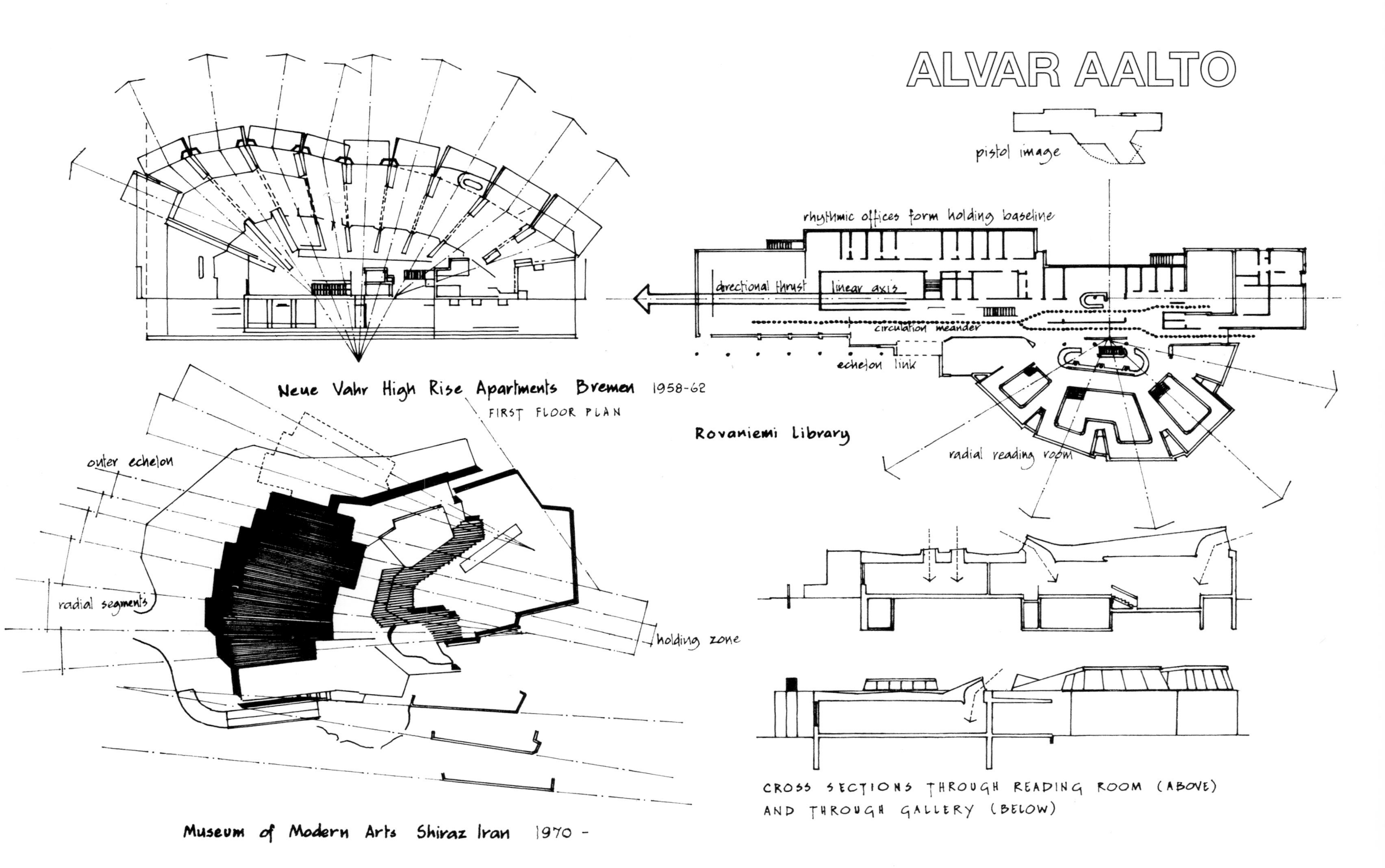

Museum of Modern Arts Shiraz Iran 1970 -

THE CLASSIC WORK

If we attempt to identify those characteristics that define the classic work, that take it beyond the ordinary, we may outline the following as being present in the major work ; 1) a mastery of technique ; 2) exceptional composition ; 3) an enduring quality ; 4) authority ; 5) either abstractly or directly, some reference to our experience of life.

Each of the arts deals with these criteria in ways that are appropriate to our sensory apparatus. Music and literature, for example, may nurture our imagination so that we respond to sounds and words by picturing something in the mind's eye. Music, in particular, can directly affect our emotions and its rhythms may be associated with the rhythmic coursing of the blood or the rhythm of the days and seasons. Painting explores the way we enjoy colour, shape and arrangement, whilst the poet might engage subtle areas of meaning that are most readily conveyed by words. Architecture involves all our senses, as for example when we walk through a courtyard with a fountain and trees. We are aware of sounds, shapes, proportions, scale, texture and pattern. We may also be subjected to a series of impressions, concerned with intimacy, privacy, power, wealth or poverty. A courtyard may have historic associations; it may suggest accademia, the church or government.

If we take the above criteria in turn, they have specific implications for each of the arts:

MASTERY OF TECHNIQUE

Although technique may be taken for granted in the arts, an enhanced level of quality may be given to major works by absolute mastery of technique. This implies mastery of the means by which intentions may be accomplished. The composer of a musical score must be familiar with the various instruments to have the necessary control of expression. In architecture such control is associated with knowledge of materials and constructional technology. The work of a master such as Alvar Aalto is exemplary in the way every detail, from window mullion to door hande, informs the final building.

EXCEPTIONAL COMPOSITION

The major work will be understood as such in part by its arrangement – in music of sounds, in poetry of words, in architecture by the articulation of the various elements. Such compositions may be rich and elaborate as in opera, or quite simple as in some poems and works of art. Because of its nature and life-expectancy, architectural arrangements may tend towards order and symmetry, or alternatively towards a dynamic balance of contrasting elements.

Robert Venturi has shown[1] that architecture can be complex, ambiguous and contradictory. He quotes examples from Mannerist and Baroque architecture in which the level of elaboration sets out to confound the usual expectations. Within necessary limits of comfort, structure and weather-proofing, such strategies impart that vitality which emerges in certain periods as a reaction against what has gone before. This oscillation, from the staid to the lively, from serenity to vigorous dramatisation and even confusion exemplifies the way in which the arts renew themselves in response to changing cultural circumstances.

AN ENDURING QUALITY

This is found in major works in the way that we can return to them again and again, to discover something fresh or to be reacquainted with familiar qualities. In fulfilling

[1] Robert Venturi, Complexity and Contradiction in Architecture, New York, 1966.

THE CLASSIC WORK

this requirement the major work may be complex or simple. Different kinds of complexity and simplicity create this enduring quality in each of the arts. The orchestral symphony consists of several contrasting but related movements; the novel consists of a series of related chapters. In each case a theme or story unfolds in a continuous linear fashion. In contrast, architecture is usually perceived as a whole, albeit consisting of a series of related parts. These may also be experienced sequentially by movement through a building.

Architecture may be complex, as for example in Richard Meier's Atheneum,[1] or relatively simple as in Bramante's Tempietto.[2] But architecture's practical and symbolic role seldom allows the kind of freedom enjoyed by the painter or musician. It is difficult to imagine an architectural equivalent to the random complexity of a Jackson Pollock painting, although Watts Towers in Los Angeles come fairly close.

Order and clarity are almost always important considerations in architecture. The need to communicate meaning usually demands a consensus architecture in which the familiarity of the language ensures shared comprehension. By this means certain styles persist, whether in civic or domestic buildings. In the sixteenth century, Andrea Palladio evolved an architectural style which has persisted to the present day. The reason for this enduring quality (as found in his Villa Capra)[3] lies in a blend of simplicity and complexity, together with the architect's careful manipulation of the communicative aspect. Palladio creates forms that are simple enough to cause no perceptual difficulties — his forms can readily be understood as wholes — they observe time-honoured architectural canons of order and symmetry, yet are embellished with meaningful decoration in the form of classical motifs. Palladio fully understood the nature of architecture, an understanding which drew extensively on Greek and Roman precedent.

1 see pages 187-231
2 see page 42
3 see page 14

AUTHORITY

To have authority, the work must inspire a confidence based on the author's command of his medium. Again this will have a different inference for each of the arts. Our confidence in Shakespeare stems from the conviction apparent in his portrayals and characterizations. Consumate technique and impeccable composition contribute, but his authority is due to a universal recognition of his mastery of every aspect of his art.

This is also the case with architecture. Authority resides in total conviction. This is particularly evident in certain periods in which every aspect of the architectural phenomenon is resolved. Kings' College Chapel Cambridge is such an example. A complete work, which integrates structure, form, proportions, decorative treatment and lighting in a way that expresses spirituality and which is perfectly at one with its setting. Such are the demands on architecture and architects that this fusion is difficult to attain and is apparent in the great periods which represent a summation of man's progress. When this occurs architecture adds authority to the purpose it serves.

On another level, vernacular architecture, or the architecture of popular taste, will have its own authority when it embraces all man's needs, practical and symbolic. In popular, universal stereotypes of domestic habitation, found in all parts of the world, authority resides in the complete rapport between programme, climate and culture. In such stereotypes, structure, materials, craftsmanship, economic forces and symbolism are all combined in a manner that emerges through the roots of the culture. This recognises the importance of tradition, the common perceptions of status and conformity and the need to convey meanings shared by all. As with a Rembrandt portrait or a Beethoven symphony, there is a concern for universal truths which transcend fashion, superficiality or contrivance. The fact that architecture is all-embracing and deals with so many aspects of existence means that it is extremely difficult for an individual architect to produce work of real authority.

THE CLASSIC WORK

REFERENCE TO THE EXPERIENCE OF LIFE

This discussion has already indicated the extent to which the major work will illuminate our perception of life. The artist, author, composer or architect will draw out and reconstitute significant aspects of experience. The way this is done will depend on the capacity of the medium, which will also determine the subject matter. Degas' portrayals of dancers heighten our perception of dance, they convey the beauty of the female form and how this may be enhanced by costume lighting and choreography.

As the framework for existence, architecture participates directly in life, and as an art form it is assessed as to the extent to which it enhances and enriches life. The close connection with practical and symbolic issues separates architecture from the other arts which may seek to inform or entertain. Architecture has a particularly responsible role, allowing less licence or self-indulgence than the other arts. It is most successful when it absorbs the life forces so that they are correctly assimilated A staircase or stair handrail must be correctly shaped to permit easy and comfortable movement. In this sense architecture is anthropormorphic — this is its connection with life. Similarly in providing shelter, comfort and order architecture directly addresses the concerns of life. Its authority and conviction depend on this ability to satisfy practical and emotional needs.

This may be manifest in subtle ways. Barry and Pugin's Palace of Westminster contains two strands of the British Parliament, the Houses of Lords and Commons. This division, separating the aristocracy from the commoner, reflects a British societal tradition. As an expression of this, the Gothic style refers to the historic continuity which the building represents. In straddling the arts and sciences, aesthetics and practicality; in dealing with symbolism and a communicative consensus, representing cultural continuity and the present, architecture expresses aspects of life directly. Like major works in the other arts, the major work of architecture will reveal a comprehensive understanding of all those life forces which must be absorbed and encapsulated in built form.

3

THE ANALYSIS OF ARCHITECTURE

ANALYSIS

This analytical methodology seeks to discover those primary organizational factors which operate in a building or project, and in so doing to reveal the preoccupations of the designer. This is done by a process of dissection which charts the existence of such factors as volumetric disposition (including the kind of geometrical system used), the circulation pattern (in many cases directly linked to the volumetric disposition, the location of key axes, both within the building and in the immediate proximity, and (where relevant) the structural system. The relevance to the general organization of the materials used, environmental considerations (sun control, prevention of heat loss or excessive gain) and the arrangement of services may also be taken into account.

These factors are analysed with reference to the purpose which the building is intended to serve, and to the kind of symbolic imagery which the building seeks to express. The analysis also takes account, again where appropriate, of cultural, technological and economic factors.[1]

An important feature of this analytical methodology is the way a building is considered in relation to its site. Site forces[2] such as the presence of a river or other topographical factors, are charted and the building's axes are related to other axes in the vicinity.

[1] It has to be stressed that analysis is a selective, subjective exercise. In this study emphasis is given to the analysis of architectural form, and only issues central to this intention are considered. Essentially any analytical investigation will focus on those issues considered specifically relevant to the subject matter. It follows from this that no two analyses will necessarily be alike, in treatment or in the emphasis given to each area under discussion.

[2] The term forces is used to indicate a weighting, a degree of intensity or energy emanating from the source. This will exert an influence on its surroundings, depending on its strength, usage, power of massing or means of making its presence felt in a situation.

The analysis relates the site forces (which include orientation, views and access), to those organizational forces identified within the building. The analysis seeks to discover how the building is conceived in relation to its site.[1] To be of most value in terms of the concerns of this study, the analysis will usually examine a major work, the task being, as far as possible, to reveal those intuitive processes which have guided the designer.

As in literary or musical analysis, major themes are sought within the work and then examined to see whether or not they are carried through consistently.[2]

[1] See G.H. Baker 'Chichester College Revisited' R.I.B.A. Journal, November 1980, pp 45-47. Also videos 'Chichester Theological College' produced by Media Services, Brighton Polytechnic. and 'The Atheneum, an analysis of form' produced and directed by Gordon Brooks, University of Arkansas, 1988.

[2] See Geoffrey Baker, Le Corbusier: An analysis of form. (Second edition 1989). Van Nostrand Reinhold (International) Co. Ltd., London.

DIAGRAMMATIC THOUGHT

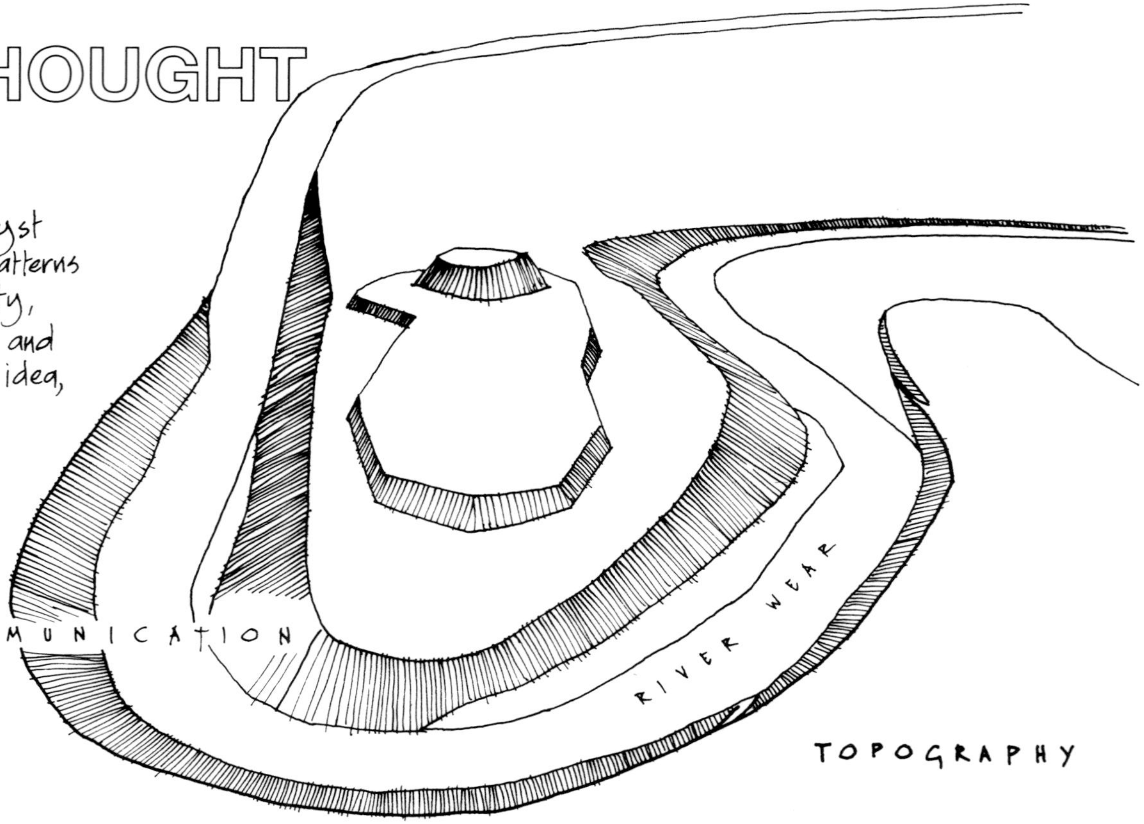

Diagrams are the essential tool of both analyst and designer. Their use encourages thought patterns capable of considerable dexterity. This dexterity, the ability to grasp the essence of a concept, and through this understanding to fully develop an idea, is central to the act of design.

DIAGRAMS :

ARE SELECTIVE

ARE ABOUT CLARITY AND COMMUNICATION

REVEAL THE ESSENCE

ARE OFTEN SIMPLE

SEPARATE OUT ISSUES SO AS TO COMPREHEND THE COMPLEX

MAKE GEOMETRIC ARTICULATION EXPLICIT

CAN QUANTIFY THE ENERGY IN BOTH SITE AND CONCEPT

ALLOW A DEGREE OF ARTISTIC LICENCE

CAN HAVE A VITALITY OF THEIR OWN

CAN EXPLAIN FORM AND SPACE BETTER THAN WORDS OR PHOTOGRAPHS

TOPOGRAPHY

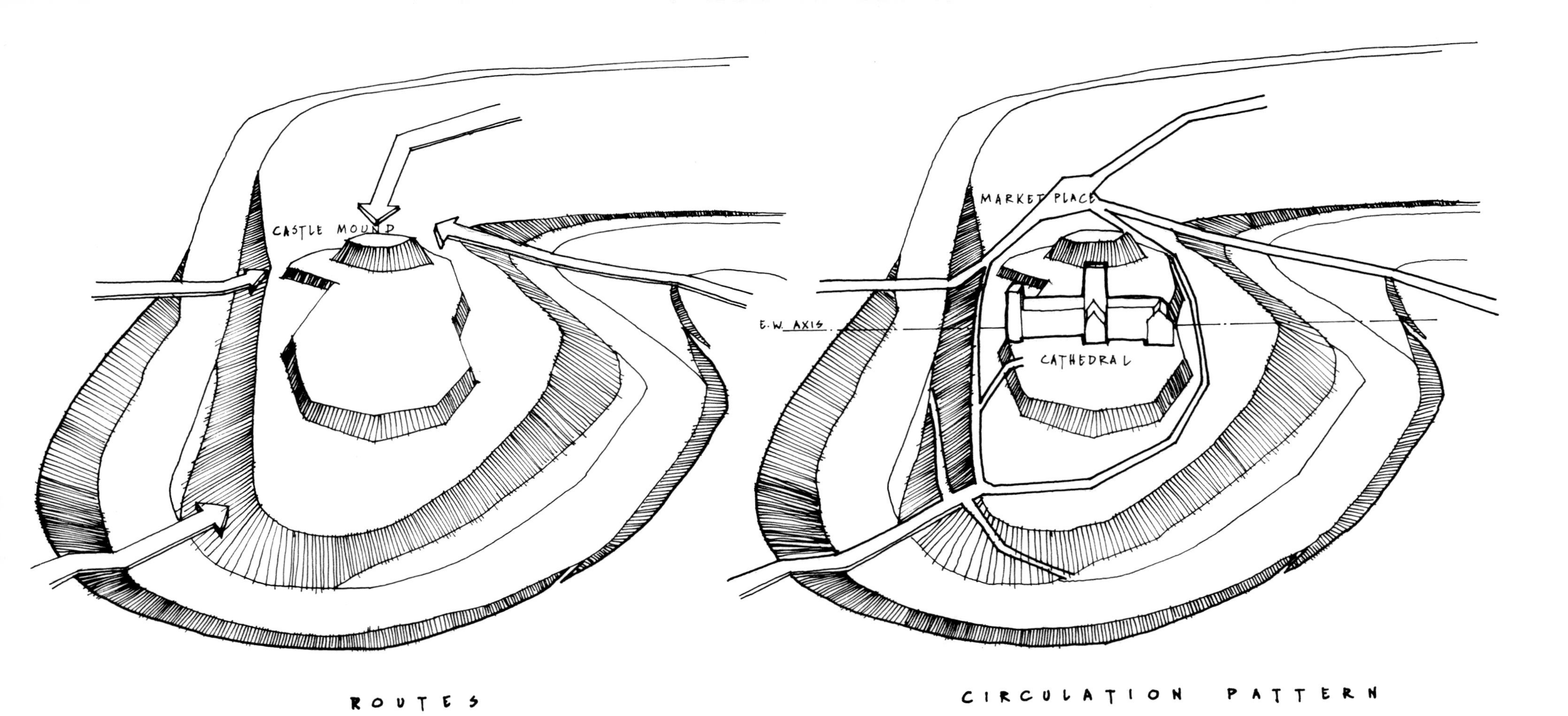

ROUTES

CIRCULATION PATTERN

An understanding of city structure can be gained by charting topography routes and circulation patterns. The city of Durham was built on the high ground of a peninsula formed by the river Wear. To the north a convergence of routes established the market place, commanded by the high ground of the castle mound. The steep banks of the river create a natural defensive barrier and on the high plateau to the south of the castle the cathedral dominates the city, its east/west axis running counter to the north/south axis of the peninsula.

SLAB TRANSFORMED

Le Corbusier's Villa Stein-de-Monzie can be diagrammatically explained as a series of transformations of a rectilinear slab.

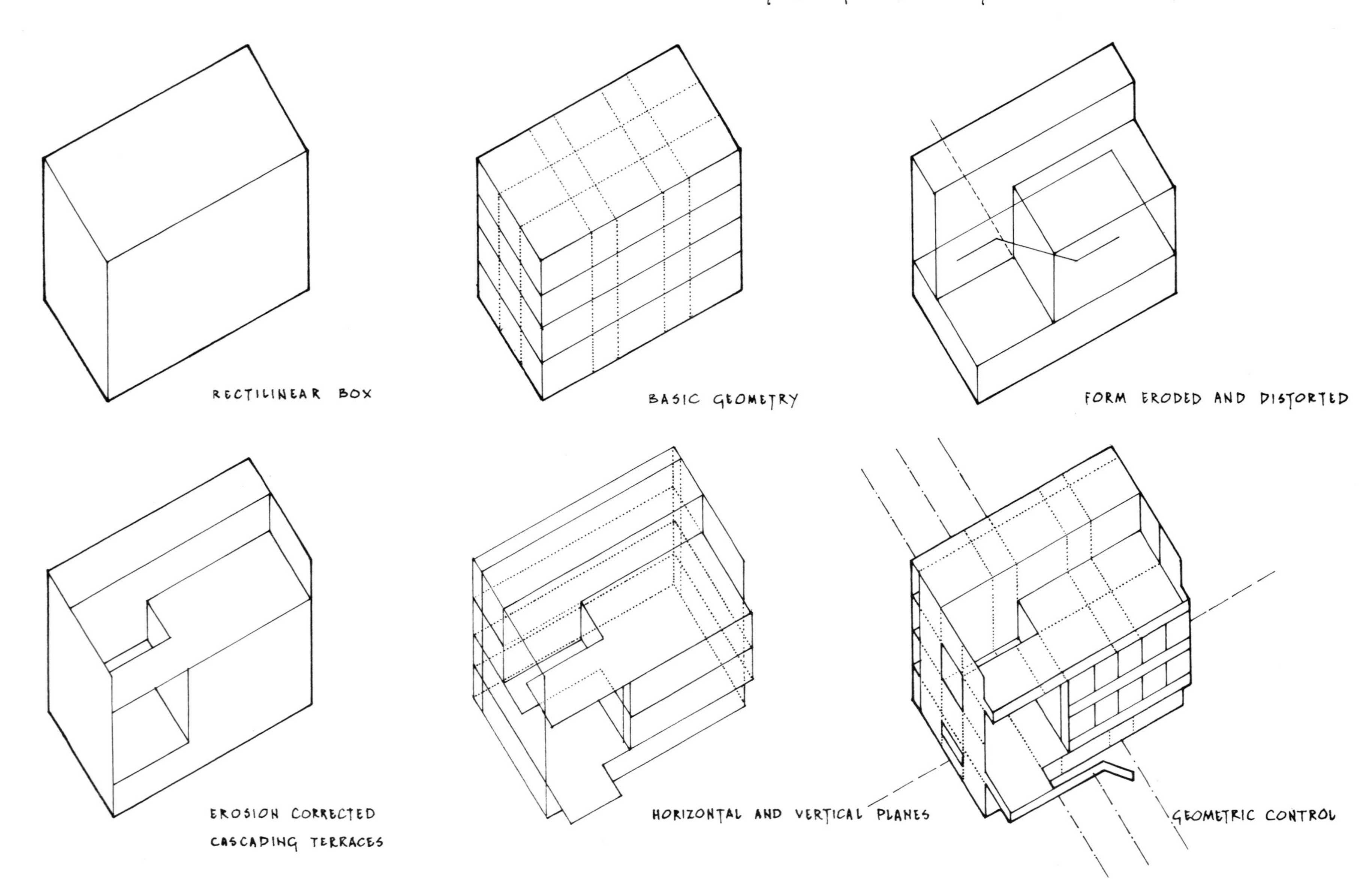

Although this analytical study does not set out to show how Le Corbusier evolved his design concept, this kind of dissection highlights issues of concern to him when the villa was designed. In this way analysis can reveal strategies and tactics used by an architect.[1]

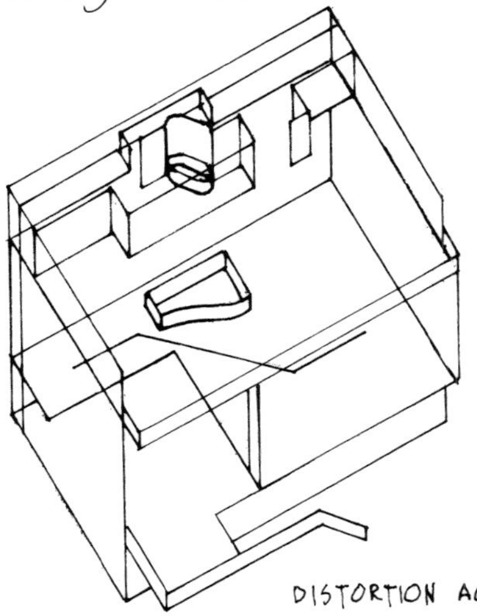

DISTORTION ACKNOWLEDGED

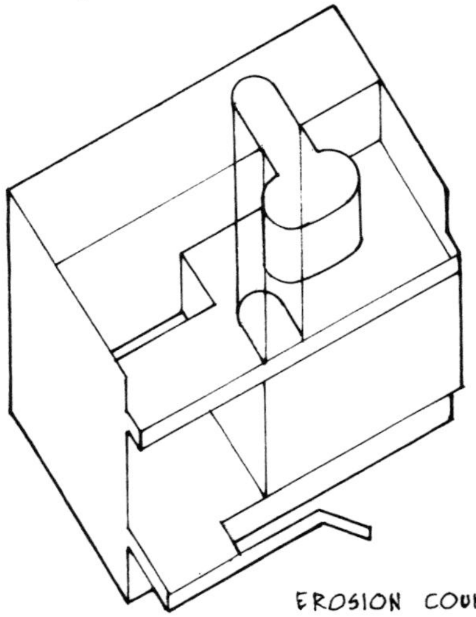

EROSION COUNTERED

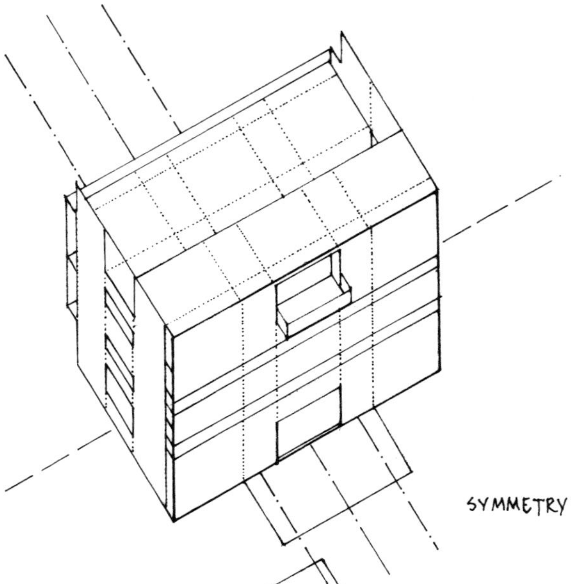

SYMMETRY

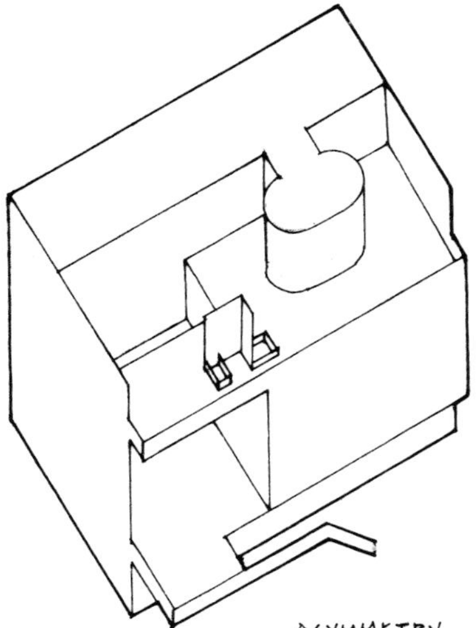

ASYMMETRY

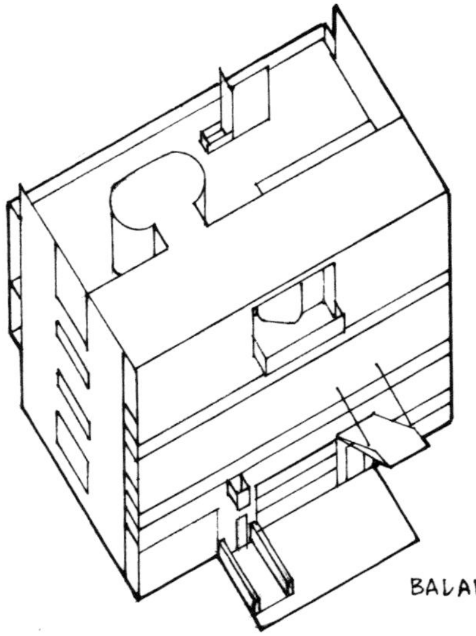

BALANCE

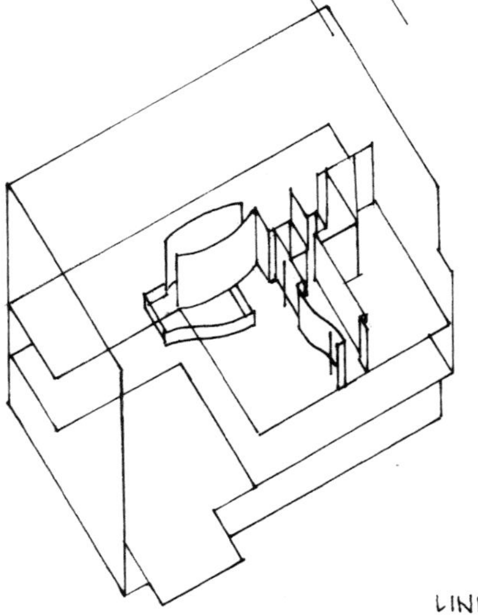

LINKAGES

[1] For a detailed analysis of the villa see G.H. Baker, Le Corbusier: An analysis of form, (Second Edition 1989), Van Nostrand Reinhold (International) Co. Ltd., London

GENERIC AND SPECIFIC FORM

Architectural form may be thought of as generic, in its original state, and specific, when the form assumes finality having been manipulated and organized to satisfy the functional demands of the programme and the particular confines or opportunities presented by the site.

Peter Eisenman has explained [1] how, when we read a square with one of its corners cut away, this is read in terms of its gestalt, as a square, which becomes the generic antecedent of the form.

Forms can be understood in relation to their generic antecedent, as when the articulation of the Monastery of St. Marie de La Tourette derives from a generic courtyard origin.

Similarly the Villa Capra may be read in terms of its square generic antecedent, reversing the courtyard of La Tourette with a centroidal core. As Eisenman points out, 'form in its generic state will provide the conceptual reference for all physical manifestations of specific form as well as give the basis for the specific ordering of this form. Form thought of in its conceptual state must acknowledge the requirements of the generic conditions.' [2]

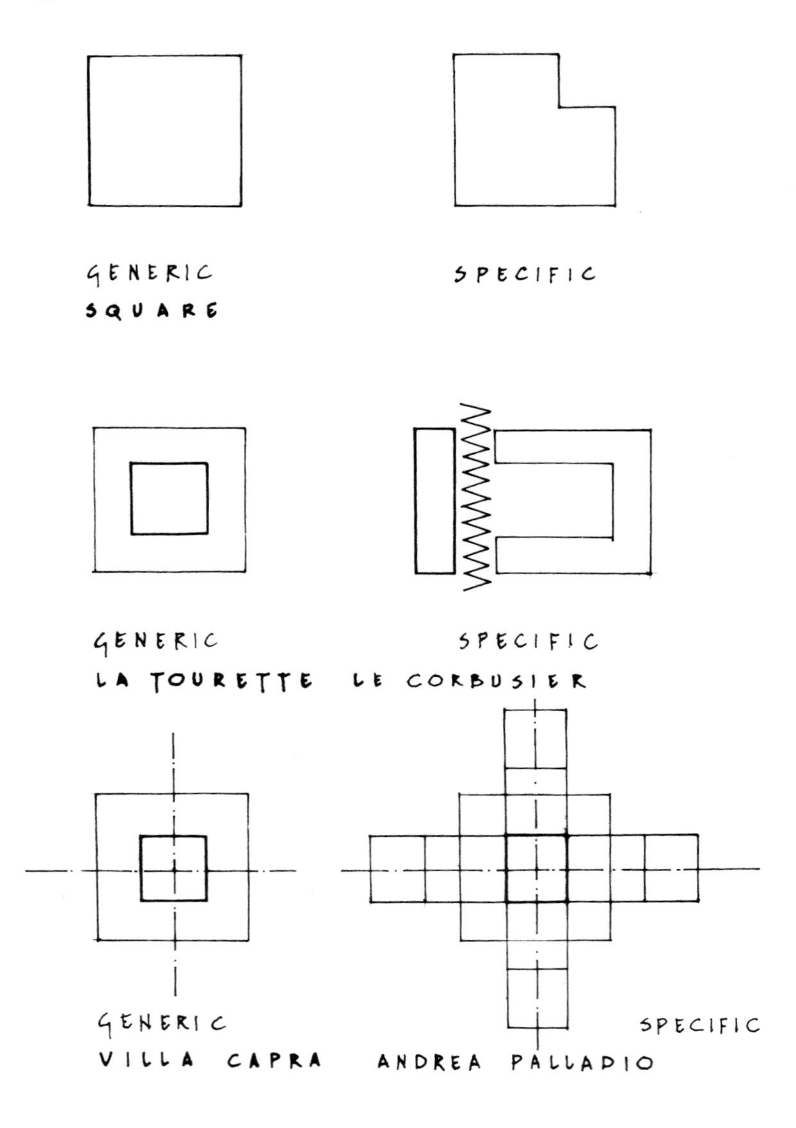

[1] P. Eisenman, The Formal Basis of Modern Architecture, Doctoral dissertation, University of Cambdridge, 1963, p. 43.
[2] Ibid., p. 42.

LA TOURETTE

The Monastery of La Tourette derives its conceptual origin from the square courtyard plan of the Cistercian monastic complex.[1] This generic form is changed by the interrelation between site forces and programmatic requirements.

From the generic square courtyard, site characteristics induce a linear condition. The program identifies a specific role for the church which is separated from the rest of the configuration. For functional and symbolic reasons the monks cells are arranged in a pinwheel formation and a linear route gives access from the monastic accommodation to the church.

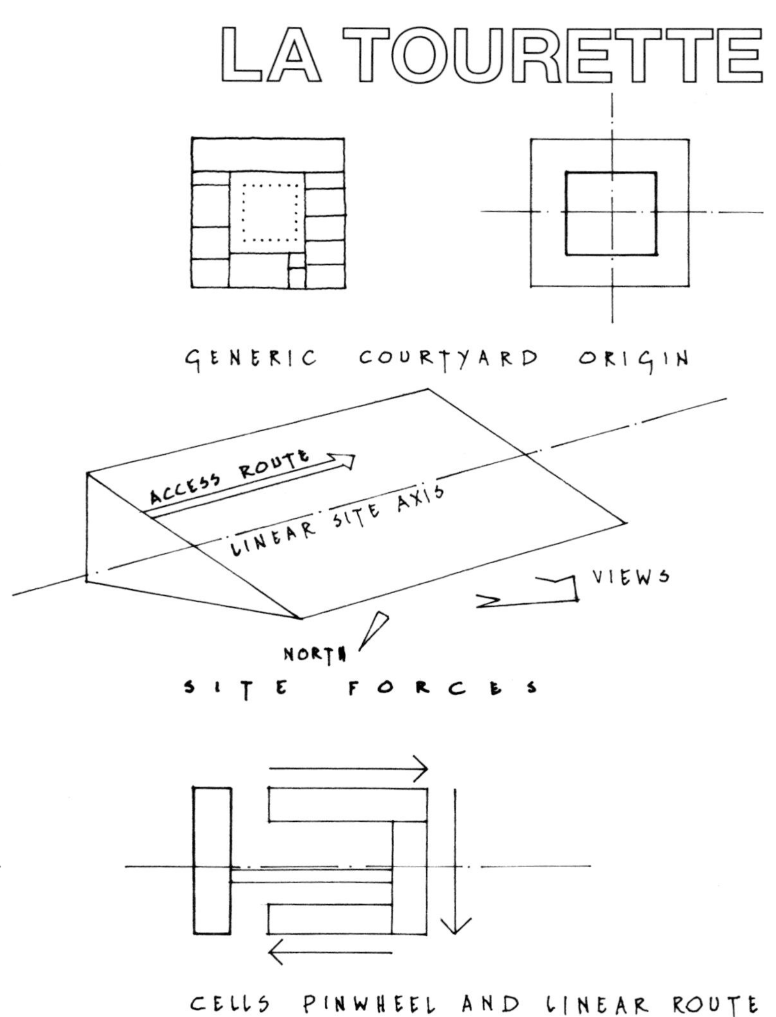

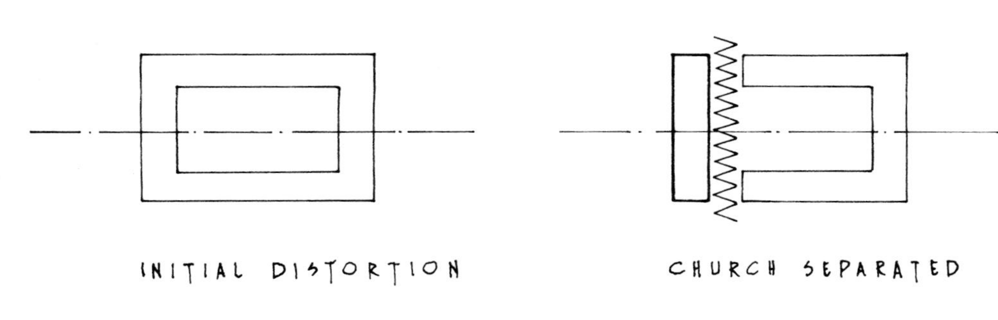

[1] Father Coutourier, acting as client for the monastery, sent Le Corbusier a sketch of the plan of a traditional Cistercian monastery. For an analysis of the design see G.H. Baker, Le Corbusier: An analysis of form. (Second Edition 1989). Van Nostrand Reinhold (International) Co. Ltd, London.

CARTESIAN GRID AND HORIZONTAL ABSOLUTE

Peter Eisenman refers to the three dimensional cartesian grid as 'the absolute reference for architectural form whether generic or specific.[1]' He explains how this grid of horizontals and verticals refers to the force of gravity and that 'everything is seen with reference to this grid whether man-made or natural.'[2]

In his study of the Greek temple temenos The idea of space in Greek architecture, Dr. Peter Martiensen refers to the horizontal absolute, as exemplified by the Greek temple platform, the flat plane on which the temple stands. The horizontal platform features strongly in the work of Jorn Utzen, particularly in his Sydney Opera House where the shells and structure rise from a horizontal podium.

In Le Corbusier's work, curved walls are frequently tensioned against an orthogonal grid, as in the Chapel at Ronchamp. In the case of both Richard Meier's and Le Corbusier's work, the orthogonal cage serves to discipline the organisation of elements. (see analysis of Meier's Atheneum, pp

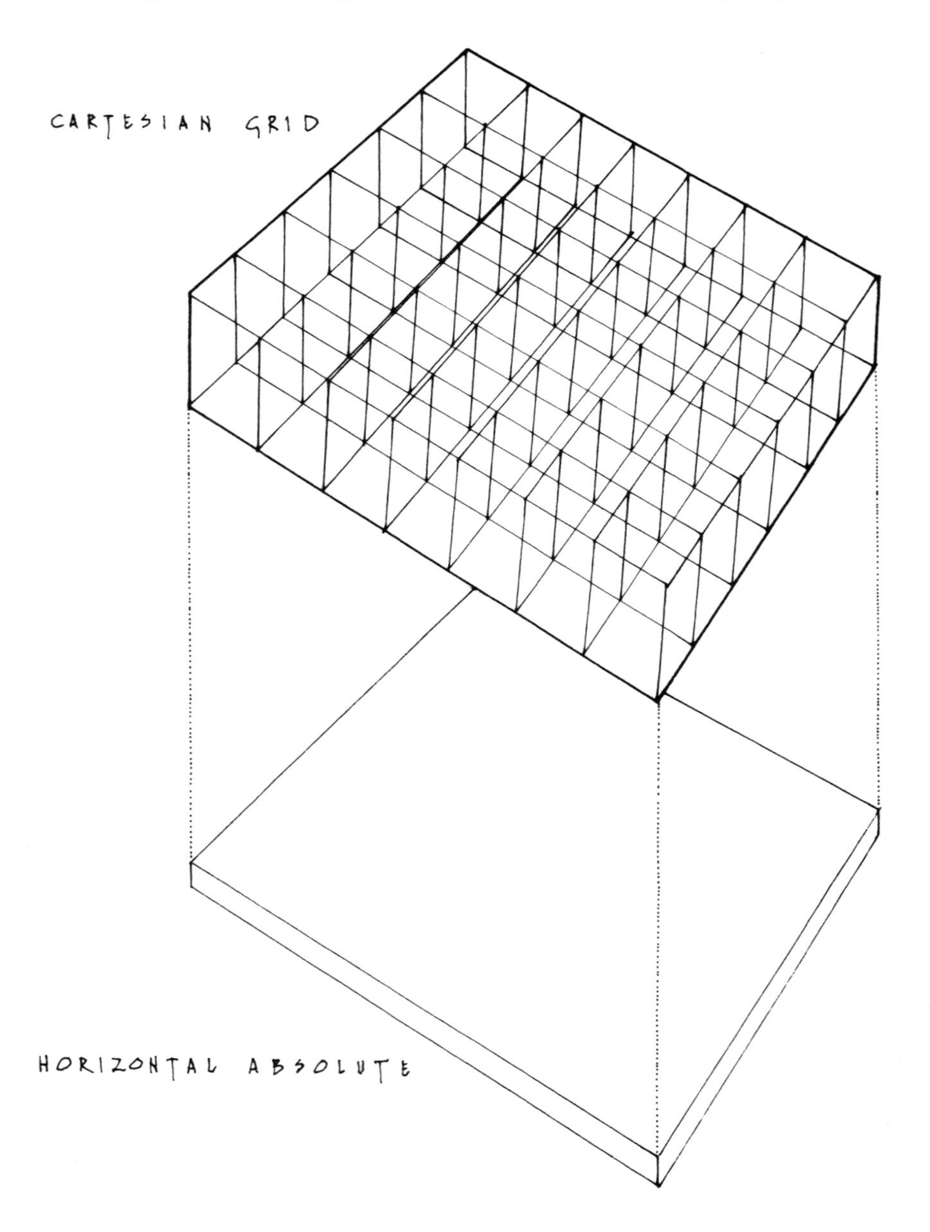

[1] Peter Eisenman, The formal basis of modern architecture, Doctoral dissertation, University of Cambridge, 1963. p. 27
[2] Ibid, p 28

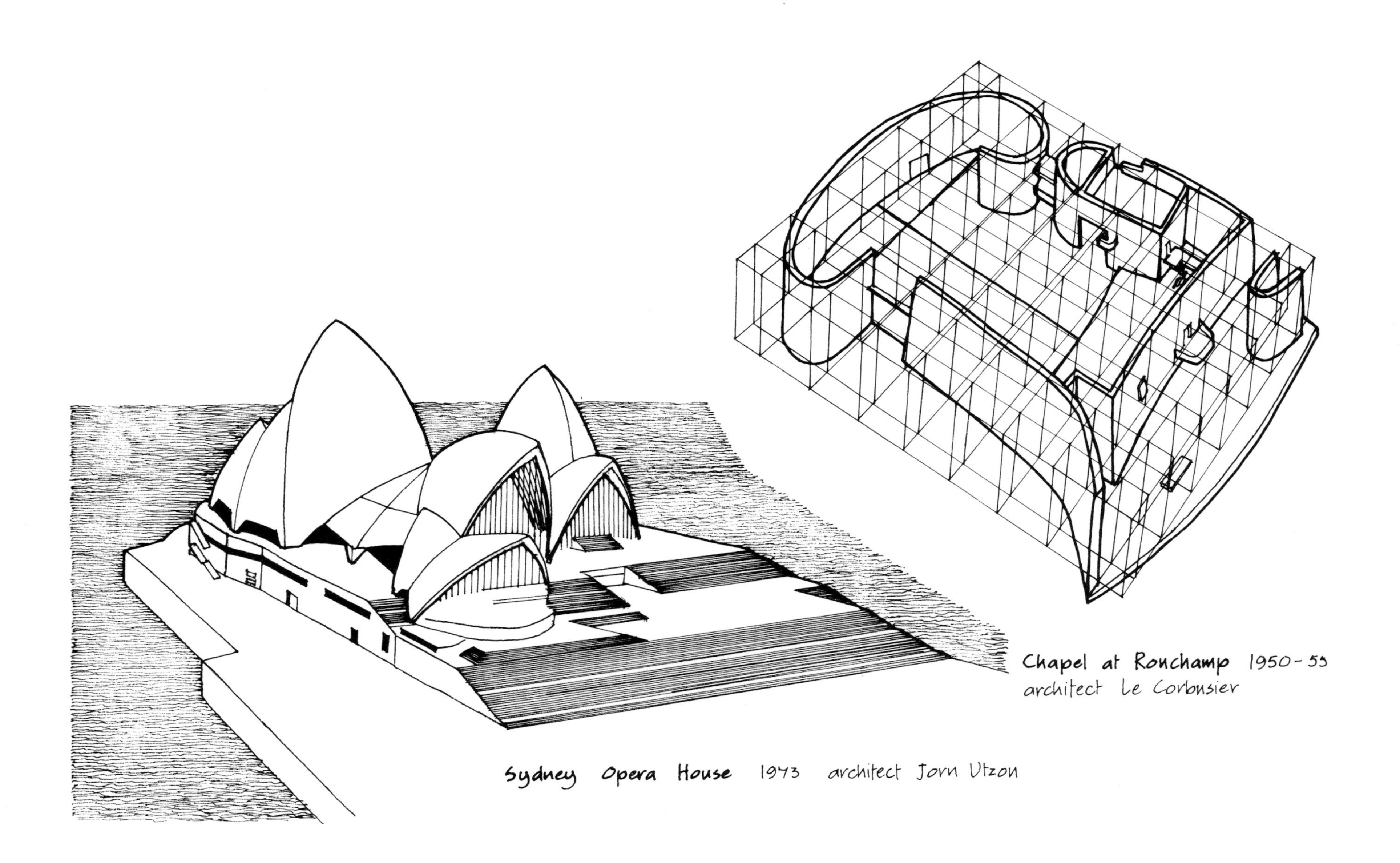

Chapel at Ronchamp 1950–55
architect Le Corbusier

Sydney Opera House 1973 architect Jorn Utzon

MASS AND SURFACE

For analytical purposes it is important to distinguish between mass and surface. Mass may be regarded as the solid component of form as exemplified in Palladio's Villa Capra at Vicenza. In contrast, Le Corbusier's studio/apartment for Amadée Ozenfant in Paris may be seen as a statement of planes.

In general Alvar Aalto states mass in his projects (see analysis of Säynätsalo, pp 153-181) whereas Mies van de Rohe is concerned with a juxtaposition of planes. The Barcelona Pavilion may be regarded as the antithesis of Palladio's mass statements in masonry, this being a consequence of the availability of steel and large glazed areas, coupled with a changed view of spatial composition due partly to the influence of modern art.

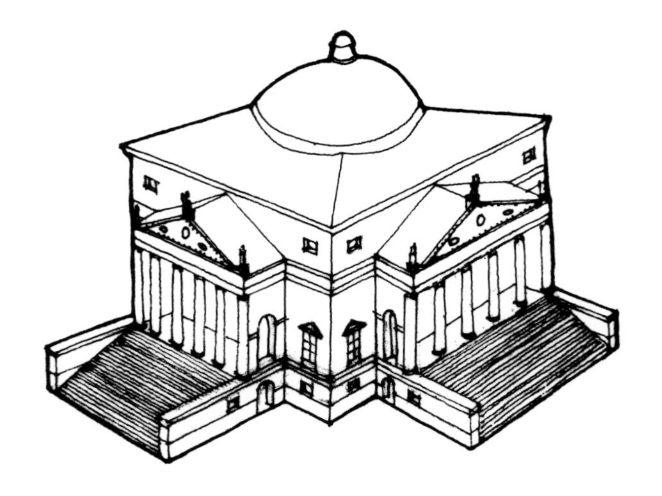

Villa Capra Vicenza 1567 architect Andrea Palladio

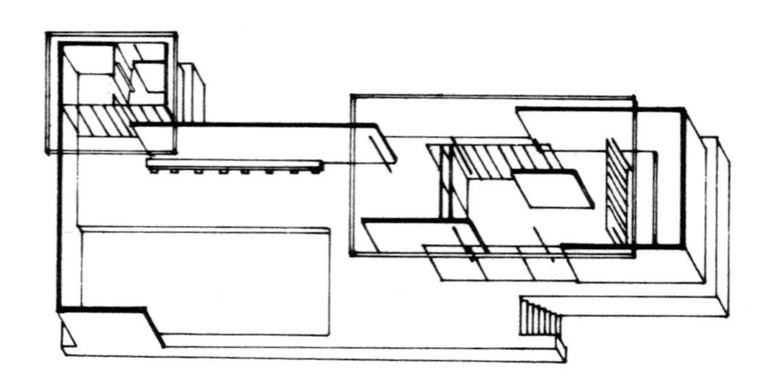

Barcelona Pavilion 1929 architect Ludwig Mies van de Rohe

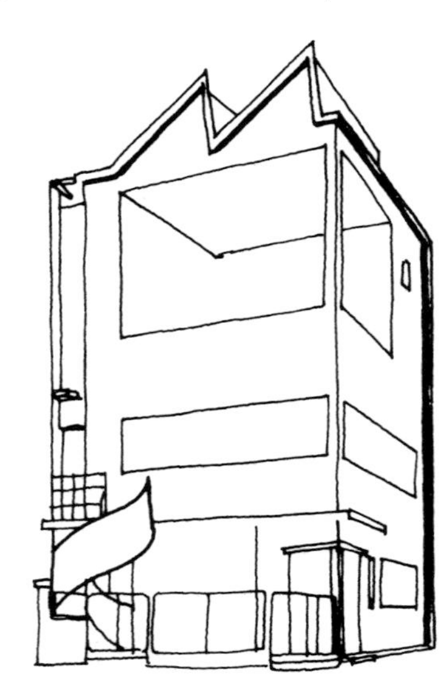

Studio apartment for Ozenfant 1922 architect Le Corbusier

Humana Building Louisville Kentucky 1982
architect Michael Graves

ARTICULATION OF THE MASS

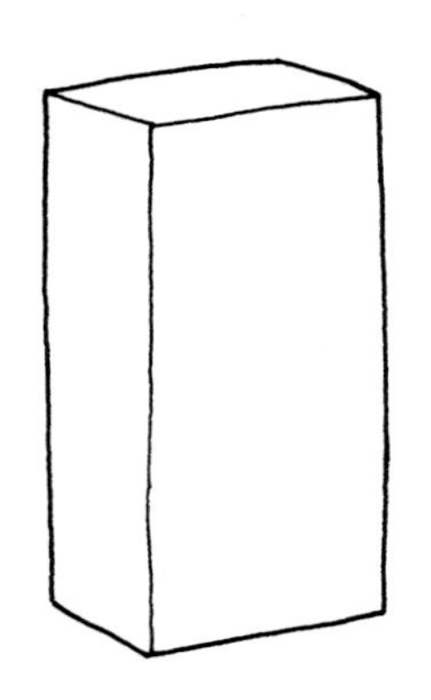

Generic rectilinear slab.

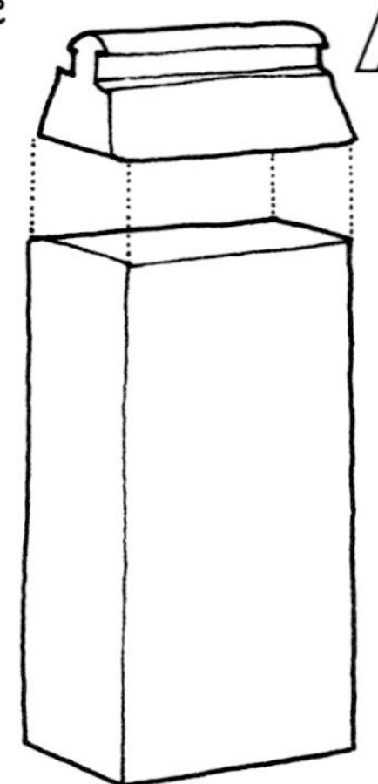

Top added to terminate the slab and also to enrich the skyline.

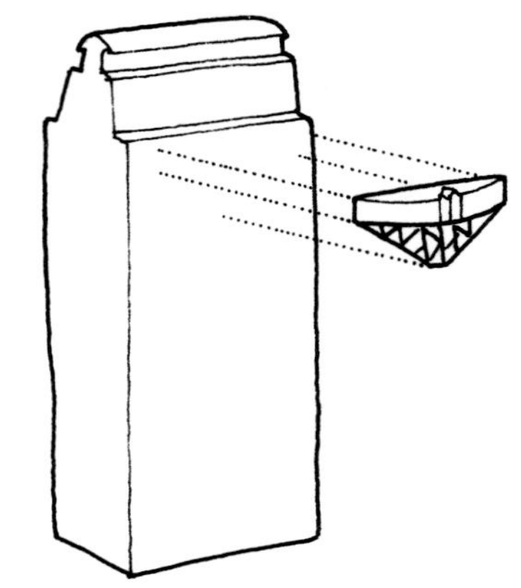

Roof garden and cantilever trusses assist the vertical termination and give a view towards the river.

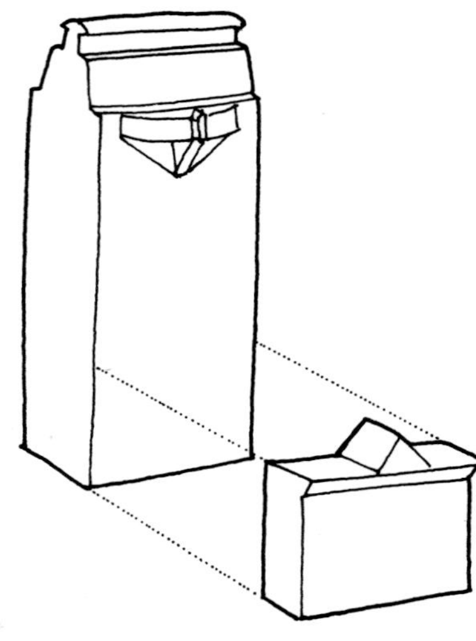

Lower section in scale with street.

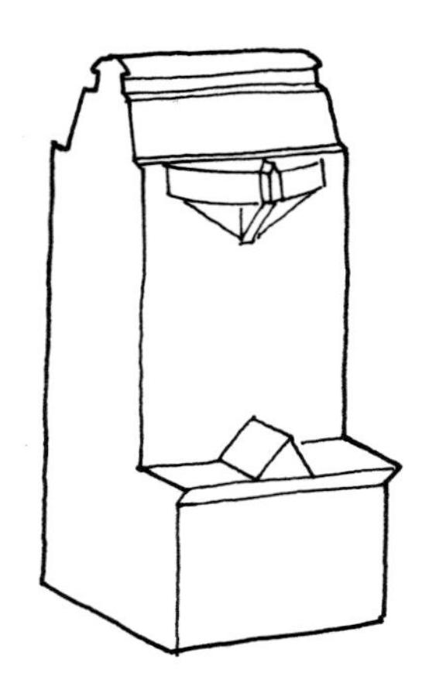

Symmetrical form requires more axial definition and reference to internal functions.

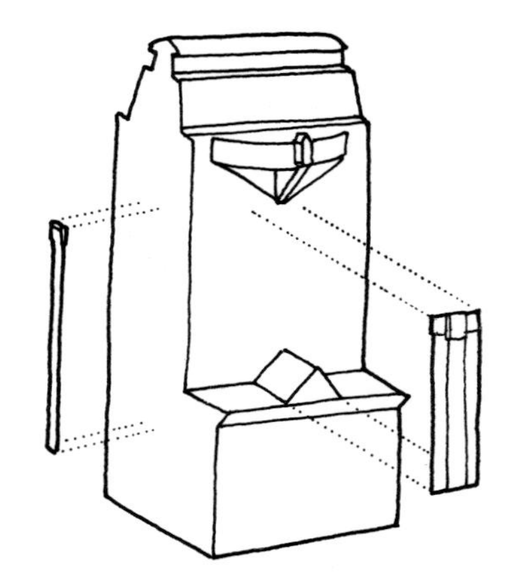

Vertical elements emphasise axiality and tie top and bottom together.

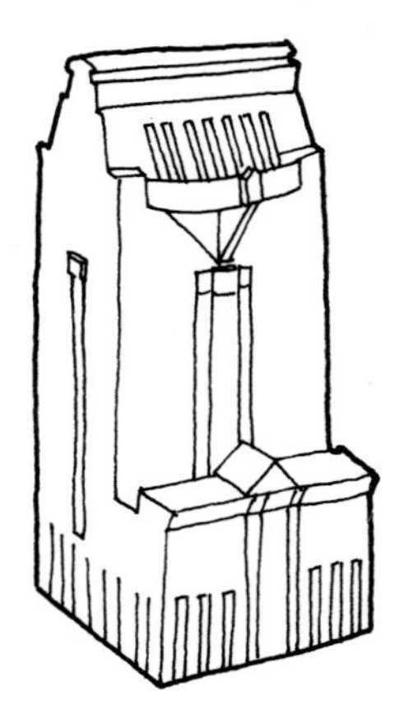

Major openings identify main spaces within the building.

Final articulation responds to context and internal functions using Graves base shaft and capital system.

CENTROIDAL AND LINEAR FORM

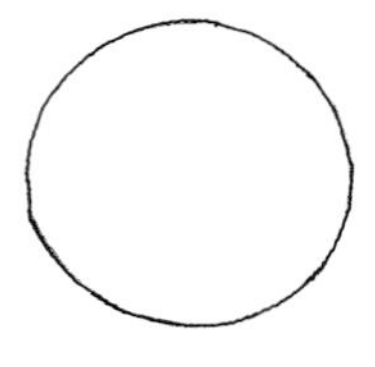
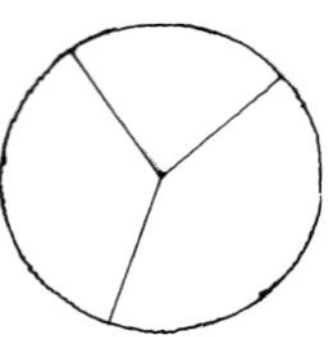
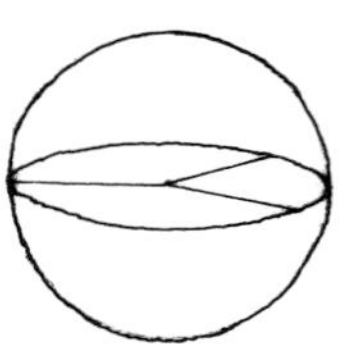

Centroidal configurations such as the sphere and the cube maintain a balance of forces as distinct from linear configurations in which the predominant force has a particular energy and direction.

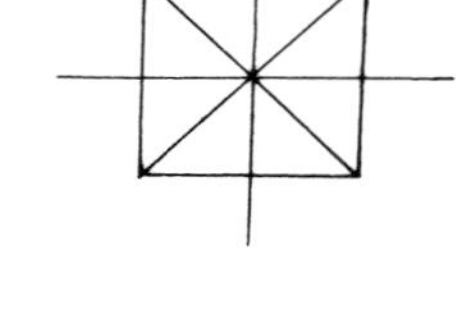
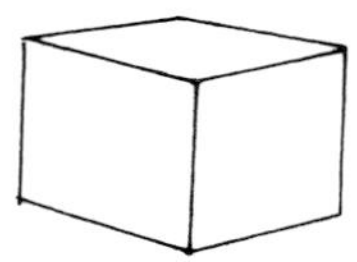
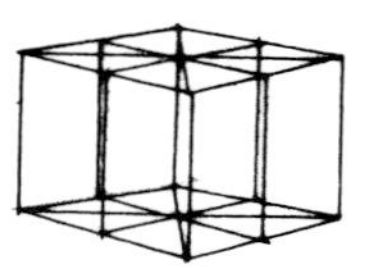

Centroidal bodies suggest repose and stability whereas linear forms imply activity.

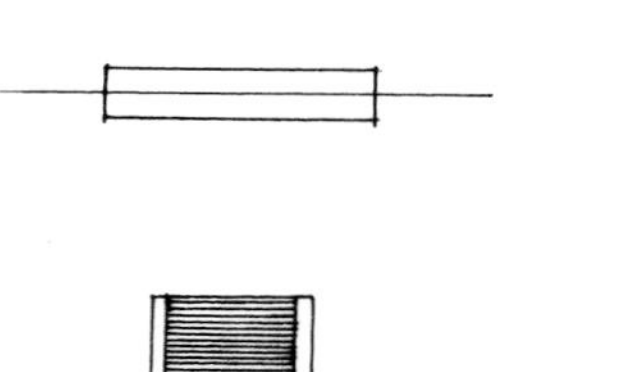
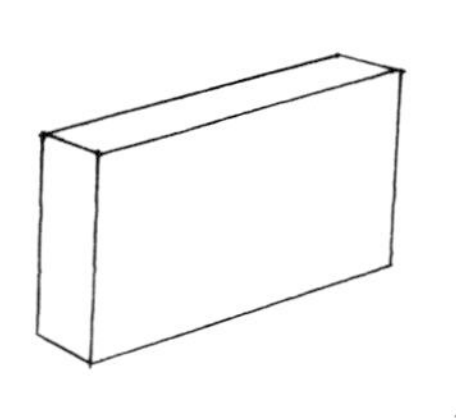
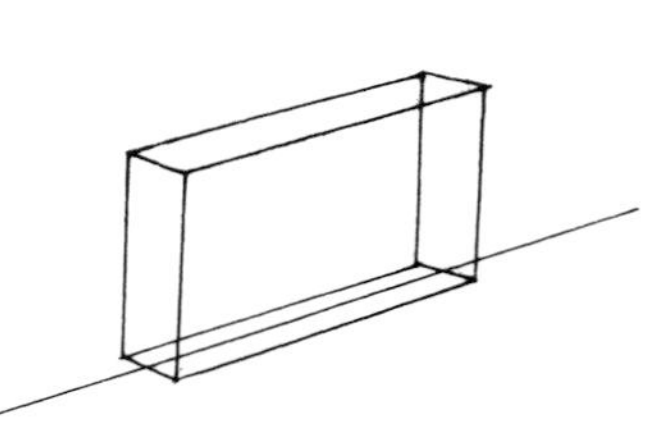

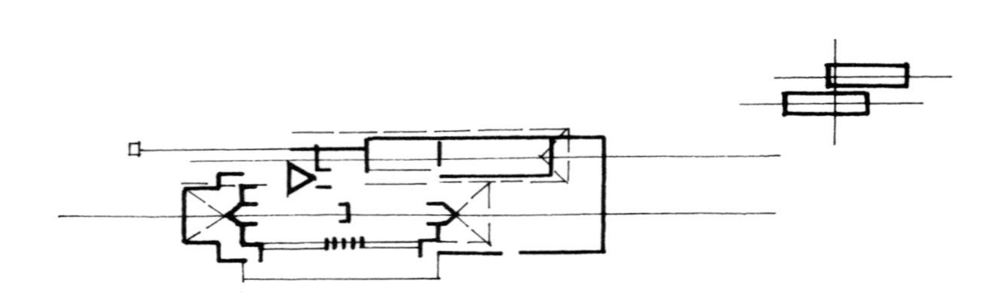

Frank Lloyd Wright's Robie house deploys two linear forms in a potentially shifting relationship.

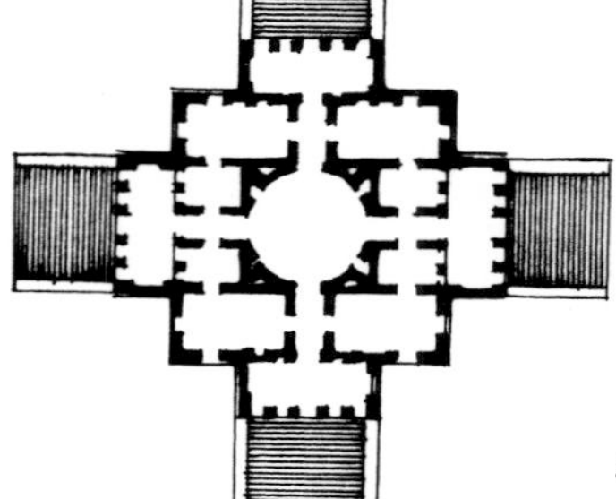
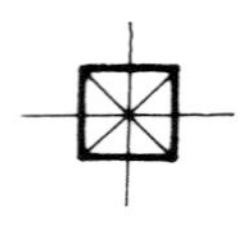

Andrea Palladio's Villa Capra is an almost symmetrical centroid.

About the dynamics of form Maurice de Sausmarez has written

> The simplest unit, a spot, not only indicates location but is felt to have within itself potential energies of expansion and contraction which activate the surrounding area. When two spots occur there is a statement of measurement and implied direction and the 'inner' energies create a specific tension between them which directly affects the intervening space.
>
> A line can be thought of as a chain of spots joined together. It indicates position and direction and has within itself a certain energy, the energy to travel along its length and to be intensified at either end, speed is implied and the space around it is activated. In a limited way it is capable of expressing emotions, e.g. a thick line is associated with boldness, a straight line with strength and stability, a zig-zag with excitement.
>
> Horizontals and verticals operating together introduce the principle of balanced oppositions of tensions. The vertical expresses a force which is of primary significance - gravitational pull, the horizontal again contributes a primary sensation - a supporting flatness; the two together produce a deeply satisfying resolved feeling, perhaps because they symbolise the human experience of absolute balance, of standing erect on level ground.
>
> Diagonals introduce powerful directional impulses, a dynamism which is the outcome of unresolved tendencies towards vertical and horizontal which are held in balanced suspension.

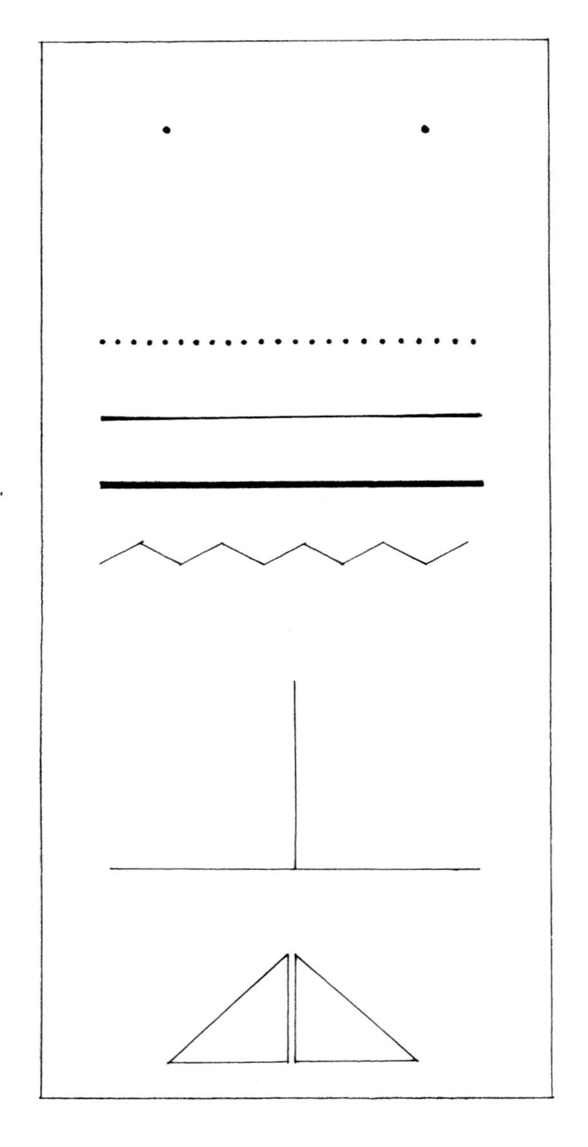

Maurice de Sausmarez, Basic Design: The Dynamics of Visual Form, Studio Vista London 1964 pp 20-22.
by permission of The Herbert Press Ltd.

CORE SYSTEMS

Architectonic arrangements may be described as systems in which the various parts are organised in relation to a thematic idea. The inherent structural nature of architecture implies a geometric organisation and the systemic ordering of architectonic form is therefore geometrical.

Centroidal core systems include the spiral – often expressed as a pinwheel – cluster and cruciform systems.

Systems provide a discipline rather than a limit. They allow for growth, they accommodate the scherzo : They can be elaborated to encompass infinite variations and complexities.

Peter Eisenman

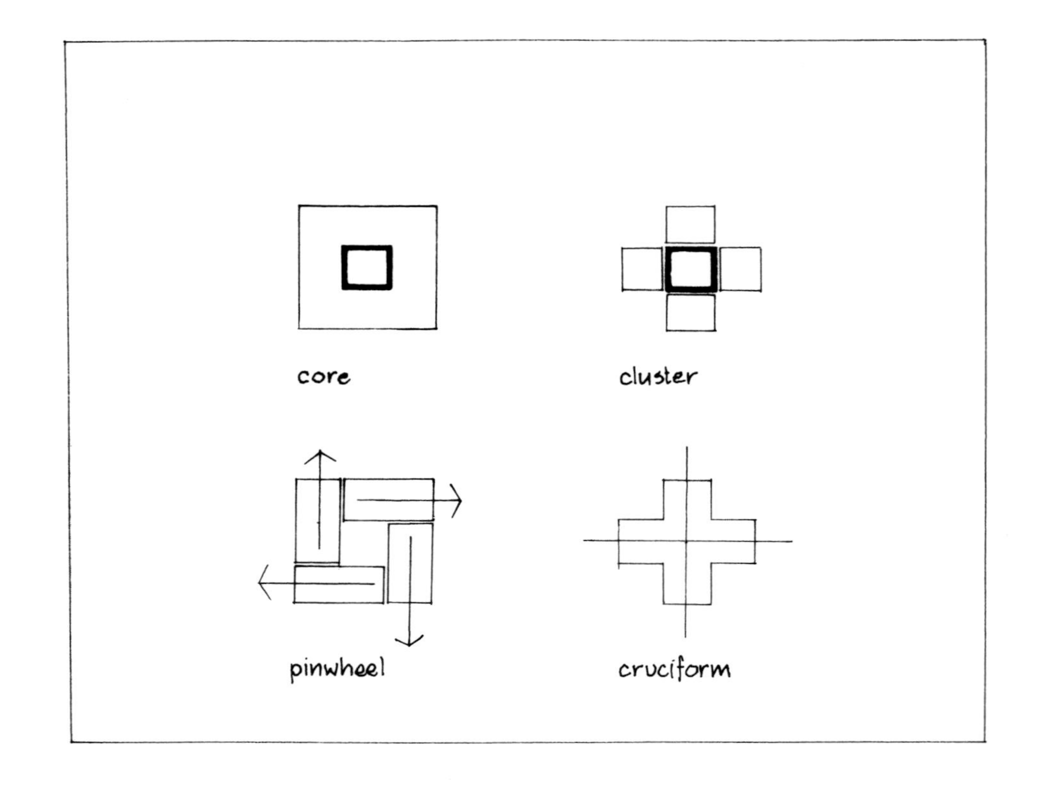

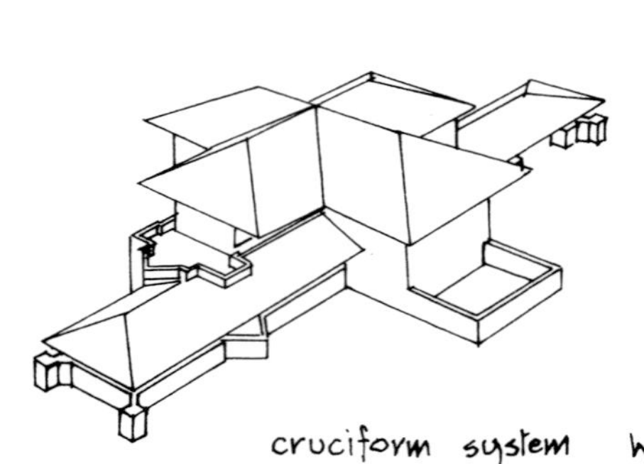

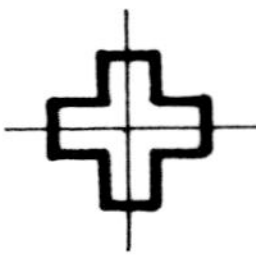

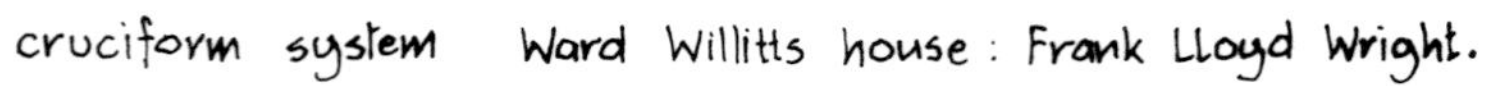
cruciform system Ward Willitts house : Frank Lloyd Wright.

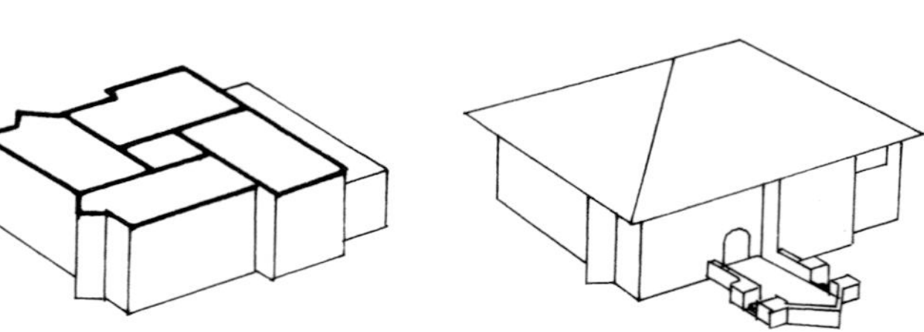
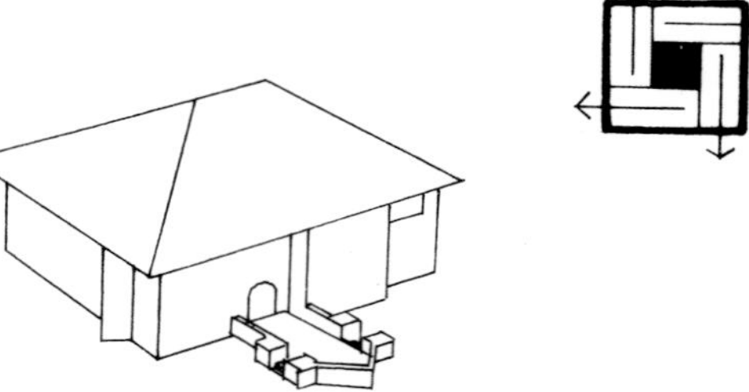

pinwheel system Arthur Heurtley house : Frank Lloyd Wright.

LINEAR SYSTEMS

Linear systems afford additive opportunities along axes. This allows for repetition and the development of rhythms. Movement becomes an important component of the form.

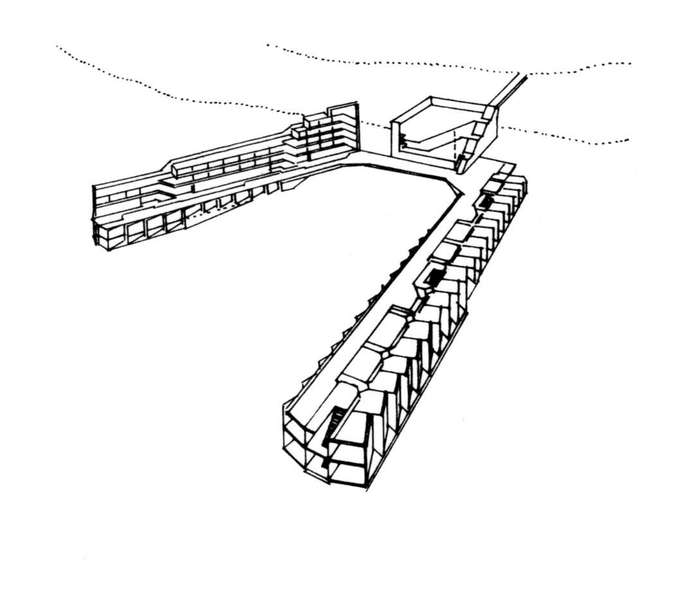

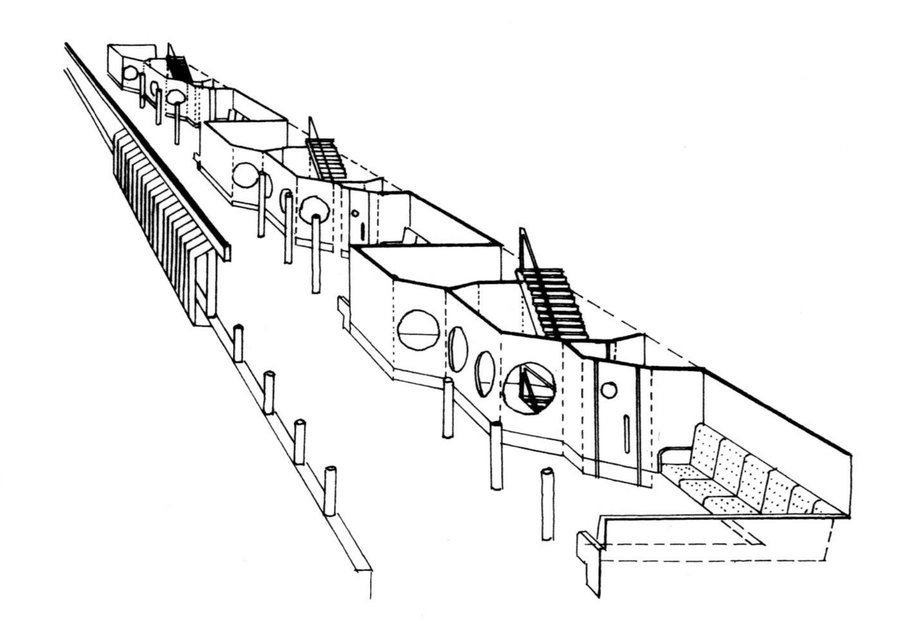

James Stirling Residential expansion for St. Andrews University 1964

AXIAL SYSTEMS

Axial ordering has formed the basis of monumental architecture since ancient times. Bi lateral symmetry with a hierarchical volumetric arrangement was the main organisational system prior to the twentieth century. During the present century axes have also played a key role in the design strategies of many architects.

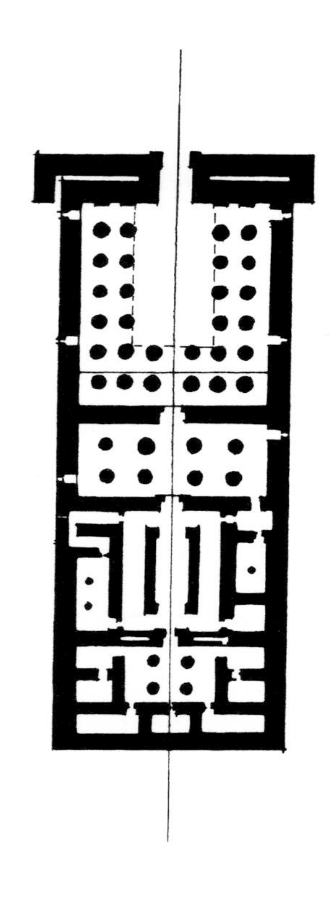

Temple of Khons Karnak B.C. 1200

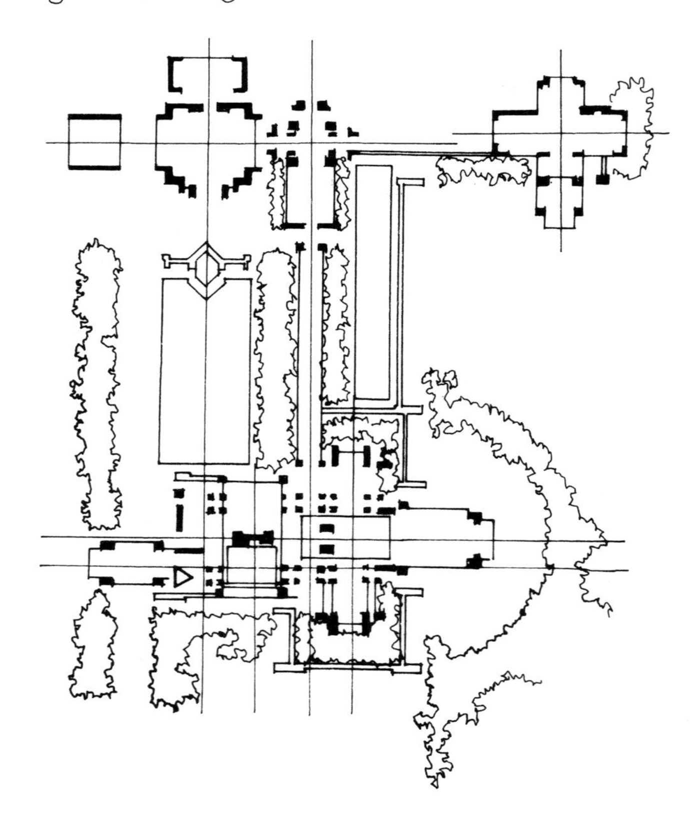

Frank Lloyd Wright Darwin D. Martin house 1904

ECHELON AND RADIAL SYSTEMS

James Stirling's History Faculty Library at Cambridge has a radial plan for the main reading room. This becomes polygonal at the perimeter and entry to the reading room is by an echelon system.

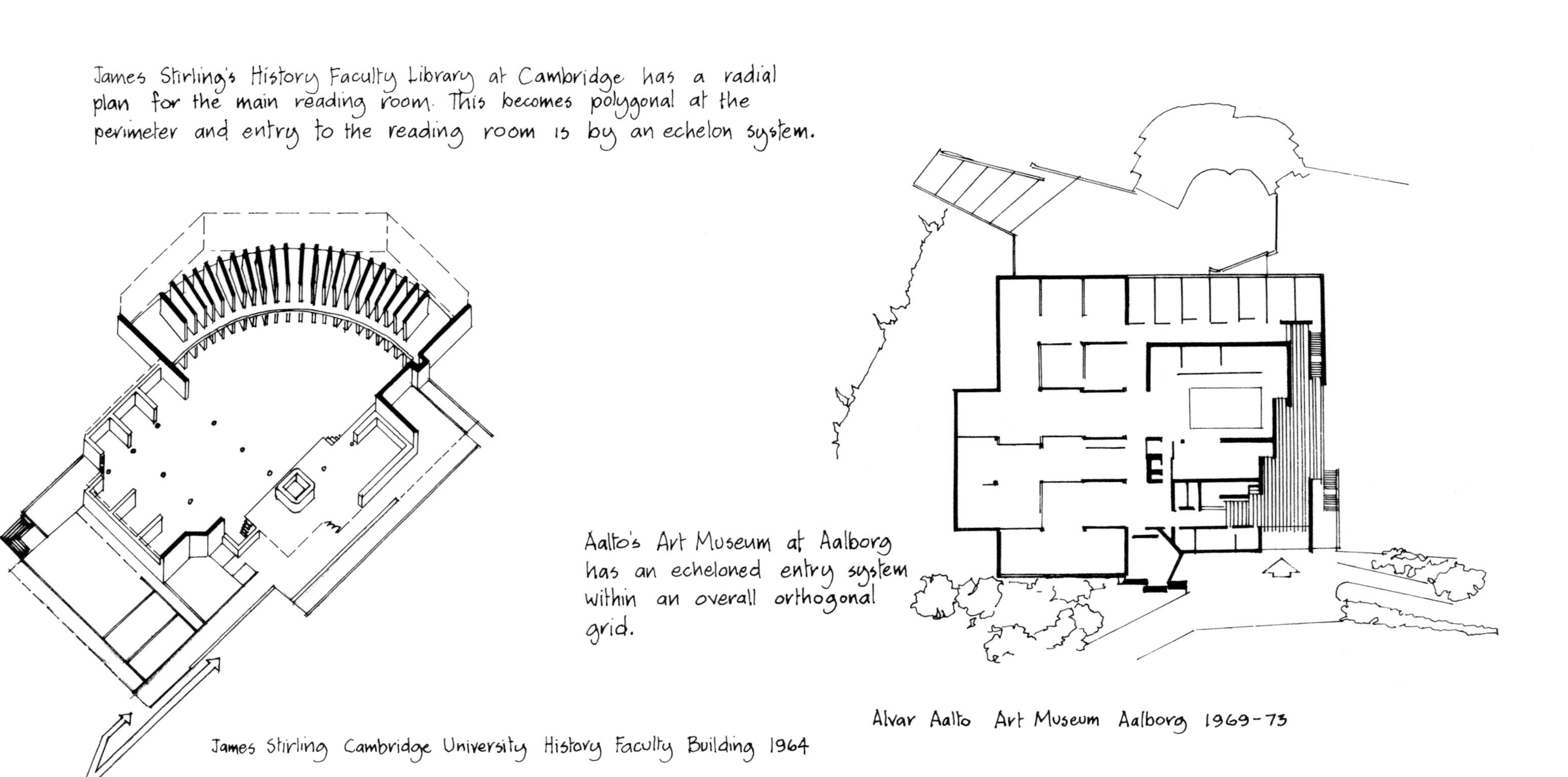

Aalto's Art Museum at Aalborg has an echeloned entry system within an overall orthogonal grid.

James Stirling Cambridge University History Faculty Building 1964

Alvar Aalto Art Museum Aalborg 1969–73

INTERLOCKING SYSTEMS

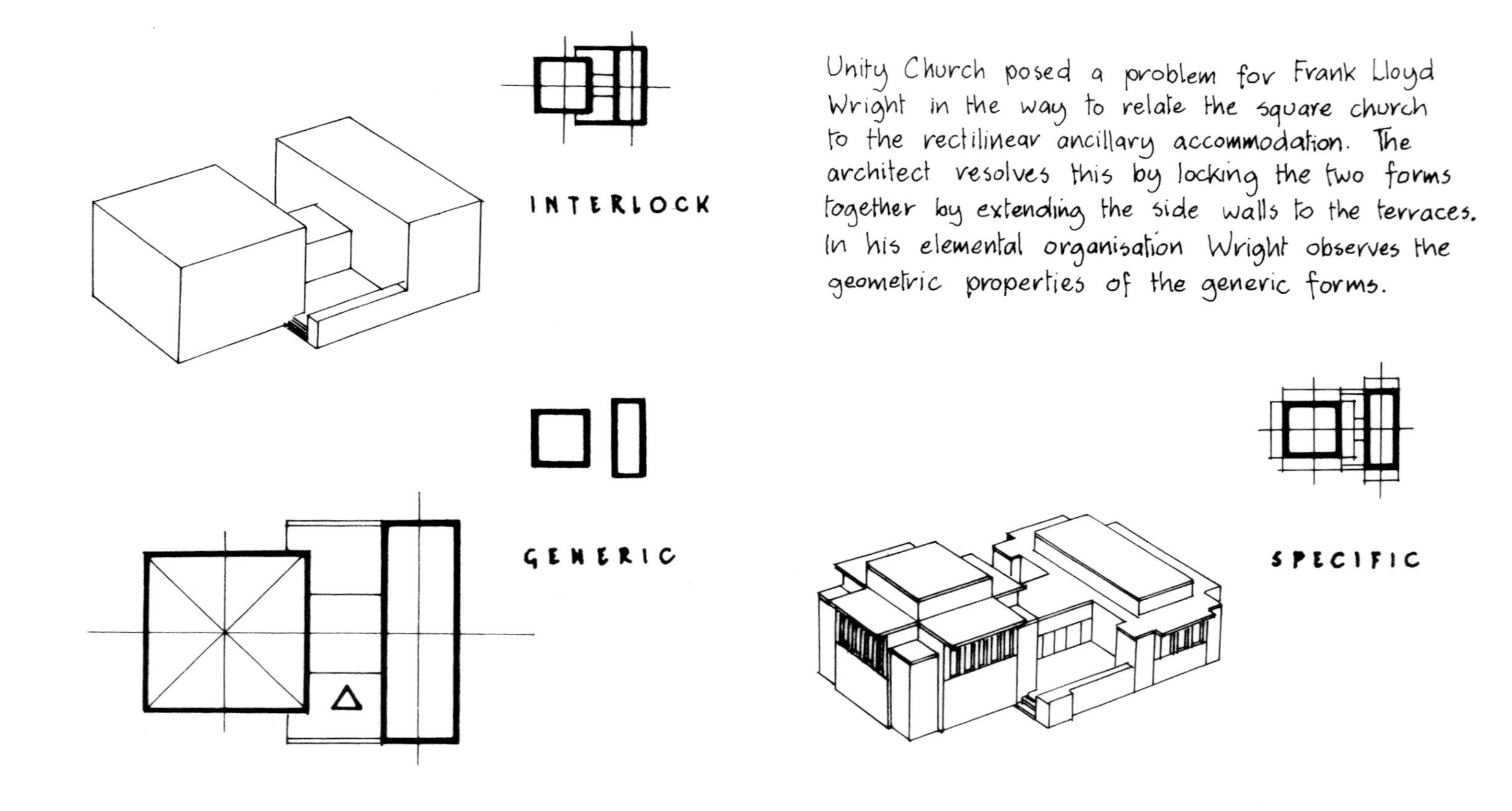

Unity Church posed a problem for Frank Lloyd Wright in the way to relate the square church to the rectilinear ancillary accommodation. The architect resolves this by locking the two forms together by extending the side walls to the terraces. In his elemental organisation Wright observes the geometric properties of the generic forms.

Frank Lloyd Wright Unity Church Oak Park Illinois 1906

FORM DISTORTION

Alvar Aalto's Cultural Centre at Wolfsburg is concerned with a centroidal problem on a linear site. The generic core form is distorted by the site to become rectilinear and in specific terms the form responds radially to the piazza by the arrangement of lecture theatres.

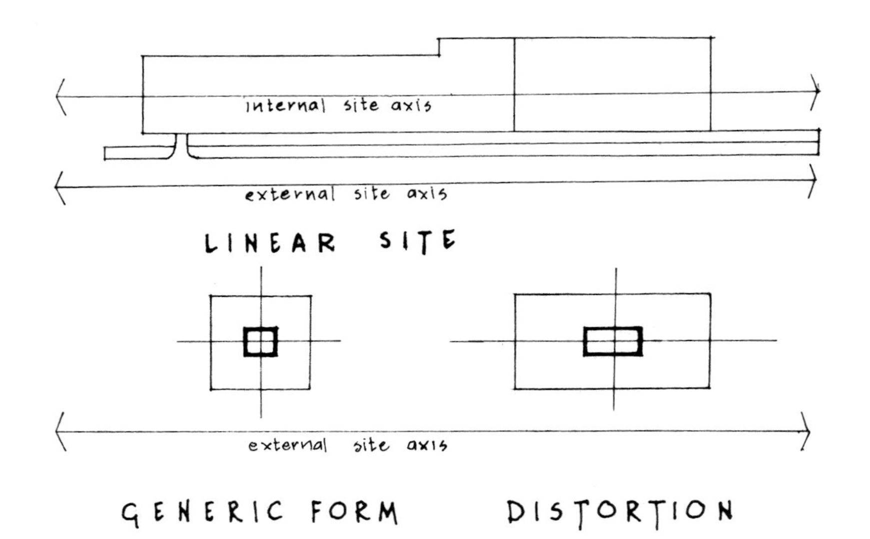

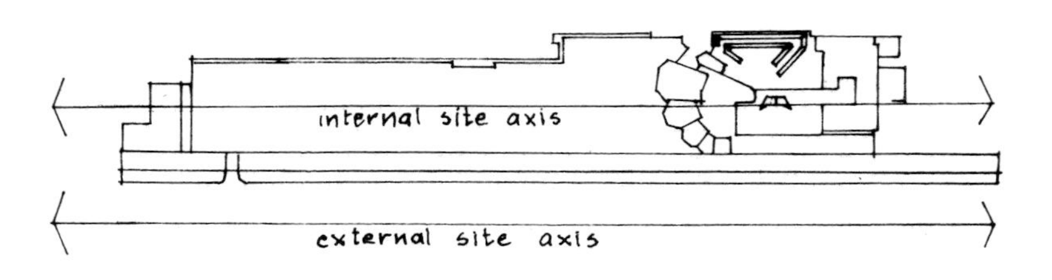

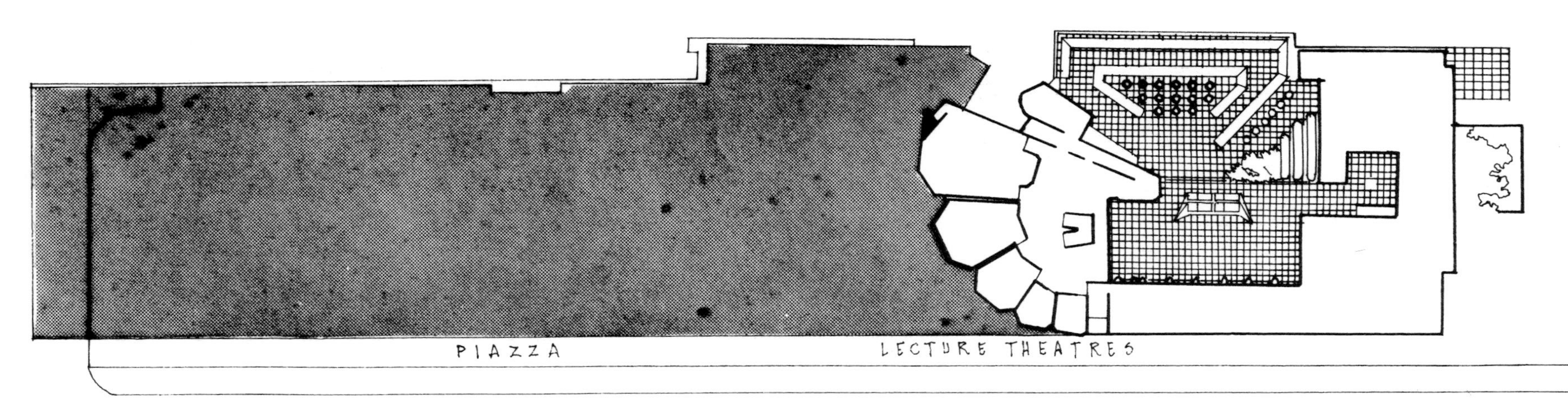

Alvar Aalto Cultural Centre Wolfsburg West Germany 1958–63

PART TWO

ANALYTICAL STUDIES

4

THE VILLAGE AND CITY IN HISTORY

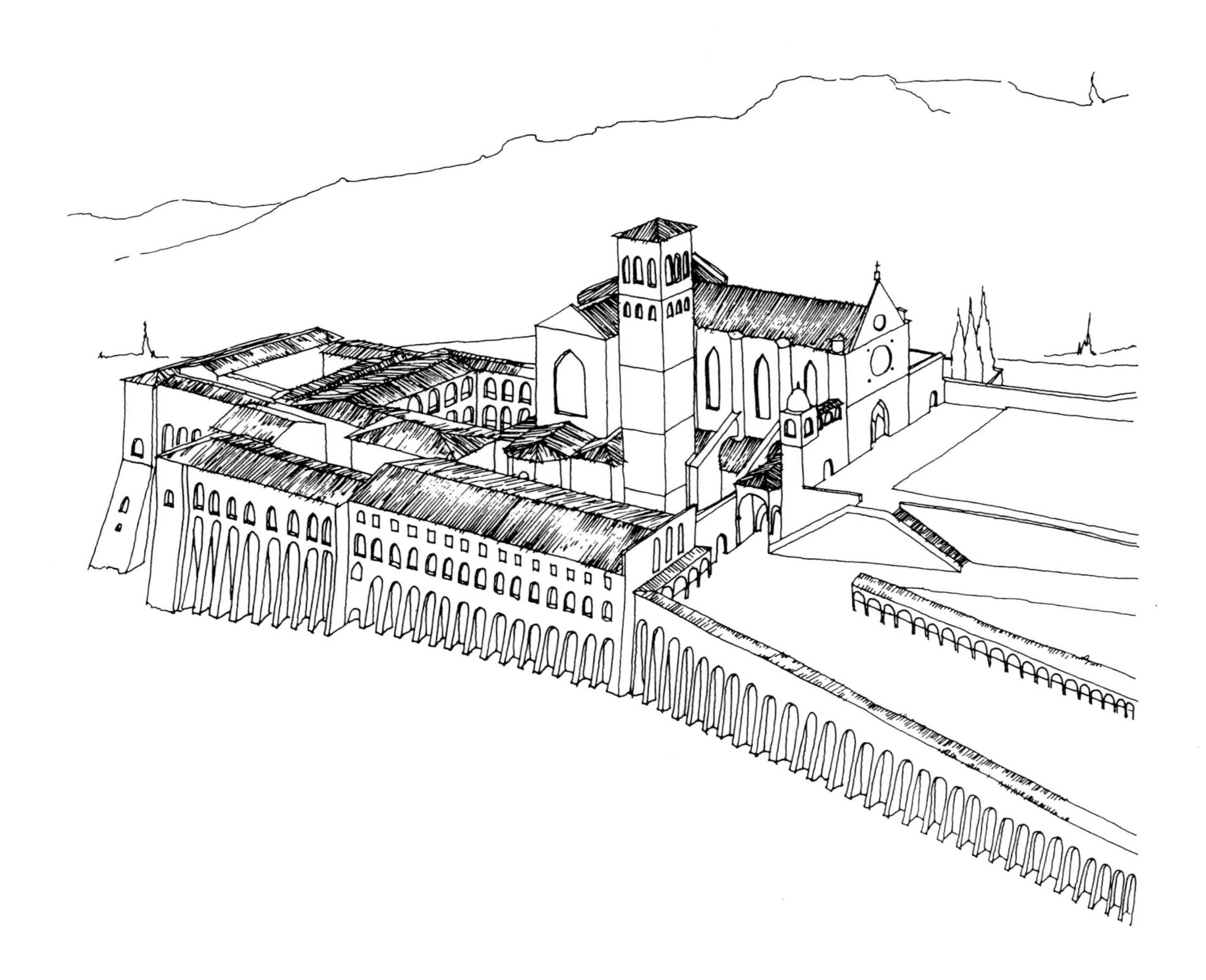

MONASTIC COMPLEX AT ASSISI

PROBLEM AND SITE

At Assisi site forces and programmatic requirements have conspired to create that total architecture so often realized in the Middle Ages. The site comprises a narrow finger of land jutting out from the long hill on which the town of Assisi stands. The monastery has two churches at its core and is linked to the town by two piazze, sculpted into the contours and providing a gap between sacred and secular. This particular problem, in this particular setting, has produced a profound synthesis, in which the monastery, the context, symbolism and cultural values are articulated in an architectural masterpiece.

GENERIC FORM

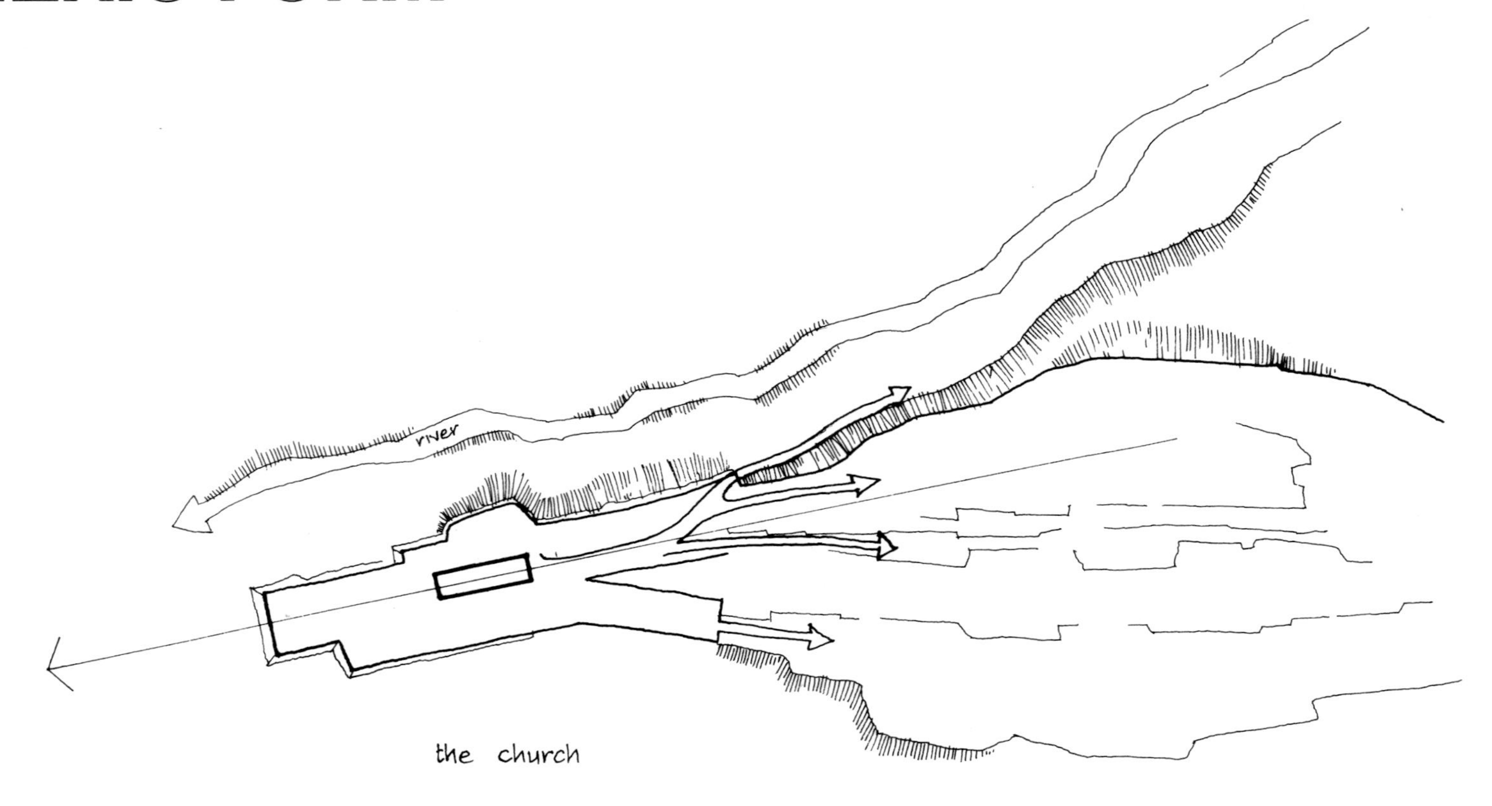

The church to the monastery at Assisi is placed within a linear site context at the end of the hill on which the town stands the generic form is linear with a dominant longitudinal axis A series of routes lead from the monastery to the town and beyond.

The above and following drawings in this sequence are after drawings by Simon Buckley

SPECIFIC FORM

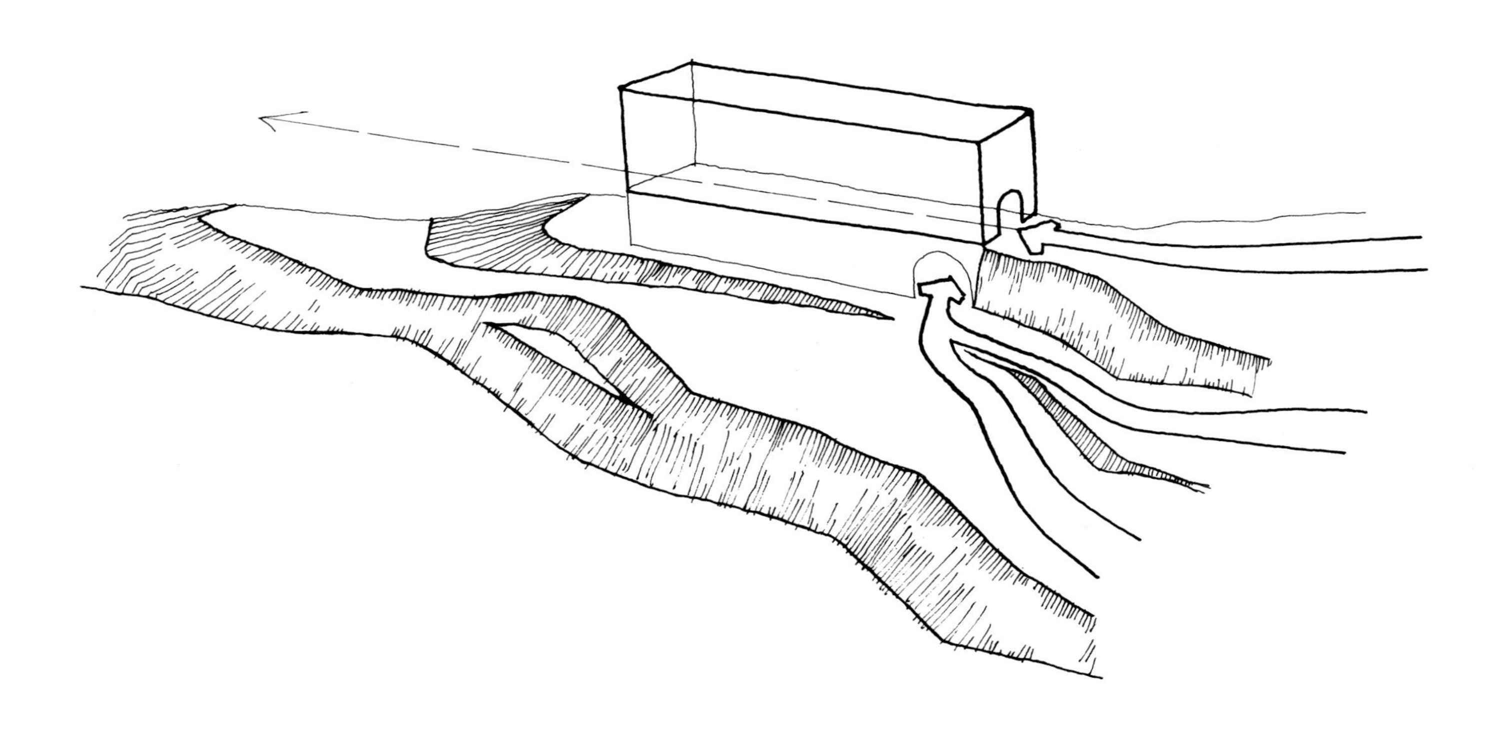

The generic linear configuration is modulated in accordance with programme and site. In specific terms two churches are provided, an upper and a lower, each on different levels.

SPECIFIC FORM

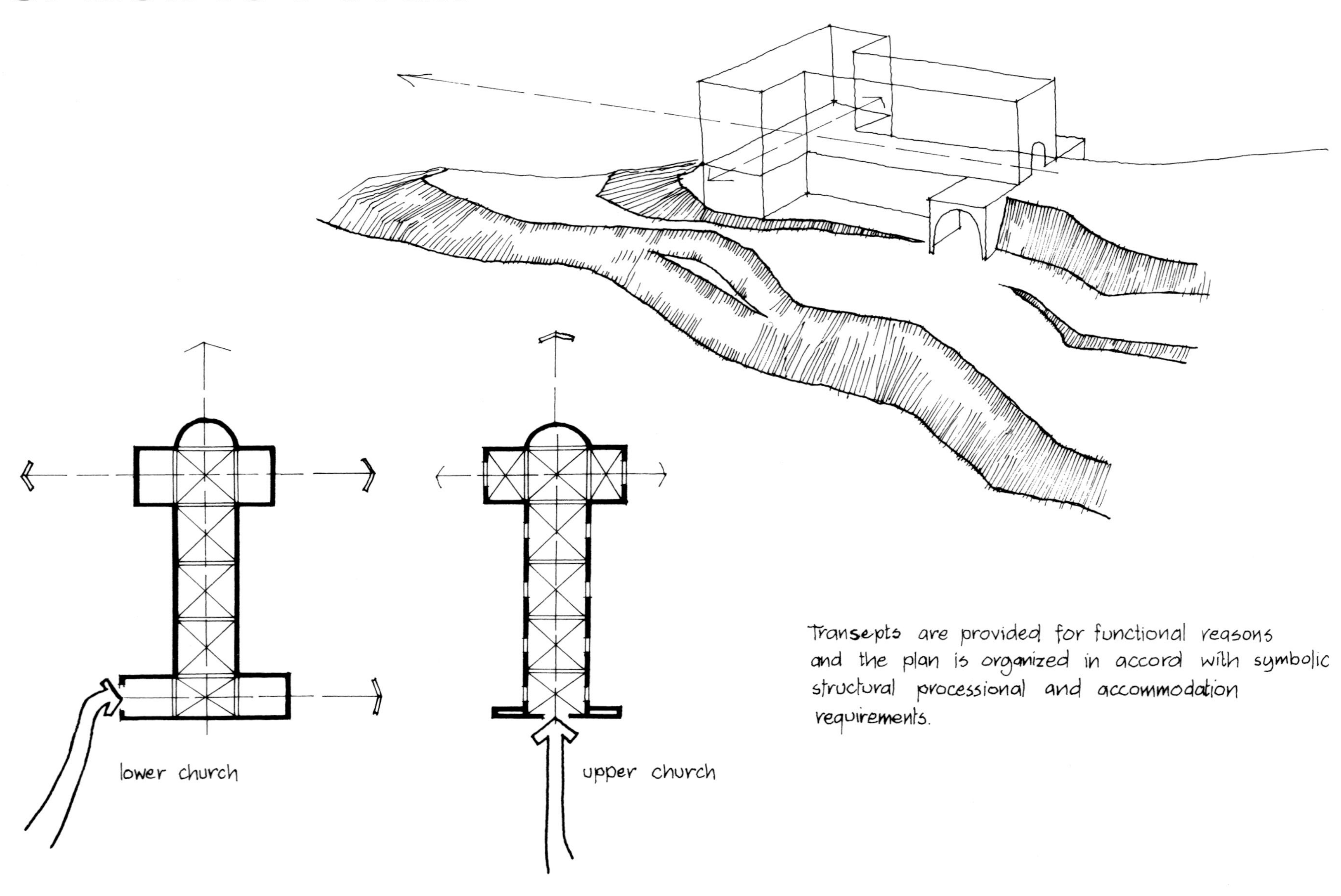

Transepts are provided for functional reasons and the plan is organized in accord with symbolic structural processional and accommodation requirements.

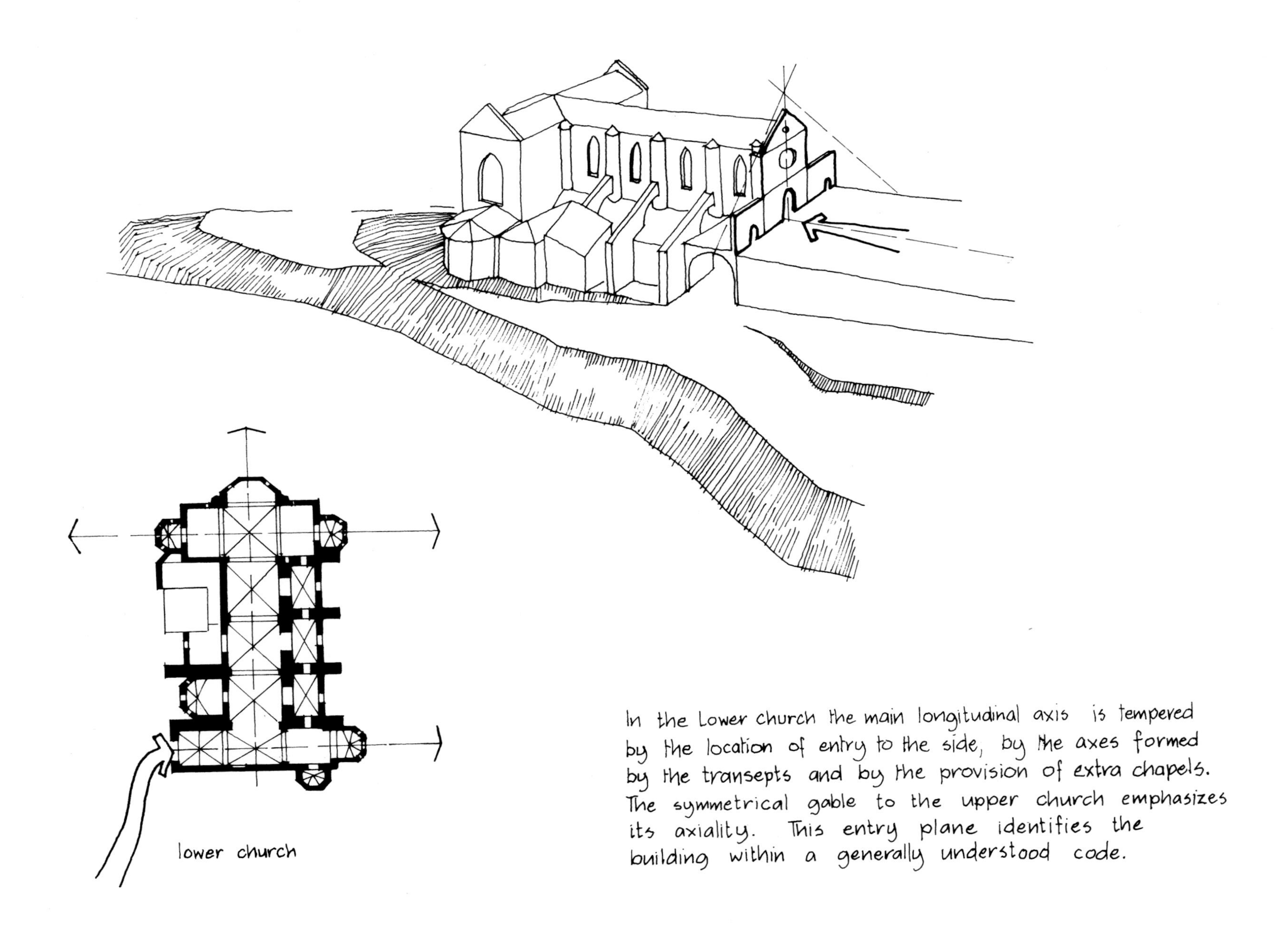

In the Lower church the main longitudinal axis is tempered by the location of entry to the side, by the axes formed by the transepts and by the provision of extra chapels. The symmetrical gable to the upper church emphasizes its axiality. This entry plane identifies the building within a generally understood code.

FORM AS SIGNAL

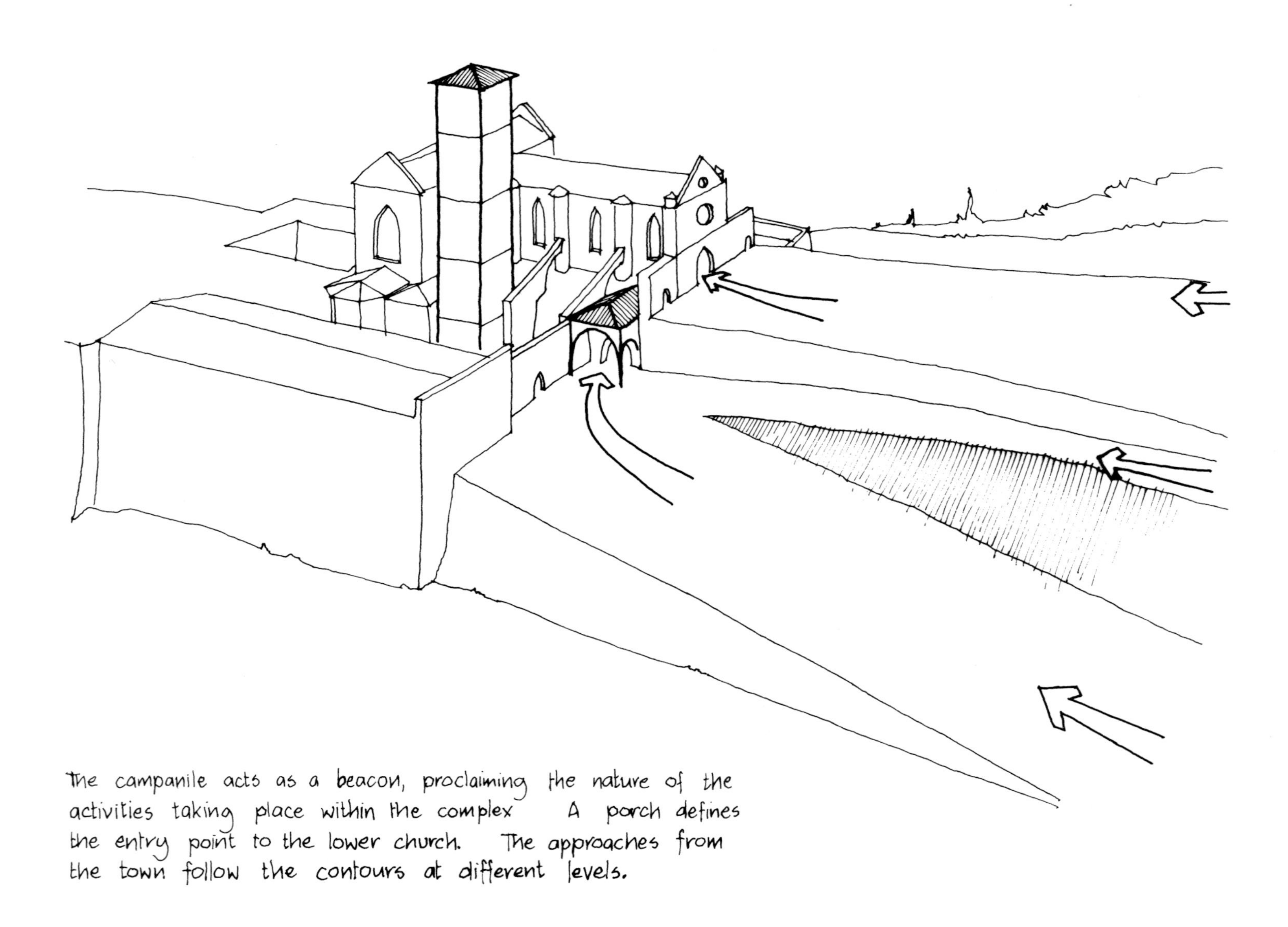

The campanile acts as a beacon, proclaiming the nature of the activities taking place within the complex. A porch defines the entry point to the lower church. The approaches from the town follow the contours at different levels.

FORM AS SYMBOL

The two piazze divide the town from the monastery, a complete symbolic break between secular and holy ground. The piazze enable a full appreciation of the position of the buildings in the landscape, whilst the facade and campanile signify the religious identity of the complex.

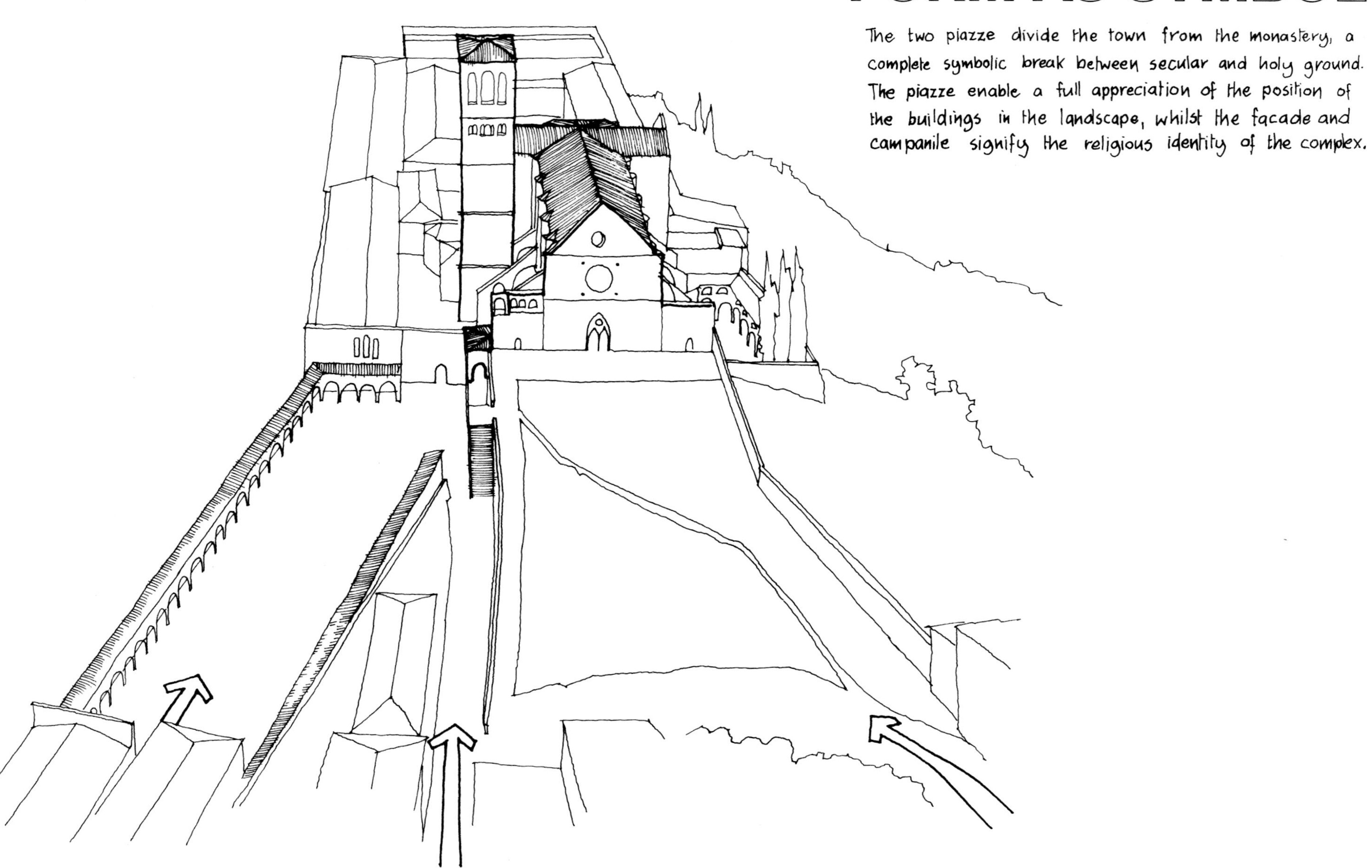

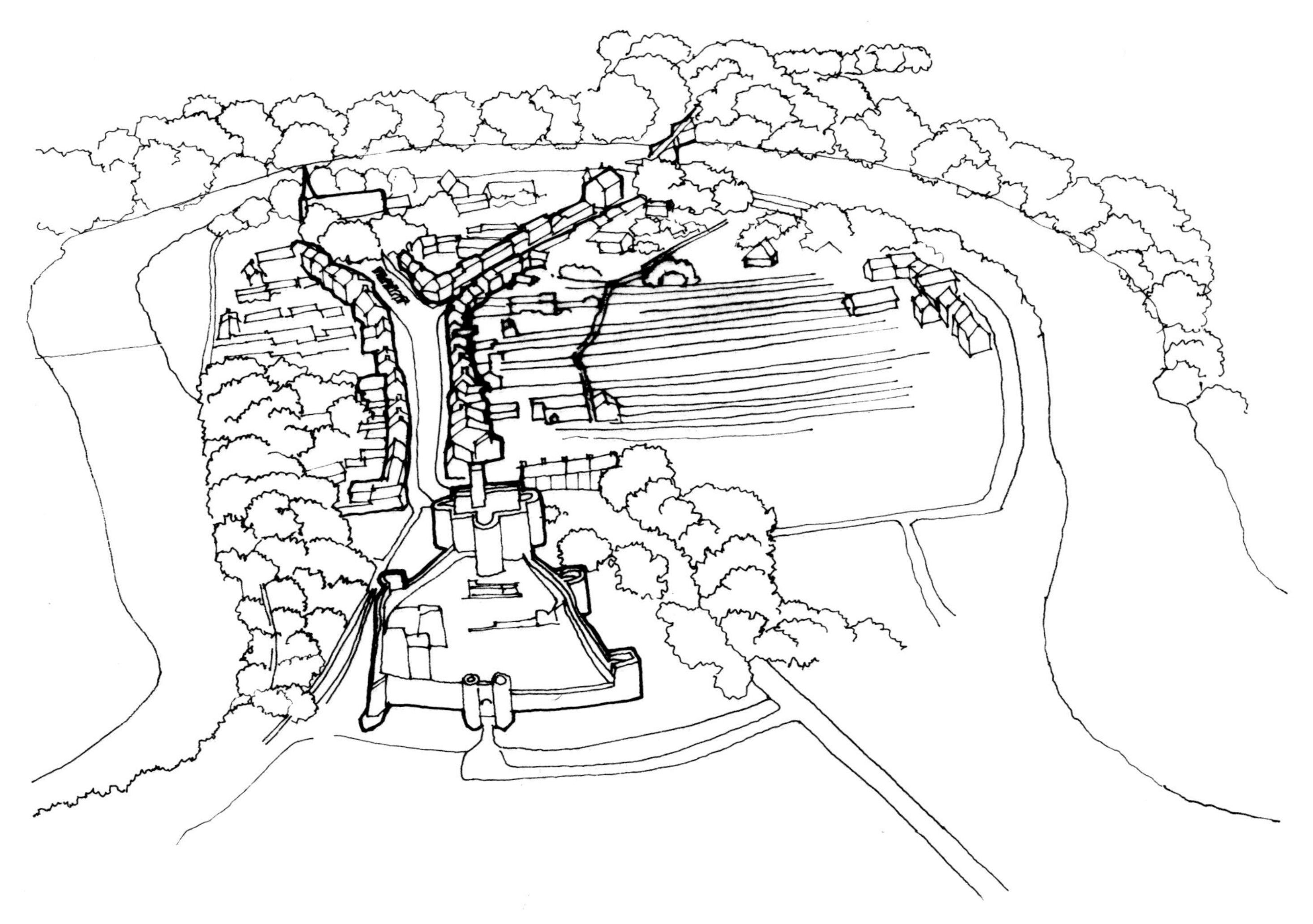

WARKWORTH, NORTHUMBERLAND

A universe created by man and for man, 'In the image of nature' . . . not, indeed by simulating natural objects, but by exemplifying 'the laws of gravity, of statics and dynamics' . . . is the spatial semblance of a world, because it is made in actual space, yet is not systematically continuous with the rest of nature in a complete democracy of places. It has its own center and periphery, not dividing one place from all others, but limiting from within whatever there is to be. That is the image of an ethnic domain, the primary illusion in architecture.[1]

1 Susan K. Langer, Feeling and Form, London, 1953, p. 97.

GENIUS LOCI AND SITE FORCES

GENIUS LOCI

Warkworth is situated in Northumberland at the northeastern tip of England. The surrounding countryside is characterized by gently rolling hills and valleys. There is a freshness about this well treed landscape blessed with considerable natural beauty. The area has less rainfall than some parts of England, with a cool climate in which winds from the south west and sometimes from the east blow for much of the year. A lasting impression of the region is of clouds scurrying across a great expanse of sky, green fields, surging rivers and a strong presence of the nearby North Sea with its sandy beaches and dune-edged coastline.

SITE FORCES

The Genius Loci of this particular location is created by specific topographical features. A bend of the river Coquet encloses a piece of land large enough for a settlement. At the narrower neck a mound rises to dominate the terrain with views on all sides. The river is the major force, the mound no less important, with man's intervention in the form of a route leading north towards Scotland and south towards Newcastle-upon-Tyne. A smaller plateau rises alongside the river to the north alongside which a bridge continues the route. Route, mound, river and the 'enclosed' piece of land suggest a 'vocation' for the kind of settlement realised in the form of a medieval village with protective castle.

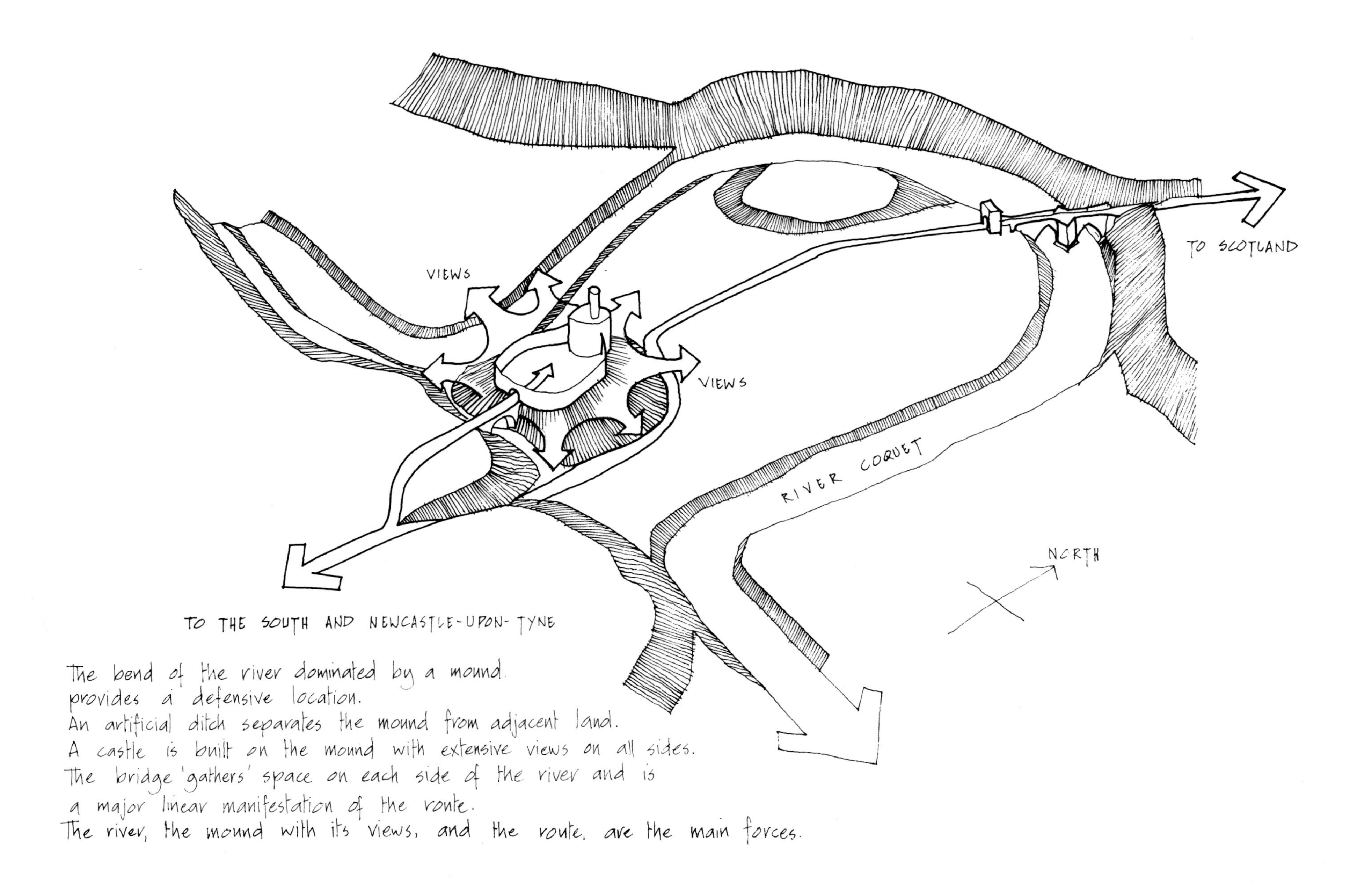

The bend of the river dominated by a mound provides a defensive location.
An artificial ditch separates the mound from adjacent land.
A castle is built on the mound with extensive views on all sides.
The bridge 'gathers' space on each side of the river and is a major linear manifestation of the route.
The river, the mound with its views, and the route, are the main forces.

CULTURAL FACTORS AND MATERIALS

CULTURAL FACTORS

The favoured defensive location almost certainly means that man would have settled in Warkwoth in pre-medieval times. The mound was an ideal location for a 'motte and bailey' castle, this being first mentioned in 1158. At Warkworth the bailey enclosure was placed to the south and a stone keep was built on the motte dominating the higher northern side. At the opposite end a ditch protects the castle against attack from the south. Castles were an integral and necessary part of the feudal system, a system in which the King had control of much of the country, the rest being maintained by barons in return for agreed services to the crown. In 1332 Warkworth was granted to Henry, second Lord Percy of Alnwick, and the Percy's built the present tower house to replace the earlier keep. (1380-90)

A small village formed on either side of the north/south route with feudal strip plots leading down to the river on either side. A church was built on an east-west axis on the small mound to the north with space around it for a graveyard. The main street is too confined for a market place so a small square is formed adjacent on the south side of the church.

MATERIALS

The use of stone, with its implications of strength leading to security, gives a monumental character to both castle and church. Stone is also used for the dwellings in the town, increasing the homogeneity of the whole.

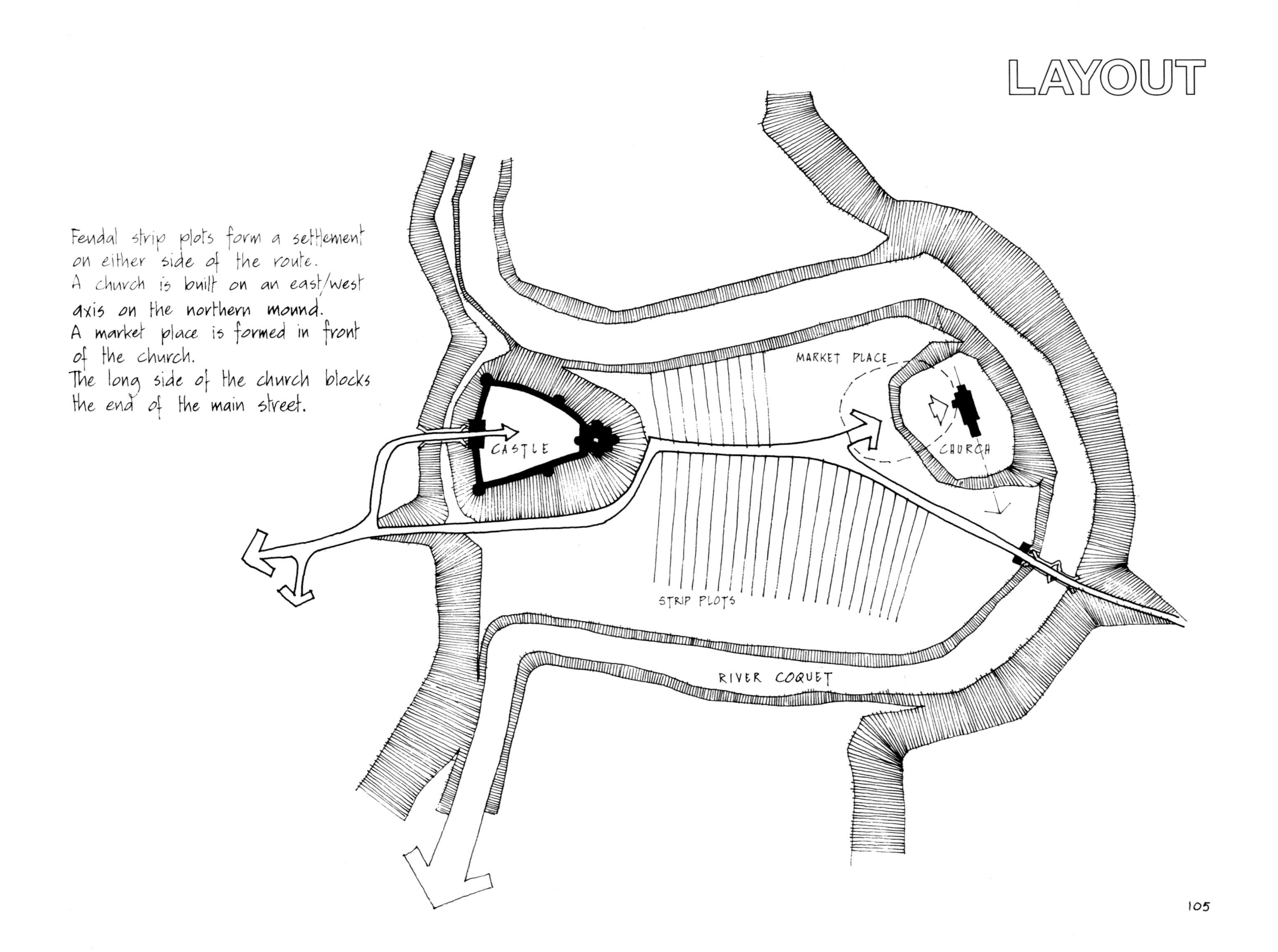
LAYOUT
Feudal strip plots form a settlement on either side of the route.
A church is built on an east/west axis on the northern mound.
A market place is formed in front of the church.
The long side of the church blocks the end of the main street.
MARKET PLACE
CASTLE
CHURCH
STRIP PLOTS
RIVER COQUET

RELEVANT ISSUES

MEANING AND POETRY
Thus church and castle form an axis, marked by their towers. Castle town and church form a homogeneous and self-contained world at a time when this would be the only world its inhabitants would know. The architecture 'concretises' the shared meanings of this society and Heidegger's poetic dimension is realised in the fusion between man's activities and nature, achieved so as to gather the properties of the place.

PROGRAMME, SITE, IDENTITY
Here the program may be said to be the need for defense, a place to dwell, and spiritual sustenance. These needs are met by an architectural response to the site and the prevailing culture. Regarding orientation, the environmental image has identity in the form of castle, village and church.

MOVEMENT AND GEOMETRY, MONUMENTAL AND VERNACULAR
In the form of the route, movement becomes a prime generator of the complex. Both castle (the keep) and church may be thought of as monumental architecture with a simple vernacular model comprising the village. Castle and church have a geometric form as befits both their structural requirements and symbolic role whilst the bridge has a pronounced linearity signalling arrival from the north much as the castle heralds arrival from the south. This clarification of boundaries already formed by the river increases the sense of protection and security so necessary at this near-border location.

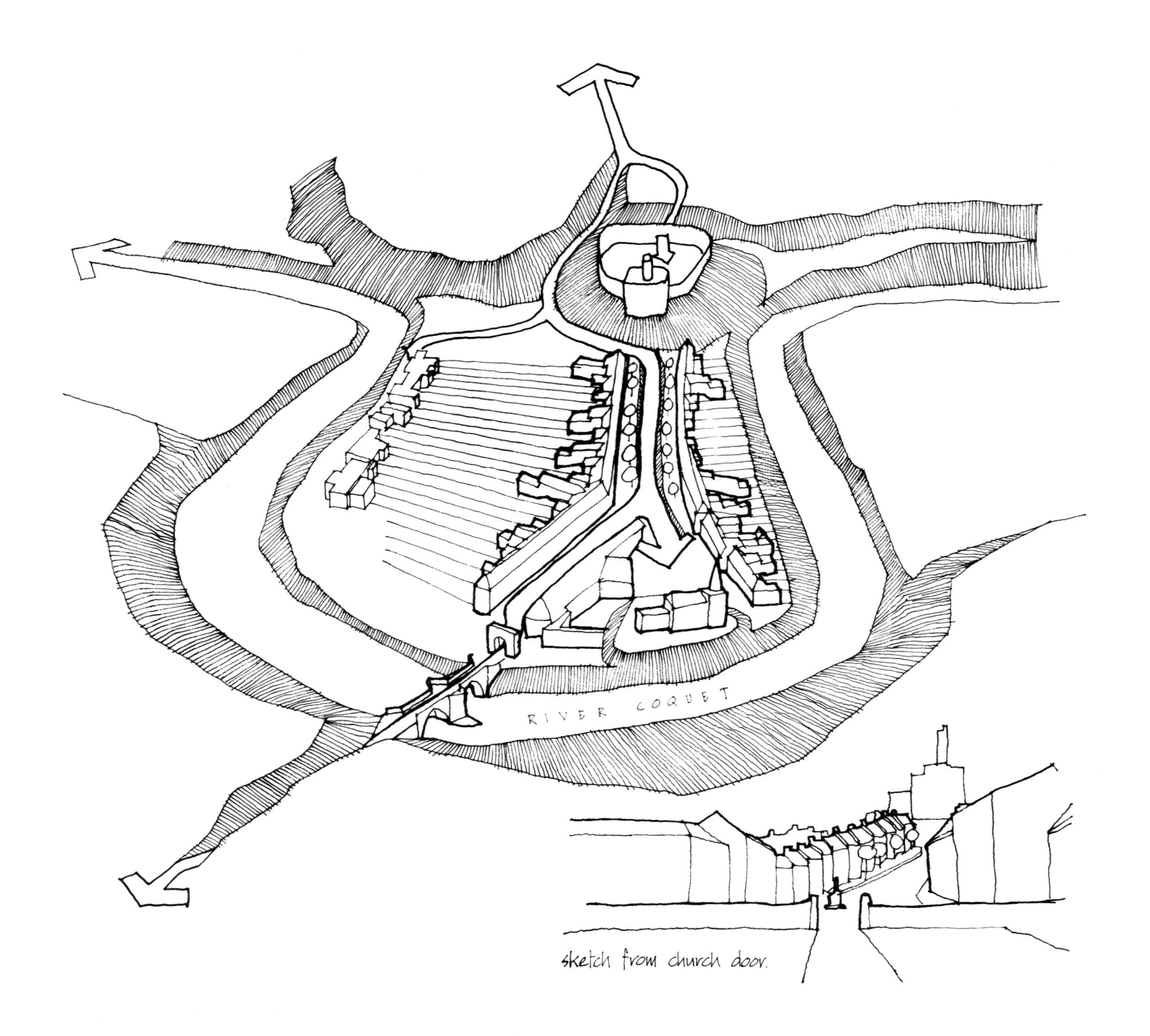
RIVER COQUET
sketch from church door.

CAMPO AND CATHEDRAL, SIENA

> The beauty of Siena is not merely the result of an unconscious or 'natural' growth; it has been consciously built up by its citizens, as a work of art, with a keen sense of unity but also with that deep respect for the inherited rights of the castes, the professions, and the clans, which is the special mark of the Middle Ages... in France and in Germany the northern Gothic period produced the cathedral as its masterpiece, Italy in the Middle Ages reached the height of communal achievement in the building of the Gothic town. [1]

The evolution of Siena typifies how religious faith, economic forces, city rivalry and a capacity to exploit the Genius Loci conspired to create a series of masterly towns and cities in Italy during the Middle Ages.

Siena, Florence and Pisa each struggled to retain the trade route between France and Rome as it passed through Tuscany. Pisa's importance lay with its harbour, and Florence was favourably located on the river Arno, but with the sea abandoning Pisa, the main rivalry was between Florence and Siena.

Throughout the 12th century the Tuscany trade route had been controlled by Siena, this being due in large measure to the trading success of the city. The resultant conflict led to war between the rival cities and to victory for the Sienese in 1262 at Montaperto.

[1] Titus Burckhardt, Siena, The City of the Virgin, London, 1960, p. 1

CULTURE AND SITE

In the 12th century the present Campo was an open space facing south, defined by a conjunction of routes and contours. Due to erosion by rain a retaining wall was built to the south, and in 1218 a master plan for the piazza was initiated. In 1288 all the houses around the square were acquired by the City with additional houses purchased in 1293.

A cathedral had been built on a hill to the west of the Campo in 1216. In 1339 it was decided to begin building a new cathedral with an extension of the chancel in the form of a new nave, running north-south. With the intervention of the 'Black Death' and escalating costs this had to be abandoned and the existing building was retained with certain ongoing additions. These included a new Baptistery, built on the lower slope beneath the cathedral choir, and a new facade, modelled on the facade of Orvieto cathedral and completed in 1377.

A new Town Hall was begun in 1297, sited in what was then the market place and which is now the Campo. The Town Hall had to face the cathedral and had to be built at the southern side of the market place. In 1297, following this decision, it was decreed that in order to create a harmonious whole all windows looking on to the Campo should be adorned with small columns.[1]

[1] Ibid., p. 24.

In the medieval city the need for protection was primarily expressed in two ways. Fortified walls provided a defensive ring around the city, and the cathedral acted as the source of contact with God, the ultimate guardian of destiny. At the height of its greatest flowering, during the 12th, 13th and 14th centuries, the inhabitants described Siena as the City of the Virgin, and the Cathedral and Town Hall symbolized the religious and temporal power of the city.

The Cathedral hovers over the city like a huge black and white striped airship, whilst lower down the slopes, nestling into the hillside, the Piazza del Campo with its Town Hall, acts as a stage for public events, its campanile rising bravely into the sky, proclaiming the civic pride of the city.

TOPOGRAPHY AND ROUTES

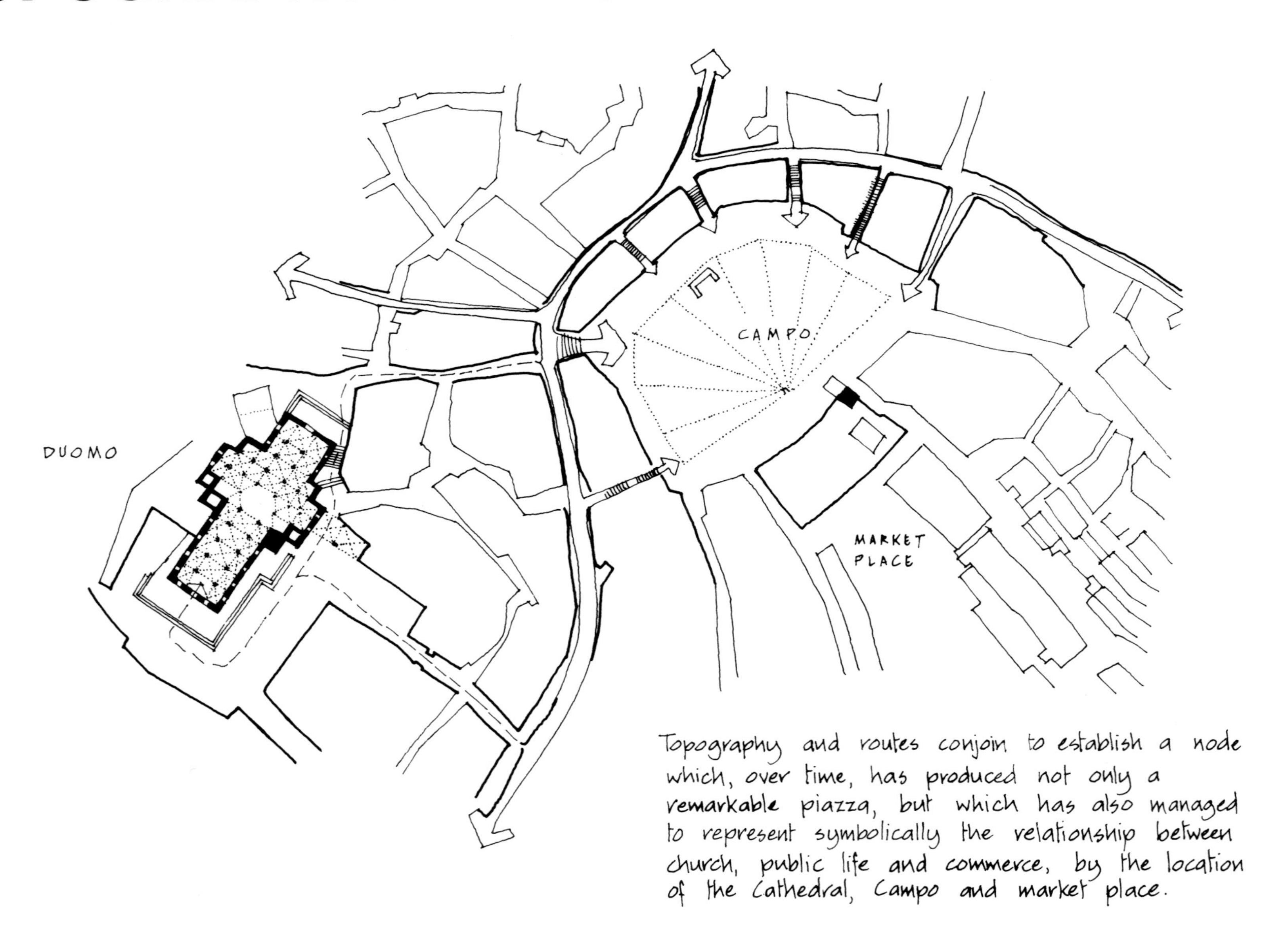

Topography and routes conjoin to establish a node which, over time, has produced not only a remarkable piazza, but which has also managed to represent symbolically the relationship between church, public life and commerce, by the location of the Cathedral, Campo and market place.

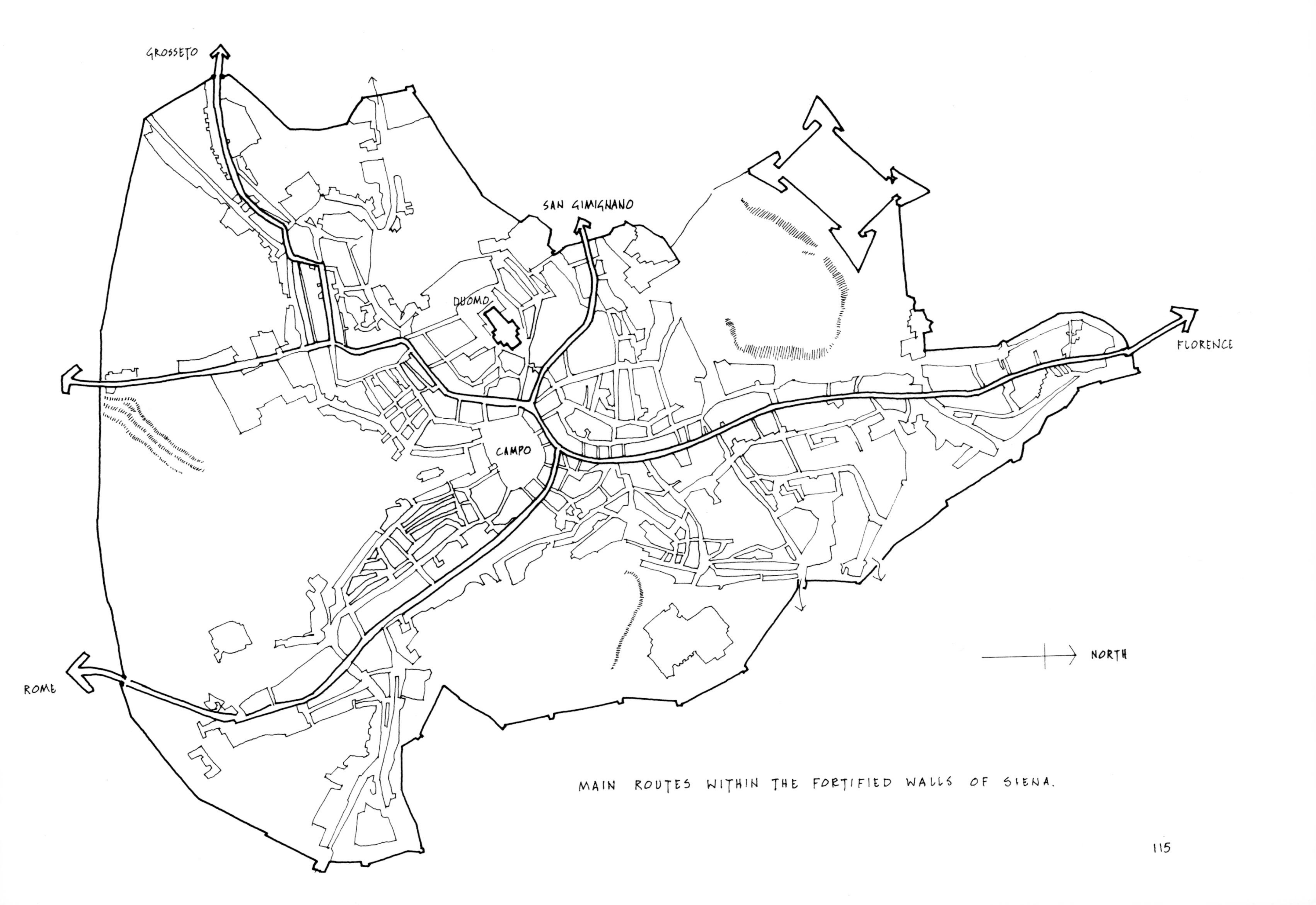

MAIN ROUTES WITHIN THE FORTIFIED WALLS OF SIENA.

CAMPO

Siena stands on a series of ridges, along which are the main routes to Florence, San Gimignano, Grosseto and Rome.

At the heart of the old city is the Piazza del Campo. From the earliest days this was a place where travellers would rest on the way to and from neighbouring cities.

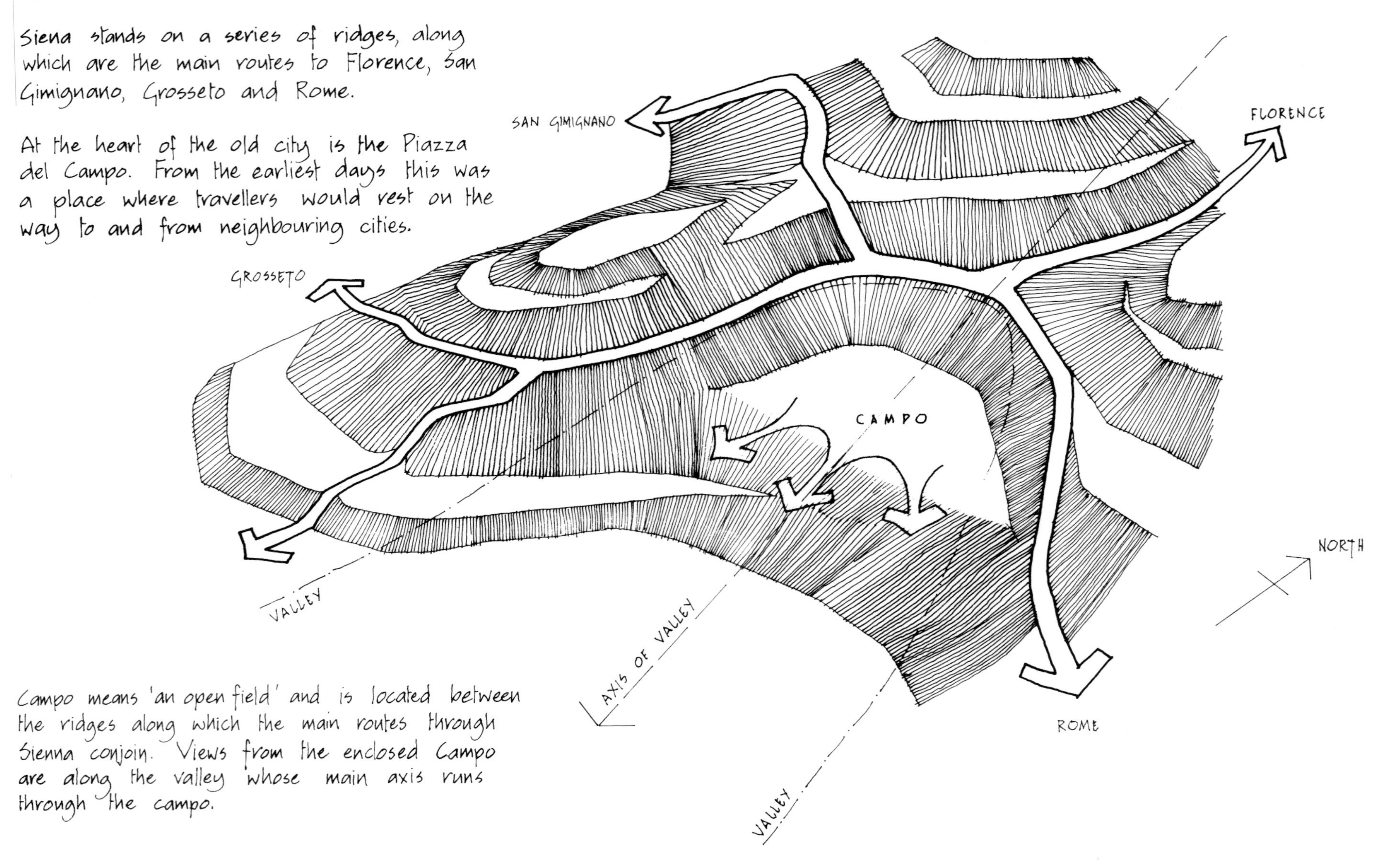

Campo means 'an open field' and is located between the ridges along which the main routes through Sienna conjoin. Views from the enclosed Campo are along the valley whose main axis runs through the campo.

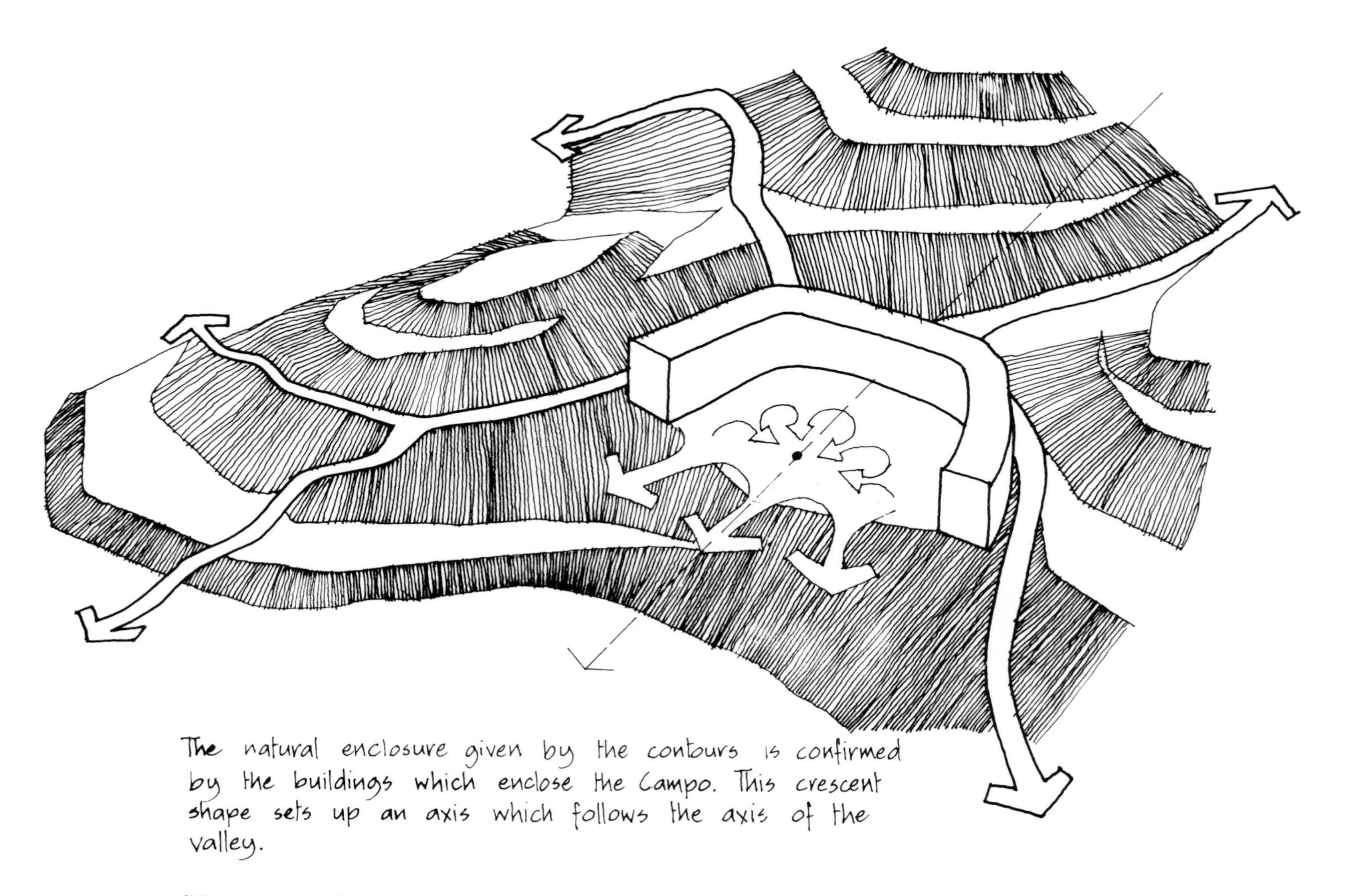

The natural enclosure given by the contours is confirmed by the buildings which enclose the Campo. This crescent shape sets up an axis which follows the axis of the valley.

The enclosed space is both inward and outward looking, with a central focal point and views down the valley.

DIAGONAL AXIS

VIEW FROM SOUTH WEST

The need for a link between the Cathedral and the Piazza del Campo is accommodated by the only major break in the buildings surrounding the square. This occurs on the western side, establishing a diagonal axis across the Campo.

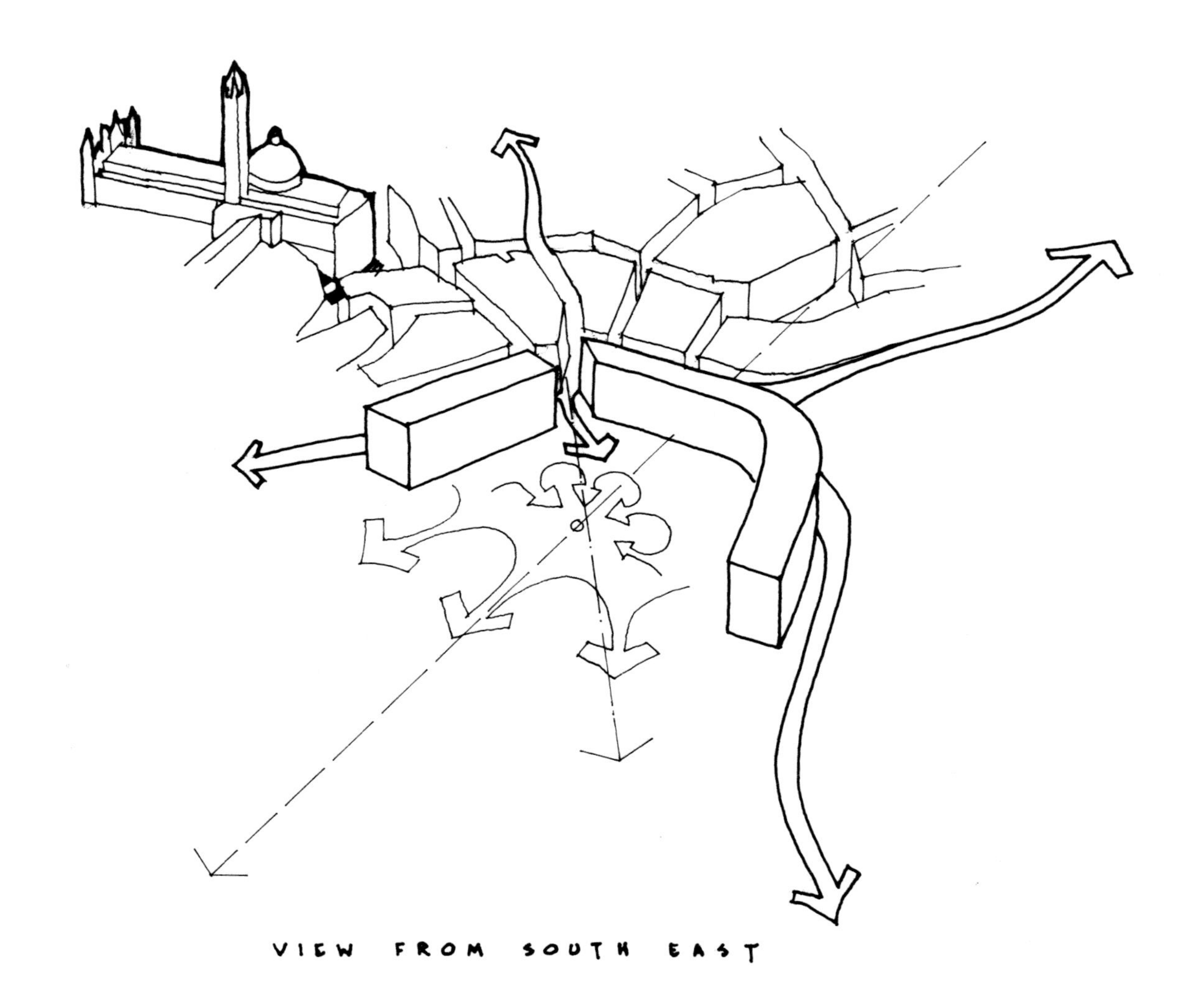

VIEW FROM SOUTH EAST

PALAZZO PUBBLICO

The Town Hall, or Palazzo Pubblico closes the southern side of the piazza, being formed of three segments which bend round to echo the shell-like sense of enclosure within the Campo.

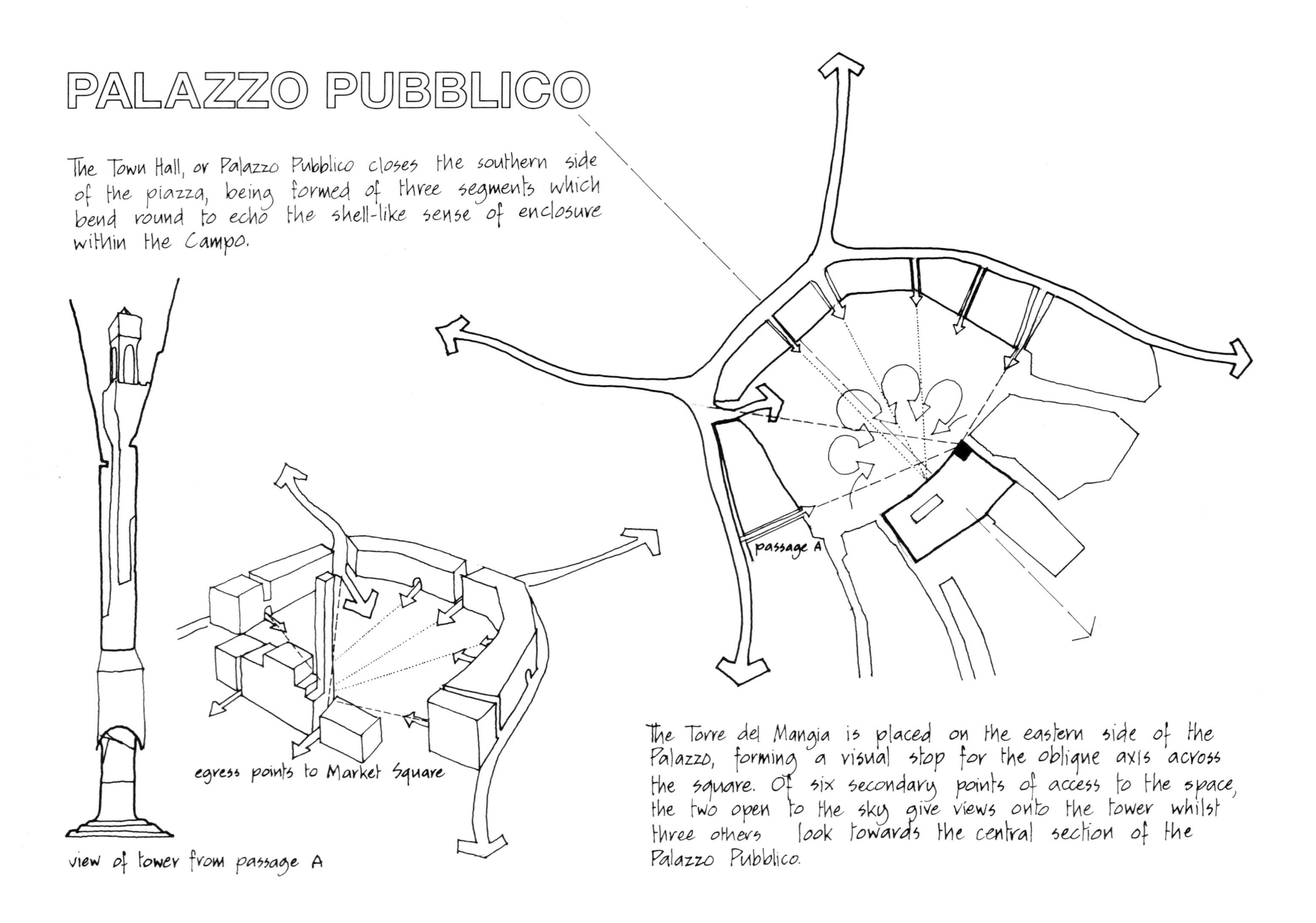

The Torre del Mangia is placed on the eastern side of the Palazzo, forming a visual stop for the oblique axis across the square. Of six secondary points of access to the space, the two open to the sky give views onto the tower whilst three others look towards the central section of the Palazzo Pubblico.

TORRE DEL MANGIA

The Torre del Mangia, as the only vertical element in the square, acts as a powerful signal, with its most elaborate treatment reserved for the top, which can be seen for miles. The clock is pulled down to relate to the piazza, of which it forms a part.

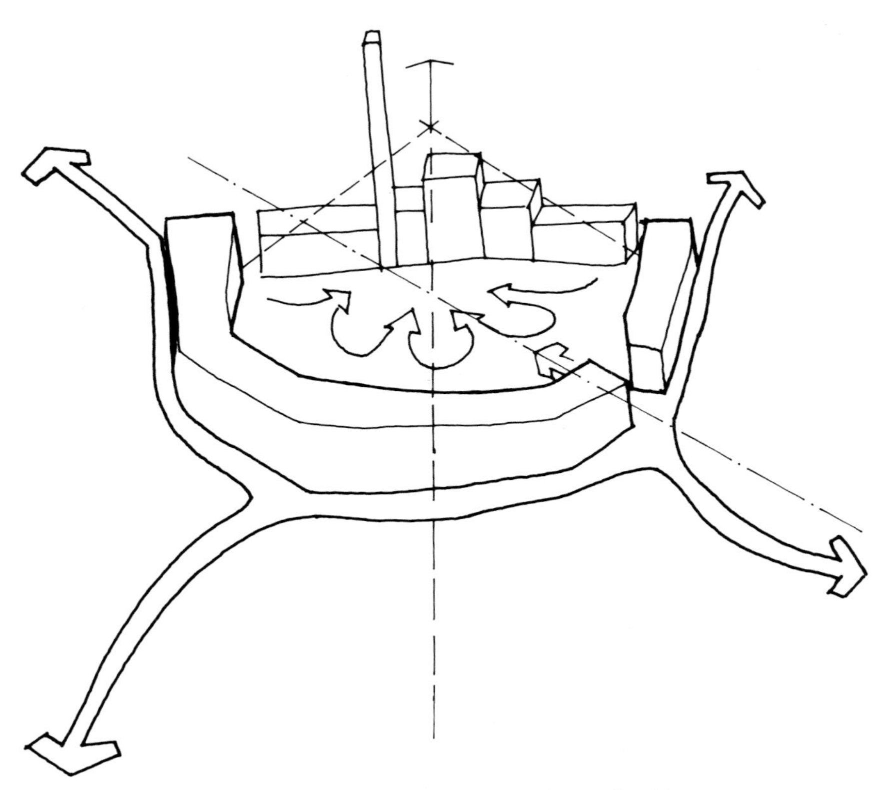

The containment on the south side of the piazza retains the focal effect and represents the importance of civic life by the pyramidal build-up and bi-lateral symmetry of the Town Hall.

FOCUS

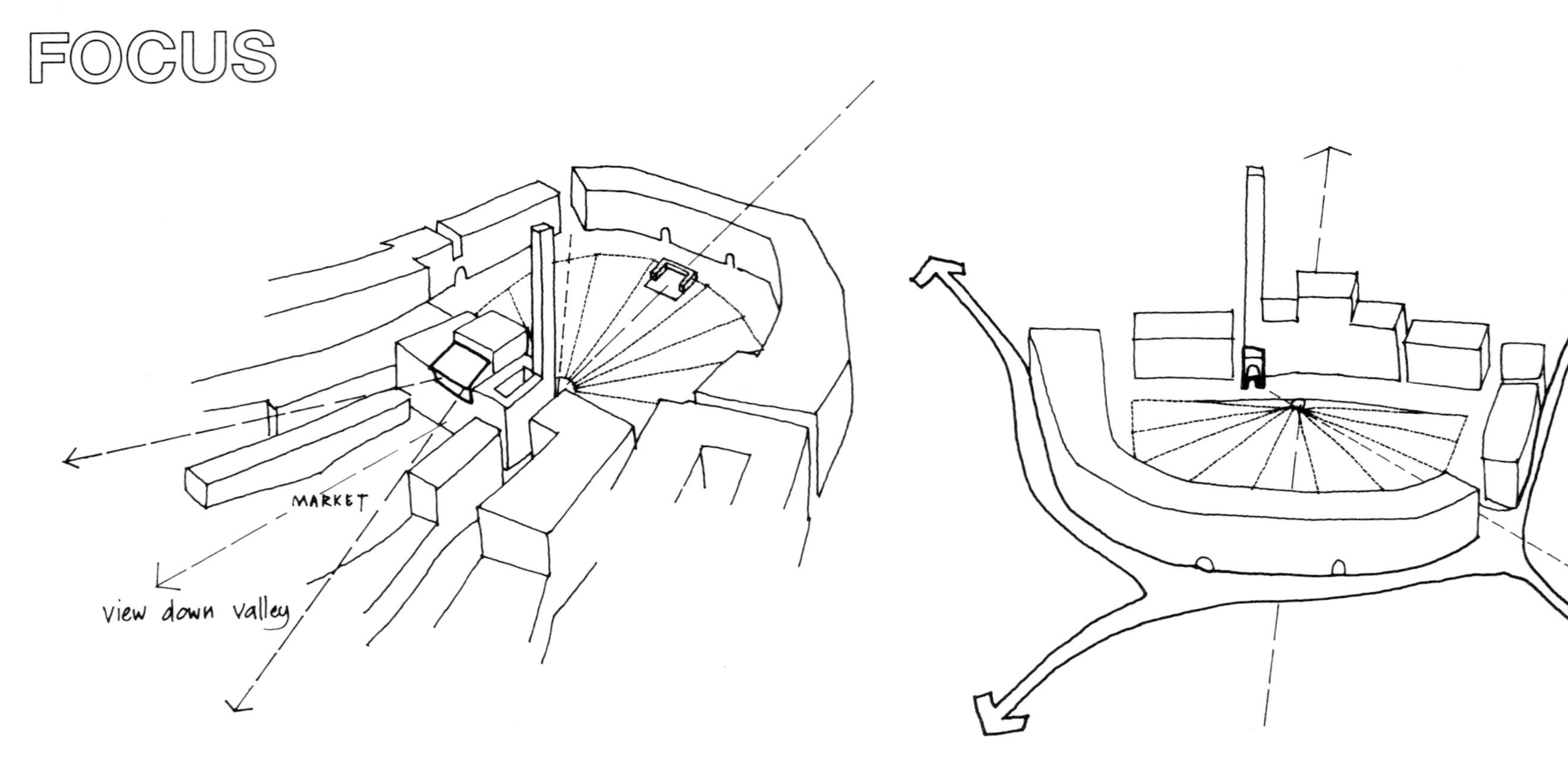

To the rear of the Palazzo Pubblico is a loggia which enjoys a view of the valley and which relates directly to the market.

At the focal point within the square is the storm drain on which the various radii of the Campo converge, these reinforcing the fan-like nature of the space and also helping to unify the piazza. Centrally on axis is the Fonte Gaia, the fountain placed low so as not to interfere with the space in the square.

If we think of the Piazza del Campo as an outdoor auditorium, the Palazzo Pubblico seems like a scene building fronted by a stage for public events. The porch at the base of the tower states its position in relation to the square much as the upper part establishes the tower and Palazzo to distant horizons.

The porch also acts as a visual stop at eye level to the oblique axis across the piazza.

The way the floor of the piazza slopes down to the storm drain intensifies the feeling of enclosure on three sides, this being confirmed by the presence of the Town Hall on the other.

Taking a section through the Campo shows that entrances from the north do not reveal the full extent of the space initially, unlike the view from the main entry point.

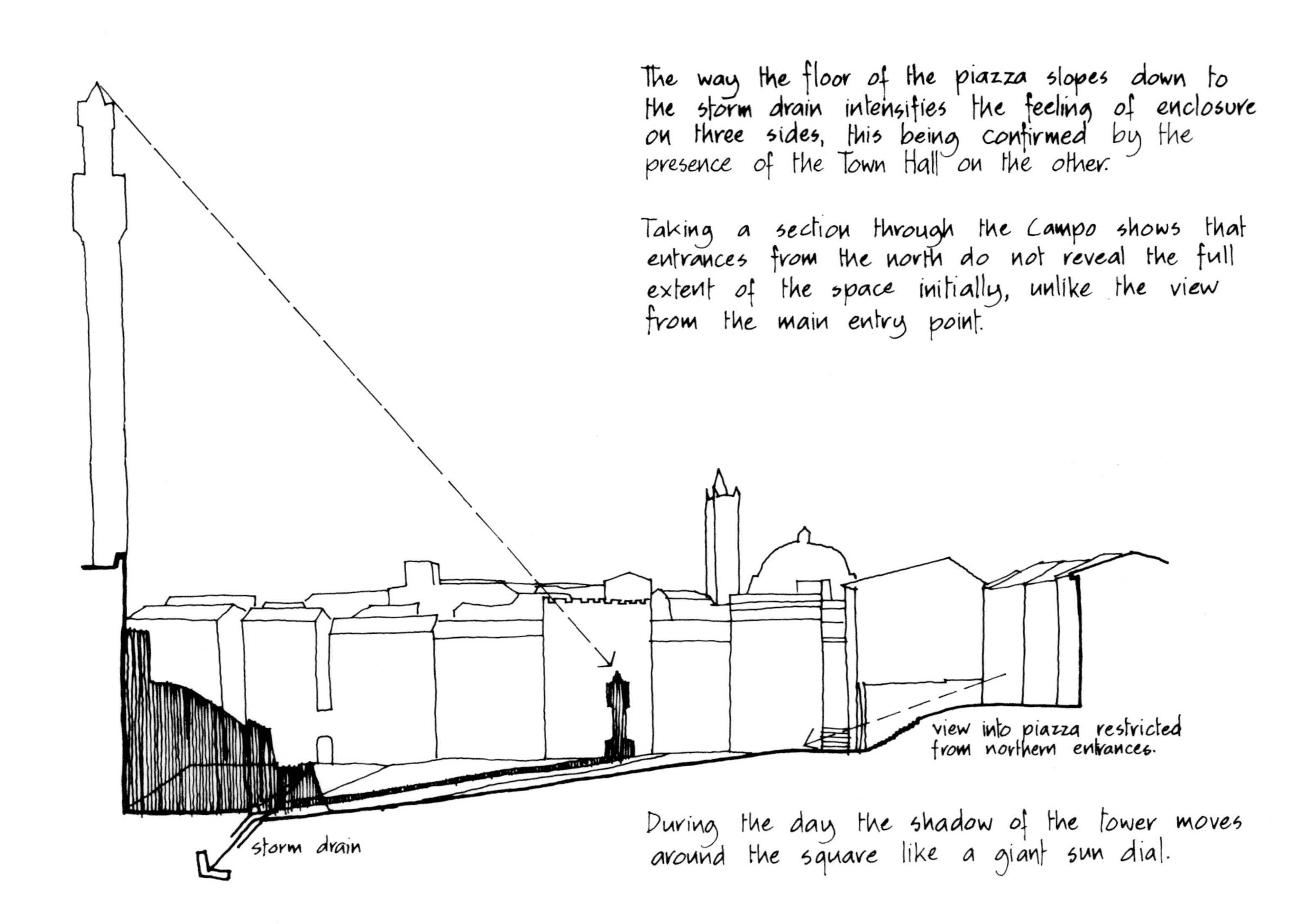

During the day the shadow of the tower moves around the square like a giant sun dial.

SECTION THROUGH CAMPO

ROUTES

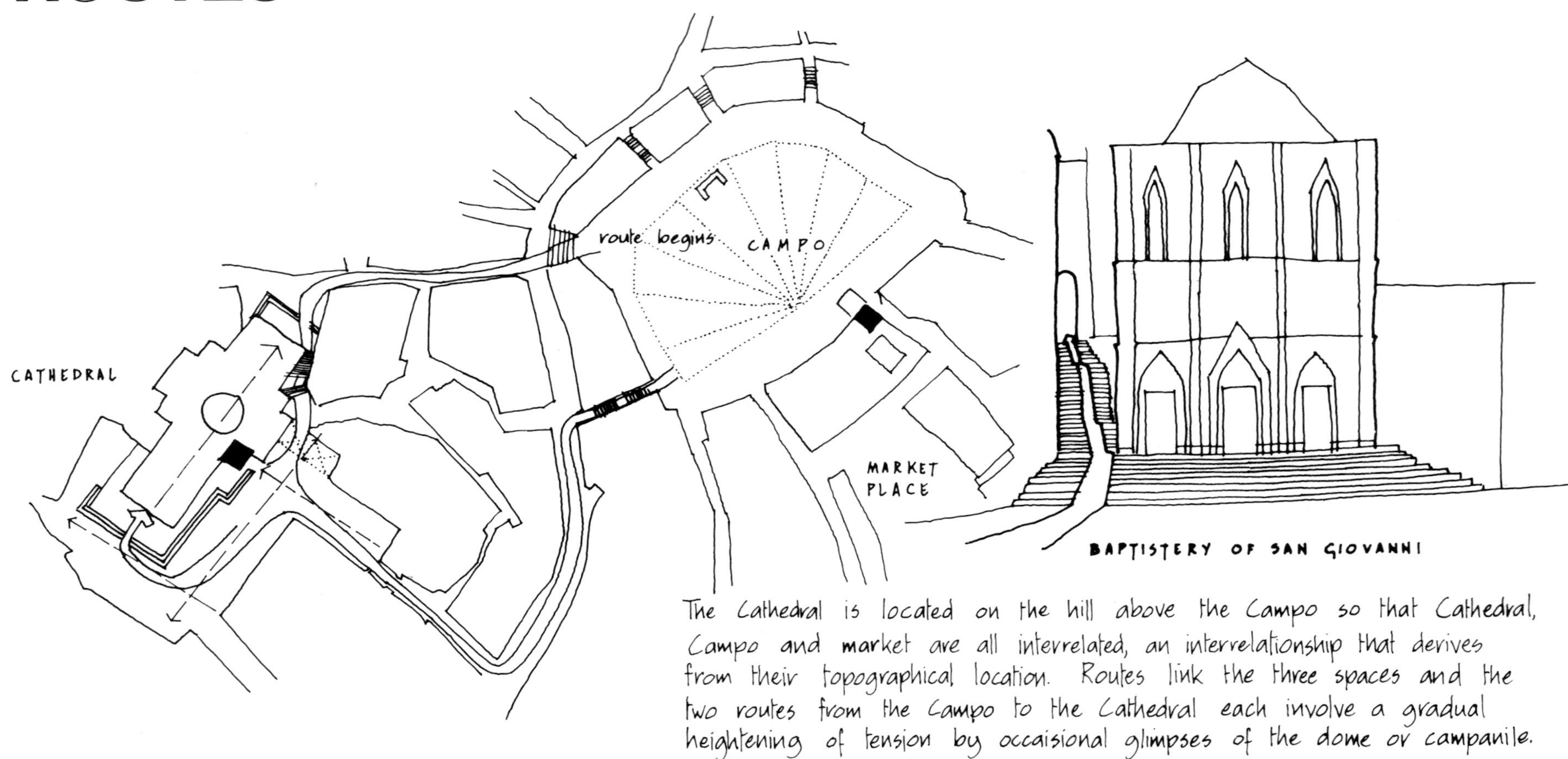

The Cathedral is located on the hill above the Campo so that Cathedral, Campo and market are all interrelated, an interrelationship that derives from their topographical location. Routes link the three spaces and the two routes from the Campo to the Cathedral each involve a gradual heightening of tension by occaisional glimpses of the dome or campanile.

The most direct cathedral approach is through the main entrance to the Campo, along the street opposite, then climbing up stairs past the Baptistery and through an arch into the space beside the Cathedral. From this point the route traverses the southern side of the Cathedral in the square formed on this east-west axis, before turning towards the Cathedral entry point.

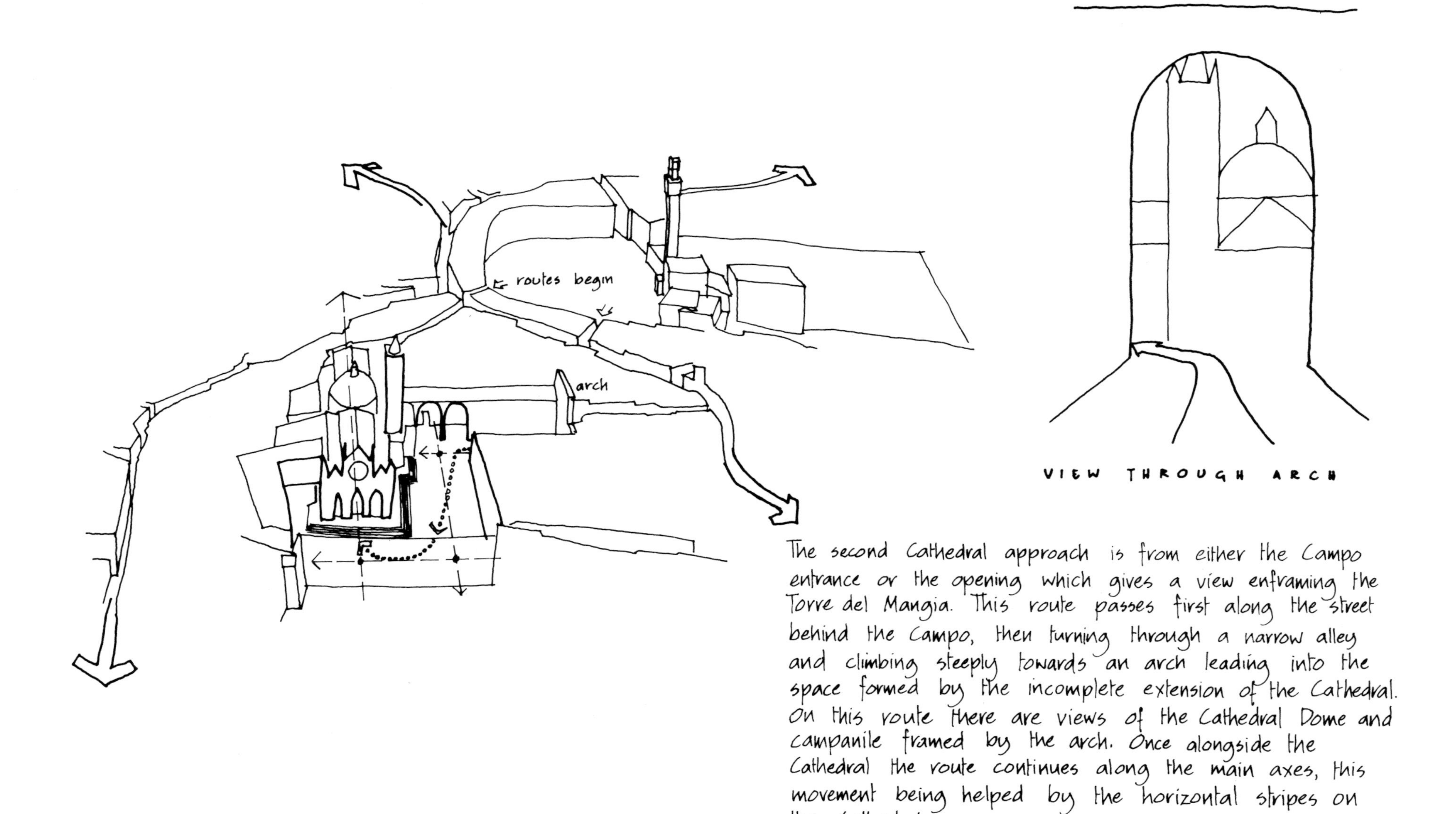

The second Cathedral approach is from either the Campo entrance or the opening which gives a view enframing the Torre del Mangia. This route passes first along the street behind the Campo, then turning through a narrow alley and climbing steeply towards an arch leading into the space formed by the incomplete extension of the Cathedral. On this route there are views of the Cathedral Dome and campanile framed by the arch. Once alongside the Cathedral the route continues along the main axes, this movement being helped by the horizontal stripes on the Cathedral.

CATHEDRAL

The final act in the progression from the Campo is the magnificent west facade of the Duomo. As with the other symbols this facade fulfils a particular role. It speaks of entry to something of great importance, the Cathedral itself.

The facade forms part of a symbol system, which includes the Cathedral dome, the campanile, and the Torre del Mangia, these two towers relating to each other as if to cite their mutual interdependence.

These forms are part of a complex interrelated spatial and volumetric network in which Cathedral, Campo and market are each separately defined, and defined appropriately by significant configurations.

That they occur in a dense built-up city fabric only increases their potency and impact, and each space is created so as to allow the major buildings in them to be properly understood.

It is an organic arrangement in which site forces combine with practical needs to form spaces and to create built objects which symbolize special aspects of life. The symbolic hierarchy is clear, and becomes the more acceptable because it forms part of the bustling network of the city.

The major buildings act as symbols which identify those aspects of life seen as important by the Sienese in the Middle Ages. Supported by sculpture and paintings, the whole city becomes meaningful and rich in form and content, in every sense reflecting the lifestyle and concerns of people at a particular moment in time.

The evolution of the Piazza S. Marco is similar to that of the Cathedral / Campo complex in Siena in the way each ensemble organizes the architecture to reflect the history of each city and its social political and religious values. In each case, a randomly disposed assemblage of dwellings is packed into the city fabric, compacted by defensive needs, satisfied at Siena by a fortified wall and at Venice by its isolation in the Lagoon.

In neither city were axial vistas possible, and any open space has to be carved out of the existing dense fabric; accordingly each piazza is in dramatic contrast to the city as a whole. Despite these similarities the cities are very different. Siena situated on a series of hills and routes in Tuscany, Venice, completely flat, surrounded by and in danger of being submerged by water. Influenced by its trading links with Byzantium, Venice has an ostentatious theatricality evidenced in the richness of its architecture and the splendour of its colouring. The city of canals is pervaded by reflective transparency, with blues, pinks, white and gold, in contrast to the brown and terra-cotta sobriety of Siena.

In contrast to the relatively anonymous architectural contributions in Siena, the power of Venice attracted the great names in architecture, painting and sculpture, with works by Carpaccio, Bellini, Giorgione, Titian, Canaletto, Veronese and Tiepolo, and buildings by Palladio, Sansovino Vignola and Scamozzi. The city comprises a fusion of the arts, reaching an architectural climax in the Piazza S. Marco, a dynamic juxtaposition of buildings and spaces that accord with the reality of needs over a period of time.

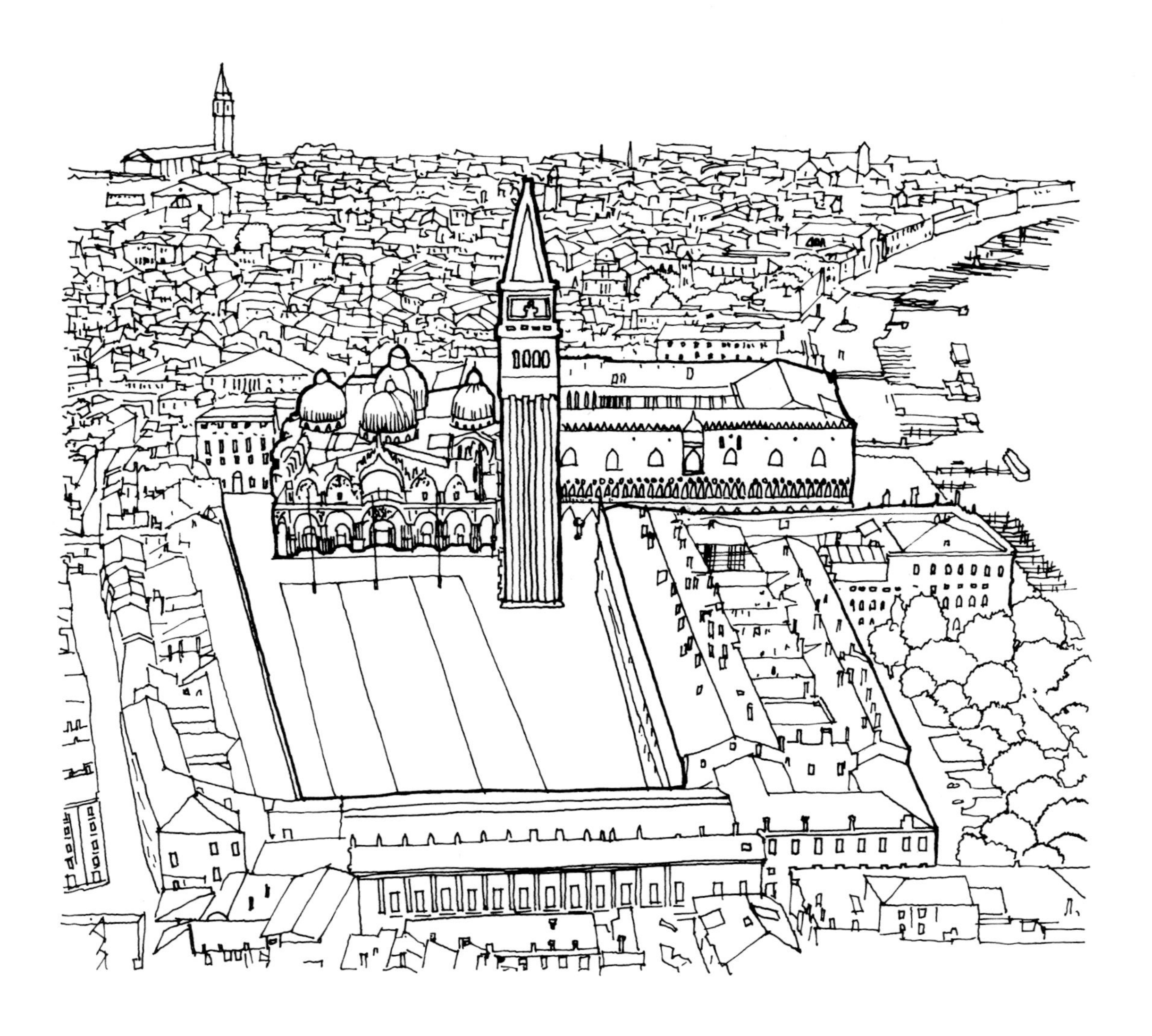

THE PIAZZA OF SAN MARCO, VENICE

SITE FORCES

WATER

The presence of so much water exerts a considerable force. To begin with there is a strong sense of continuous horizontality and during Spring and Summer the sparkling animation of the canals and blue Aegean sky charge the city with unusual effects of light and shade. The air of unreality provided by the setting is increased by symbolic connotations associated with islands. Originally the settlement was seen as a temporary refuge, an escape from the mainland, and islands inevitably suggest those romantic associations which often produce picturesque or exotic responses.

ROUTES AND VIEWS

The site is centrally located in relation to the entrance to the Grand Canal, with a direct route to the commercial area at the Rialto. The close proximity of the islands of S. Giorgio and Guidecca opposite give a sense of containment externally. There are views from the site towards these islands and towards the arrow-head point of the mouth of the Grand Canal. On approaching the site by boat the site affords sufficient frontage to be able to make a grand gesture similar to that in cities where space allows axial vistas, whilst internally there is sufficient containment for the creation of an enclosed 'private' domain. The potential for interaction between internal and external is exploited and refined by successive contributions over several centuries.

THE SITE

The site is surrounded on three sides by a labyrinth or 'maze' of buildings and routes. This mysterious disorder contrasts with the order and clarity of the piazza. The complex exploits the dramatic confrontation between these two opposing 'worlds'.

ROUTES

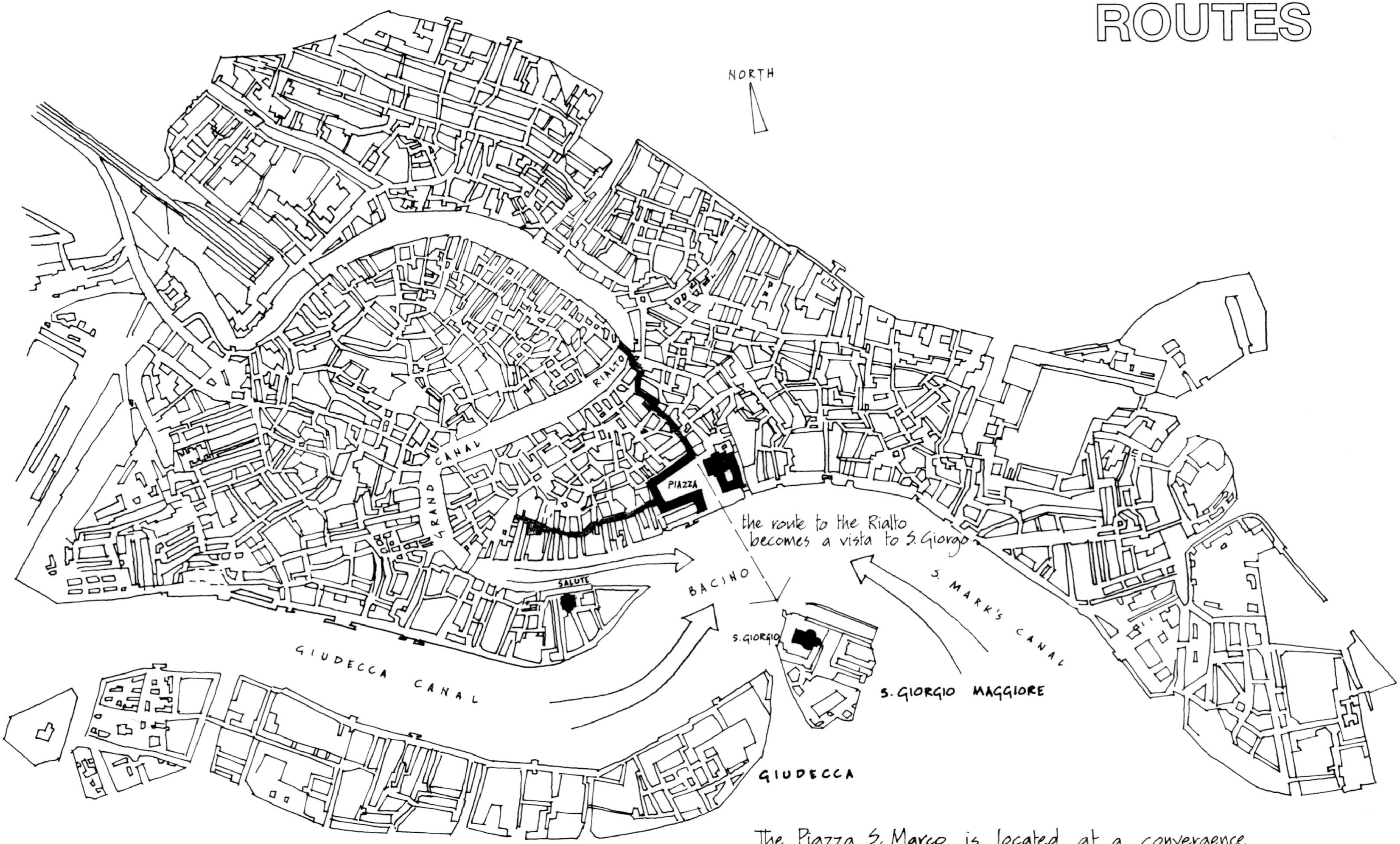

NORTH

RIALTO

GRAND CANAL

PIAZZA

SALUTE

BACINO

S. GIORGIO

S. MARK'S CANAL

GIUDECCA CANAL

S. GIORGIO MAGGIORE

GIUDECCA

the route to the Rialto
becomes a vista to S. Giorgio

The Piazza S. Marco is located at a convergence of routes and acts as a focal point adressing the city and the water.

ORIGINS

The first Piazza San Marco was formed in the space fronting the earlier Basilica. A campanile was begun in 888, but until the late twelfth century, a canal, just beyond the campanile, limited the size of the square. The fortress-like Doge's Palace is a reminder of the defensive origins of the city.

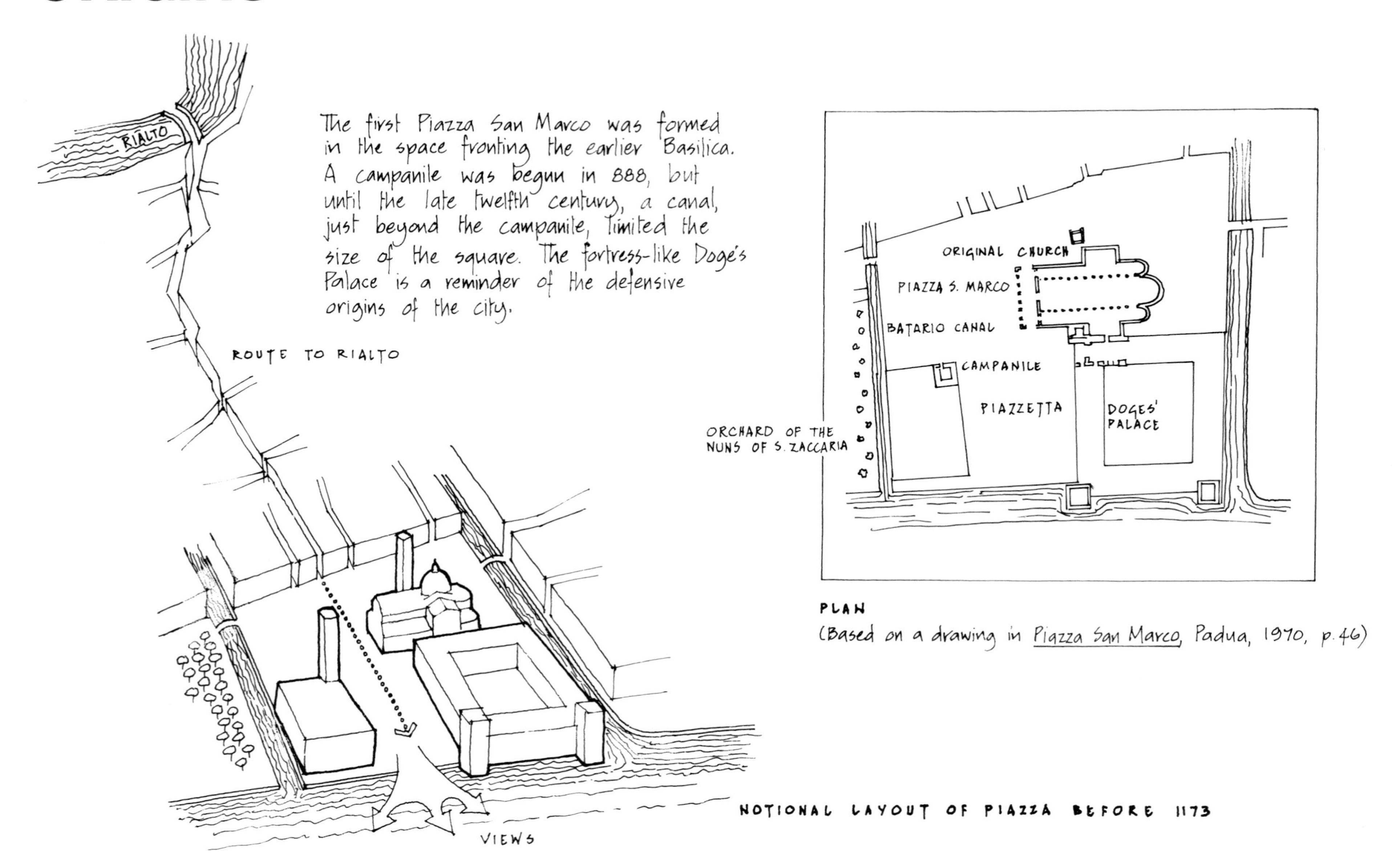

NOTIONAL LAYOUT OF PIAZZA BEFORE 1173

PLAN
(Based on a drawing in Piazza San Marco, Padua, 1970, p.46)

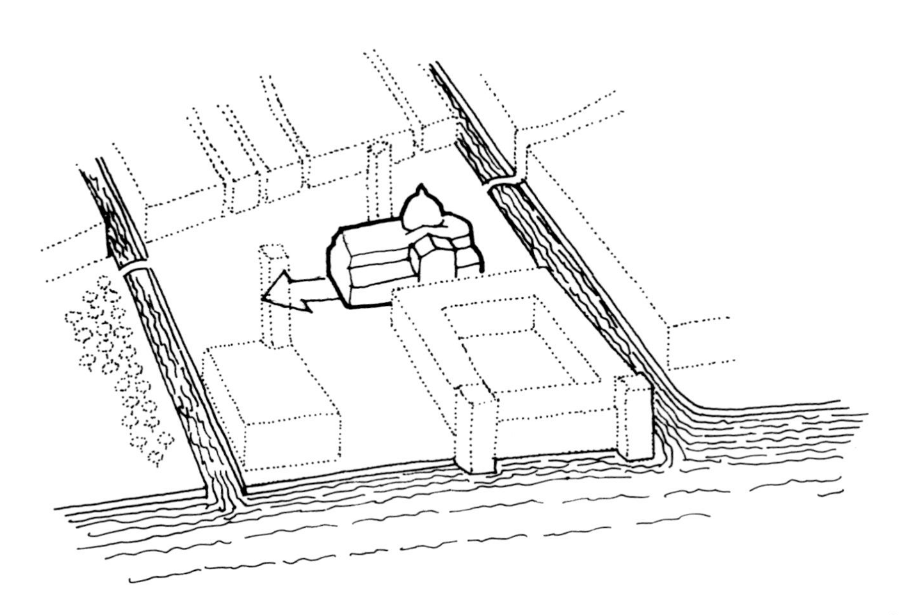

1) The establishment of the Basilica of St. Mark as the dominant mass with its main facade facing onto the piazza.

SITE FACTORS

Although far from complete, and unrecognisable as we now know the square, this embryonic state of the piazza contains the basic ingredients which do not change with time and which, when sensitively developed, ultimately ensure the success of the complex.

In essence these comprise nine important factors:

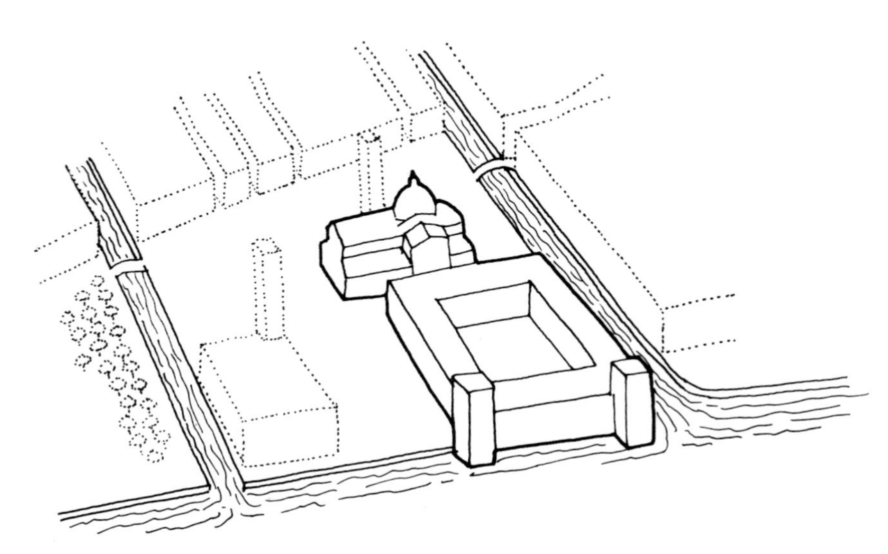

2) The combined linked masses of the centroidal Dogés Palace and Basilica on approximately the same orthogonal grid.

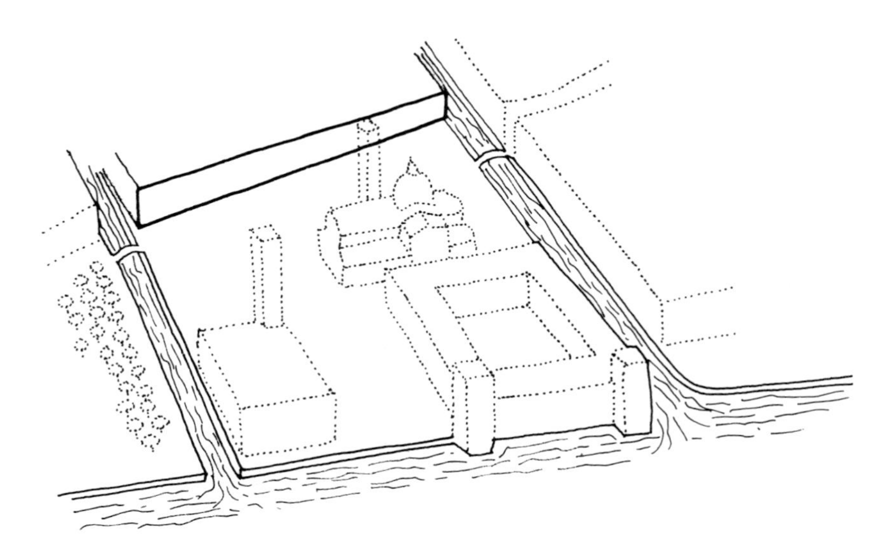

3) Containment of the north side of the piazza by a continuous plane at an oblique angle.

SITE FACTORS

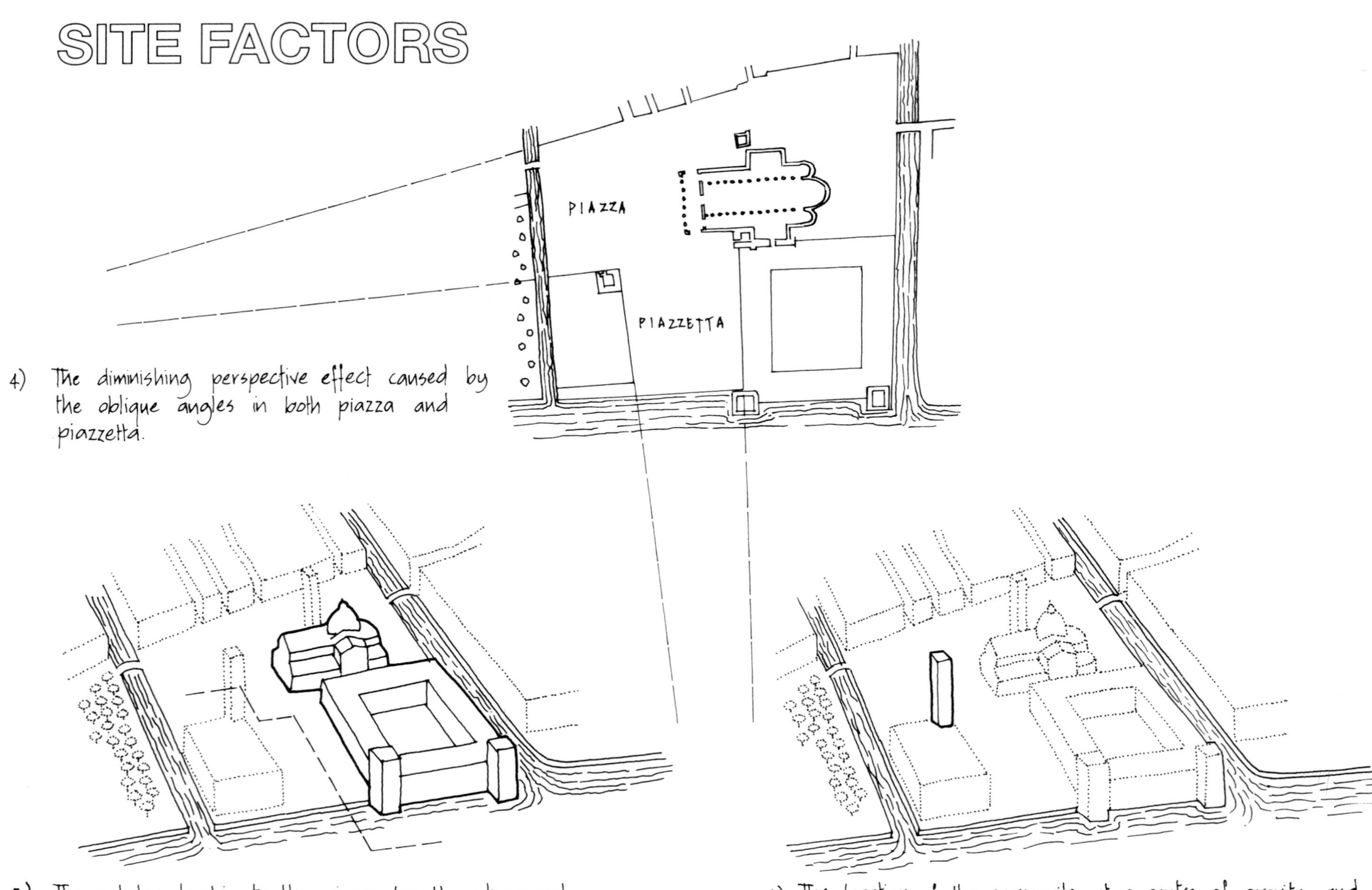

4) The diminishing perspective effect caused by the oblique angles in both piazza and piazzetta.

5) The echelon lead-in to the piazza by the staggered alignment of the Basilica and Doge's Palace.

6) The location of the campanile at a centre of gravity and right angled pivot point in the ensemble.

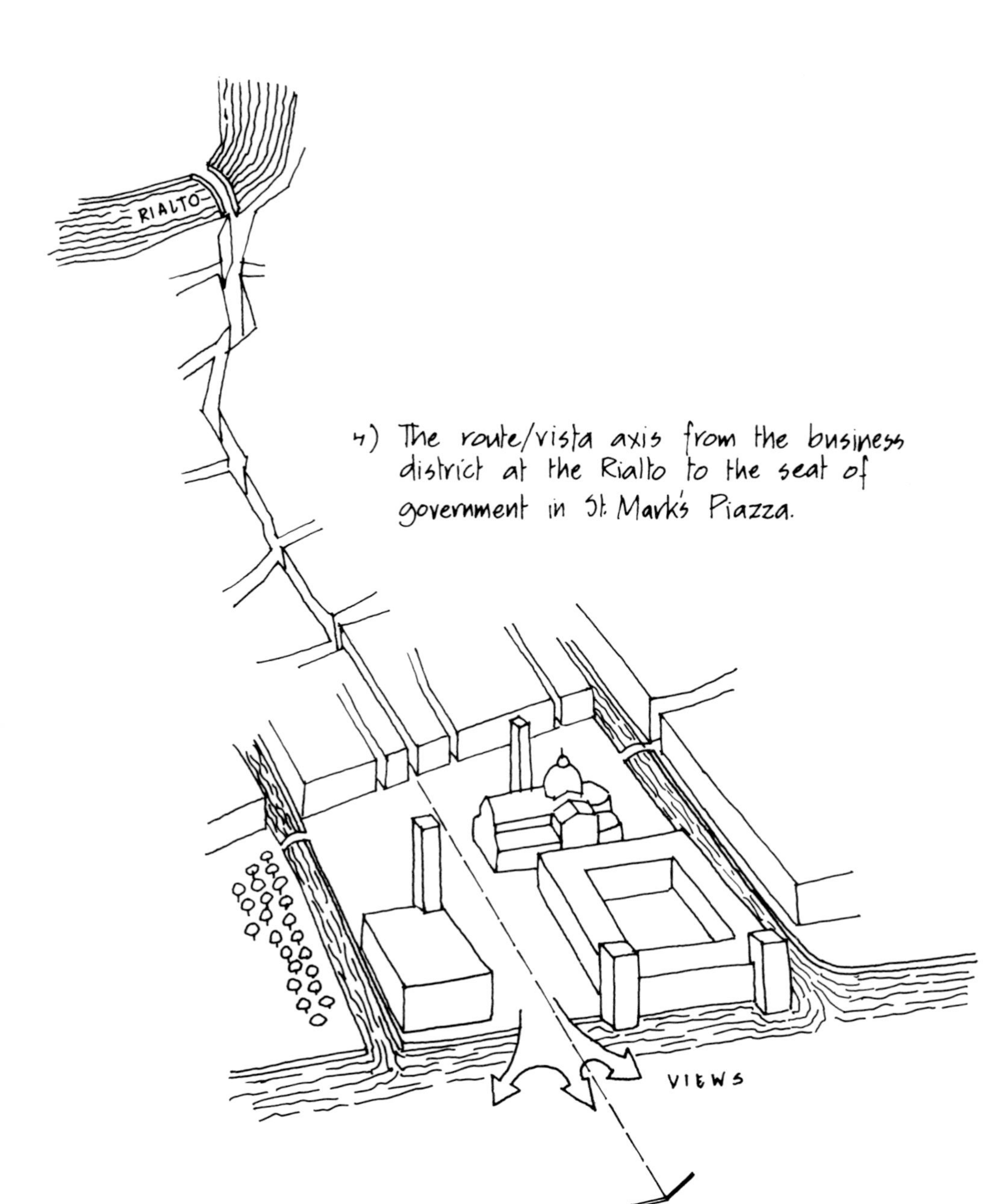

7) The route/vista axis from the business district at the Rialto to the seat of government in St. Mark's Piazza.

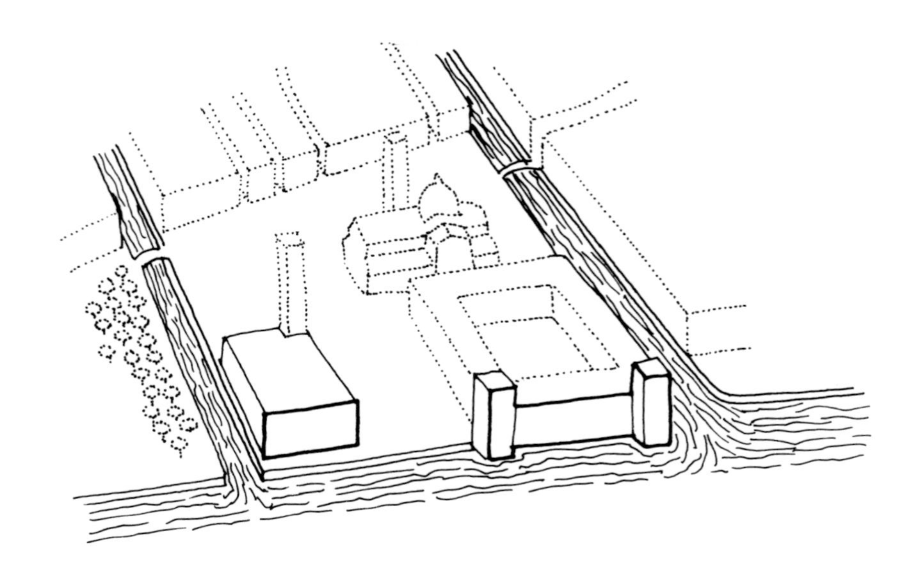

8) Facades which face the Bacino

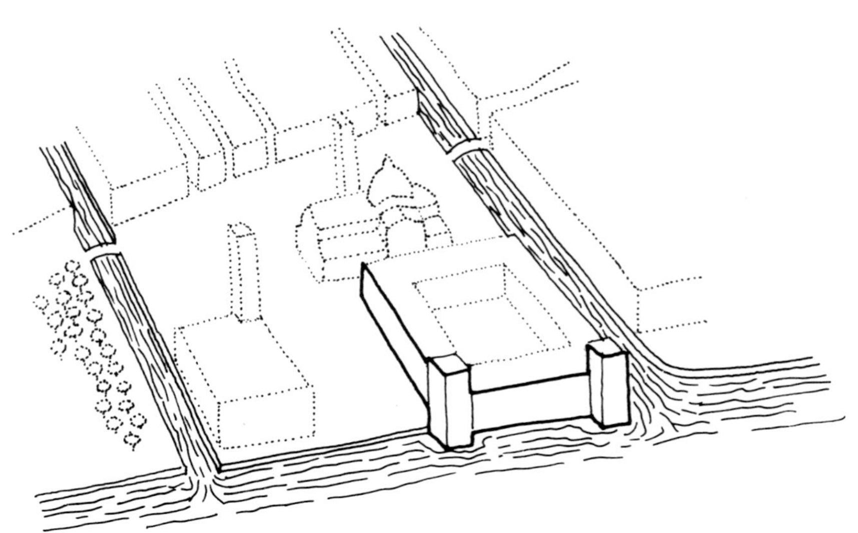

9) Twin facades on the Doge's Palace facing both Piazzetta and Bacino

ELEMENTS COMBINED

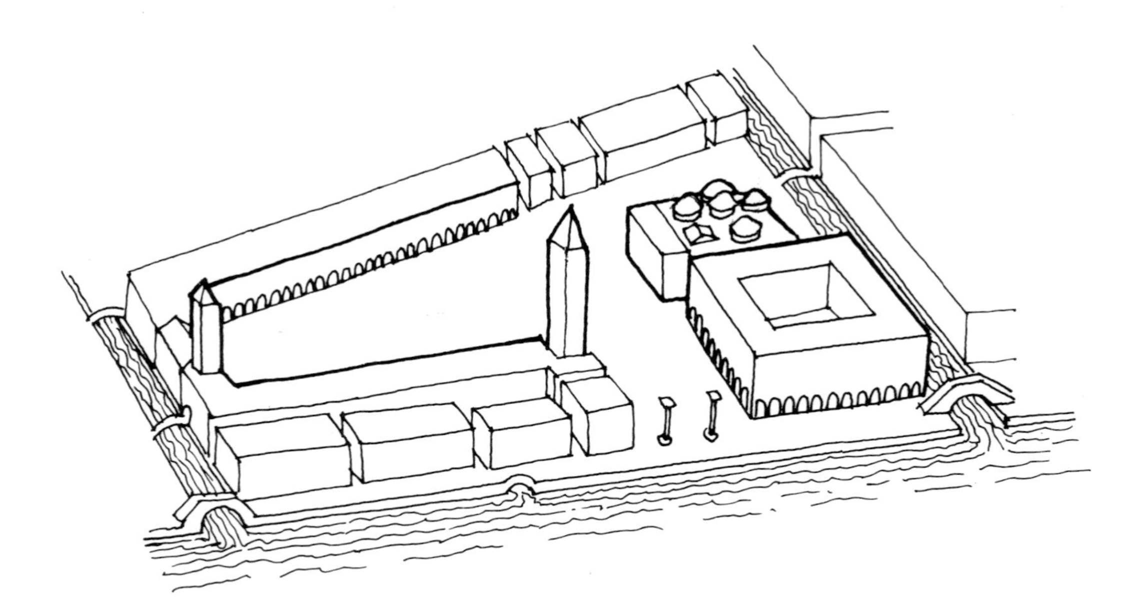

In 1173 Sebastiano Ziani, the Doge, bought the land containing the Batario canal, and a competition to organise the space was won by Nicolo Barattiero who had built the giant granite columns at the end of the Piazzetta.

The canal was filled in in 1176 to almost double the size of the square and the church of S. Geminiano was moved back and rebuilt to form the western edge of the new paved piazza.

It was decided to have covered walks to enclose the piazza and houses and shops were arranged around the space, the houses being assigned to the nine Procuratori de Supra, officials who were in charge of St. Mark's and its properties. By the beginning of the fourteenth century, there was a covered walk all the way round the square, and during this period the Piazza S. Marco was the largest and best organized city square in Europe.

On the north side of the square, the first Procuratie, (built in the 12th century) had an arcade with 50 openings, making it a considerable medieval monument which lasted 350 years.

The south and west sides of the Doge's Palace were finished by 1424. The 500' long Procuratie Vecchie was built between 1480 and 1517 by Bartolomeo Buon the Younger and Sansovino began his library in 1536 to complete the Piazzetta. Sansovino also designed the Loggetta at the base of the Campanile.

The Clock Tower by Loducci was erected in 1499 and the three flagpoles with Leopardi's bronze bases were erected in 1505.

After Sansovino's death, Scamozzi finished the Library and built the Procuratie Nuove, begun in 1584, in the process detaching the Campanile and increasing the size of the square.

Under Napoleon, the church of S. Geminiano was pulled down enabling completion of the piazza on its west side.

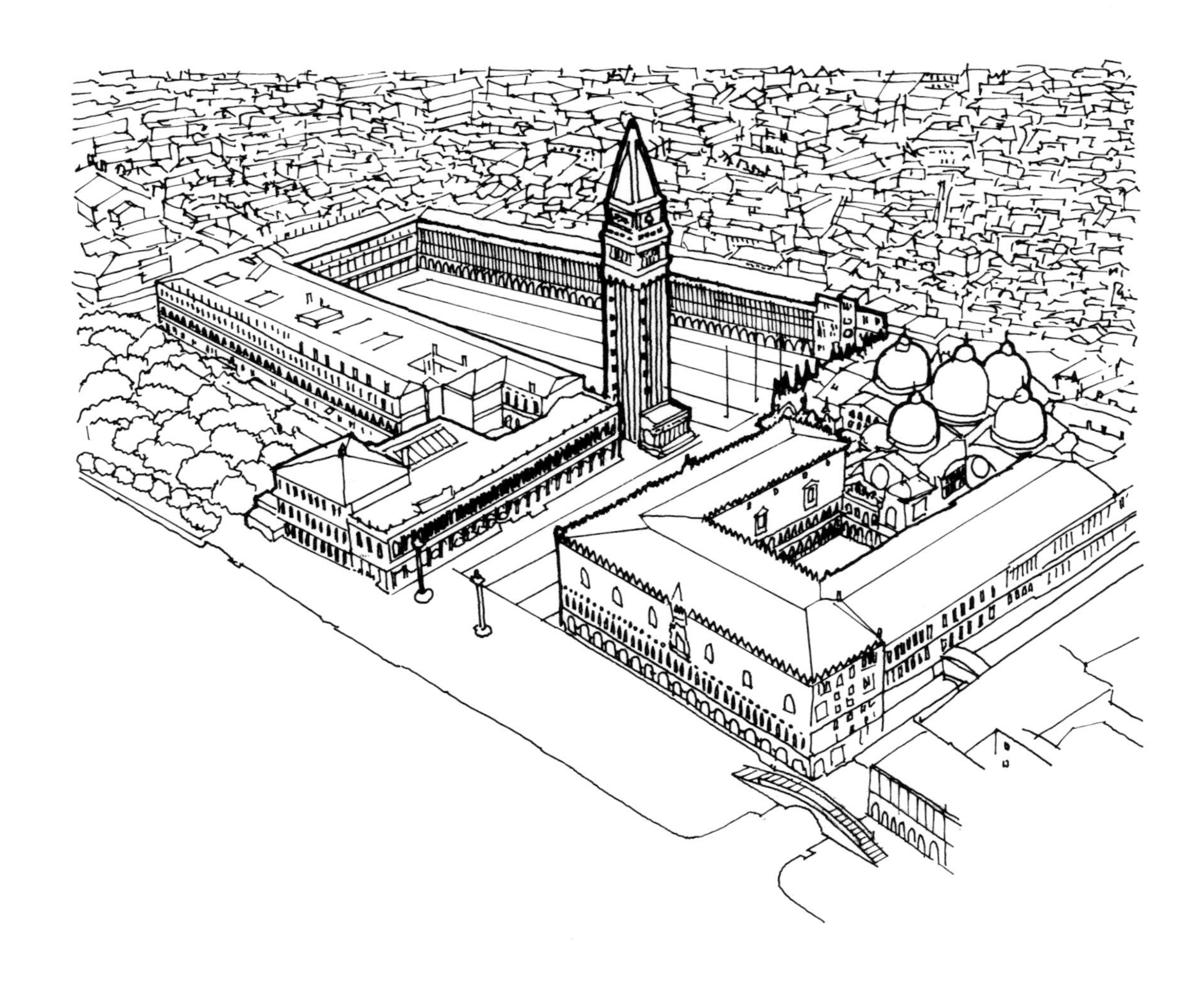

CENTROIDAL MASS

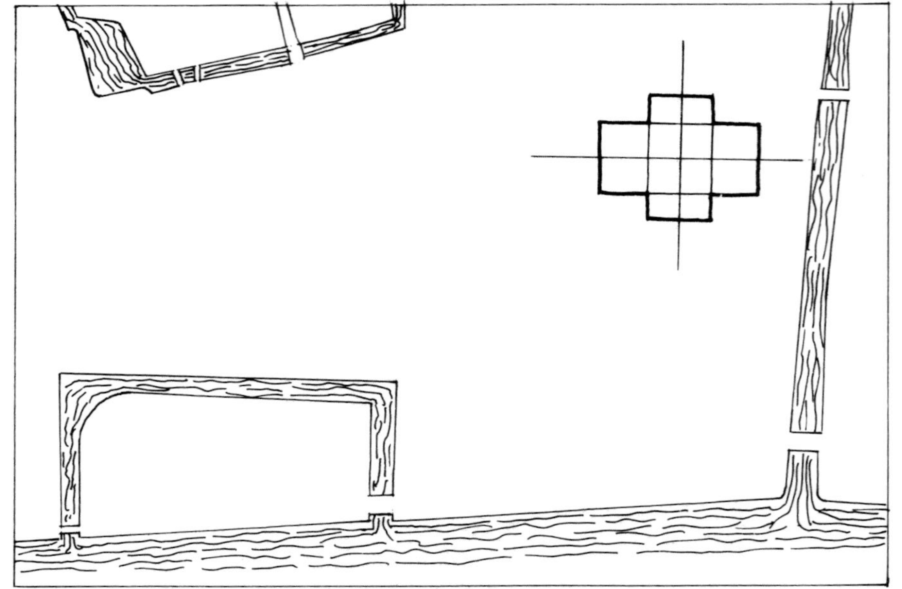

In the final assemblage of elements, the site may be read as a flat platform with canals restricting the boundaries to the north south and east

The Greek Cross plan of St. Mark's establishes a regular bi-laterally symmetrical form which has the inherent potential to dominate the space.

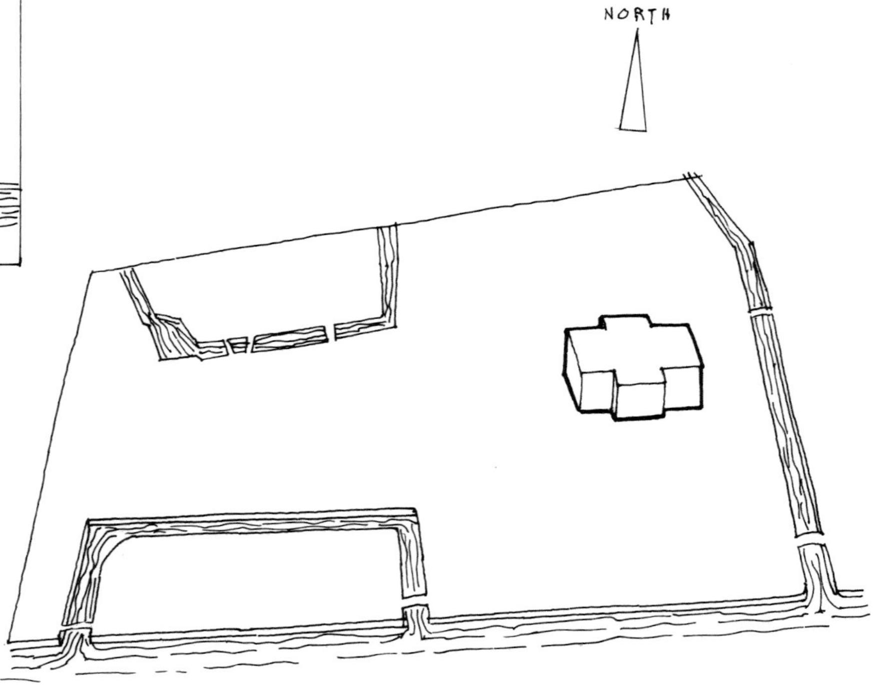

EXOTIC DOMINANCE

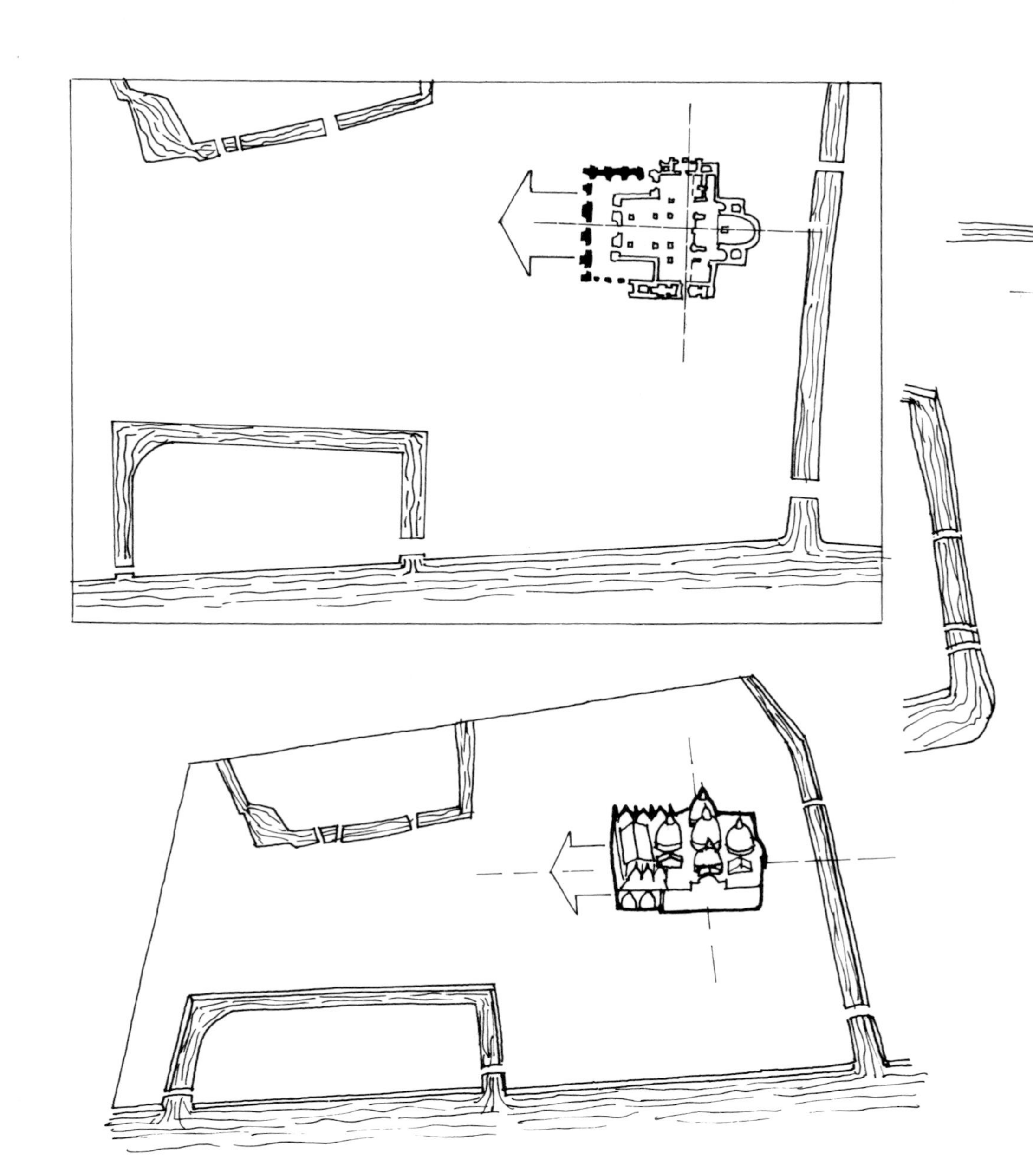

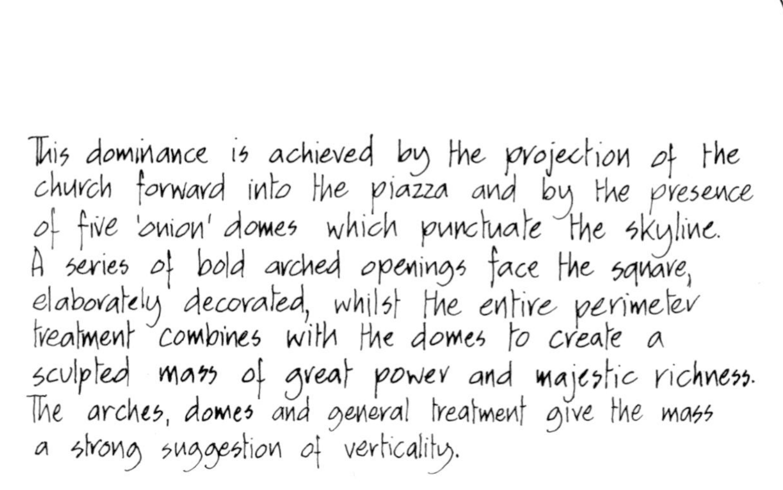

This dominance is achieved by the projection of the church forward into the piazza and by the presence of five 'onion' domes which punctuate the skyline. A series of bold arched openings face the square, elaborately decorated, whilst the entire perimeter treatment combines with the domes to create a sculpted mass of great power and majestic richness. The arches, domes and general treatment give the mass a strong suggestion of verticality.

INTERLOCKING CONTRASTING MASSES

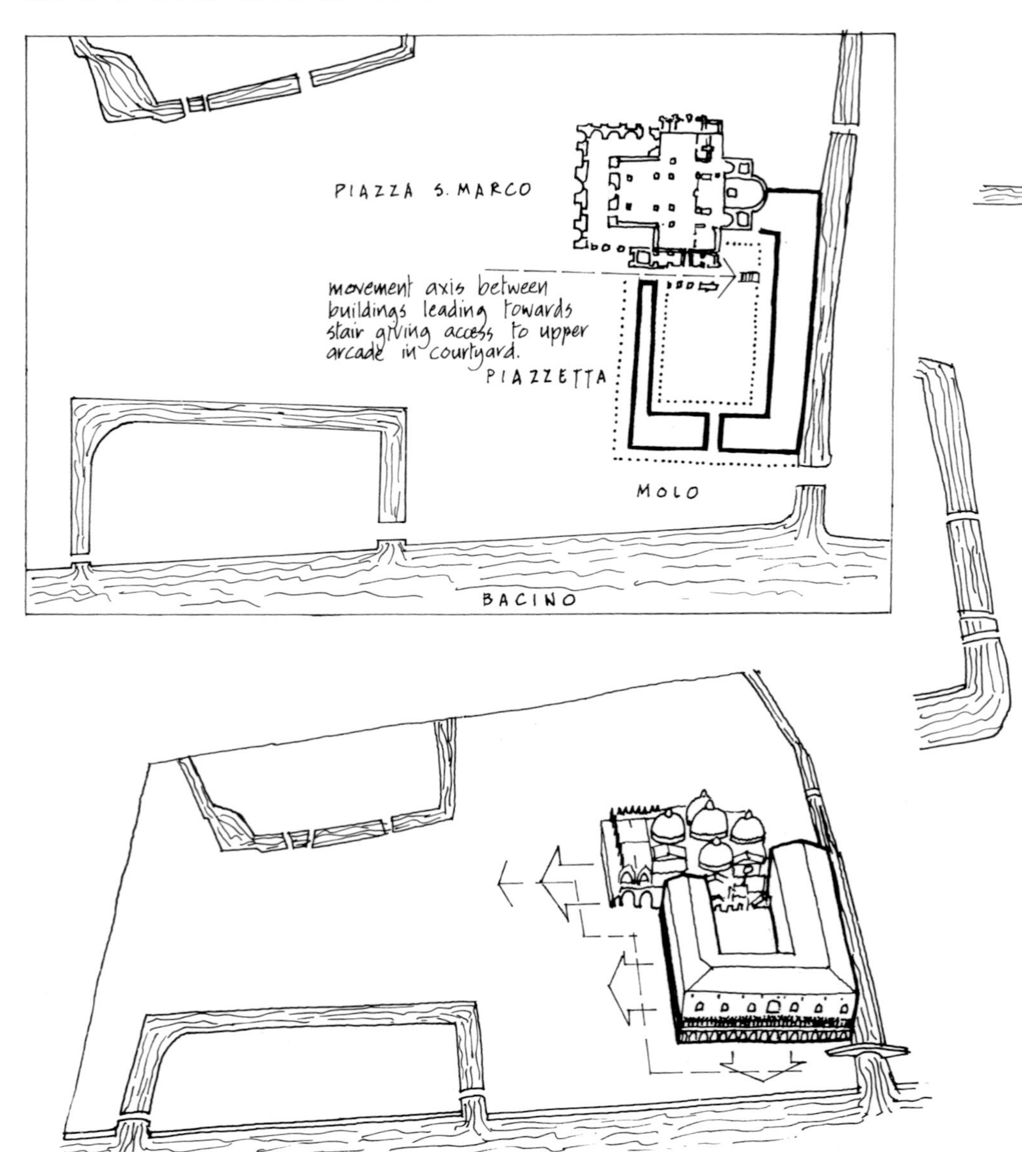

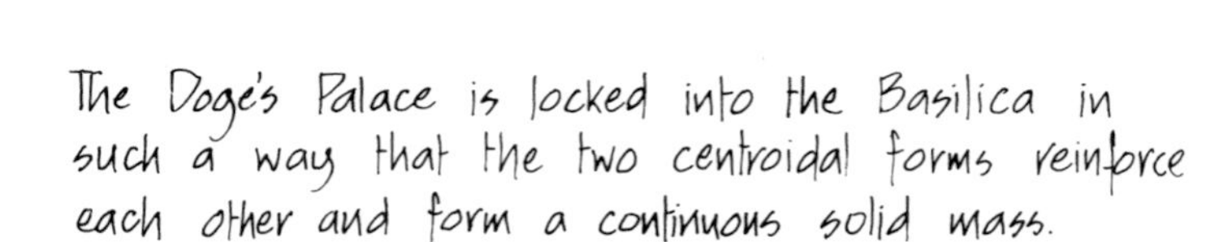

The Doge's Palace is locked into the Basilica in such a way that the two centroidal forms reinforce each other and form a continuous solid mass.

The Basilica remains dominant, the courtyard erosion of the Palace reducing its mass content. If St. Marks responds to the Piazza, the Doge's Palace responds primarily to the sparkling waters of the Bacino, yet it also faces the Piazzetta in an echelon arrangement which guides movement towards the Piazza.

Arcades enrich the Palace at the lower levels, giving the upper mass a floating effect, and the insistent columnar rhythm also guides movement from Molo to Piazza. If the Basilica is earthbound with a vertical emphasis, the Palace is horizontal and has a 'floating' sense of linearity despite its centroidal configuration.

CIRCULATION NETWORK

The forms lock together to form a composite whole.

At the point of interlock a circulation route pierces the complex and rises by the Scala dei Giganti to the second floor level of the inner cortile of the Doge's Palace.

A further route around the courtyard at ground level gives access to the Basilica. The network of circulation routes links Palace to Basilica and links both to the Molo and Piazzetta.

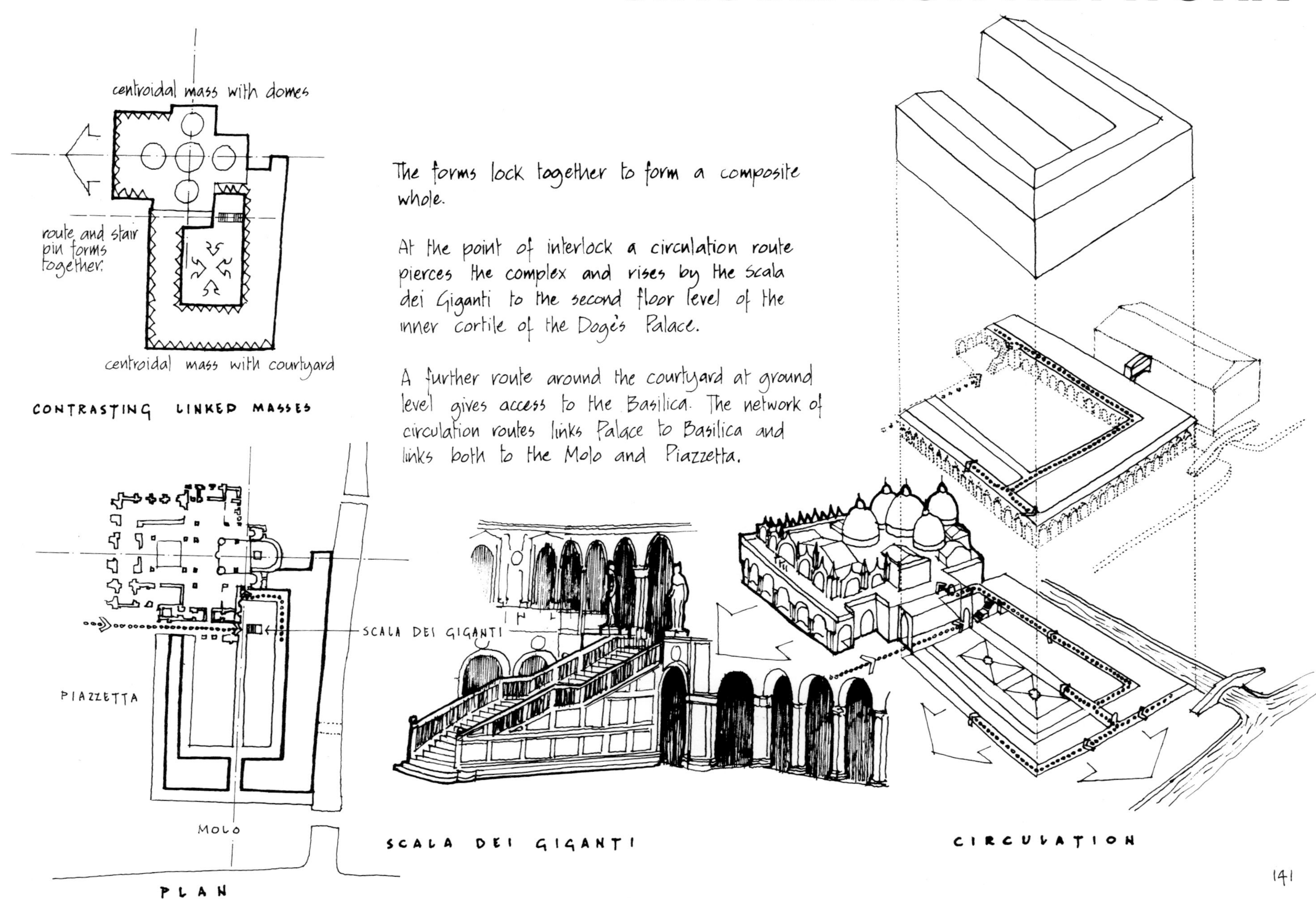

MOVEMENT

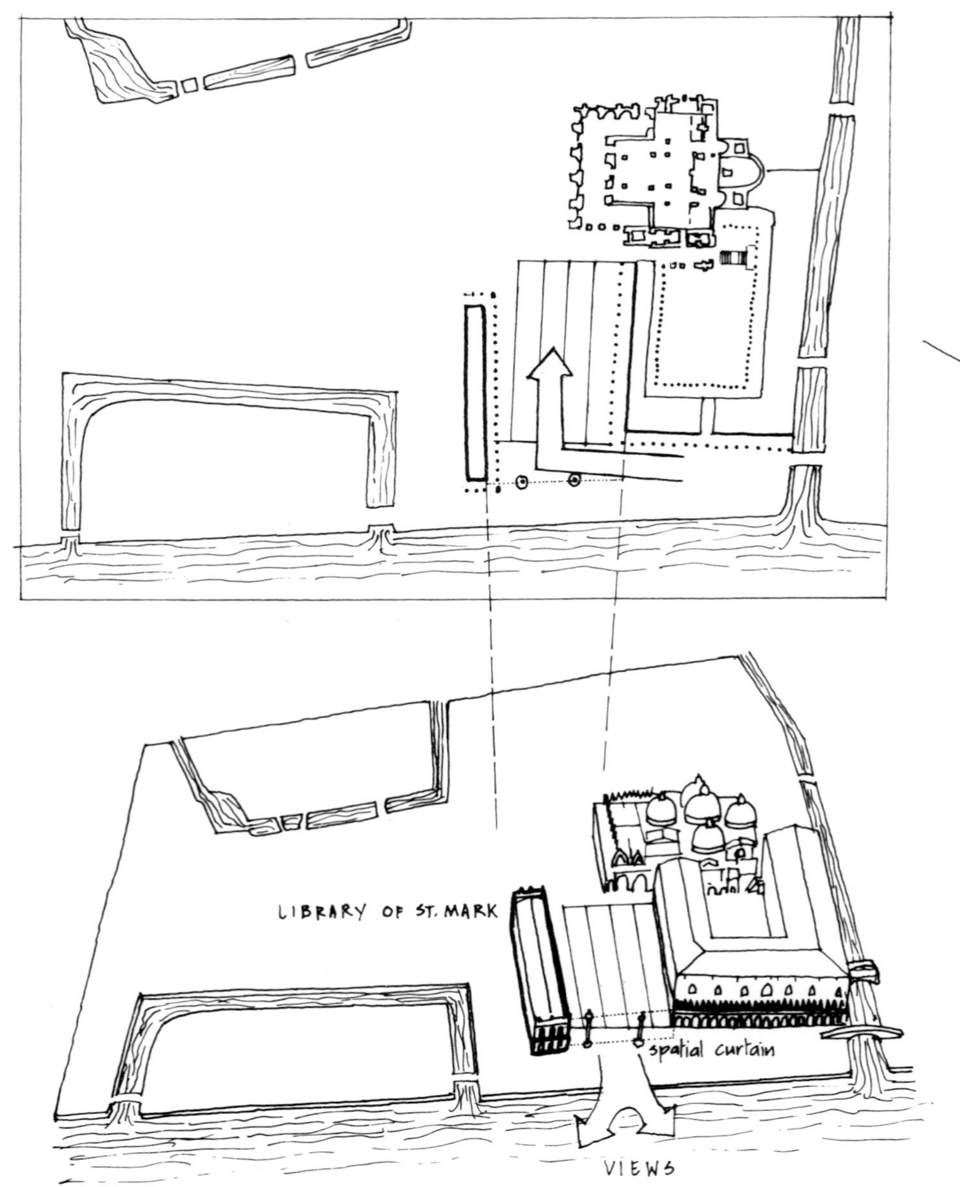

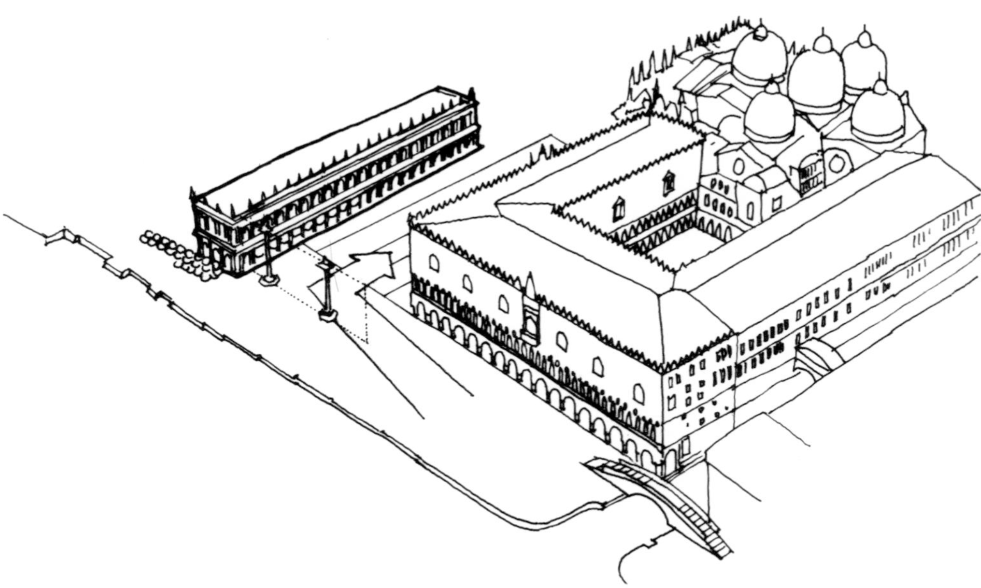

The forward projection of Sansovino's Library turns movement into the Piazzetta. The colonnades of both Library and Doge's Palace direct this movement which is also assisted by the pattern of the floor paving.

The two columns at the end of the Piazzetta form an implied spatial curtain which helps to define the edge of the Piazzetta and also provides a frame for views outwards. The sense of framing is assisted by the diminishing perspective effect of the differing angles of the Library and Doge's Palace.

OBLIQUE PLANE

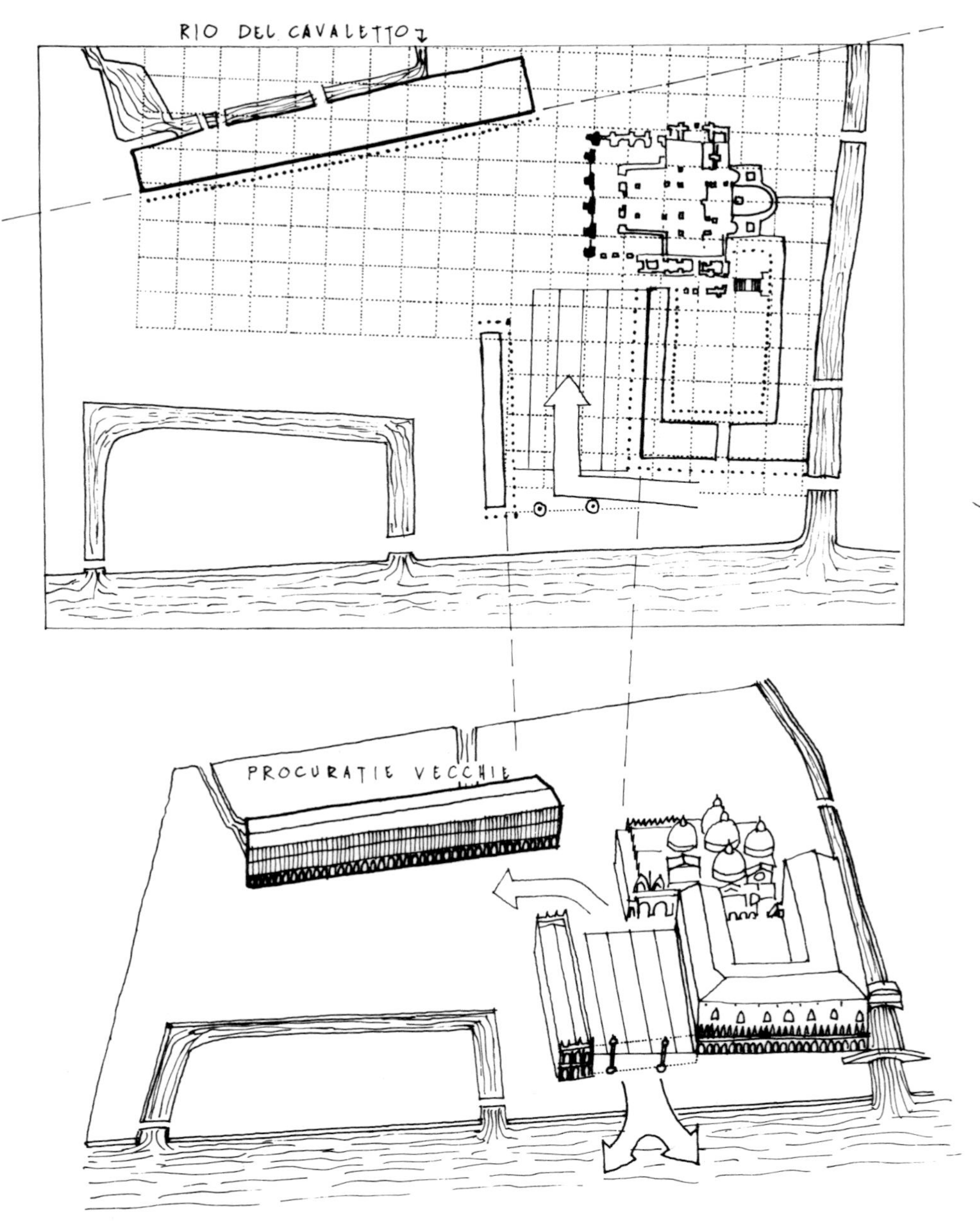

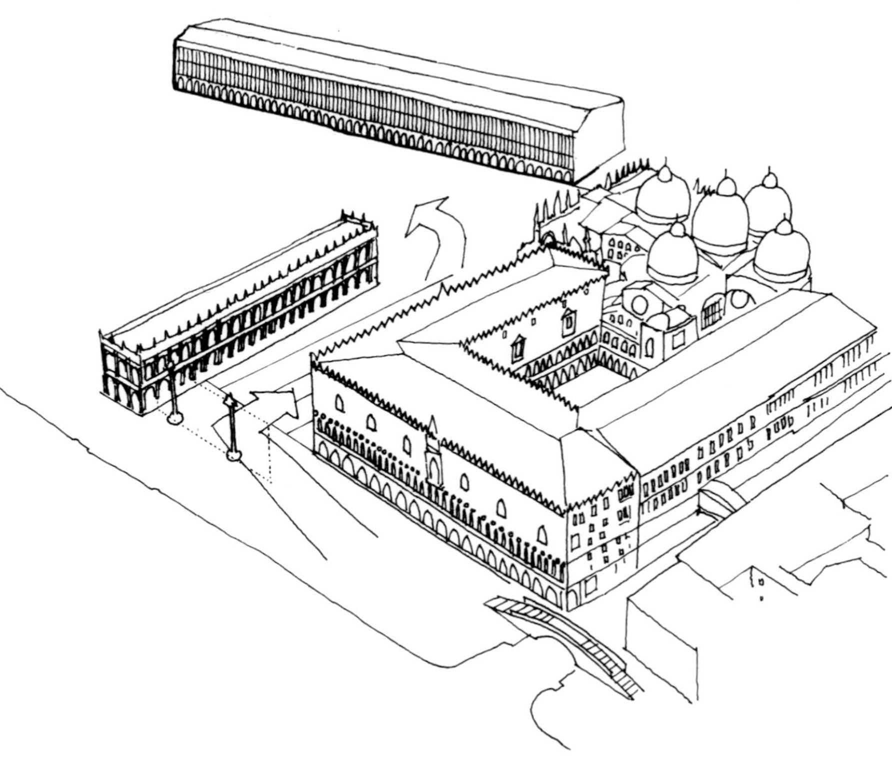

The combined dominant centroidal masses, St. Mark's Basilica and the Doge's Palace, establish an implied orthogonal field determined by their respective facades facing St. Marks' Piazza and the Piazzetta.

Restricted in its location and alignment by the Rio del Cavaletto at its rear, the Procuratie Vecchie fronts onto the north side of the piazza. Although in consequence a product of circumstances, the facade makes a dramatic oblique planar interaction with the orthogonal field which turns movement into the Piazza.

ENCLOSURE

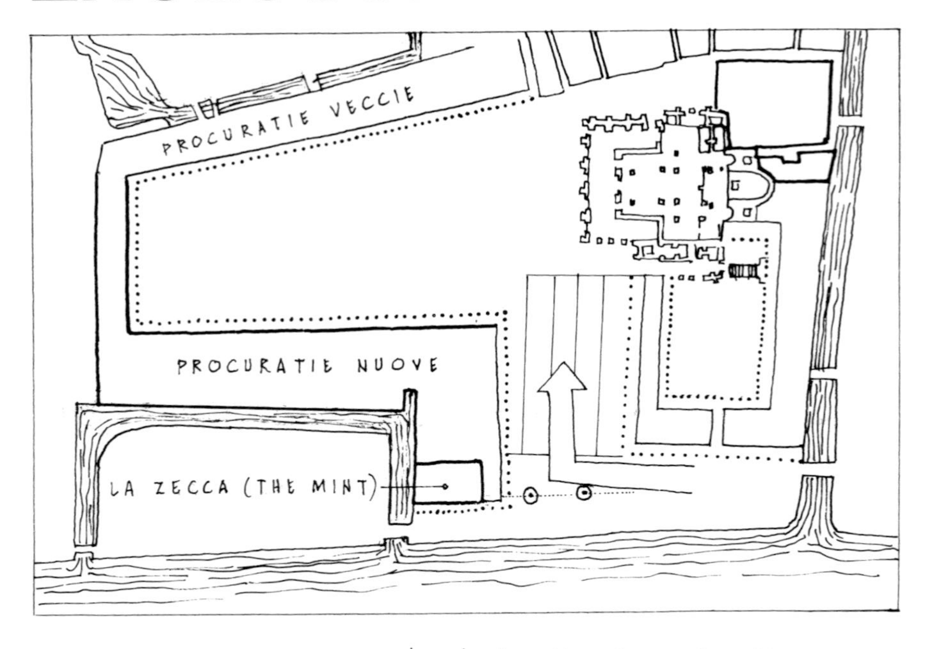

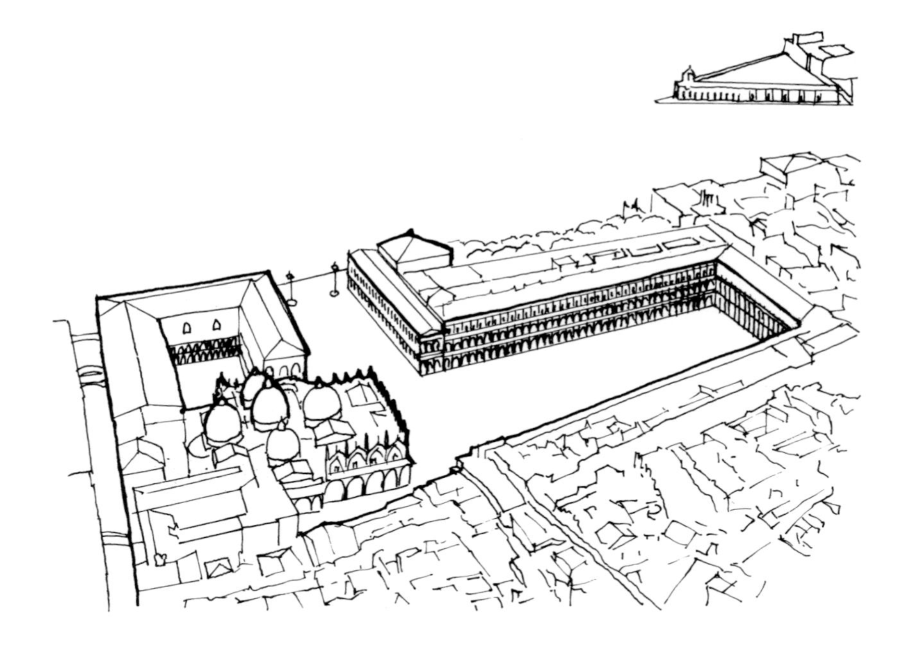

St. Mark's Square is completed by the Procuratie Nuove on its southern side by Scamozzi, who completed the Library after Sansovino's death. Scamozzi's design of the Procuratie picks up the scale and rhythm of the Library but adds an extra floor to strengthen this side of the square.

The format is continued across the west side but is reduced to two storeys to match the height of the Procuratie Vecchie.

The sturdy centroidal mass of La Zecca (the Mint) by Sansovino provides a secure termination of the complex on the side facing the Bacino.

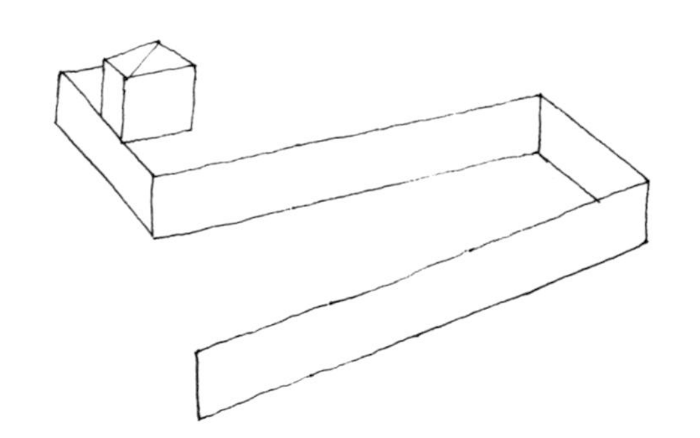

POSITIVE/NEGATIVE OBLIQUE/ORTHOGONAL

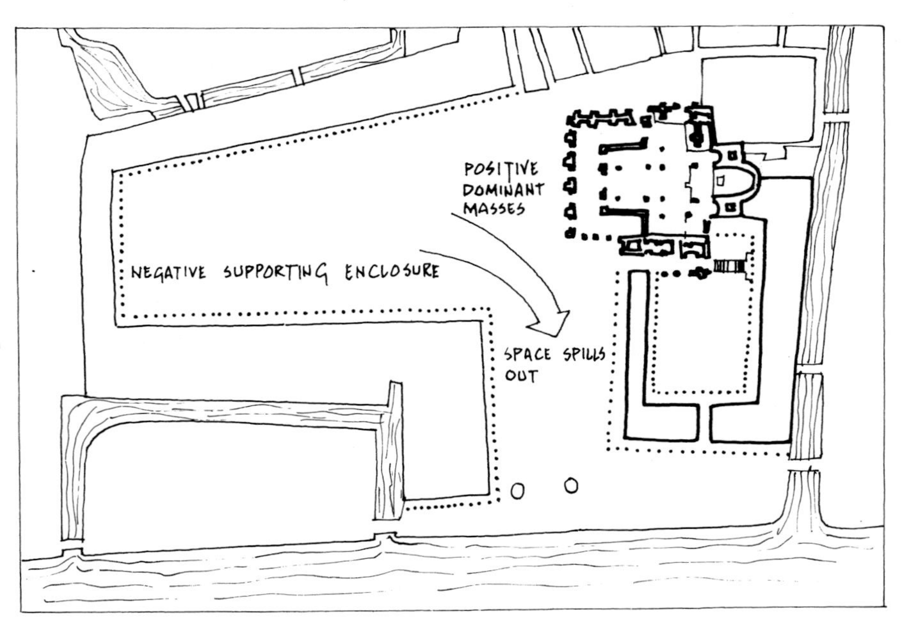

The complete enclosure, with a more or less continuously regular roofline, contains the Piazza S. Marco and the western edge of the Piazzetta. The effect is of linear horizontality, these planes, with a strong rhythmic component, acting as a passive background to the main events which dominate and generate each space, the Basilica and Doge's Palace. This dual megastructure, with its echeloned alignment, fashions the positioning of the two spaces, with the Piazza spilling over into the Piazzetta at its south east corner.

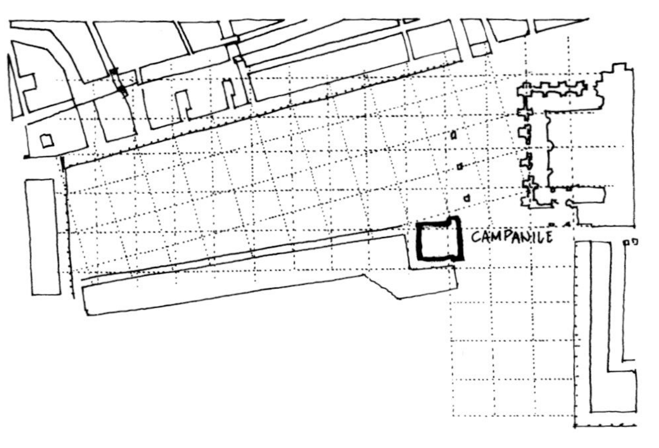

The above plan of the piazza in about 1500 (taken from Lotz, Italienische Plätze) reveals the basic dilemma which is presented by the oblique alignment of the Procuratie Vecchie.

This stems from the way the oblique field so engendered, and which leads appropriately visually towards the Basilica, conflicts with the orthogonal field established by the Basilica and Doge's Palace. (Both fields are dotted in over the plan)

At this point in time, before Scamozzi's Procuratie Nuove, the Campanile is shown wedged into the southern side of the square.

PIAZZA

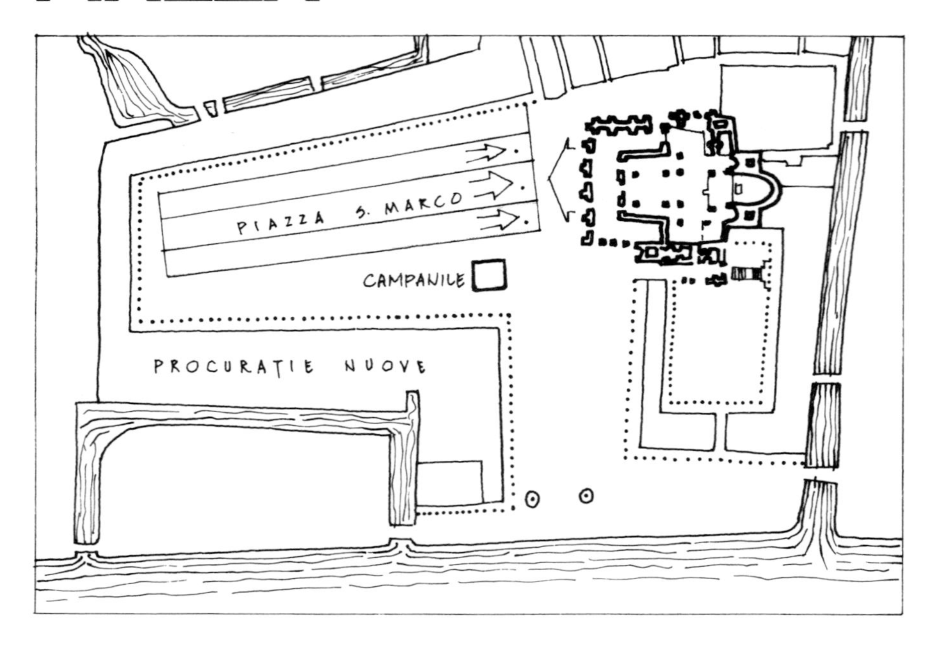

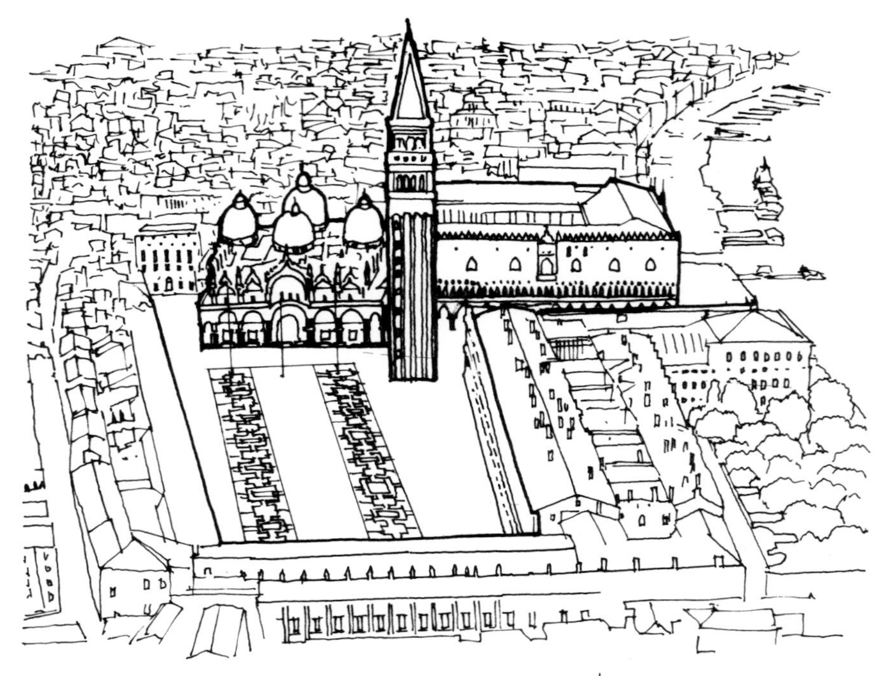

The positioning of the Campanile, detached by Scamozzi from the adjacent Procuratie Nuove, clearly defines and separates the Piazza from the Piazzetta. By breaking away the Campanile, the planar enclosure of both spaces is allowed to continue uninterupted, giving a sense of continuity from Piazzetta to Piazza.

By its location, the Campanile helps to contain the Piazza and acts as an element framing the Basilica, which addresses the Piazza at an angle. Any doubt as to which field, orthogonal or oblique, should operate in the square, is resolved by the floor paving, which reinforces the oblique facade of the Procuratie Vecchie and directs the space, obliquely, towards St Mark's.

Scamozzi's alignment of the Procuratie Nuove, however, retains the orthogonal characteristic and the turn to the Library is a right angle. This orthogonal reading is not quite that of the Basilica and Doge's Palace; this axial shifting, sometimes slightly, sometimes boldly, is a major feature of the ensemble, animating the mass-space-planar relationships with a subtle dynamism.

The diminishing perspective induced by the angle of the Procuratie Vecchie exaggerates the apparent length of the square, this being enhanced by the close spacing of the hundred columns in the arcade.

PIAZZETTA

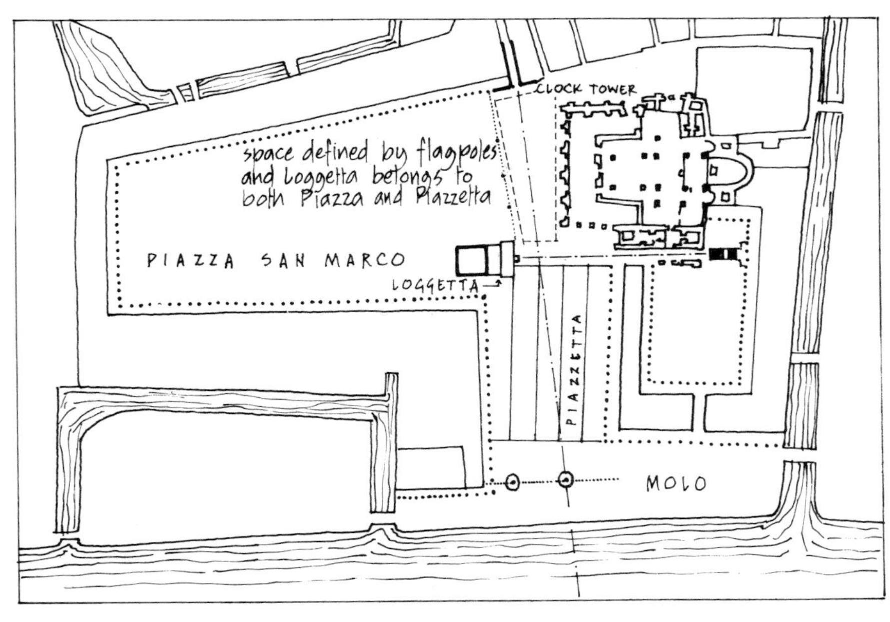

The positioning of the Campanile also defines the Piazzetta as a linear space with its axis running approximately north/south. At the northern end the axis is concluded by the Clock Tower by Coducci, whilst to the south the axis runs through the easterly column which defines the edge of the Piazzetta as it meets the Molo. Further definition is provided by the three flagpoles fronting the Basilica. These flagpoles also enframe the Basilica as foreground incidents when St. Mark's is viewed from the Piazza.

Sansovino's Loggetta, at the base of the Campanile, confirms the directional nature of the tower by ensuring that it faces the Piazzetta. This intervention, whilst retaining continuity of the axiality of the Piazzetta, further subdivides the space by creating a space fronting St. Mark's which belongs to both Piazza and Piazzetta.

The positioning of the Campanile also concludes the axis which pins the Basilica and Doge's Palace together and which leads to the Scala dei Giganti. The Campanile, therefore, whilst establishing the spatial definition of both Piazza and Piazzetta, forms part of the Basilica/Doge's Palace group and by its separation, does not belong to the planar enclosure around these spaces.

In its verticality, the Campanile relates directly to the vertical emphasis apparent in the Basilica, in this sense acting in contrast to the horizontal planar enclosure around the Piazza. Like both Basilica and Doge's Palace it is a major event, an object in the space and not simply an enclosing element. Placement of small windows to the left on each facade of the Campanile implies a sense of rotation, not inappropriate to its pivotal position and role.

MOVEMENT

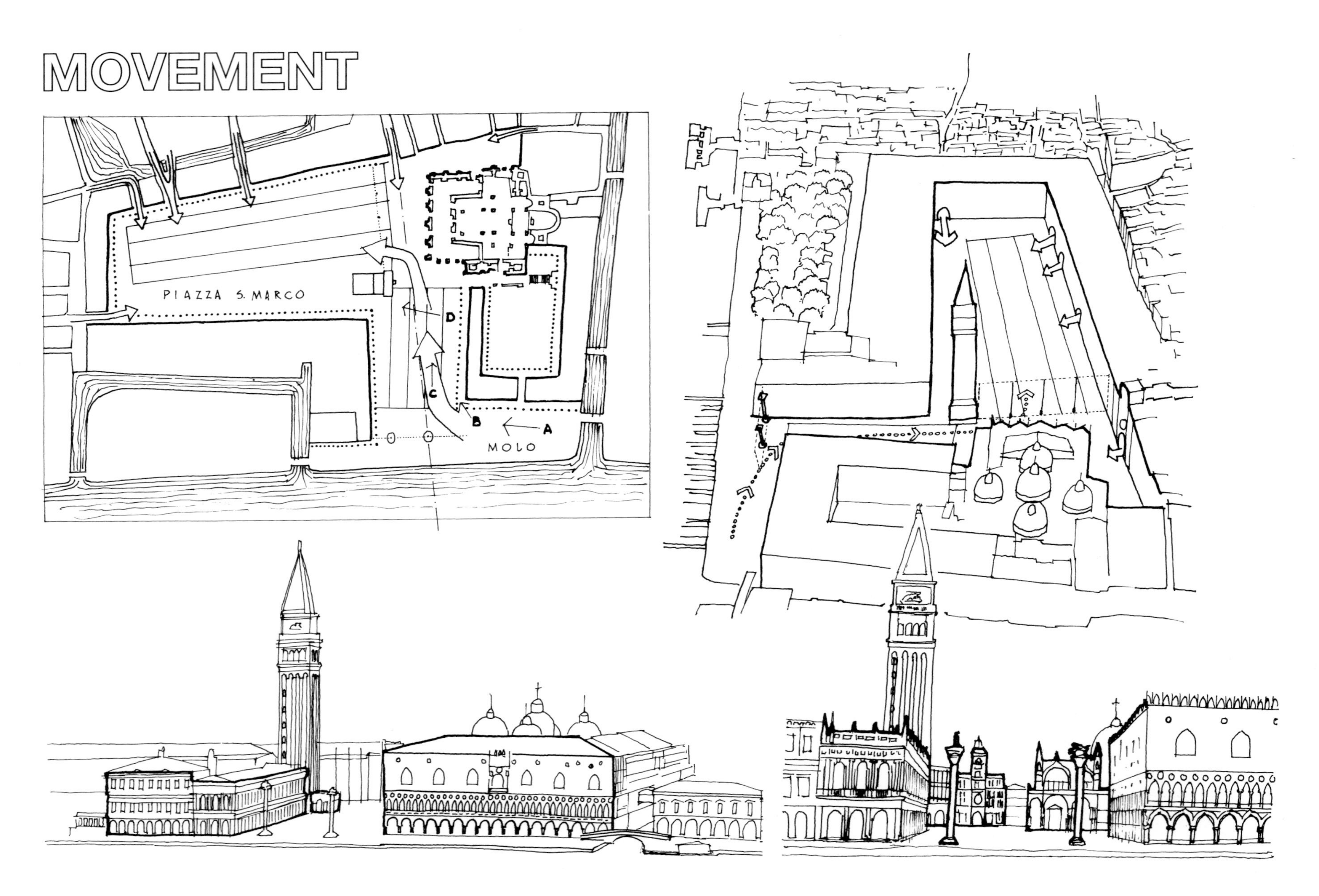

VIEWS FROM BACINO

FROM MOLO TO PIAZZA

VIEW A

VIEW B

VIEW C

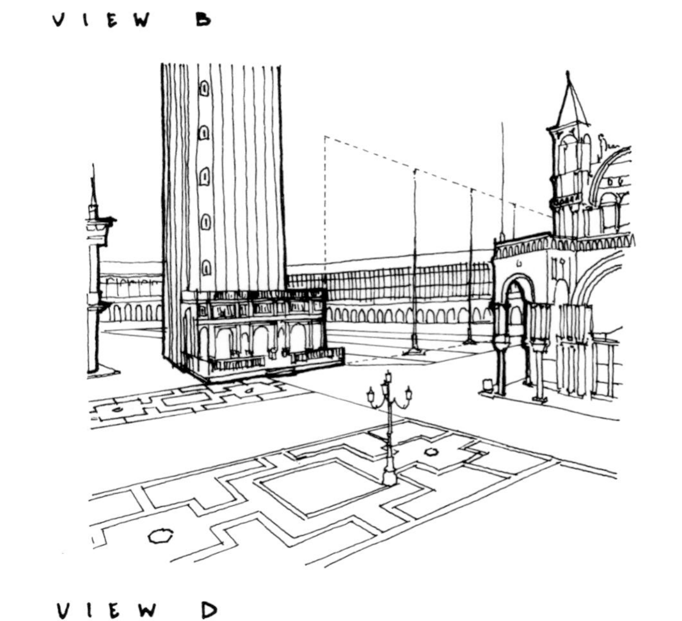

VIEW D

VIEWS

The two most dramatic entry points into the Piazza occur as important routes emerge into the space at the south west corner and through the Clock Tower opening.

At the south west corner the view of St. Mark's and the Campanile is framed by an arch of the arcade surrounding the Piazza. Following movement through the 'maze' of narrow streets the drama and magnificence of this view is one of the finest in all architecture.

VIEW A

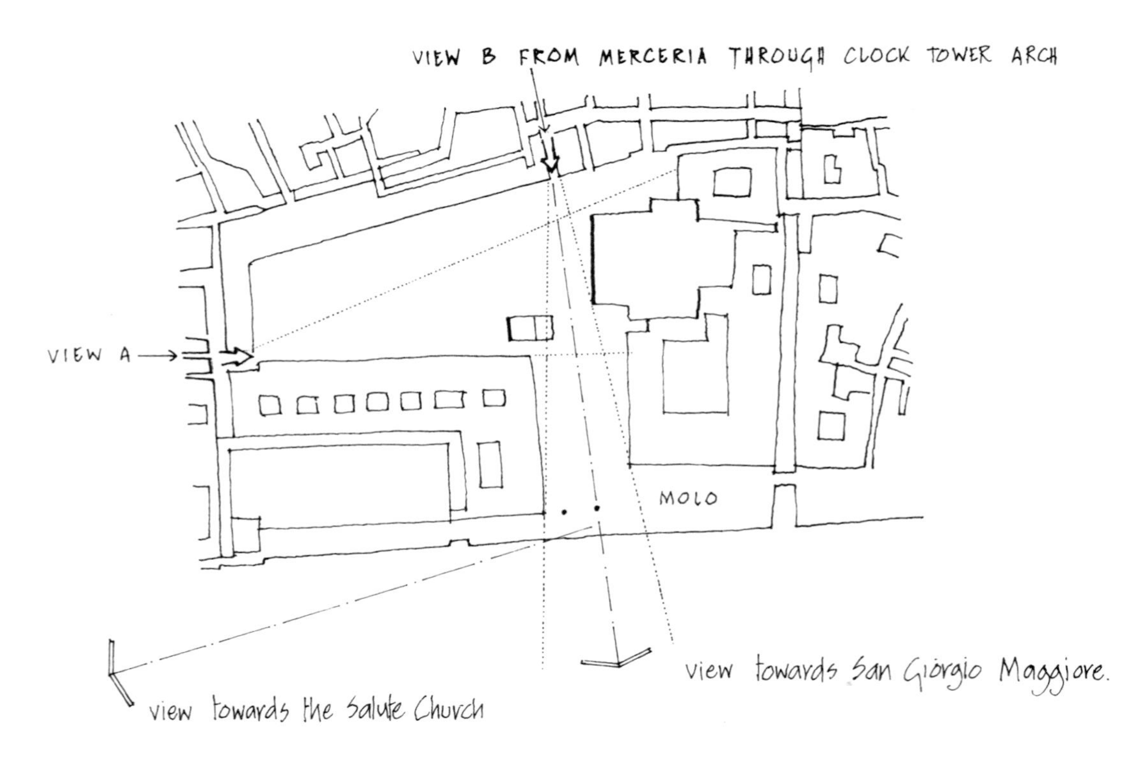

After taking the route from the Rialto along the Merceria, the view through the arch of the Clock Tower is also a compelling visual event. Framed by the twin columns the axial vista leads towards San Giorgio Maggiore, focusing on Palladio's domed church. On reaching the Molo the view to the right is of the entrance to the Grand Canal and the Salute church.

VIEW B

VIEW FROM CLOCK TOWER

INTERPRETATION

The Piazza S. Marco is an outstanding example of those qualities which ensure successful urban design. The reason for this has much to do with the way the role of architecture has been understood and fully expressed. Briefly stated, the Piazza addresses those issues of symbolism, pragmatism and the Genius Loci with which architecture is primarily concerned.

Successive contributions by gifted architects, selected by informed and responsible patronage, have produced an architectural masterpiece which operates on all levels demanded by the art. The time dimension has added to the totality in a manner that is entirely appropriate, because one of architecture's most important tasks is to represent both past and present aspects of a culture. This is particularly evident in the way each successive addition has respected the existing situation whilst managing to provide a positive and sensitive contribution.

That these additions have not always joined on to their neighbour immaculately (as with the corner junctions inside the Piazza) only adds to the vitality of the whole. Each architect has impressed his own personality on the ensemble and has been able to preserve the unity of the totality. The authority of the complex has much to do with the way each addition has responded to the specific conditions and requirements of its time.

If we consider the various buildings separately, each has considerable presence. The Basilica and Campanile are contrasting masses, each of which has a dominant role within the complex. There is a clear similarity with the Palazzo Pubblico and Torre del Mangia at Siena in the way these elements address both their respective piazzas and also signal the power and pride of their cities to distant horizons.

The Basilica expresses its Byzantine origins with an exotic imagery that celebrates both the power of the church and the vitality of the culture which it served. The exuberant majestic exterior contrasts with the mysterious solemnity of the interior, demonstrating that difference between light and darkness which must have coloured human experience in medieval times, when life was precarious and God so necessary.

If the Basilica speaks both of church and government, and is correctly dominant within the complex, the Doge's Palace fulfils another role, poised as it is, on the edge of both the Bacino and Piazzetta. The Palace has its Gothic vigour spiced with an Eastern ebullience which reflects and is reflected into, the sparkling blue waters which it faces. The Palace exemplifies the vitality of Gothic architecture, its inherent energy being fuelled by the powerful rhythm of its arcades, this animation being supported by the richness of its pattern and decoration.

Sansovino's Library is a perfect foil to the Palace, its elegance and sophistication contrasting with, yet complimentary to, the Gothic 'naievety' and extravagance of its neighbour. These buildings underscore the evolutionary advance in human consciousness from the Middle Ages to the Renaissance, yet, although separated by their respective world views, each design is strong and assured, the Library squat, compact, horizontal, with its own rhythms and rich decoration managing to be as powerful as its larger, elevated neighbour.

INTERPRETATION

Maintaining the Renaissance sobriety of the Library, the Piazza continues the Piazzetta theme of contrast between background and foreground. Whereas in the Piazzetta this is evident in the difference between Library and Doge's Palace, in the Piazza the enclosure is by buildings uniform in tone, containing the square as a receptacle for people and events, and above all for the Basilica. St Mark's provides the foreground, asserting itself not only by the richness of its three-dimensional form, but also by the way the evening sun adds visual warmth to the colored mosaics facing the piazza.

Of especial importance in the Piazza is the obliquely angled Procuratie Vecchie. Not as rich sculpturally as the other two sides of the square, it has its own power, due partly to its oblique angle in relation to the other elements and partly to the insistant columnar rhythm of the arcade, these combined factors increasing the apparent length of the square.

The Clock Tower is appropriately picturesque in a Venetian sense. Whilst forming part of the Procuratie Vecchie, it cleverly stops the Procuratie rhythm and establishes an identity which expresses a dual function, that of clock and archway to a major route from the square. By raising the central section, containing clock and arch, the Tower concludes the axis leading through the Piazzetta to San Giorgio Compared to the Procuratie, of which it remains a part, the Clock Tower is light hearted, a delicate balance being struck between its playful figures and colouring and the dignity of the arcade alongside. This mixture, of correct seriousness and an emotive theatricality, is also present in the relationship between the St Mark's/Doge's Palace group and the rest of the buildings in the complex.

Such juxtapositions give the complex humanity and ensure that it speaks to us on several levels, expressing a broad range of sensory experience. Sansovino's Loggetta has a 'weighting' which belies its size, acting as meeting point, viewing pavilion, termination of the axis towards the Scala dei Giganti, and also managing to turn the Campanile, (otherwise directionally negative) towards the Piazzetta, and the two main buildings, Basilica and Doge's Palace.

The Piazza San Marco cannot adequately be discussed in stylistic or design terms but rather in terms of its extraordinary capacity and content. As with many great works of the human imagination, the ensemble balances formality and informality, unity and diversity, energy and control. We are presented with an architectural equation in which massing, surface treatment, movement progression and symbolic content fully engage the senses. To this must be added the magical time dimension which transports frail twentieth century man back to a glorious episode in his past.

In a description of Venice as seen through the eyes of the painter Giorgione, John Ruskin wrote:

> "Have you ever thought what a world his eyes opened on... when he went down, yet so young, to the marble city - and became himself as a fiery heart to it? A city of marble did I say? nay, rather a golden city paved with emeralds. For truly, every pinnacle and turret glanced and glowed, overlaid with gold or bossed with jasper... A wonderful piece of world. Rather itself a world... A world from which all ignoble care and petty thoughts were banished... No foulness nor tumult, in those tremulous streets... No weak walls could rise above them; no low-roofed cottage, nor straw-built shed. Only the strength as of rock, and the finished setting of stones most precious. And around them... still the soft moving of stainless waters... Above, free winds and fiery clouds raging at their will; - brightness out of the north, and balm from the south, and the stars of the evening and morning clear in the limit of arched heaven and circling sea."

J. Ruskin, The Stones of Venice, Vol 2 London 1896 p 183.

5

ANALYTICAL STUDIES OF BUILDINGS

ALVAR AALTO TOWN HALL AT SAYNATSALO
1950-61

ALVAR AALTO

Of those architects considered to have been pioneers of modern architecture, the works of Frank Lloyd Wright and Alvar Aalto most closely correspond with the proposition advocated in part one of this book, that architecture results from an interaction between programmatic requirements, the Genius Loci and the culture in which the architecture exists.

To some extent this is true of Le Corbusiers work, but his belief in universal solutions leading to standardization and his artistic as opposed to 'building' approach to design, place his output outside the central concerns of Wright and Aalto, each of whom made a significant contribution to the domestic architecture within his own culture. In this, these architects can be compared with Lutyens, who in his early houses similarly proposed an architecture rooted in his native land and owing inspiration to both landscape and tradition.

However, with regard to the traditional architecture within their respective cultures, a major point of departure for both Wright and Aalto was the desire to establish a fresh approach to the manipulation of internal space, and especially to redefine the relationship between inner and outer space.

In the case of Wright and Aalto, these explorations resulted in what has been termed an organic architecture, in which the elemental organization responds to internal requirements and external conditions simultaneously, each architect seeking to lock his building into its immediate topography.

In so doing, each architect uses a different kind of geometry. In Wright's work the organization is often controlled by systems which ensure homogeneity and unity as a direct result of the geometry itself. This is evident in his use of axes, the pinwheel and interlock

Aalto's work, by comparison, is more relaxed, less geometrcally deterministic and more malleable, concentrating particularly on how ensembles interact with the landscape. There is an inner as well as an outer 'fluidity' in the way elements merge into each other, corresponding closely to D'Arcy Wentworth Thompson's description of cell growth.[1] Aalto often gathers his elements around a central foyer or court[2] and uses radial configurations in combination with linear forms.[3]

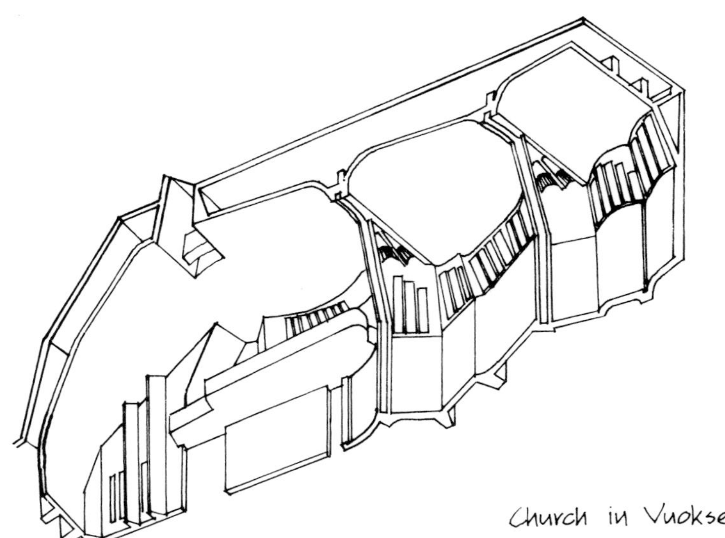

Church in Vuoksennisca (Imatra) 1956-59
(after an axonometric from Dizionario Enciclopedico di Architettura e Urbanistica, 1968-69.)

[1] Discussing the form of any portion of matter Thompson describes this as a 'diagram of forces,' explaining how an Amoeba tends 'to be deformed by any pressure from outside.' He refers to the fluid state of the organism and how its shape responds to forces exerted upon it. D'Arcy Wentworth Thompson, On Growth and Form, Abridged Edition, ed. by T. Bonner, Cambridge University Press, Cambridge, 1961, pp. 11, 12.

[2] See page 84

[3] See page 62.

ITALY AND FINLAND

The town hall at Säynätsalo is one of Alvar Aalto's most representative works in that the small complex of brick and timber buildings around a court encapsulates several themes which developed during his career. These themes can be traced back to two powerful influences on him, the one resulting from a trip to Italy in 1924 when he visited Florence, Padua and Venice, the other being the pervasive effect of the landscape of his native Finland.

In 1926, explaining the importance to him of Italian hill towns Aalto had written: 'The town on the hill . . . is the purest, most individual and most natural form in urban design.'[1] The Italian hill town remained a source of inspiration throughout his life and became so interwoven with his perception of the Finnish landscape that he often read the latter in terms of the former: 'Central Finland frequently reminds one of Tuscany, the homeland of towns built on hills' and in a description of how villages in Finland could be transformed, he explains how when he sees these villages, in his mind's eye he would 'make the church stand out as a more dominating element among the houses by building a little colonnaded square in front of it or by raising its spire. (The open square surrounded by architecture, is one of the most powerful rhythmic accents available in hilly country).[2] In 1924 he wrote:

> Arriving at daybreak in a town which we have never been in before, we realize that there are laws, traditions, customs and details in this hustle and bustle which, just like the other phenomena of our day and age, are not just the movements of atoms, but energy directed into these channels and supervised by more developed individuals . . . Nothing does a town greater honour than a well-developed public life and beautiful, functional 'public places,' not the least of which is the market hall, the nerve center of its food distribution and morning bustle.[3]

1 Quoted from Göran Schildt, Alvar Aalto, The Decisive Years, New York, 1986, p. 13.
2 From Göran Schildt, Alvar Aalto, The Early Years, New York, 1984, p. 210.
3 Ibid., p. 253.

Aalto had taken particular note of the vertical accentuation given by the campanile to the Italian hill town, and again applying the principle to his homeland wrote:

> Take an example, Ronnimäki Hill, which dominates the countryside around Jyväskylä, would only need a white campanile (tower) near (not at) the top for the whole area to acquire an extremely refined character. Even a lookout tower would do, but not one of those needlelike towers which function as a point of observation but not as an object of it. [1]

Despite the fact that the hillside on which the Säynätsalo town hall was sited had a very gentle slope which could not be compared to an Italian hill town, Aalto's design brings together several strands of his thoughts inspired by the visit to Italy. These include the notion of the town on a hill with the tower as a landmark, the enclosed court, the potential of stairs and the way architecture can mirror the vitality and express the essential character of a town.

[1] Ibid., p. 209.

SITE FORCES

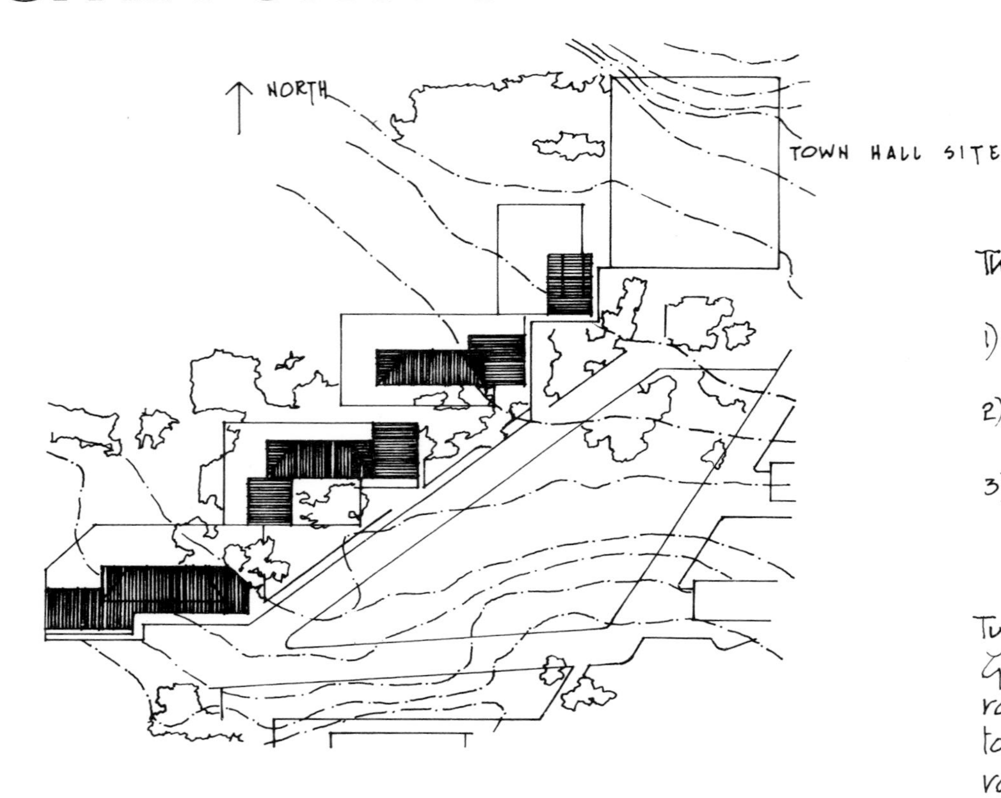

PROPOSED SITE PLAN (not as built)

The main characteristics of the town hall site are:

1) The contours which delineate a gentle slope within a landscape of pine trees.
2) Two obliquely aligned routes which traverse the contours as they rise up the hill.
3) The layout of housing, echeloned alongside the routes but deployed rhythmically within the discipline of an orthogonal grid.

Typically Aalto's layout intended to reinforce the Genius Loci by strengthening linkages between routes, contours and the architecture. Responding to the setting of pine trees with their sense of randomness and verticality, Aalto proposes low horizontal buildings laid out in an informal yet ordered fashion.

The proliferation of trees on the hillside gives a strong sense of nature on the site. This is not, therefore, the typical urban site as would normally be the case for a town hall, but instead represents an unusually direct interaction between man's activities and nature.

CENTROIDAL MASS

The town hall is situated at a nodal point where the routes conjoin to form the town square.

A centroidal form is proposed for the town hall, so positioned as to terminate the echeloned blocks of housing which lead towards the node.[1]

The oblique route and its supporting echelon rhythm of housing together constitute a powerful external vector inducing pressure on the centroidal town hall.

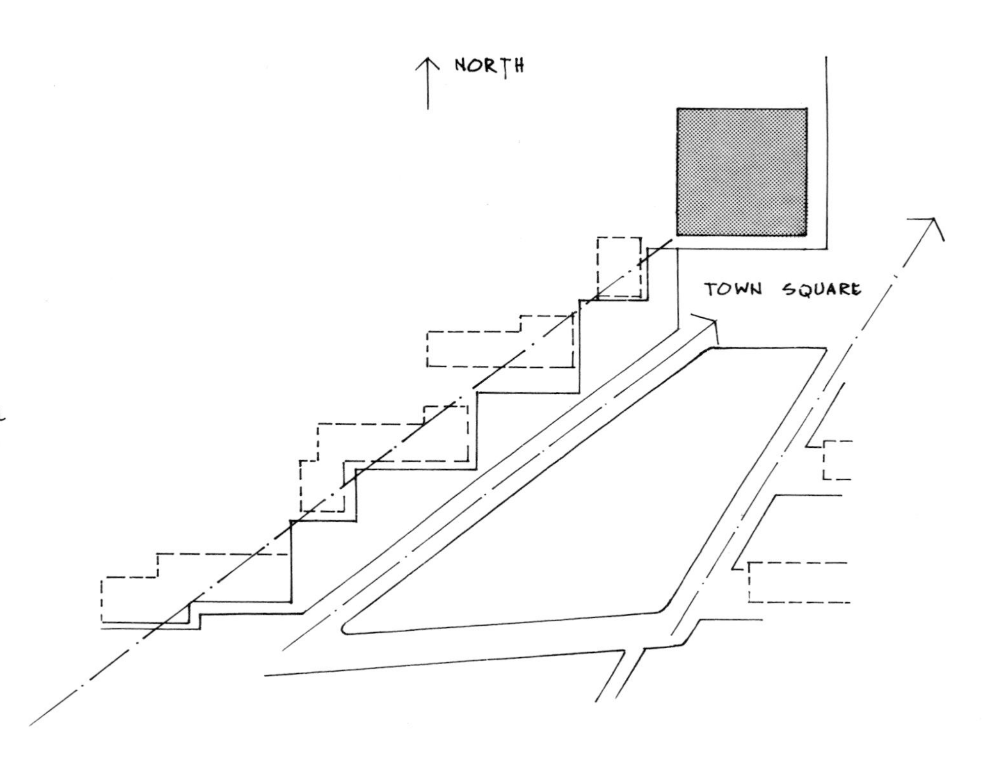

[1] see Peter Eisenman, doctoral thesis, The Formal Basis of Modern Architecture, Cambridge University 1963 p. 150

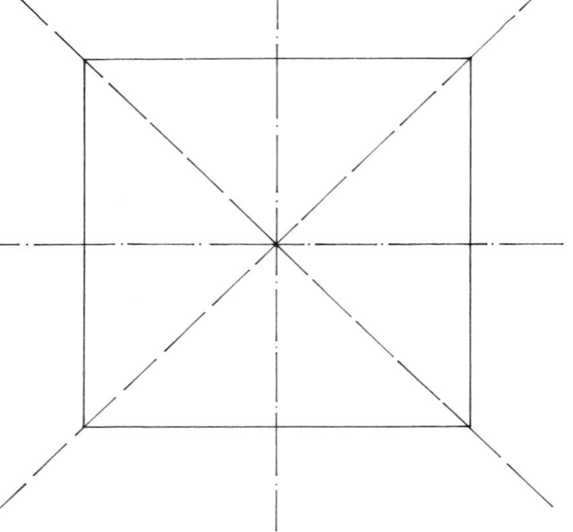

The generic form is centroidal, a symmetrical form with equal axes.

external vector

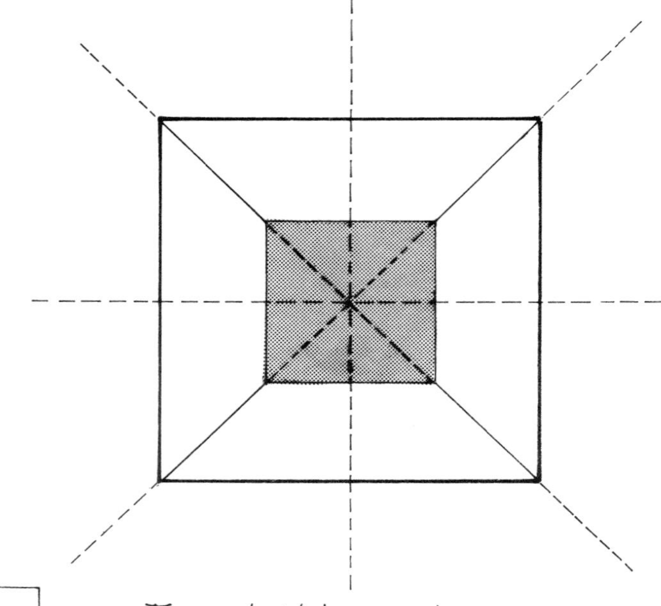

The centroidal mass becomes a courtyard. Sloping roofs point inwards to strengthen the feeling of enclosure. Echeloned housing produces an external vector which affects the form on the diagonal.

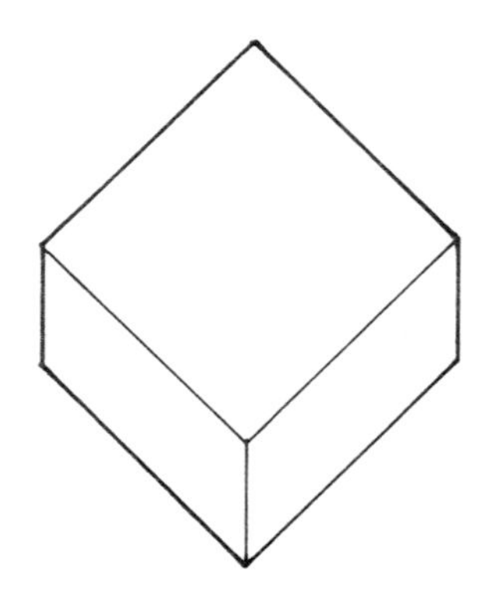

CONFIGURATIONAL READING

A symmetrical centralized mass eroded at its core or nucleus.

SYMBOLIC READING

A courtyard is a sheltered refuge which may suggest a sense of community. Diverse elements may be unified and become homogeneous around an enclosed courtyard.

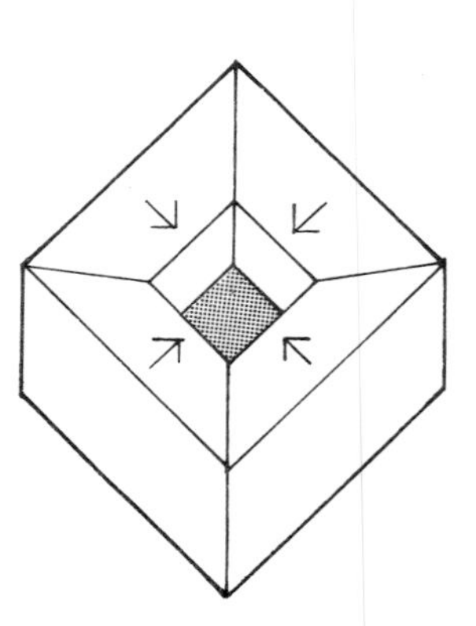

BACK

lateral axis

Dominant facade

FRONT

EFFECTS OF SLOPE

The directionality of the slope changes the form so that the south facing facade assumes a dominant role. The form becomes directional.

The internal court is raised to provide two levels of accommodation.

On a slope the centre of gravity shifts to pull back the internal lateral axis.

lateral axis pulled back as centre of gravity shifts

NORTH

SOUTH

Inner court raised

SECTION

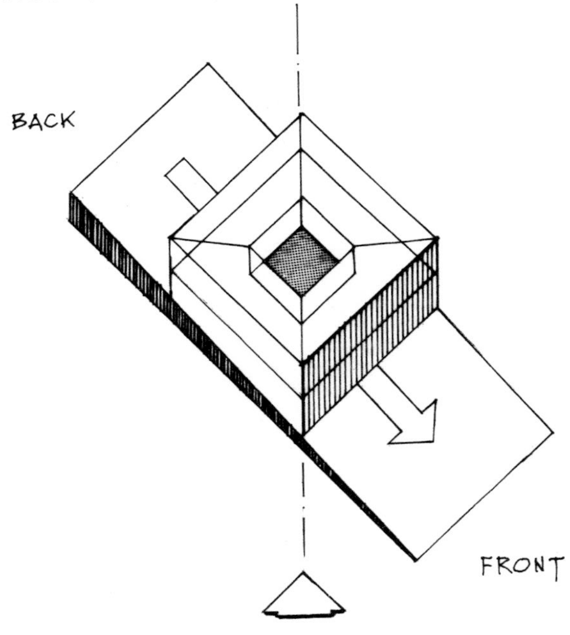

CENTROID FRACTURED

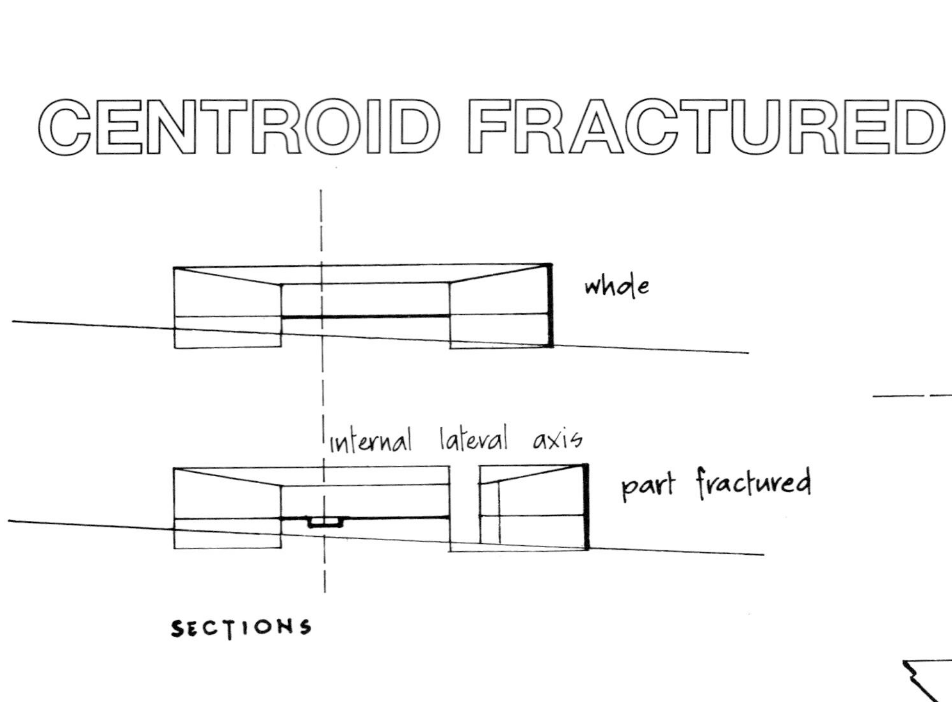

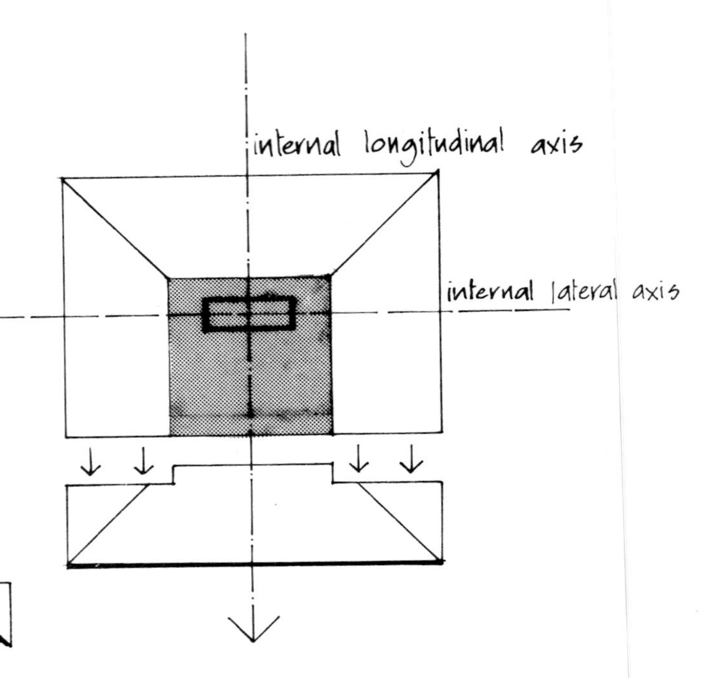

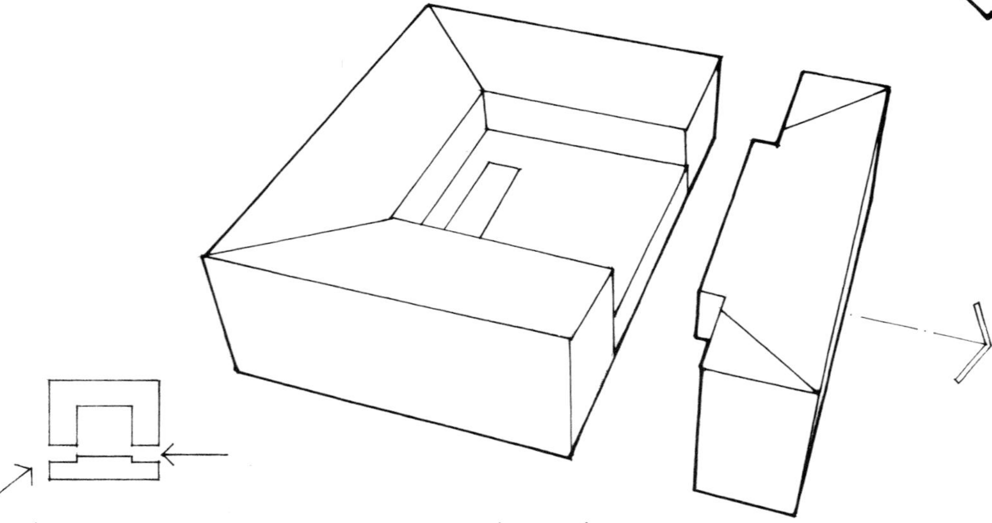

The centroidal form is fractured by pulling away the southern side.[1]

A pool is placed within the courtyard where the internal axes meet. The form remains bi-laterally symmetrical and directional.

CONFIGURATIONAL READING

Fracture suggests possibility of tension between triple-sided court and separated part. Slightness of fracture retains gestalt of centralized mass with eroded nucleus.

SYMBOLIC READING

Courtyard enclosure and unity retained but court now accessable.

[1] Eisenman argues that the library is sliced away from the court as a result of two lines of force, one from the east, the other from the south-west, these emanating from entry points at these corner junctions. Ibid., p. 152

ACCESS

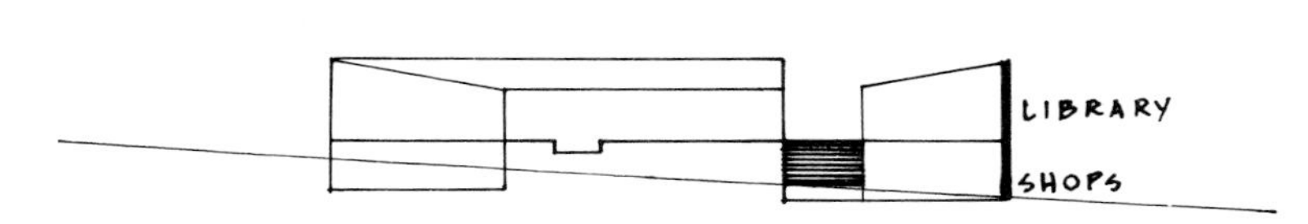

SECTION

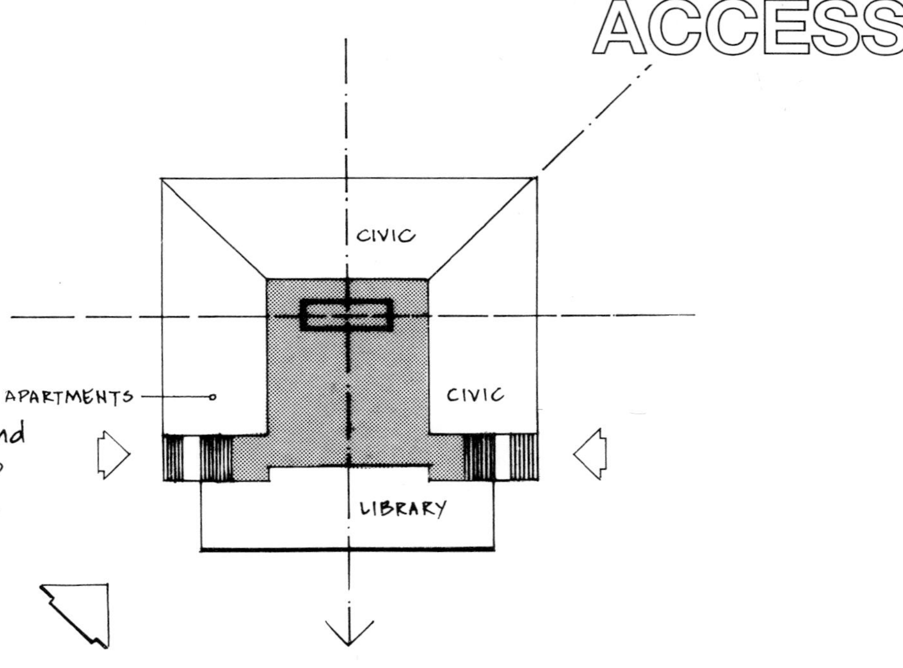

ACCOMMODATION
The upper level is concerned mainly with civic and public activities with shops on the lower floor to the south and east. Apartments are placed in the western block.

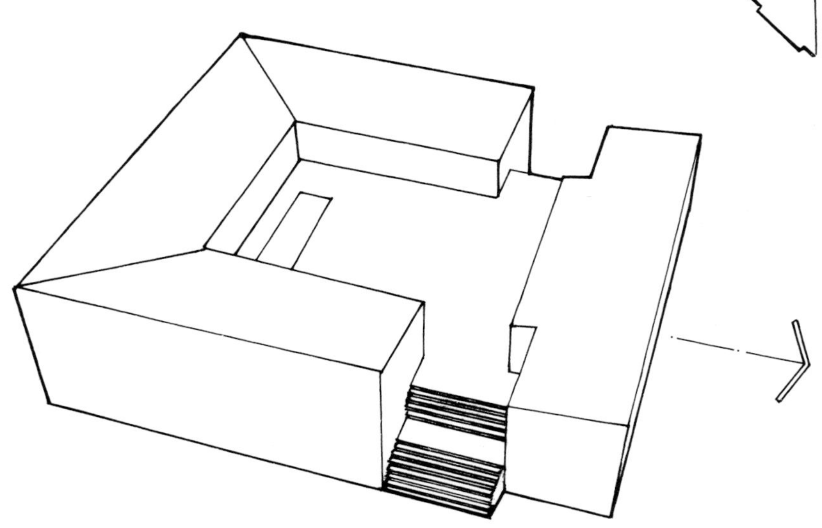

Stairs give access to the court at the point of fracture. The south block is reduced in width but remains 'locked' into courtyard.

CONFIGURATIONAL READING
The form is bi-laterally symmetrical and the centralized mass with an eroded core remains as a gestalt. Where the southern block 'locks' into the court, the space at either side spills down in the form of stairs.

SYMBOLIC READING
Contact is established between the inner private world of the court and the exterior without diminishing the sense of shelter and privacy.

COUNCIL CHAMBER

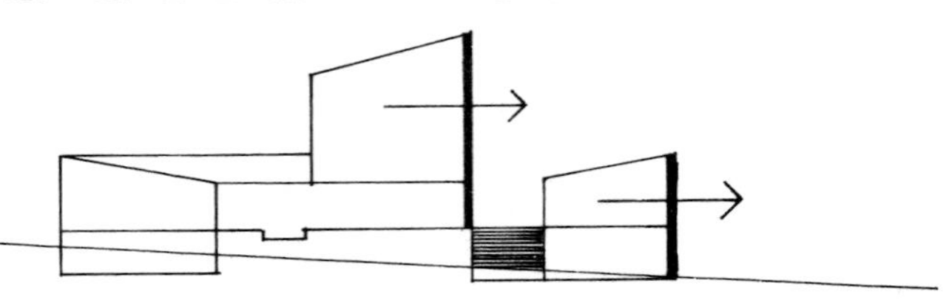

SECTION

Council chamber roof points in same southerly direction as does the fractured block.

secondary entry

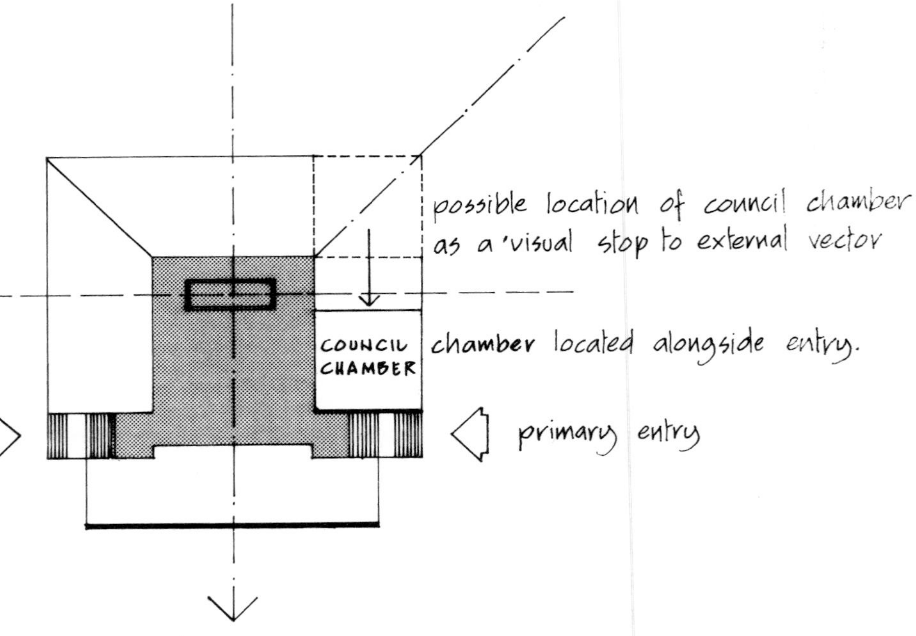

The council chamber has a key role in the complex, partly due to its importance, but also because a large volume is needed to house its activities.

This allows the architect to provide a focus within the complex and also to provide a visual stop when seen from the approach route.

To do this, the chamber could have been placed on the oblique axis in the north east corner. Instead the chamber is located at the point of fracture, alongside the stair access from the public space. This relationship to the point of entry gives this particular entry added importance.

approach route direction

SYMBOLIC READING

As the main element, the Council Chamber dominates.

CONFIGURATIONAL READING

The bi-lateral symmetry is distorted.

external vector

SPIRALS

The council chamber acts as the pivot for two spiralling movements, both anti-clockwise, one ascending around the chamber, giving access en route, the other spiralling around the court as a glazed corridor which continues internally.[1]

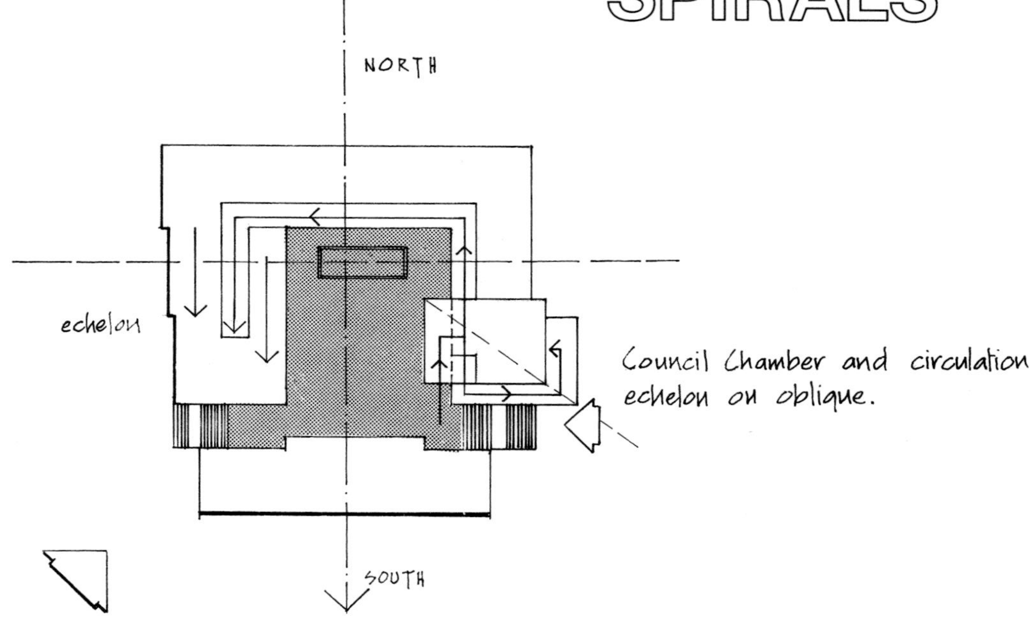

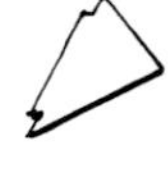

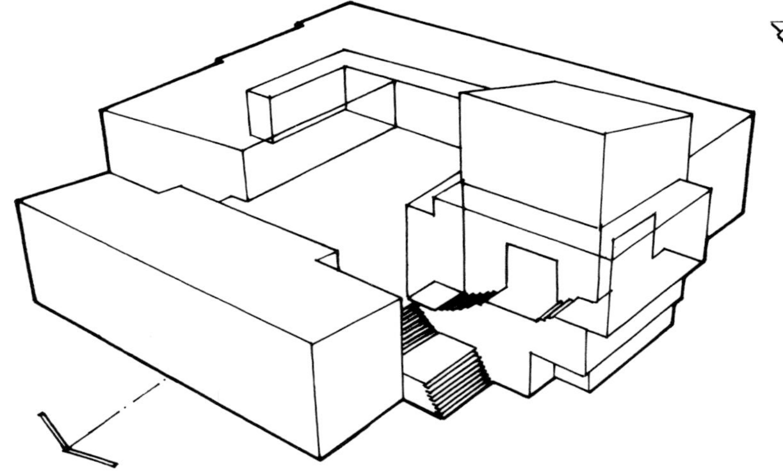

[1] Eisenman compares this spiral movement system to Le Corbusiers Pavillon Suisse, explaining the latter as the 'control of a pattern of behaviour, movement of people, which is external to the fabric of the building yet enforced on the observer by the presence of the building ... For Aalto the spiral movement is a quality of the work itself, the control of the volumetric arrangement by a perceptual reference to a generic spiral.' Ibid., p. 155.

SYMBOLIC READING

The spirals represent movement and in this case enclosure.

CONFIGURATIONAL READING

The Council Chamber pins one corner of the court. The courtyard spiral exerts pressure which threatens to close the south-western corner. An echelon on the west facade forms part of this pressure and the entire west side is strengthened to balance the mass of the council chamber. The council chamber entry point at court level extends out to form an enclosed corner of the court to the north-east. The pool is shifted off axis towards this corner.

FLOW

The attempt to close the court at the south-west corner is prevented by a build-up of internal pressure within the court which flows out of the space in a cascade of steps on the diagonal.[1] This flow, like a powerful current, shapes its 'banks' so that the edge of the west block is cut back sharply. The sharpness of this fractured edge is complemented by a straight stair leading to the apartments in the west block. A projection and setback create a contained zone within the court.

[1] see Eisenman, Ibid., p. 157.

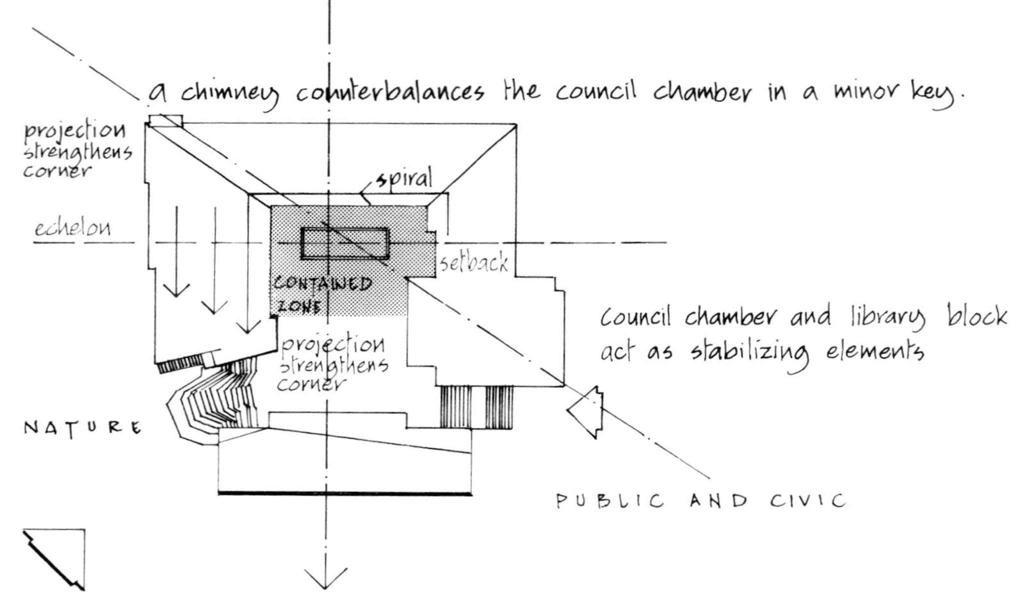

PUBLIC AND CIVIC

southern block roof is distorted by acute fracturing at south-west.

NATURE

stair pulled towards external vector

oblique external vector

SYMBOLIC READING

The court may be interpreted either as a 'lake' which cascades outwards at its southern extremities, or more literally as a secluded garden with grass and planting. The contorted stair links the private world of the court with its landscape and symbolizes the organic energy inherent in Aalto's work. The stair, flowing on to the slope and into nature, contrasts with the regular formal stair leading from the public square to the civic realm of the council chamber.

CONFIGURATIONAL READING

The volumes which enclose the court are distorted by the pressures created. The southern block remains a stabilizing element linked to the council chamber.

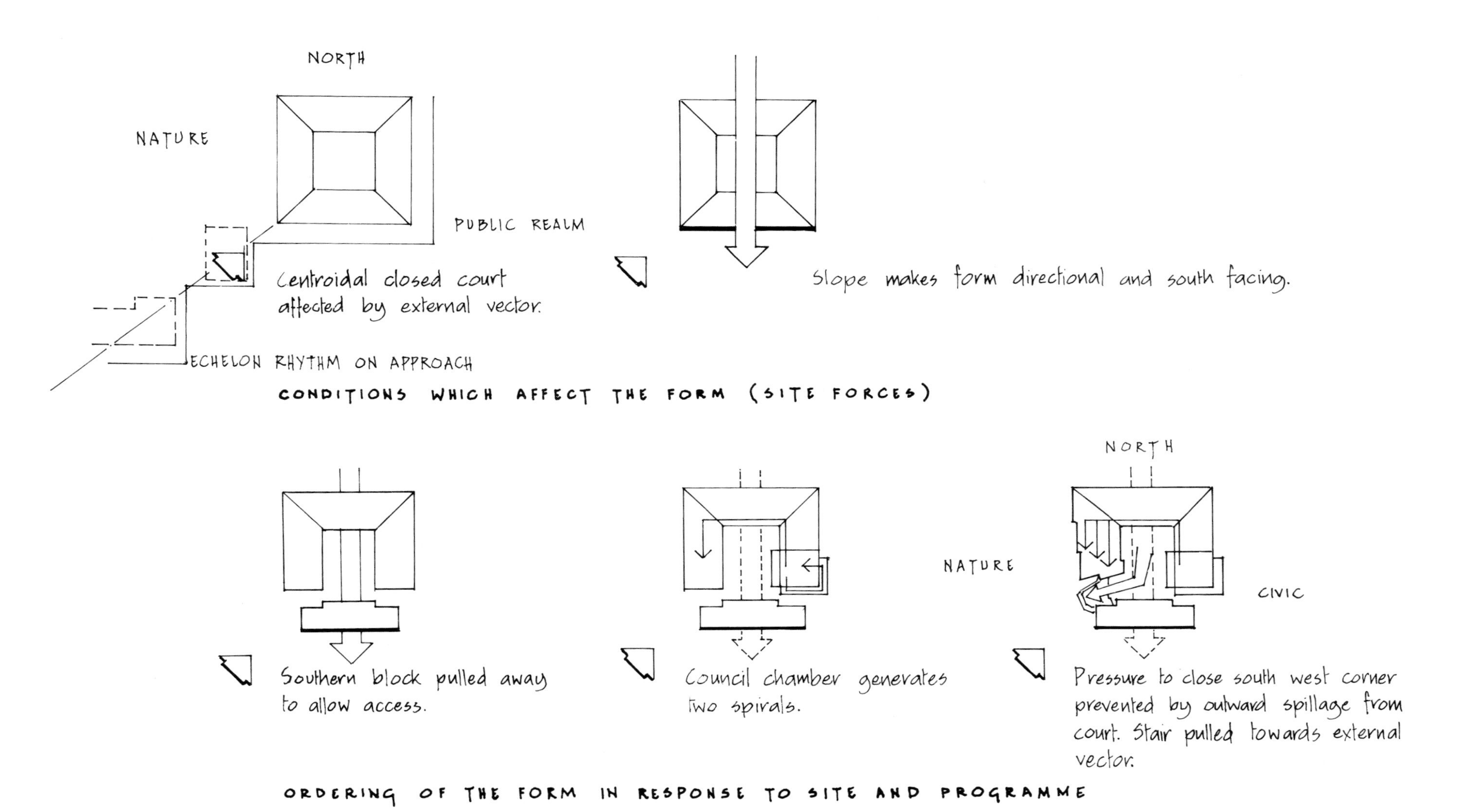

There are similarities in the courtyard treatment at Säynätsalo and Le Corbusier's monastery at La Tourette (1957-60). For an analysis of the monastery see G. H. Baker, Le Corbusier: An analysis of form, (Second edition, 1989), Van Nostrand Reinhold (International) Co. Ltd., London, pp. 267-298.

DIAGONALS

As Eisenman points out,[1] the circulation corridor is fully glazed on two adjacent sides of the court, whereas the other two sides have windows placed in solid walling. This reaffirms the diagonal condition imposed by the external oblique vector.

The library is extensively glazed on its southern side, affirming the south-facing frontality of the complex.

Had this glazing faced the court the effect would be to destroy the internal court reading in terms of the external vector and would also have consolidated the introversion of the complex.

With the actual fenestration deployment, two site conditions are satisfied, 1) the effect of the oblique vector on the court, and 2) the south-facing frontality induced by the slope.

The diagonal condition within the court is part countered by the opposite diagonal generated by the council chamber echelon and terminated by the chimney.

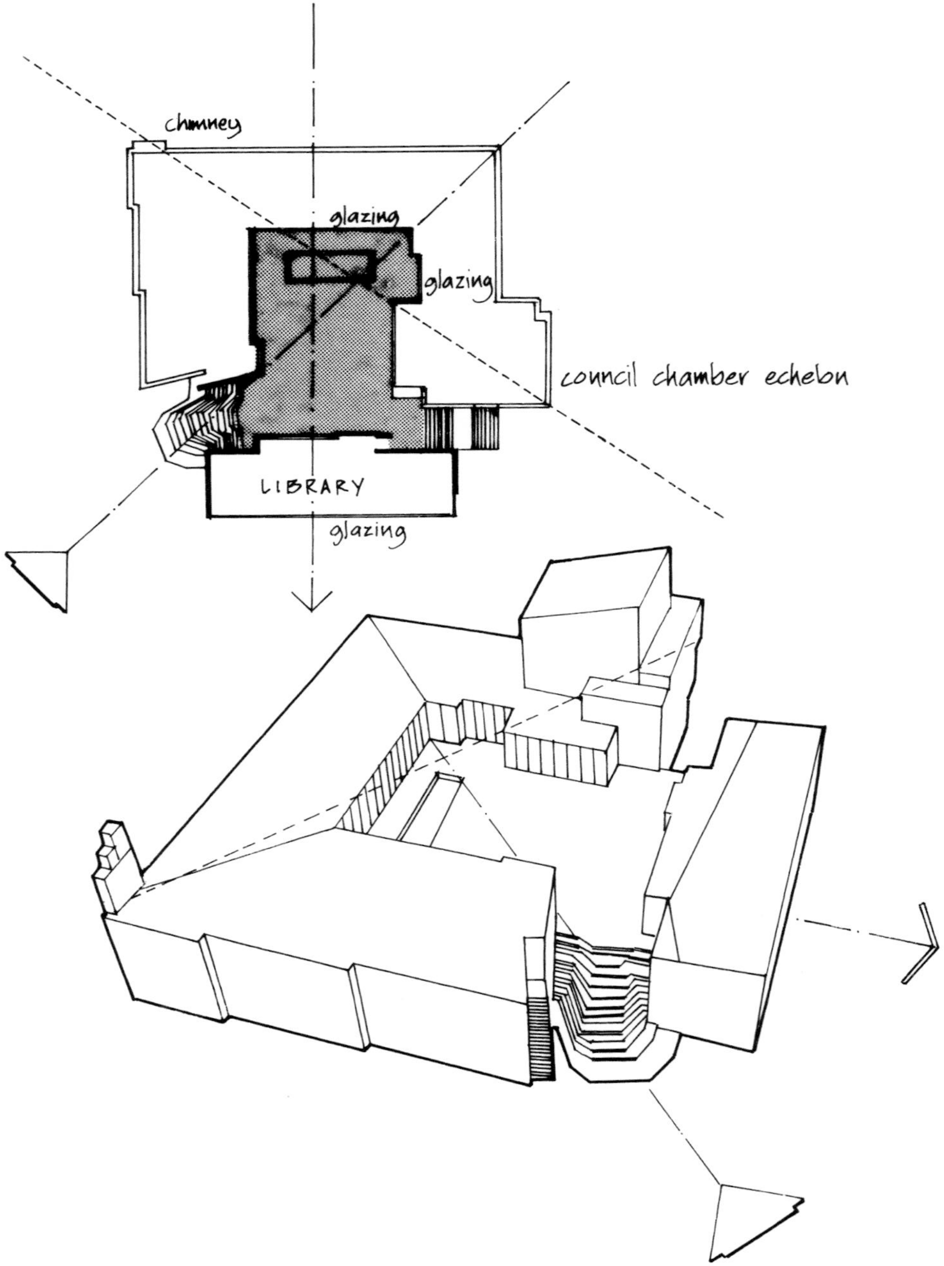

chimney
glazing
glazing
council chamber echelon
LIBRARY
glazing

[1] Ibid., p. 154.

STABILIZING ELEMENTS

The council chamber and library act as stabilizing elements which counter pressures within the court. The lateral axis is developed in each configuration, by an outward cantilever in the council block, and by a linear deployment in the library.

The council chamber ensemble is locked on to the library by a pergola which turns movement into the civic suite. A brick paved area (visually aligned with a projection from the library) is placed alongside the pergola on a similar north-south axis. This supports the locking effect of the pergola and indicates a shift in the centre of gravity towards the south east corner.

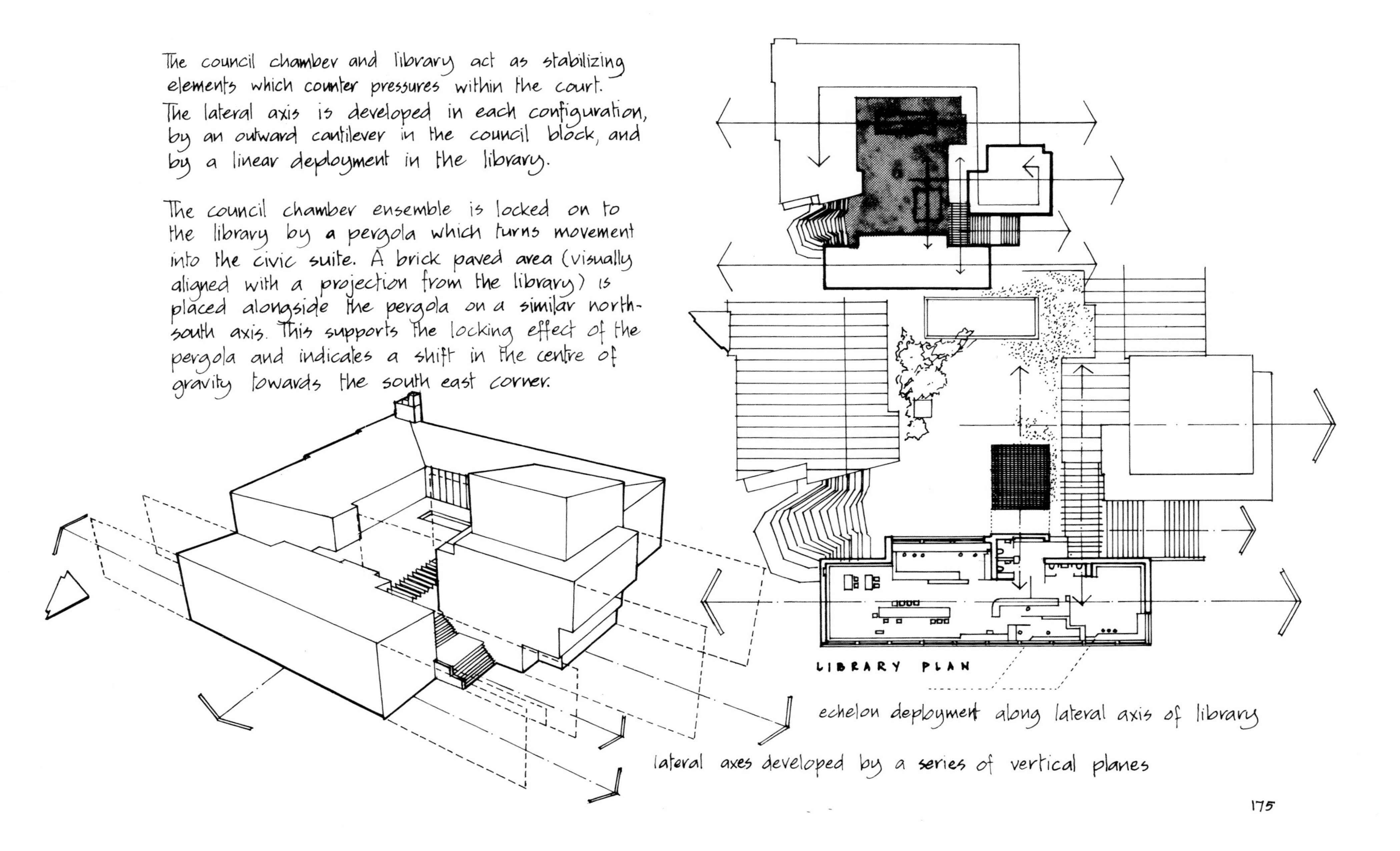

lateral axes developed by a series of vertical planes

COUNCIL CHAMBER

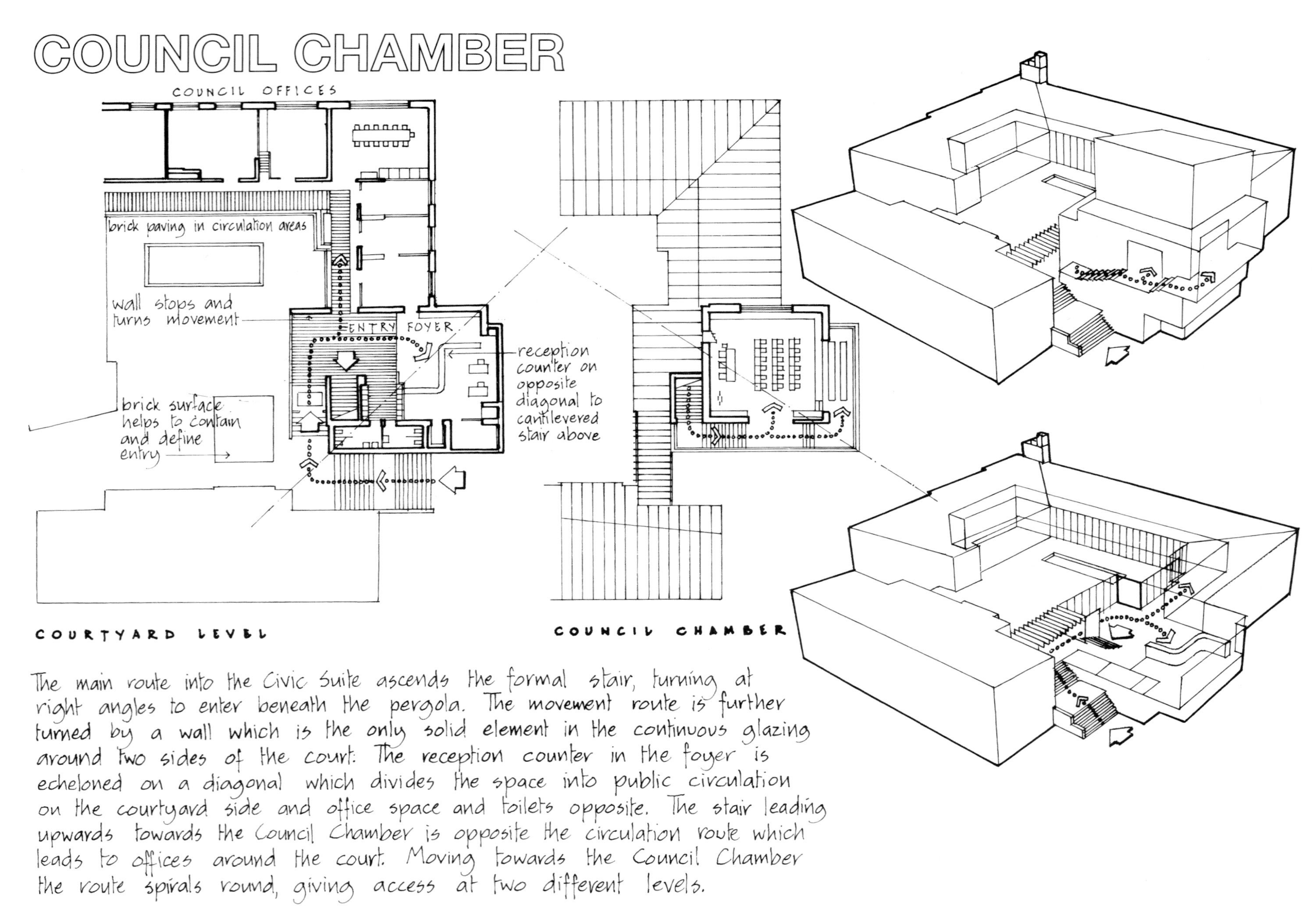

The main route into the Civic Suite ascends the formal stair, turning at right angles to enter beneath the pergola. The movement route is further turned by a wall which is the only solid element in the continuous glazing around two sides of the court. The reception counter in the foyer is echeloned on a diagonal which divides the space into public circulation on the courtyard side and office space and toilets opposite. The stair leading upwards towards the Council Chamber is opposite the circulation route which leads to offices around the court. Moving towards the Council Chamber the route spirals round, giving access at two different levels.

BOX TRANSFORMED

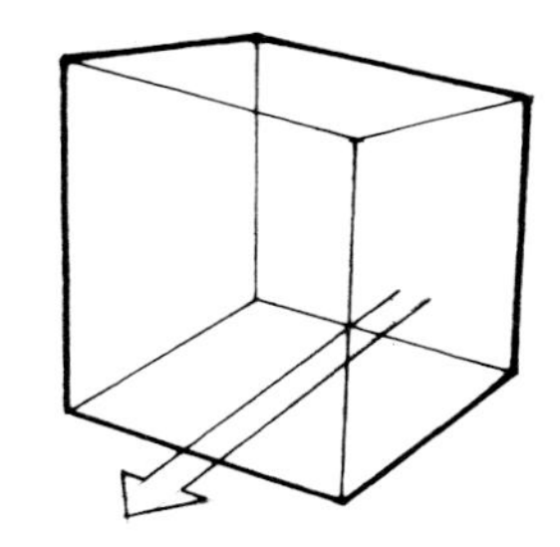

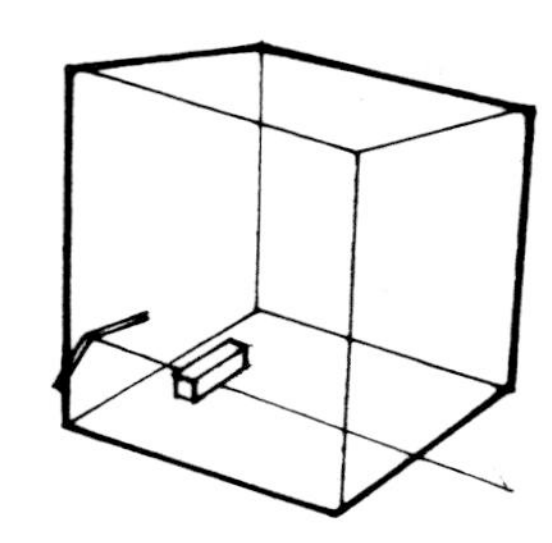

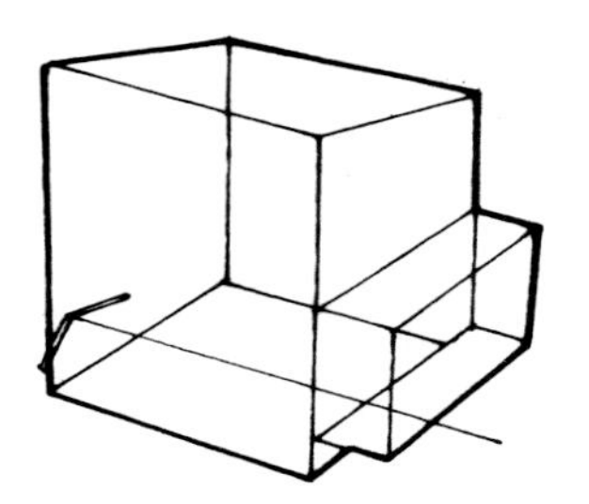

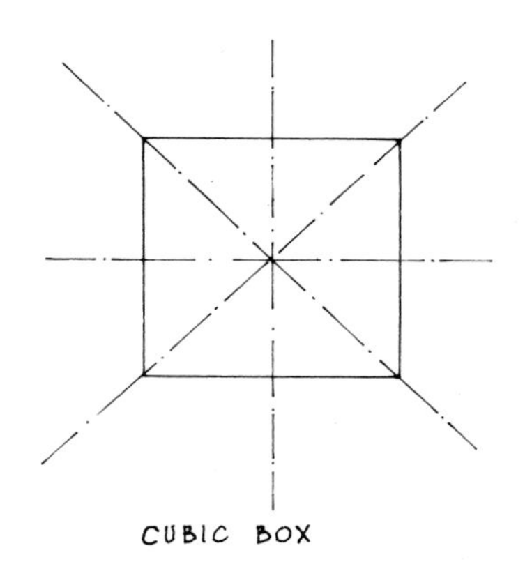

CUBIC BOX

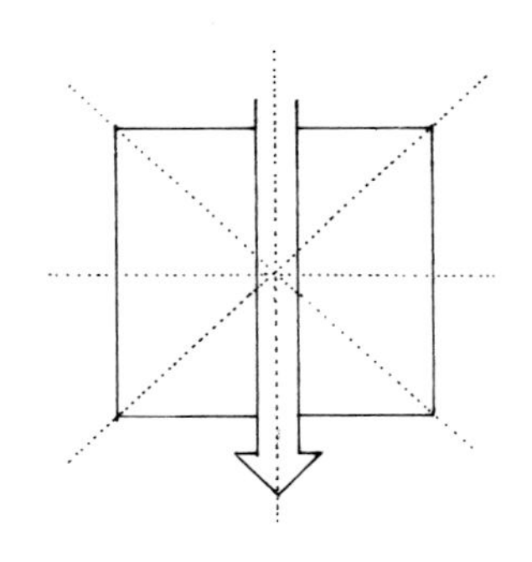

DIRECTIONAL NORTH / SOUTH

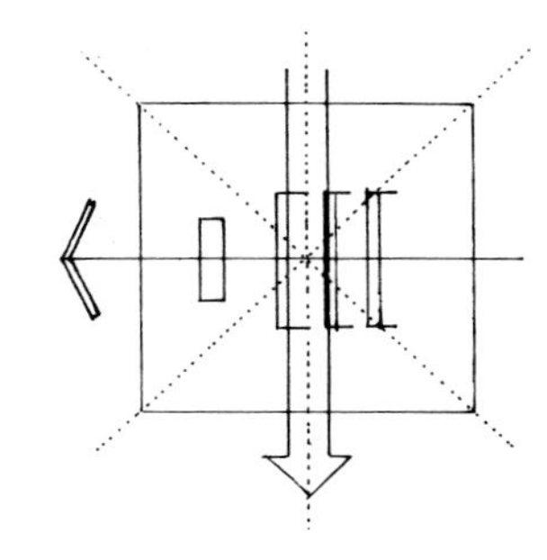

CHAMBER ALIGNED EAST/WEST

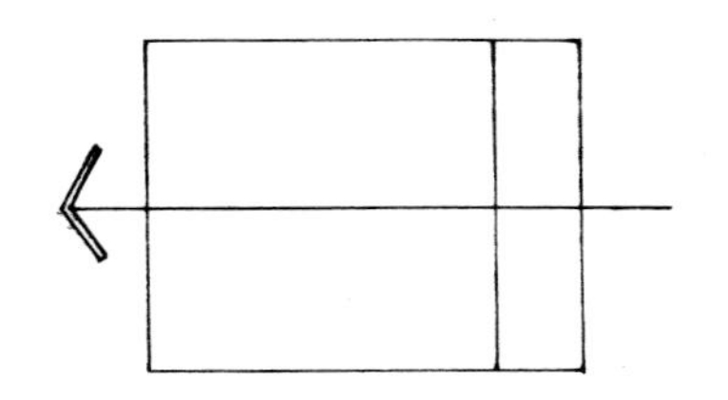

REAR ADDITION

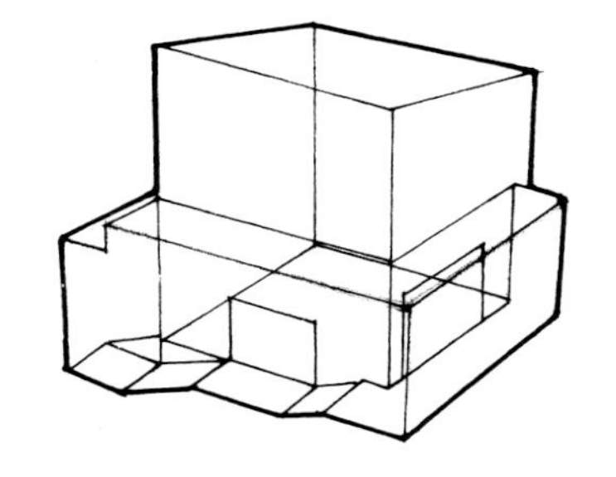

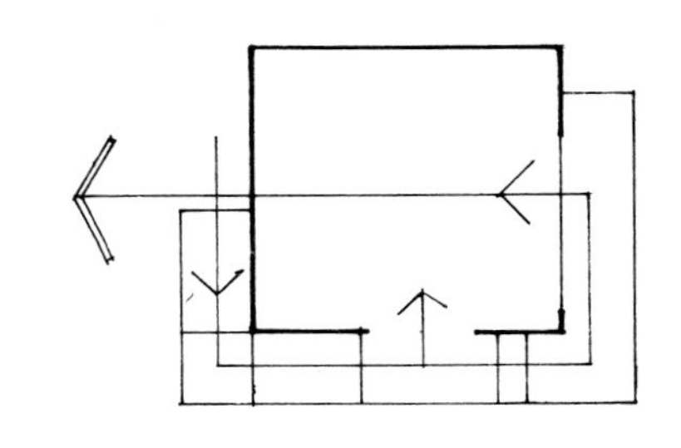

CIRCULATION SPIRAL

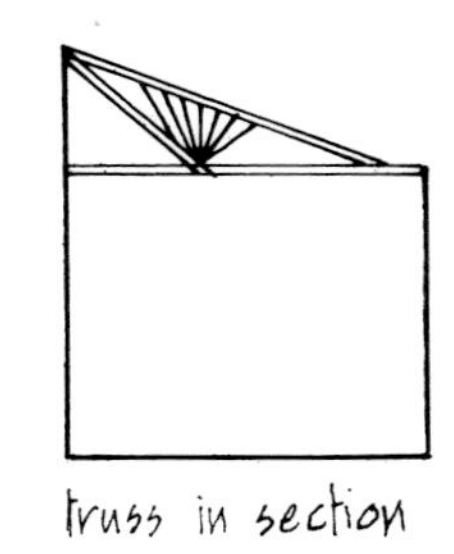

secondary beams

trusses from below.

primary supports

ROOF SUPPORTED BY OUTSTRETCHED 'FINGERS'

ENERGY

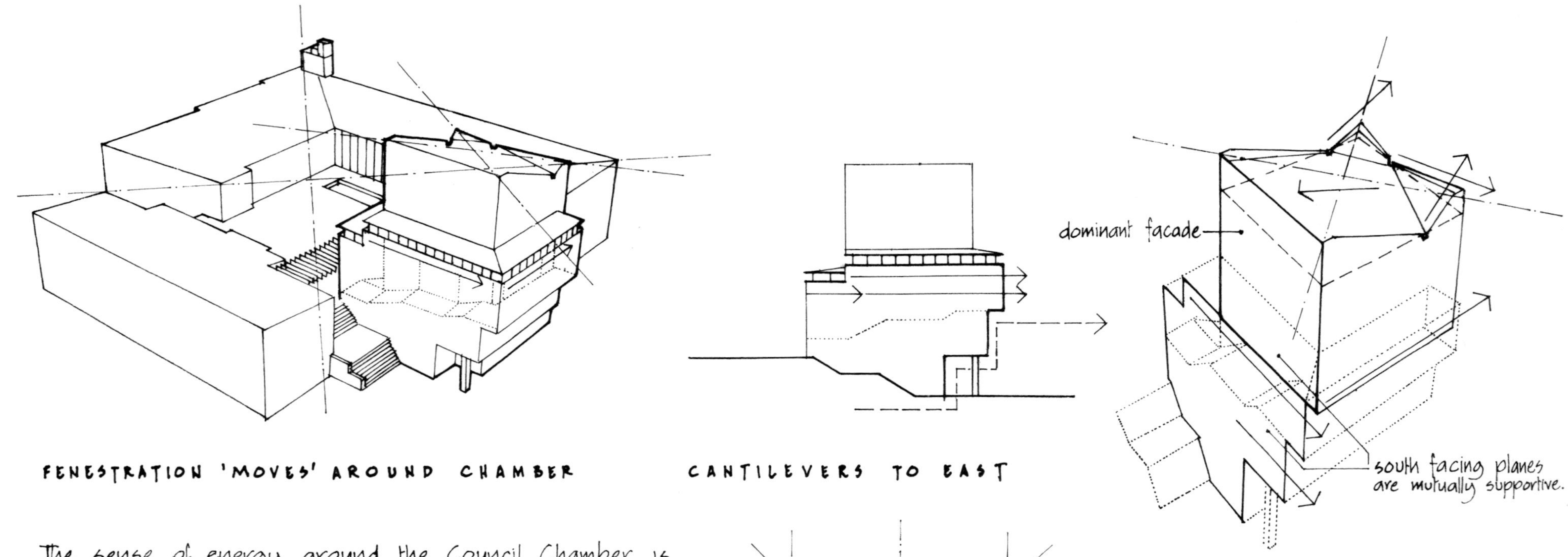

FENESTRATION 'MOVES' AROUND CHAMBER

CANTILEVERS TO EAST

The sense of energy around the Council Chamber is developed in several ways. The horizontal slit windows lighting the spiralling route highlight and reinforce the sensation of movement.

Lateral pressure to the east is developed by the double cantilever of the southern plane alongside the entry stairs.

The roof of the chamber dips down from south to north but also ascends again at each corner whilst taking a further dip on the northern side.

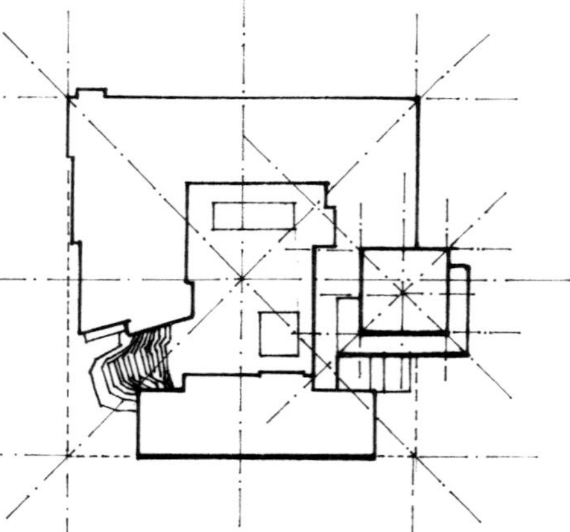

ROOF FALLS AND RISES IN 4 DIRECTIONS

Council Chamber and generic form each have orthogonal and diagonal characteristics of a square plan.

COUNCIL CHAMBER

SYMBOLIC READING

At the heart of the ensemble and the community, the Council Chamber expresses its importance by its configurational arrangement. The plan is ordered and axial in an east/west direction. It is approached by a 'ceremonial' route after ascending the formal stair externally and the spiral route internally.

On the interior, the roof celebrates the aspirations of communal government with an emotive gesture in the form of the trusses, which speak of the trees and proud craftsmanship of the region.

The Chamber is the most expressive statement in the ensemble, representing order in its plan and energy in its three dimensional dynamism. The spiral movement symbolizes protection and heightens the importance of the Chamber itself.

Externally the upward tilt of the roof adds to the power and monumentality of the form. To the rear, the multidirectional pitches are similar to the roof trusses in evoking both the complexity and idealism of communal government.

CONFIGURATIONAL READING

The roof pitch gives the form a predominately south-facing role which conforms with a major characteristic of the complex. This alignment is reinforced by the power of the forward projection of the southernmost plane as it is extended by the spiralling route. This plane exerts pressure on the entry stair, whilst the cantilevers push the form out to the east, further strengthening the perceptual impact of the form.

To the rear of the roof, the corner treatment acknowledges the oblique characteristic of the complex. The spiral 'wrap-around' reiterates the orthogonal nature of the court and participates in the double spiral system generated by the chamber.

The chamber is therefore in a pivotal position, being pulled by two spirals, one around the court, the other around itself. The cubic form, with its roof rising (in different ways) to all four corners of the mass, is strong enough to resist any attempt to be pulled out of position by the spiral movement systems.

PERCEPTUAL FACTORS

Aalto's deployment of forms in the Säynätsalo Town Hall seems linked to his close examination of the Italian hill town. The complex offers a series of visual experiences concerned with discovery as movement from either approach into the complex is carefully controlled. The organization of the massing provides several messages, amongst which are suggestions of mystery, complexity, energy, monumentality, informality and repose.

Jeremy Blake has considered these issues in an analysis of perceptual factors in relation to each approach to the building.[1] Blake explains how the Council Chamber provides a visual incident when approaching from the west, with the opening leading to the raised court creating a desire to explore. Blake asserts that had the mass expressing the chamber been insignificant, the composition would have failed, particularly if the space had been allowed to leak out at the eastern entry point.

Blake goes on to illustrate how a larger mass would provide the necessary visual stop, but that this would remain unsatisfactory if the space could still leak out.

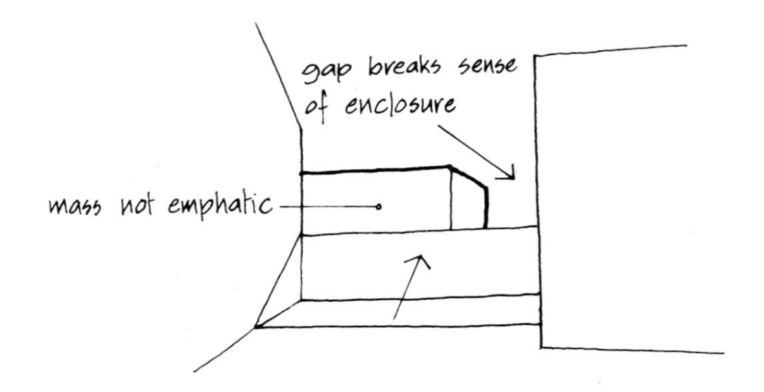

1) **APPROACH FROM THE WEST**
DESIRE TO ENTER AND EXPLORE, BUT WEAKNESSES IN COMPOSITION WITH SIZE OF DISTANT MASS AND GAP WITH VIEW OUT BREAKING SENSE OF ENCLOSURE.

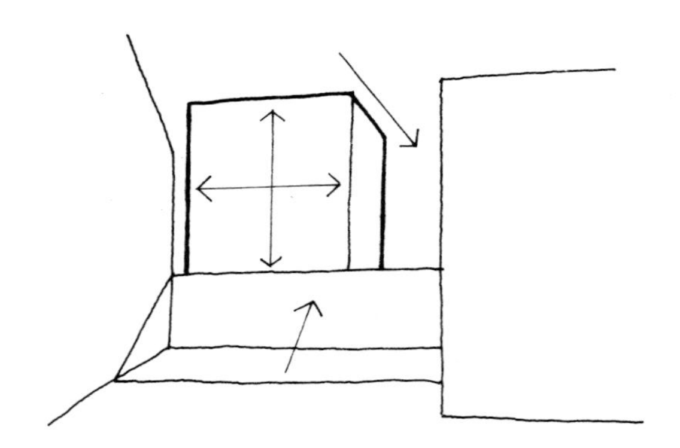

DRAWINGS AFTER J.M. BLAKE.
CAPTIONS BY J.M. BLAKE.

2) INTRODUCTION OF LARGE MASS ASSERTS SENSE OF FULL STOP ALTHOUGH WEAKNESS STILL EXISTS WITH VIEW OUT. RELATIONSHIP OF MASSES MORE EQUAL AND STATIC. PERMANENCE AND CALM.

1 Jeremy M. Blake, 'Articulation, Alvar Aalto, Village Hall Säynätsalo,' Dissertation, School of Architecture, University of Newcastle-upon-Tyne 1976

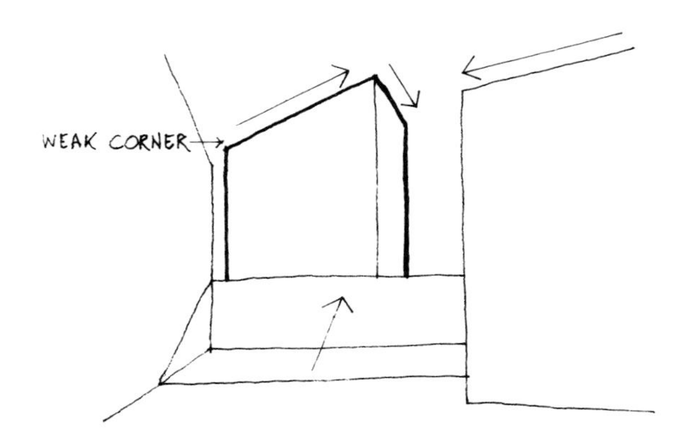

3) VITALITY AND DRAMA BY CONTRASTS IN DIRECTION OF PITCHES AND OBLIQUE APPROACH UP STEPS. DOMINANT FACADE WEAKENED BY VIEW LEAKING OUT AND BY ANGLE OF VISION.

4) FURTHER VITALITY BY STEPPING OF SIDE MASSES. SENSE OF ENCLOSURE WITH MYSTERY OF PARTS UNSEEN. UPWARD ENTRY REINFORCED BY STAIRS TO APARTMENT. WEAK CORNER OF COUNCIL CHAMBER STRENGTHENED.

5) COUNCIL CHAMBER ROOF DIRECTIONS STABILISE THE MASS YET MAINTAIN EMPHASIS ON FRONT FACADE. THE EYE IS LED TOWARDS ENTRANCE UNDER PERGOLA AS WELL AS TOWARDS WHAT IS OUT OF SIGHT IN RAISED COURTYARD. THERE IS A COMPLETE FUSION WITH THE SITE BY THE IRREGULAR FLIGHT OF GRASS COVERERED STAIRS. THE MASSES ARE RESTRAINED AND DOMESTIC YET THEY MAINTAIN A SENSE OF VITALITY AND MONUMENTALITY.

CONCEALMENT AND MYSTERY

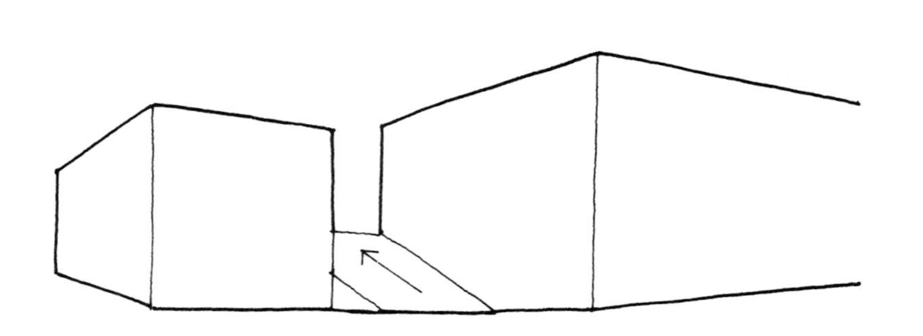

1) **APPROACH FROM THE EAST**
MYSTERY OF EXPOSED YET ENCLOSED SPACE HEIGHTENED BY RAISED CENTRAL AREA. DESIRE TO ENTER AND EXPLORE.

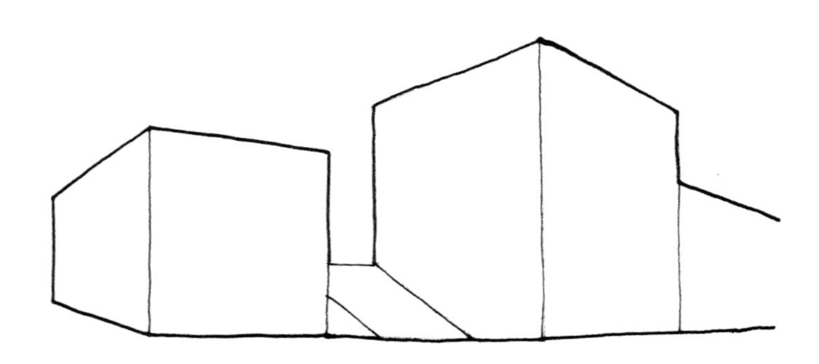

2) LARGER BUILDING MASS INCREASES DRAMA OF CONTRASTS IN THINGS SEEN AND NOT SEEN. APPROACH INTO RAISED COURTYARD MADE MORE MONUMENTAL AND MYSTERIOUS. NO SENSE OF FRONT OR REAR.

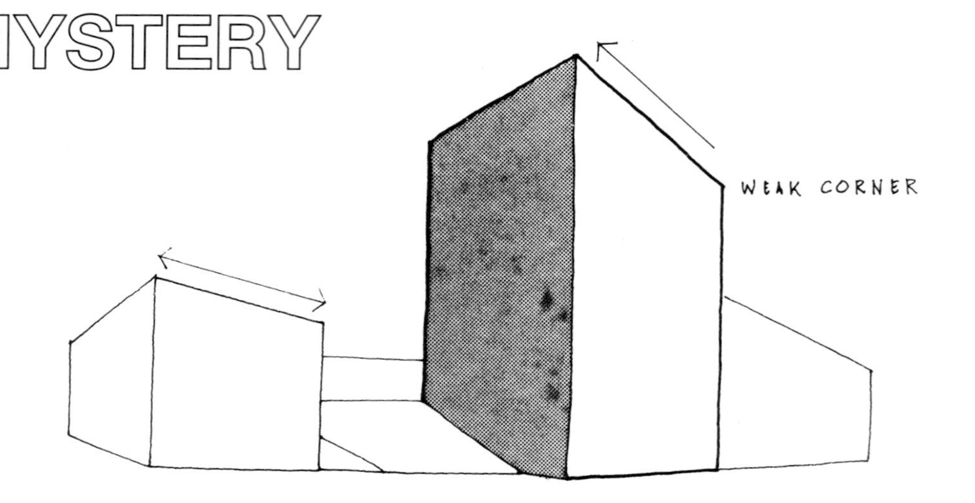

3) THE ROOF PITCH OF THE COUNCIL CHAMBER CREATES ASSERTIVE AND DIRECTIONAL 'FRONT' FACADE. HOWEVER LOWER POINT OF MAIN MASS SEEMS WEAK AND FORM REMAINS SIMPLISTIC.

DISCOVERY BEYOND

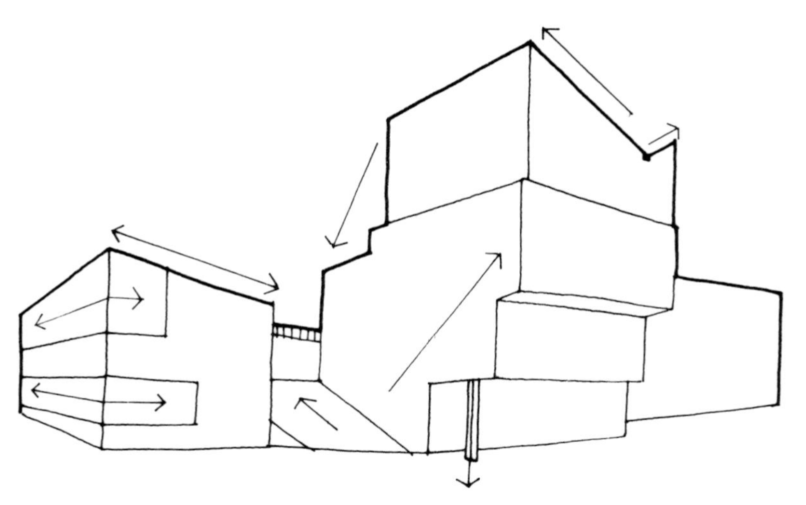

4) SENSE OF MYSTERY CONFIRMED BY PERGOLA WHICH ACTS AS GATEWAY TO UNSEEN UPPER LEVEL. MONUMENTALITY OF MASS MAINTAINED BUT CENTRAL ELEMENT BROKEN DOWN TO INDUCE SCALE AND VITALITY. CONTRAST BETWEEN OBLIQUE UPWARD ENTRY AND OUTWARD PULL OF COUNCIL CHAMBER CIRCULATION. COLUMN EMPHASIZES RELATIONSHIP WITH GROUND. WEAK CORNER OF COUNCIL CHAMBER ROOF STRENGTHENED. FENESTRATION IN SOUTHERN (LIBRARY) BLOCK TURNS CORNER AND POINTS TOWARDS ENTRY STAIR.

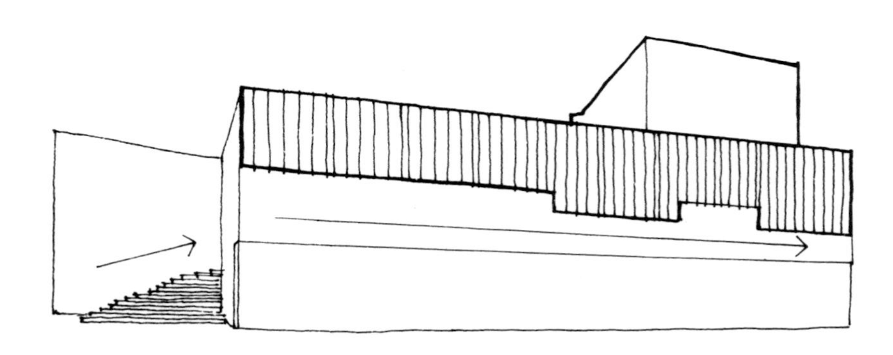

5) FROM THE CIVIC SQUARE THE ASSERTIVE RHYTHMIC SLATTED FACADE DOMINATES. BUT THE MASSING OF THE COMPLEX DRAWS THE EYE BEYOND — TO THE LEFT THE UNSEEN BECKONS AS THE CONVOLUTED STAIR INDICATES ENTRY, WHILST THE TWO LOWER PARTS OF THE SLATTED WINDOW MULLIONS DRAW THE EYE TO THE RIGHT. IN THIS DIRECTION THE CHAMBER AWAITS DISCOVERY.

BOLD AND DEFIANT

CIVIC APPROACH UP A GRANITE STAIR. FACADES BOLD AND ALMOST DEFIANT YET RESTRAINED BY SCALE OF WINDOWS AND PROJECTIONS. SENSE OF PERMANENCE AND CALM AS WELL AS MYSTERY AND AUSTERITY.

Blake's analysis of movement towards the building underscores the way Aalto uses massing to control the visitor. On approaching, the courtyard, with its detached southern block, suggests something beyond, an idea confirmed by the visually evident Council Chamber.

Aalto's forms are arranged so as to draw the visitor forward in ways that are appropriate to each approach route and his surface treatment locks the complex into the site in a manner that is specific to every part of the building.

Aalto also deals with the emotional responses of the observer, and as Blake points out, the complex manages simultaneously to suggest monumentality, a degree of domesticity, permanence, calm and vitality.

Aalto's design approach deals with the programme, the Genius Loci and meaning. His use of brick and timber has a cultural reference in that these materials are widely used in Finland. In its form, the building expresses the life of the community, and its relationship to the setting speaks of the strong sense of the landscape that pervades this country of forests and water.

LIGHTING

Aalto's lighting philosophy takes account of specific needs within the complex and the way fenestration affects surface treatment and massing.

In the Council Chamber a large window lets in light from the north, whilst an echeloned window admits western sun. On the periphery, strip windows at high level light the circulation route which moves around the edges of the chamber.

The large northern window is placed centrally on the wall surface, giving a sense of symmetrical stability to a facade with a roof which pitches sharply upwards. As this is the rear of the mass, the erosion of wall surface caused by such a large window is appropriate, allowing the main weighting to be at the south-facing dominant side of the configuration. This northern plane is a clear stop to the modelling around the chamber, which builds outwards to the east and south, the spiral of the route being clearly indicated by the 'ribbon' of glazing.

The small echeloned window to the west filters the light so that the low rays of the western sun do not shine directly into the chamber. Its surface location does not erode the mass, which retains its power on the courtyard side, and its size gives scale to the facade.

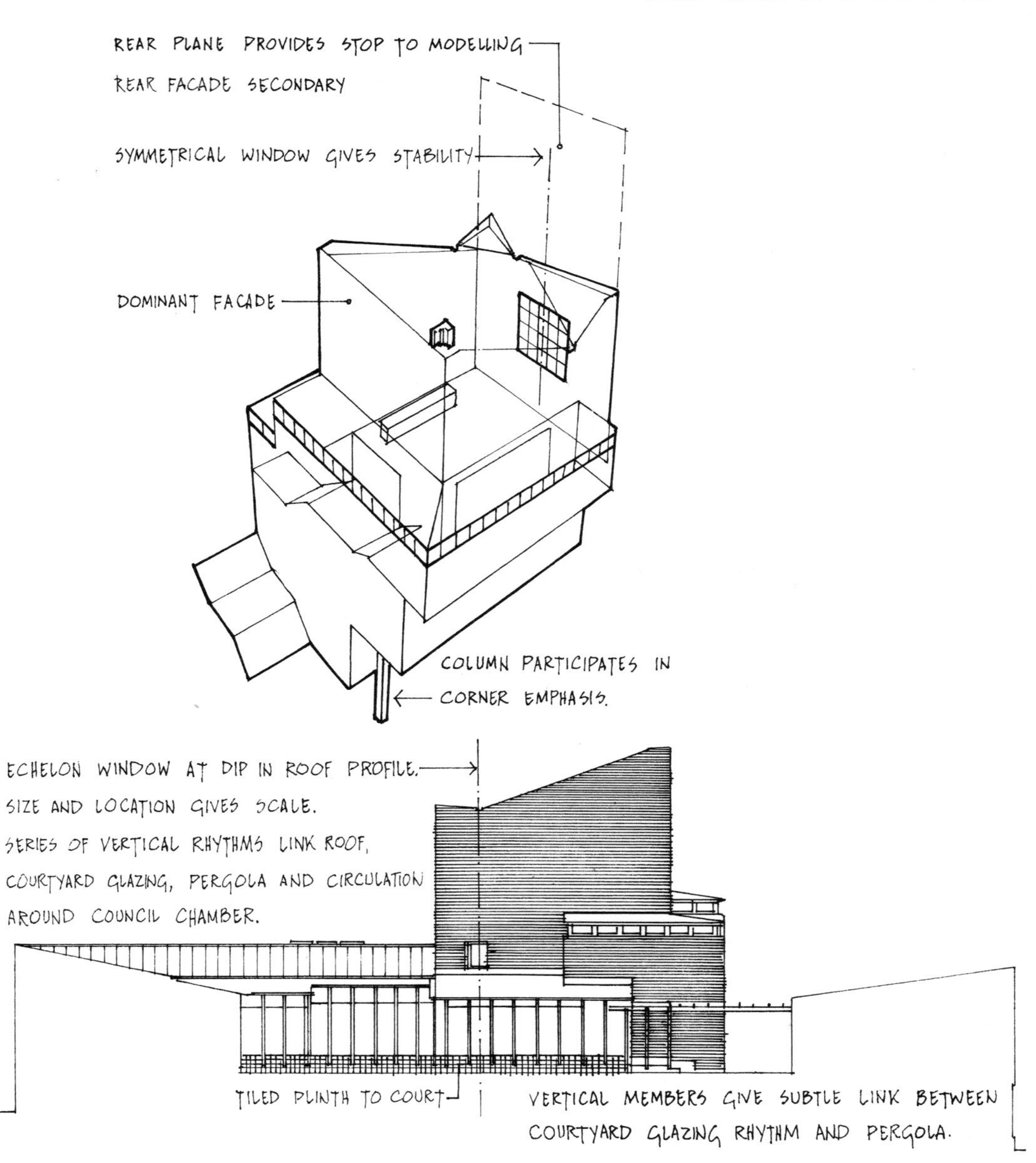

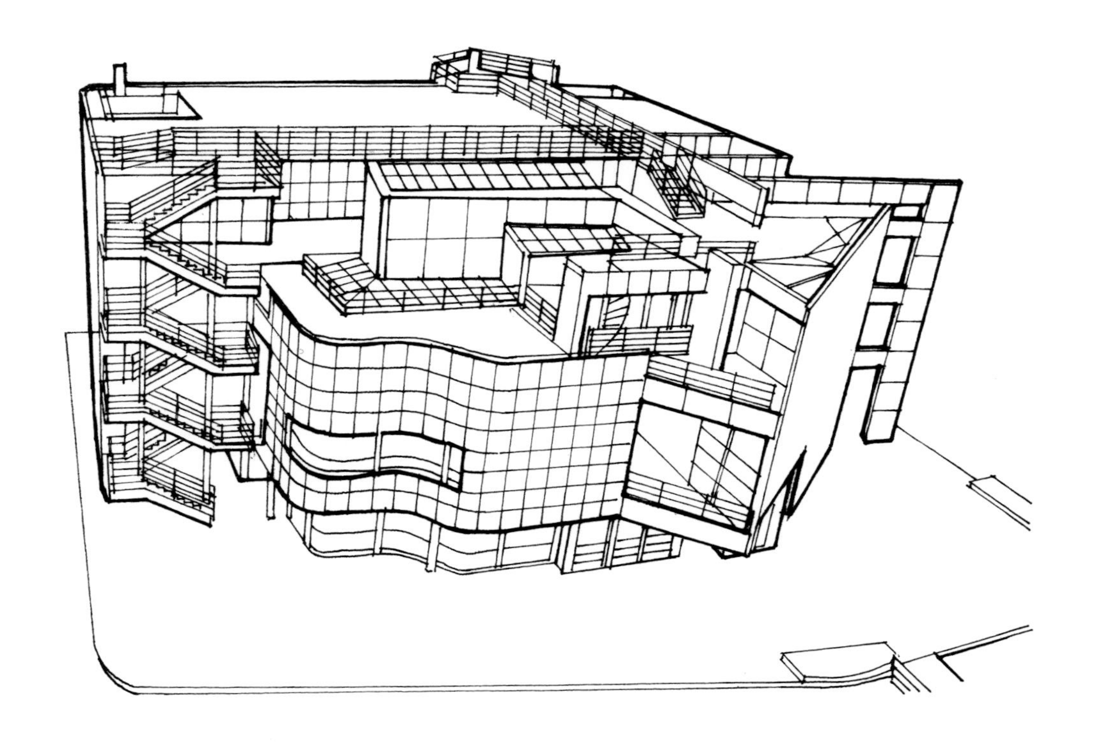

RICHARD MEIER
THE ATHENEUM NEW HARMONY 1975–79

RICHARD MEIER

If Säynätsalo is a consummate demonstration of Aalto's organic architecture, Richard Meier's Atheneum at New Harmony, Indiana, similarly encapsulates the salient characteristics of the architect's personal style.

As Kenneth Frampton has explained,[1] Meier's work falls into an American tradition following on from the work of such influential Europeans as Mies van de Rohe and Walter Gropius. Frampton points out that a third generation of American architects have developed a style relating 'more to the Romantic end of the American ideological spectrum than to the Neoclassical ethos stemming from Mies.'

This third generation, continuing 'the tradition of the International Style through its independent return to pioneer sources,' comprised a group of three, Peter Eisenman, Michael Graves and Richard Meier. Later the group extended to John Hejduk and Charles Gwathmey.

Eisenman, Graves and Meier[2] were originally influenced by Colin Rowe, particularly by his interpretations of Le Corbusier's villas of the late twenties, and if Graves has shifted his position significantly away from these models, a modified Corbusian influence still pervades the work of Richard Meier.

[1] K. Frampton, Introduction to Richard Meier Architect, Buildings and Projects 1966-76, New York, 1976, p 7.

[2] Ibid., p. 8.

Typical of Meier's early work, the Smith House at Darien, Connecticut, although built in timber, has a distinctly Corbusian flavour in its compact organization, abstract imagery and sculptural presence. The house also demonstrates central principles of Meier's design strategy in the clarity and rigour apparent in his diagrammatic categorization of programme, structure, circulation, enclosure and entrance.

However, if a direct comparison be made between the Smith House and two of Le Corbusier's more canonical works, the Villa Savoye and 'Les Terraces', (the Villa Stein de Monzie at Vaucresson), the differences are as important as the similarities.[3]

Le Corbusier's villas, although fully exploring the interaction between volume and space, using transparency and erosion of the mass as means of extending contact between the villas and their landscape, are characterized by three distinct 'restrictions.'[3] First, the use of concrete establishes its own kind of plasticity resulting in a strong sense of mass; second, Le Corbusier's adherence to the Greek classical tradition gives him a greater reliance on axiality as a discipline, resulting in his work having an inevitable monumentality; third, Le Corbusier's villas (including the Jaoul Houses) have a strong sense of horizontal stratification. By comparison, the Smith House is more

[3] See my analyses of Le Corbusier's villas in Le Corbusier: An analysis of form. (Second edition 1989). Van Nostrand Reinhold (International) Co. Ltd., London.

THE SMITH HOUSE

relaxed, more concerned with planes rather than mass and has a vertical rather than horizontal reading. The house evokes images of the American domestic tradition of Richard Neutra in particular, whose expansive and glamourous houses suggested an openness and opulence that is American and not European. Although as compact as Le Corbusier's villas, the Smith House is more permeable, but in its elaborate interplay of mass and membrane the house has a Corbusian richness of articulation.

These characteristics are retained in other important works, notably in the House at Old Westbury, so strongly reminiscent of the International Style, and in the Douglas House, which extends ideas generated in the Smith House.

Meier's plastic virtuosity and the capacity of his architectural language is demonstrated throughout his work, and the Atheneum, presenting a different kind of opportunity as a public building, has, like Le Corbusier's artist's residences, the right ingredients for Meier in being a very special kind of commemorative museum / information centre. This special quality emerges from the nature of the programme, with its historical and idealogical associations, and the site, these enabling Meier to exploit an articulation system based on circulation and an orthogonal grid to form a typically complex and elaborate statement.

THE SMITH HOUSE
DARIAN CONNECTICUT 1965-67

PROGRAMME

The town of New Harmony was founded by George Rapp and his followers in 1818. The Harmonists, as they were called, came from Wurttenburg in Germany. They were intensly religious, industrious, and believed it was necessary to create a harmonious world to prepare for Christs second coming.

This religious community was self-sufficient and was based on agriculture and the making and selling of goods and merchandise. They lived communally, so everything could be shared – no rich, no poor, everyone to be equal.

In spite of its prosperity, there were problems, and so in 1825 New Harmony was sold to the Scottish philanthropist, Robert Owen. He sought to further those ideals on which his utopian community of New Lanark in Scotland had been based. Owen, like Rapp, was committed to the idea of a model community and attracted a wide following of scientists and educators.

This rich heritage and commitment to religion, science and education, powerful and universal utopian ideals, provided the roots for a community that embodied the spirit of energy and those heroic visions on which America was founded.

These idealistic beginnings to the town of New Harmony have continued through the nineteenth and into the twentieth century and it is presently enjoying a renaissance based on tourism. This influx of visitors has given cause to restore the historic buildings as reminders of the town's cultural heritage, but also to build a centre-piece – the Atheneum – for its historic district.

This tourist information centre at once expresses the modernity of the twentieth century, but also contains subtle clues to the past and has a pivotal role in the understanding of the town's complex history.

The architect, Richard Meier, was asked to conceive a building as a place in which the public would become aware of the uniqueness of this historic town. He was asked to provide a building which would use modern materials and techniques and which would give visitors a sense of excitement as they arrive at the town.

SITE FORCES

The Atheneum site is at a point where the river and the town interact with each other; the site is at the edge of the town, between it and the river. Because the river floods to varying levels each year, the site is raised on a shallow plateau. From this elevated location, views are in an arc around the site with good views towards the river and the town.

The river surges at an angle to the town, this being apparent in the way the bridge bends to cross the river, its angle being at variance with the town grid.

The placement of the Atheneum on the edge of the town by the river is appropriate because this way the town is preserved intact and the building can express those intellectual ideals on which the town was founded in an entirely modern way.

These two forces, town and river, are quite different. The river is broad, a powerful surging force bordered by trees and cornfields. It is visually compelling and the best views are towards it.

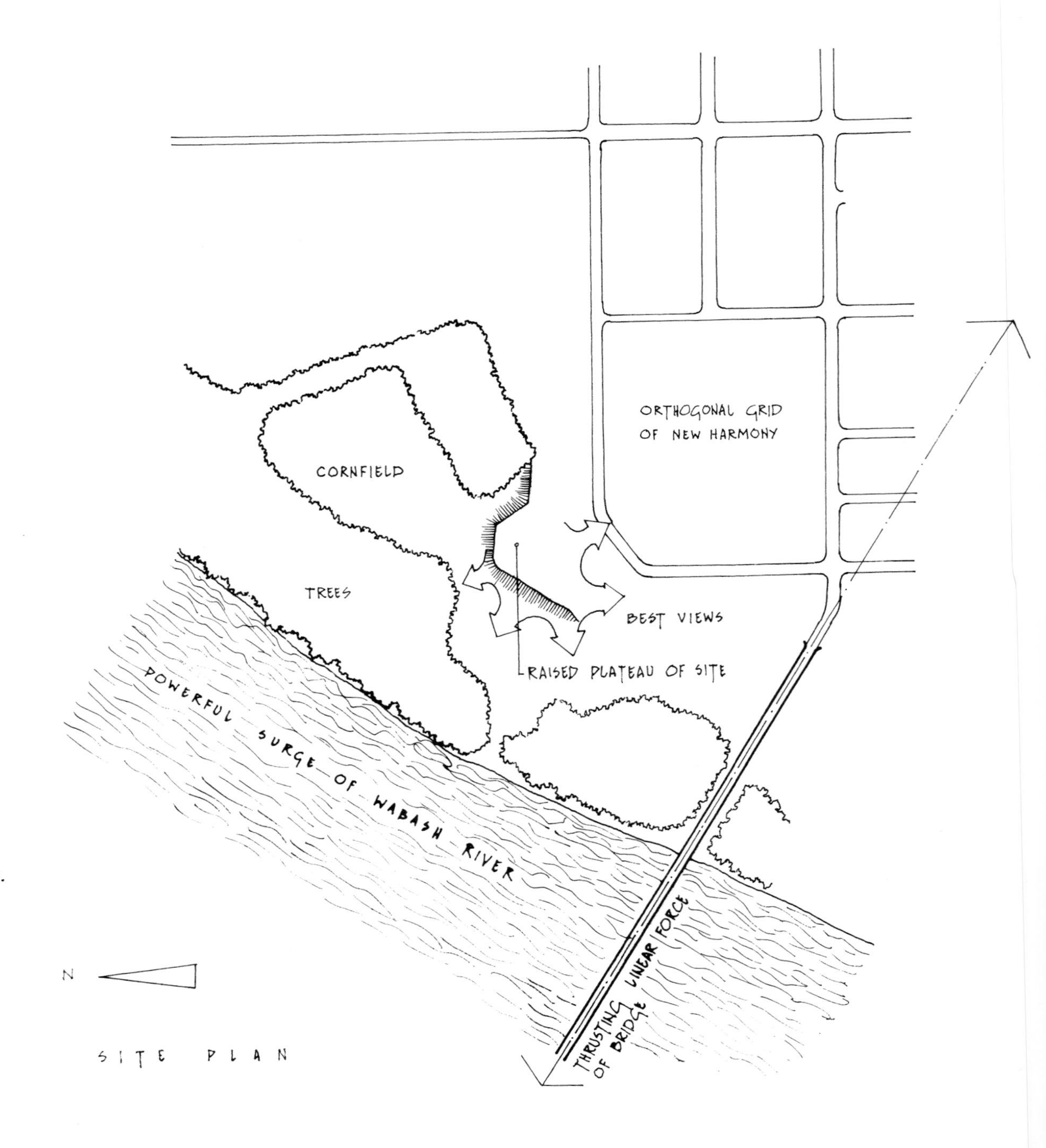

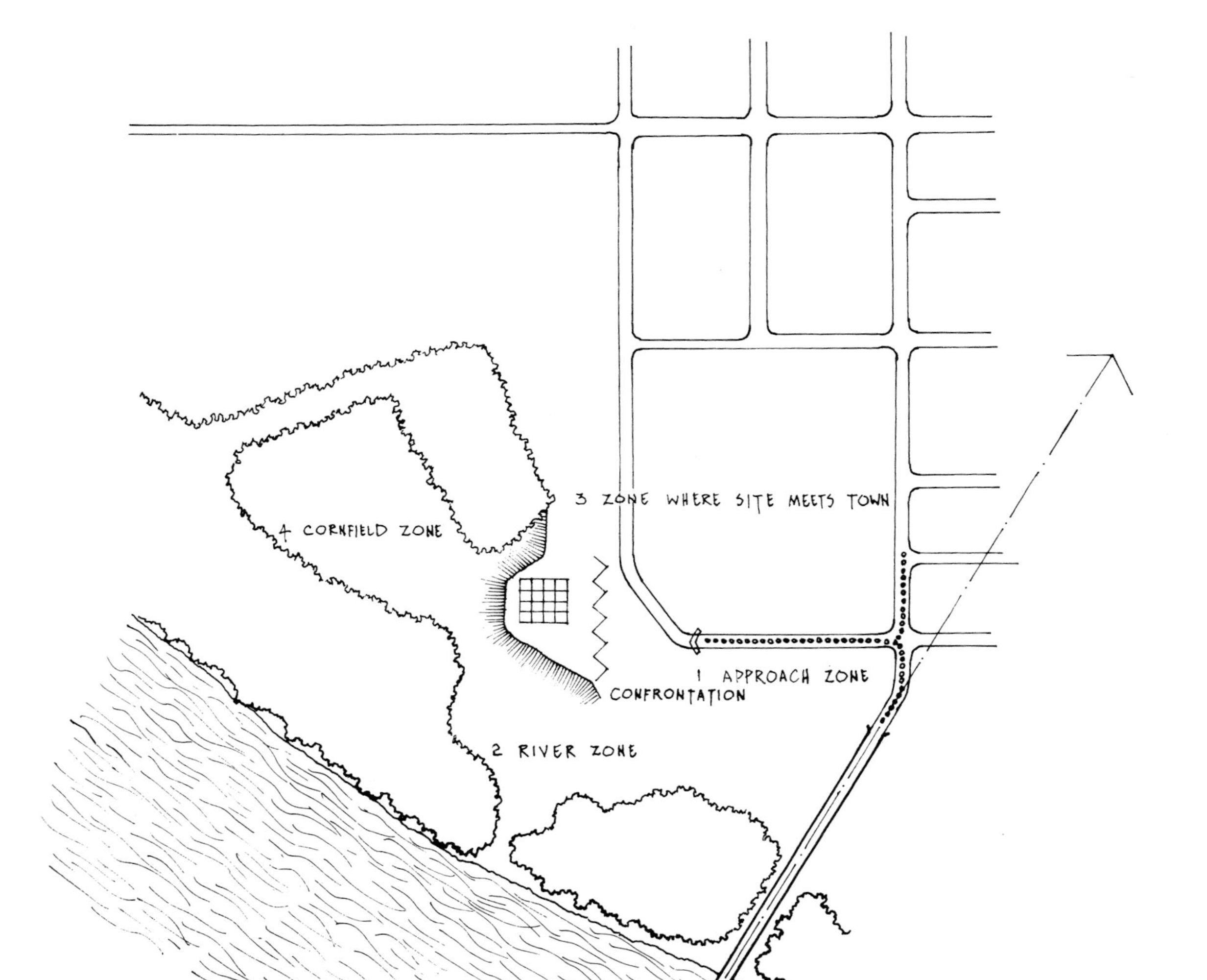

ZONES

By contrast, the town is a more placid ordered affair. It has a regular grid and is a product of man's imagination. So the task of the building is to mediate between man, as expressed through his intellectual idealism and the powerful and beautiful forces of nature.

The way the bridge crosses the river at an angle seems to symbolize this interaction between man and nature. If we think of the site as a series of zones, there are four of these. First there is the zone of approach from the town. Most visitors arrive along the road forming the central axis of New Harmony, then turn at right angles towards the building. Secondly there is the zone between the building and the river, this being a symbolic access route from the river. Third there is the zone where the site meets the town, and fourth there is the area to the northeast, a cornfield surrounded by trees. Giving priorities to these zones, the approach is most important because this is the first point of contact, of confrontation, between visitor and building. Second is the river zone, where the building relates to the river and takes advantage of the views. Third is the zone where site and town meet, and fourth, the cornfield zone to the north and northeast.

ORTHOGONAL GRID

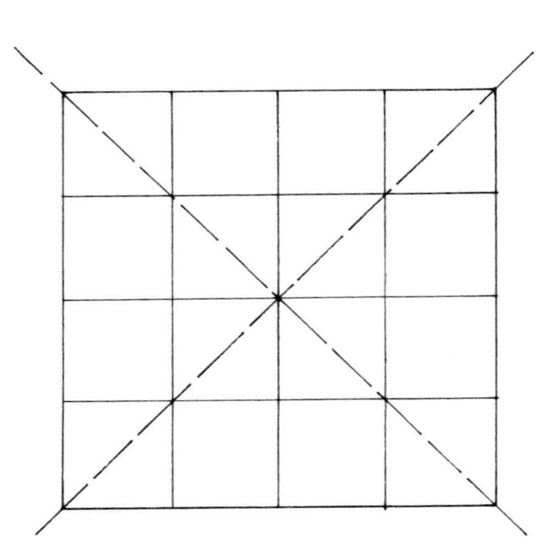

GENERIC SQUARE

Given the site conditions, Richard Meier exploits the opportunities by placing a square box on the site plateau with a structural grid adhering to that of the town grid. It is regular, symmetrical and orthogonal.

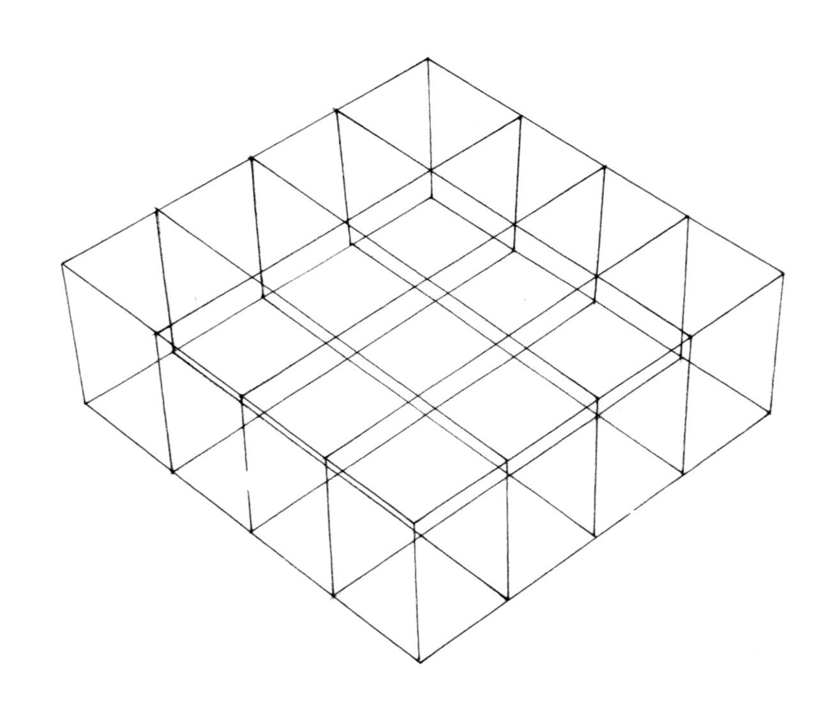

REGULAR SYMMETRICAL ORTHOGONAL

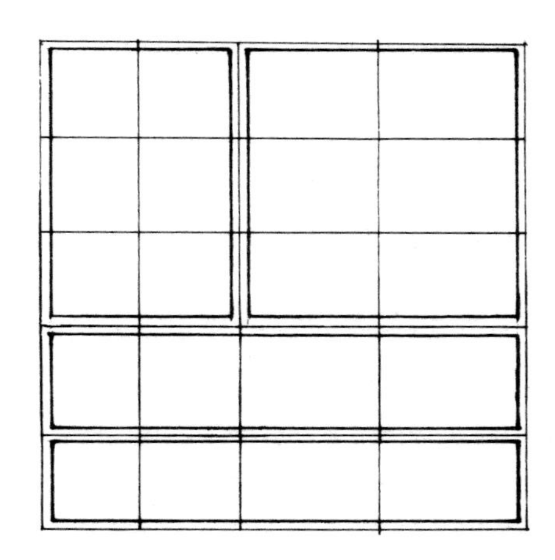

FOUR ZONES

The regularity of the orthogonal grid changes to accommodate internal functional needs resulting in a changed module. The new grid system can be subdivided into four distinct zones.

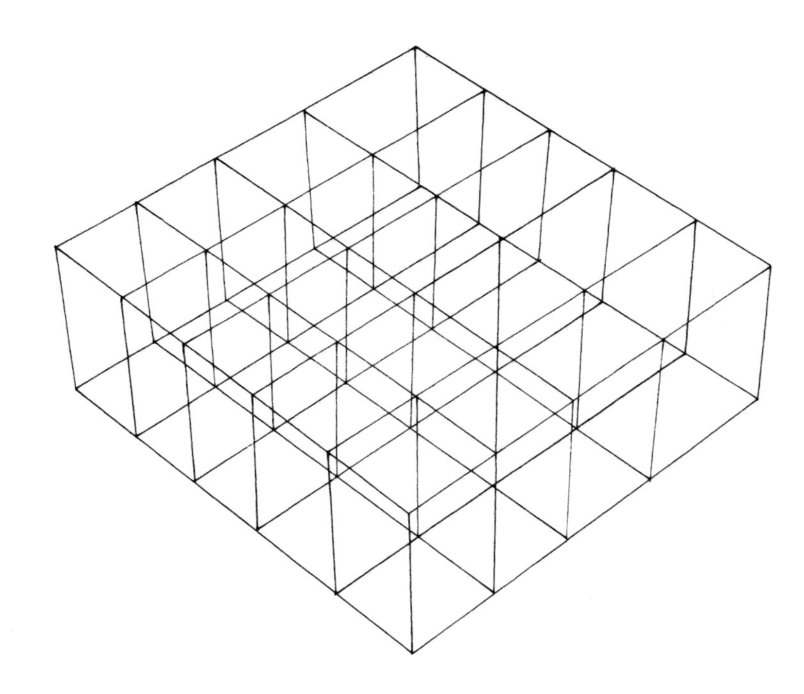

ADJUSTMENT TO ORTHOGONAL GRID

VISUAL RANGE

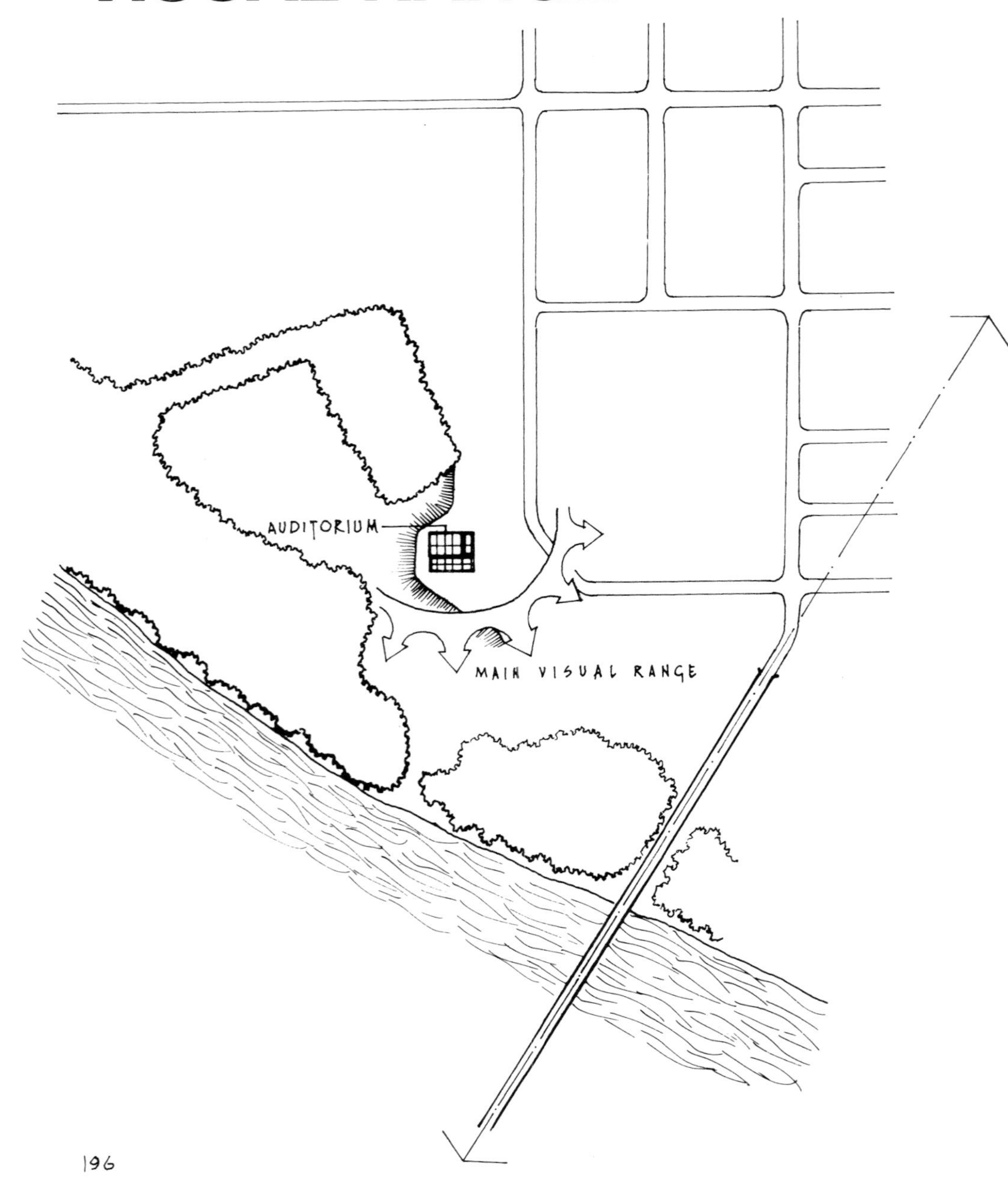

Accepting the prime visual opportunities as extending in an arc from north to southeast, Meier places the closed box of the auditorium on the northeastern side of the site.

AUDITORIUM

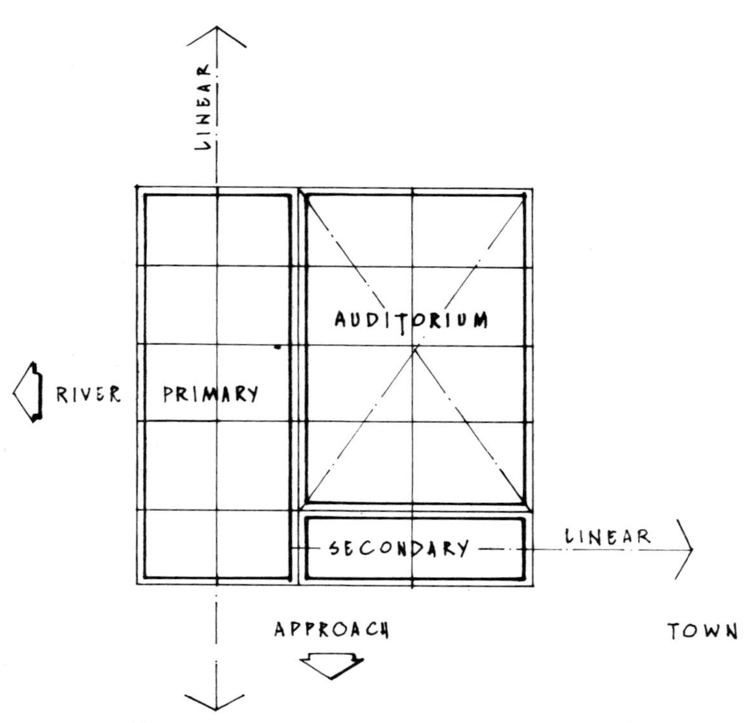

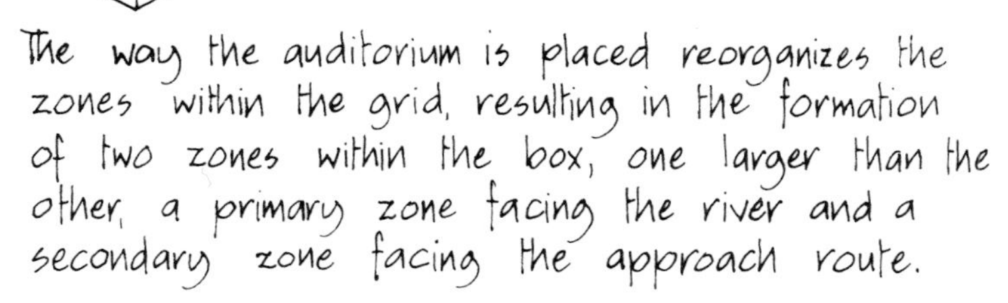
The way the auditorium is placed reorganizes the zones within the grid, resulting in the formation of two zones within the box, one larger than the other, a primary zone facing the river and a secondary zone facing the approach route.

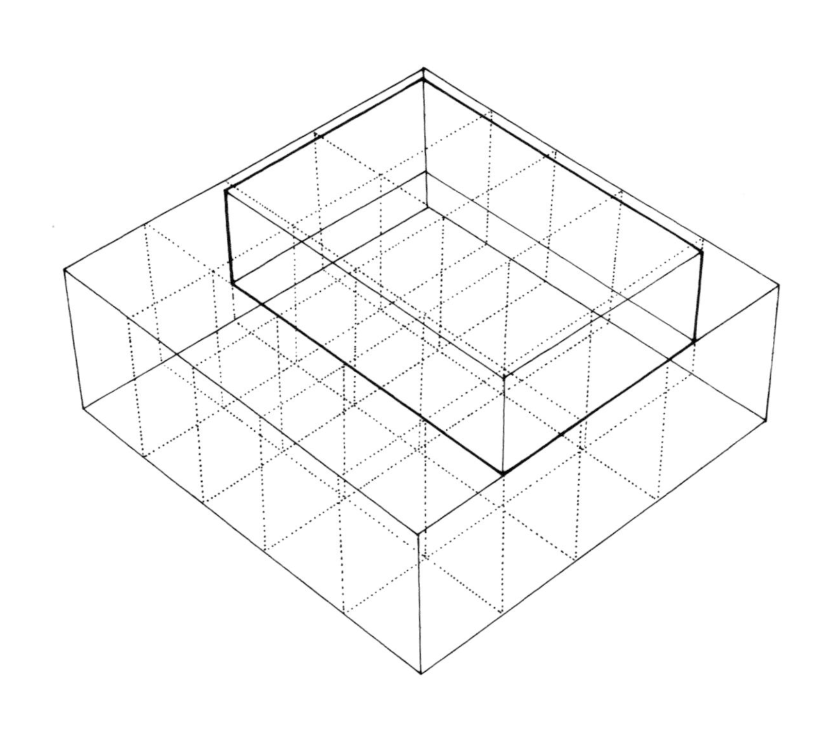

RAMP

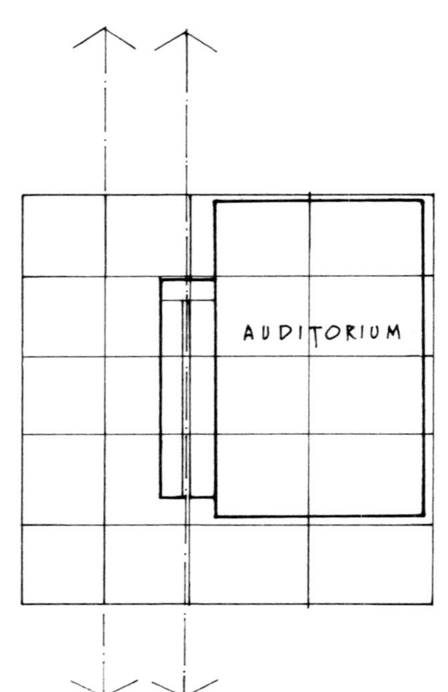

A ramp is placed adjacent to the auditorium so that it reinforces the linearity of the primary zone.

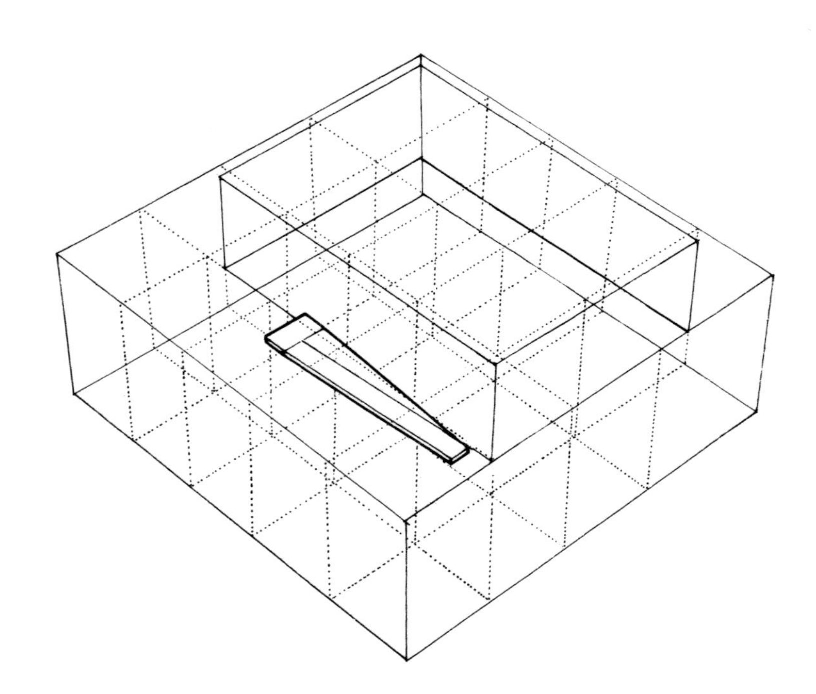

TILTED AXIS

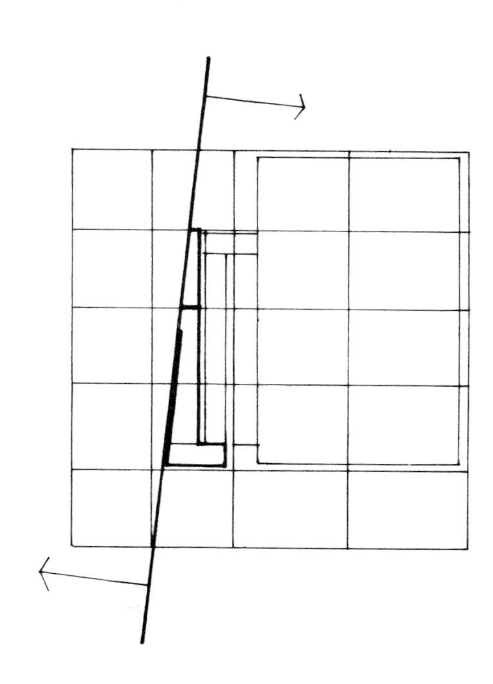

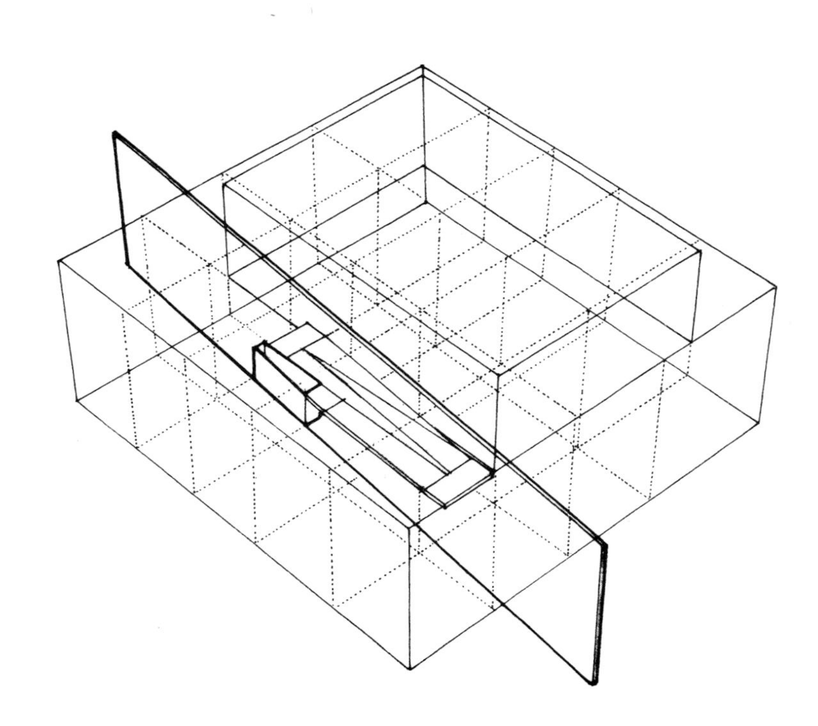

A 5° angle is introduced to the design so that the ramp adjusts to the new alignment. A core is formed where the two grids meet.

ROUTES

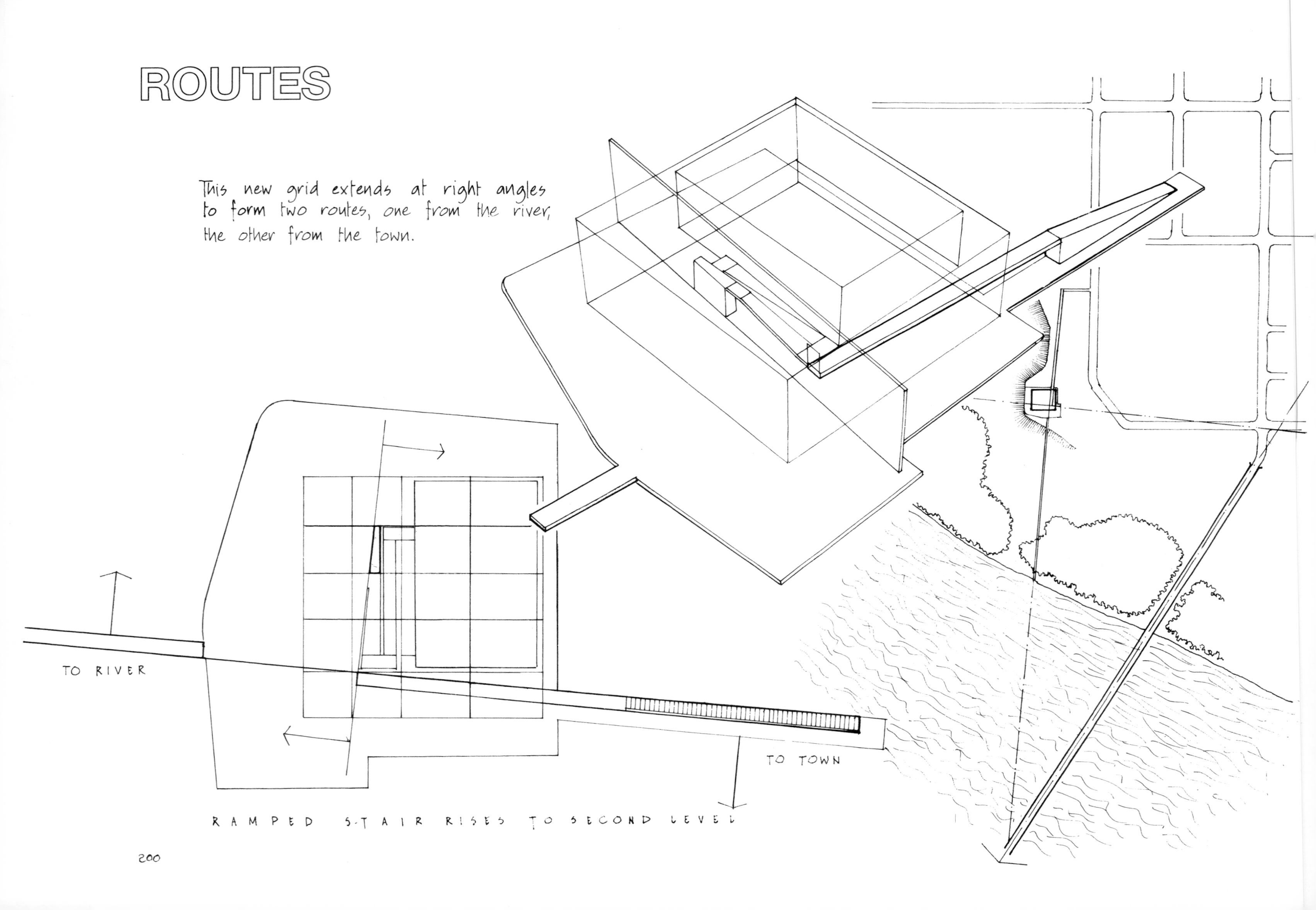

This new grid extends at right angles to form two routes, one from the river, the other from the town.
TO RIVER
TO TOWN
RAMPED STAIR RISES TO SECOND LEVEL

STAIR AND SCREEN

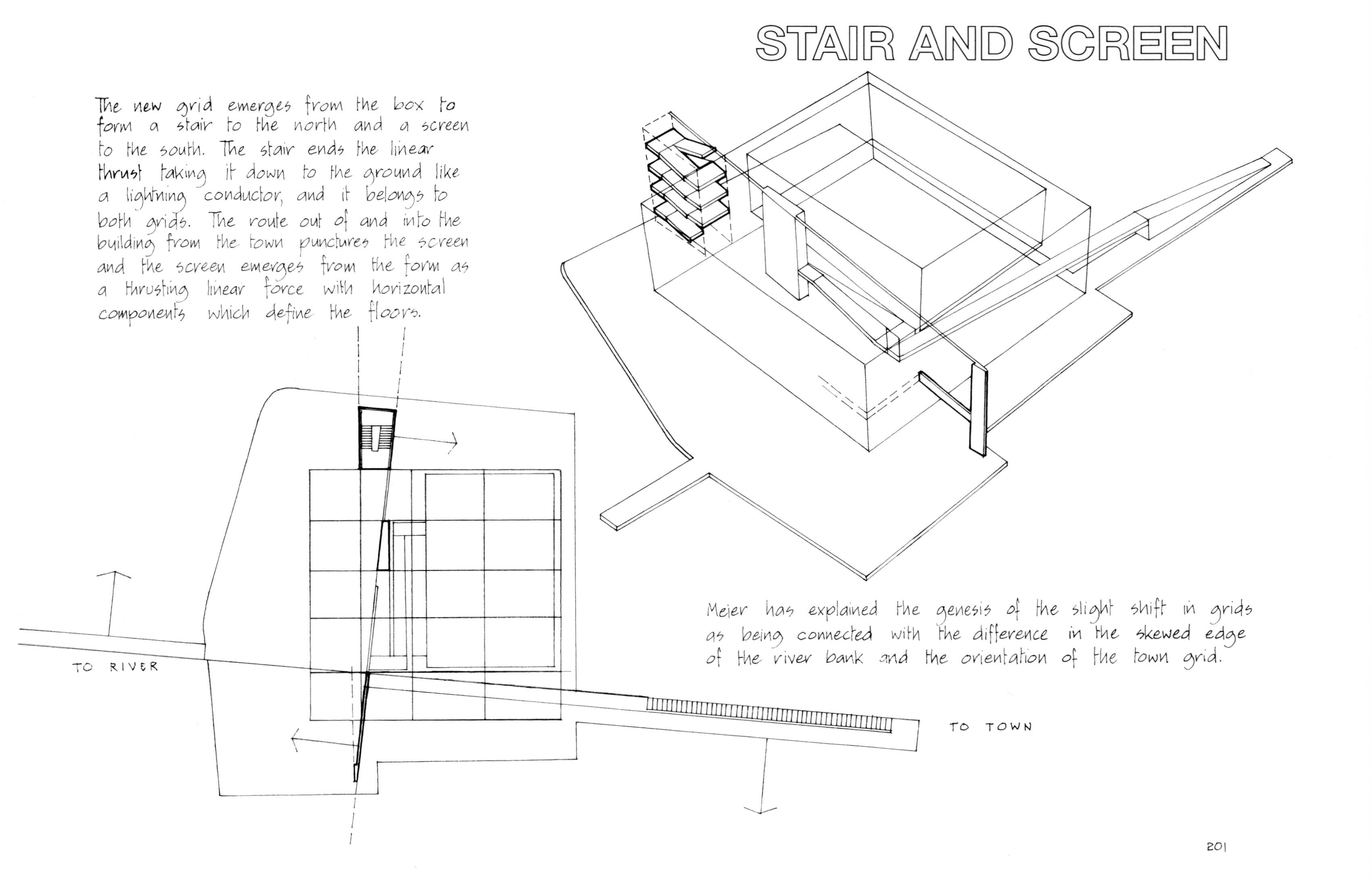

SQUARE OVERLAY

A more radical rotation of a slightly larger square is placed across the first, tilting the form even further. Within these rotational forces the original grid and auditorium act as stabilizing elements.

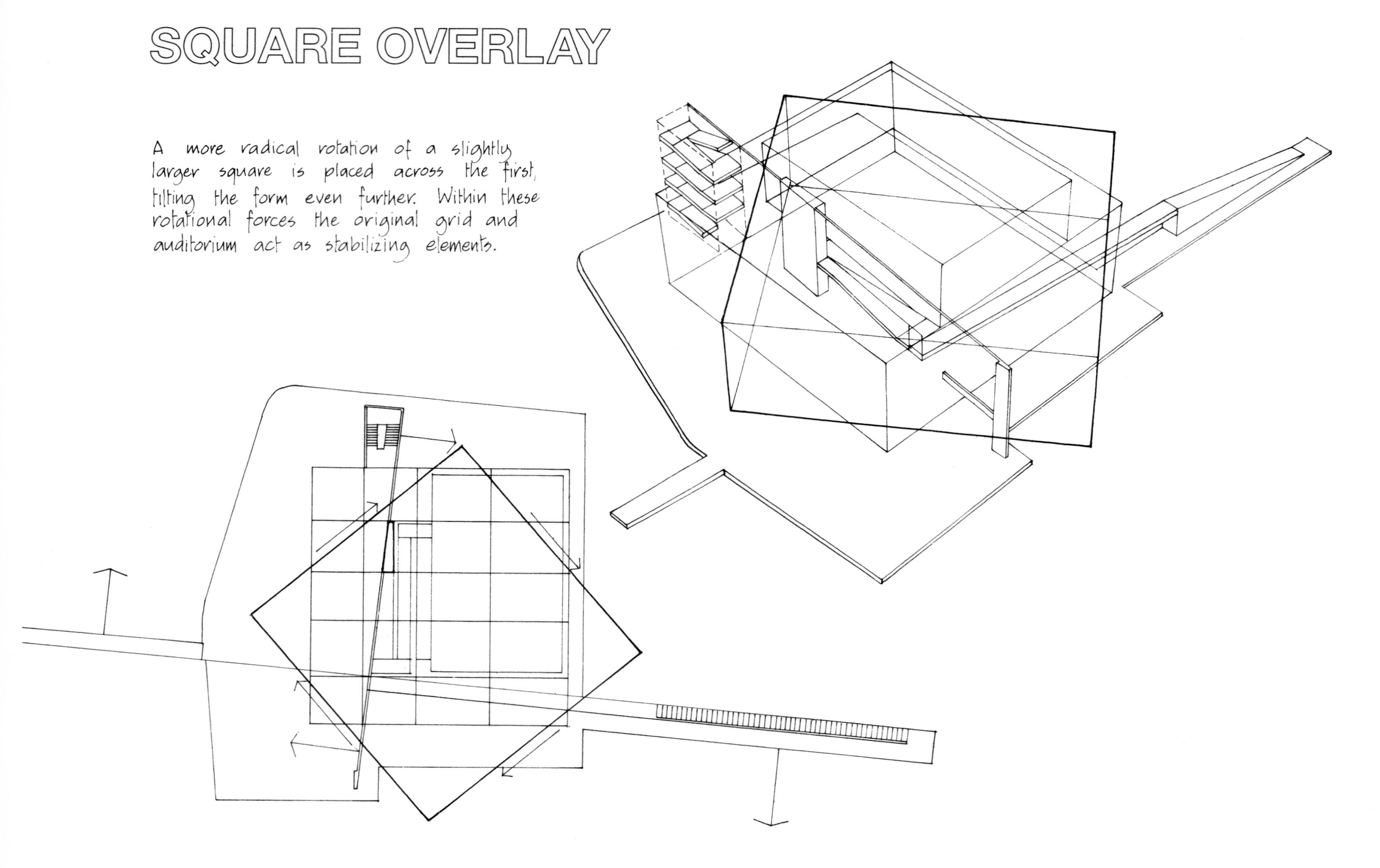

SCREEN AND STAIR

A screen delineates the square to the southwest giving expression to the turning moment. The corner is stated by the horizontal edge to an observation deck so that the vertical screen and horizontal edge come together to form a thrusting axis pointing along the original grid towards the river.

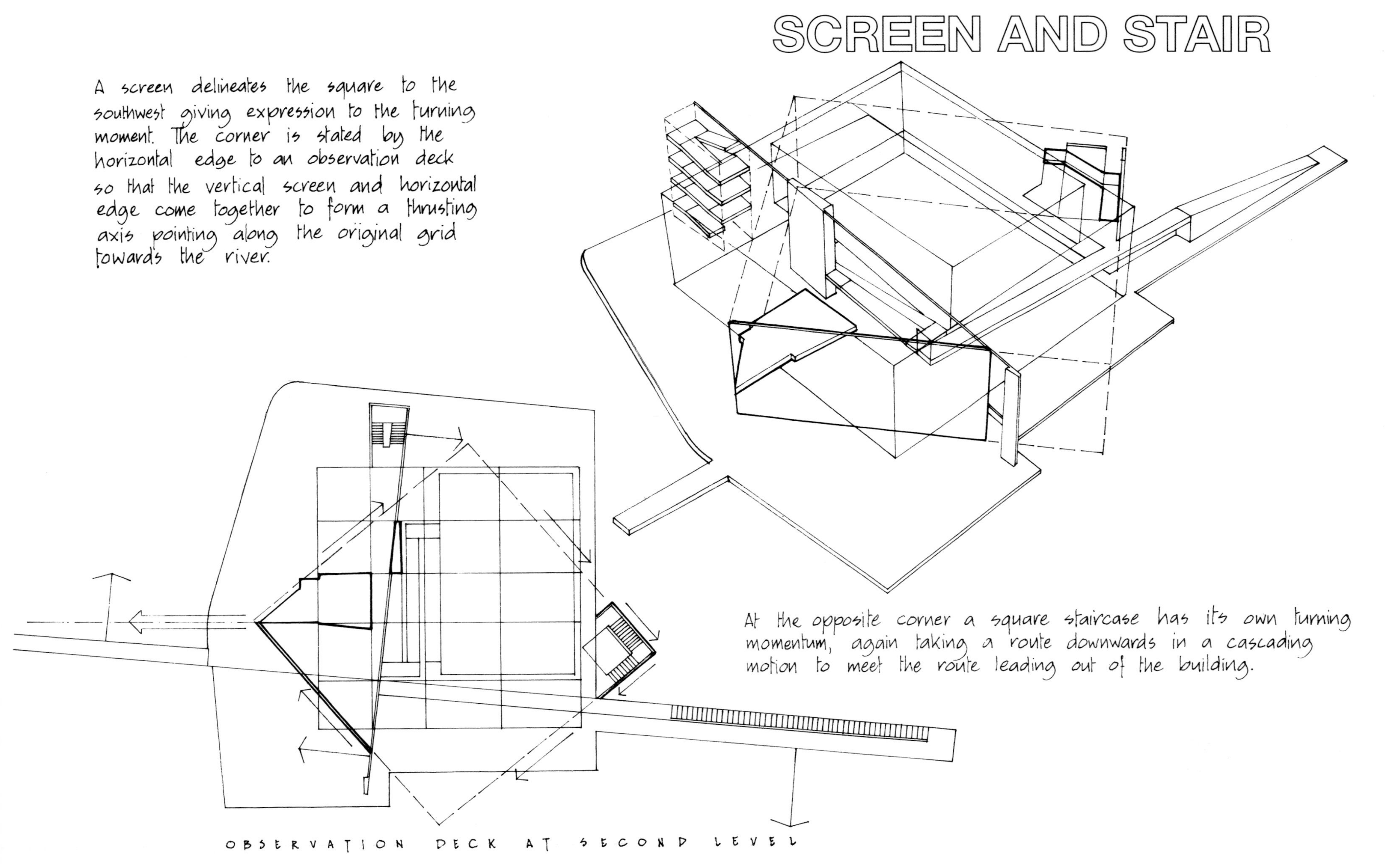

At the opposite corner a square staircase has its own turning momentum, again taking a route downwards in a cascading motion to meet the route leading out of the building.

OBSERVATION DECK AT SECOND LEVEL

APPROACH

The rotated square forming the screen provides a planar barrier, which upon arrival to the building turns the eye towards the river.

On approaching from the parking area, the eye and movement is turned towards the river. The approach route is at 90° to the screen, which prevents any view into the building.

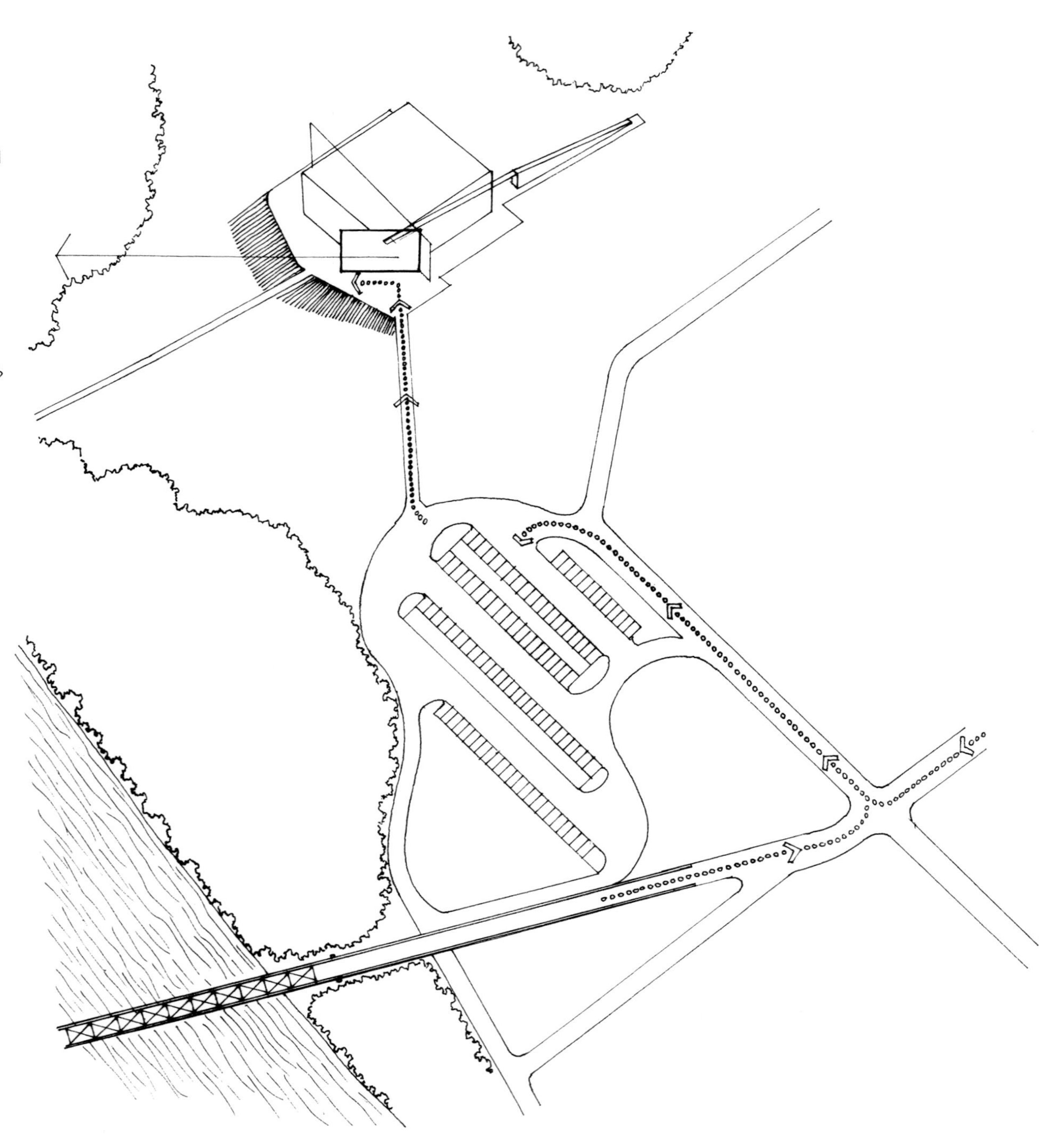

ENTRANCE

The screen is cut away to allow the insertion of an entry box. The large scale of the screen is used to attract the eye towards the entry box, this having human scale.

The entry box is aligned with the auditorium and is just off the movement axis on the route towards the building from the river. It provides a visual focus as the visitor moves towards the building, either from the river or from the car park.

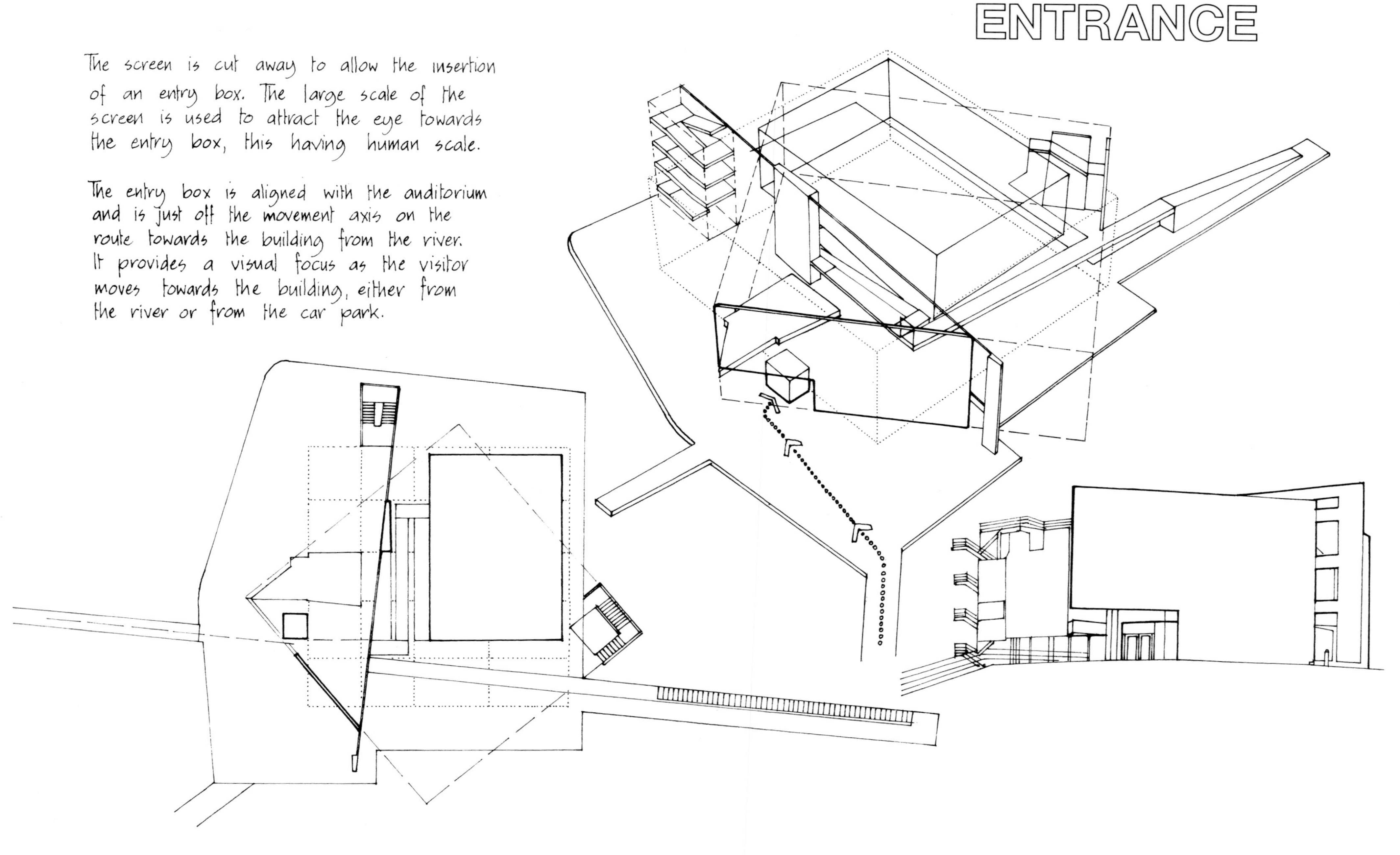

HOVERING PLANES

Just above entry, a triangular gallery is placed so that the floor plane is above that of the adjacent observation deck. These horizontal planes meet at the corner, giving two sharp edges to reinforce the sharp edge of the vertical planar screen. This corner of the building resembles the prow of a ship and thus reinforces the prevailing shipboard imagery of the whole composition.

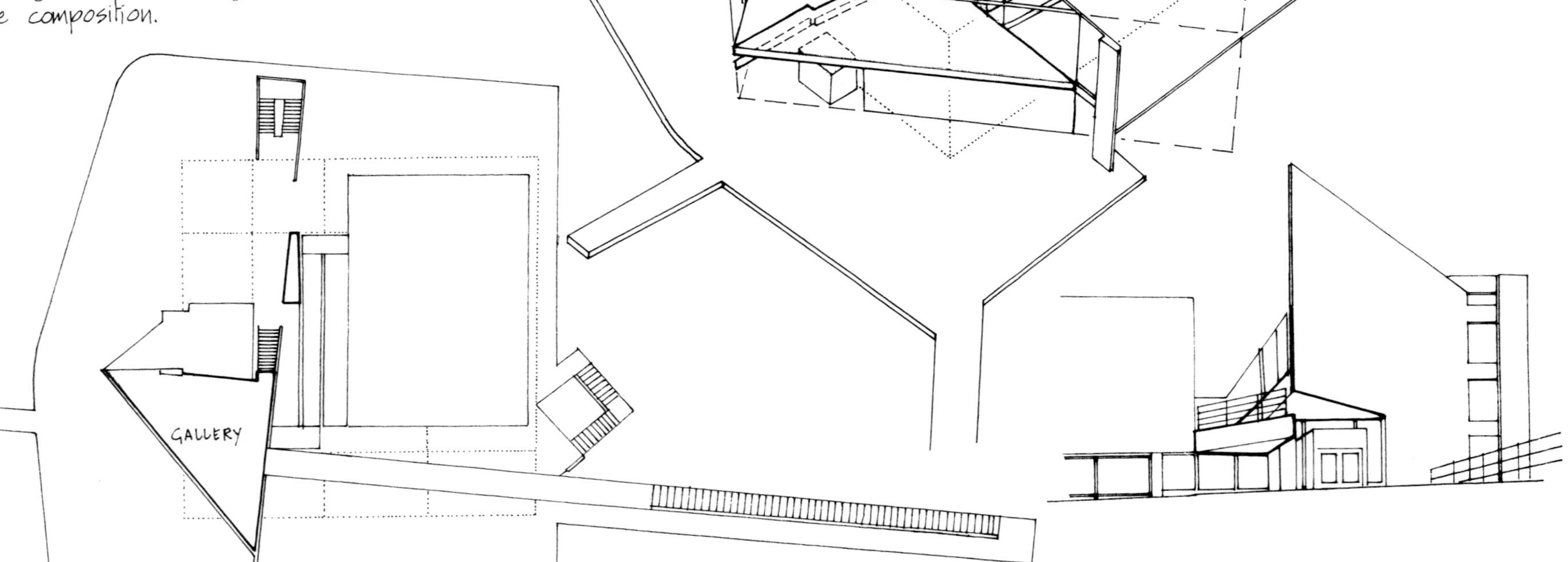

SECOND LEVEL PLAN

DYNAMIC CORNER

A further triangular plane hovers above as part of a roof observation deck. This locks back onto the vertical plane as part of a dynamic juxtaposition of planes at entry.

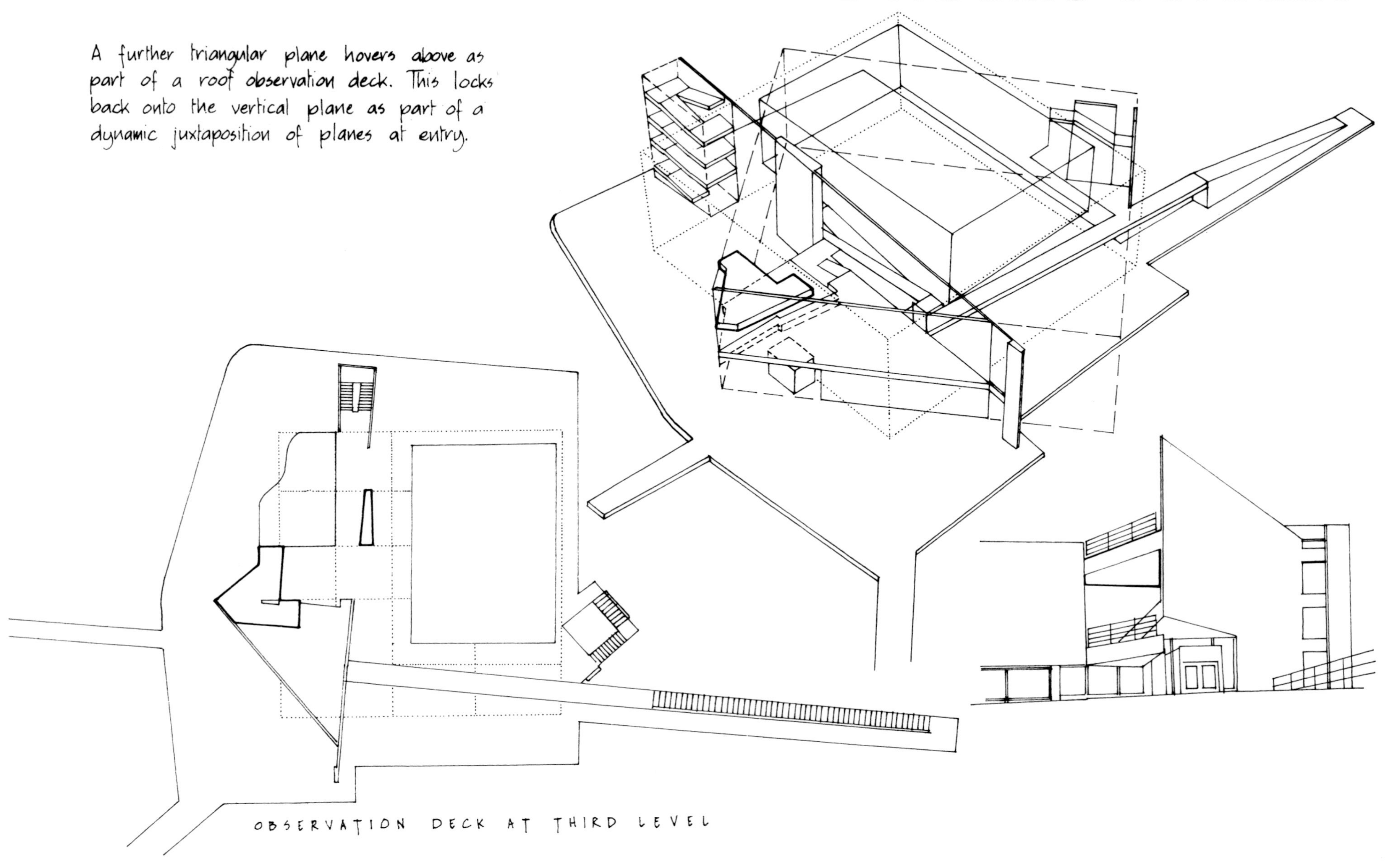

OBSERVATION DECK AT THIRD LEVEL

CURVED GALLERY

Adjacent to this vigorous clashing of planes, a curved box hovers above ground level, its wavy form responding to the river. This box provides a contained viewing gallery, its curved ribbon window framing views of the river. The serene curved solidity of the box contrasts with the animated series of planes alongside.

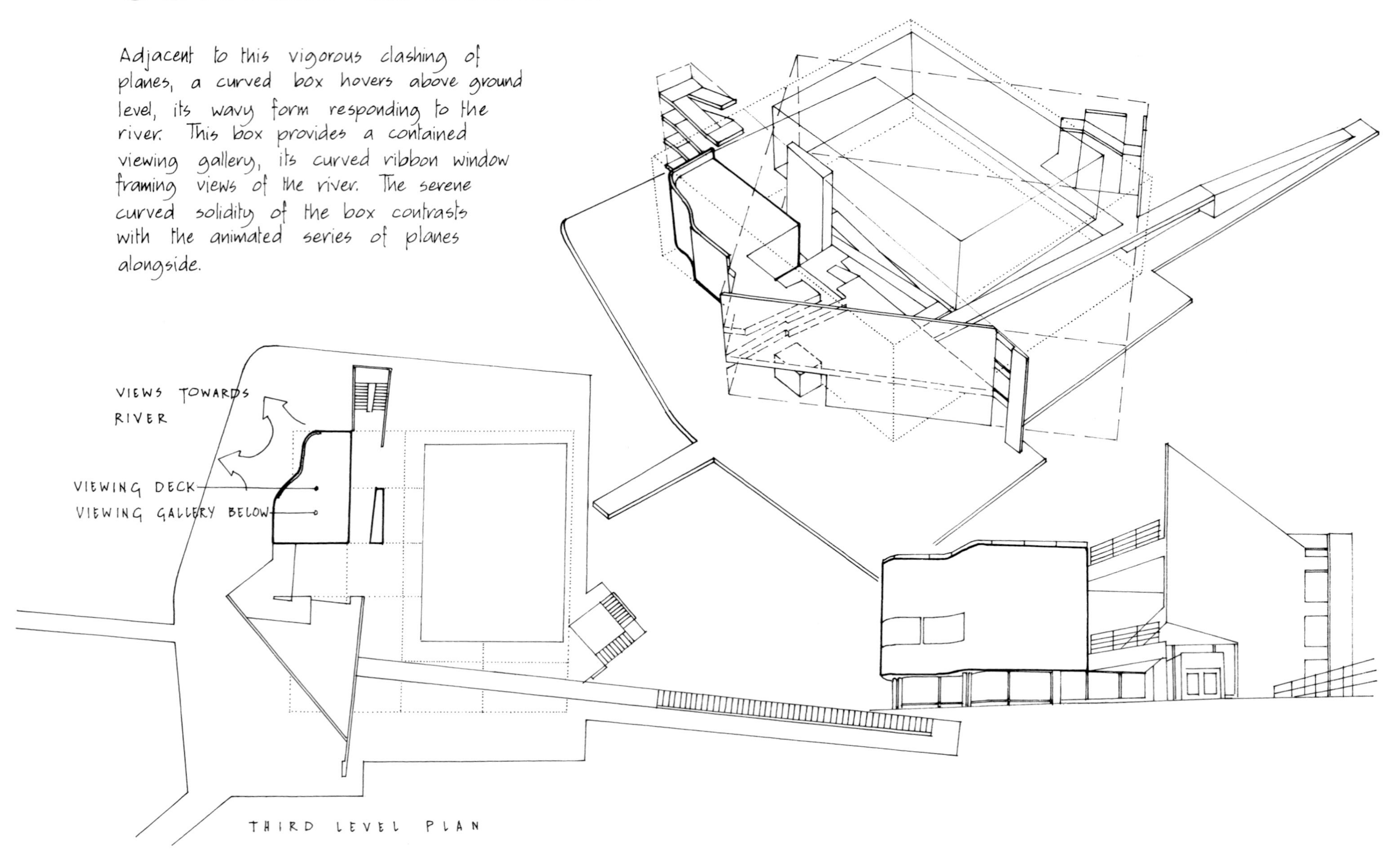

THIRD LEVEL PLAN

LIGHT WELL

Between the curved viewing box and triangular gallery, the observation deck forms one side of a light well into the building so that light penetrates down into the sides of this space and also into the central circulation space formed by the ramp. A stair links the deck level with the gallery.

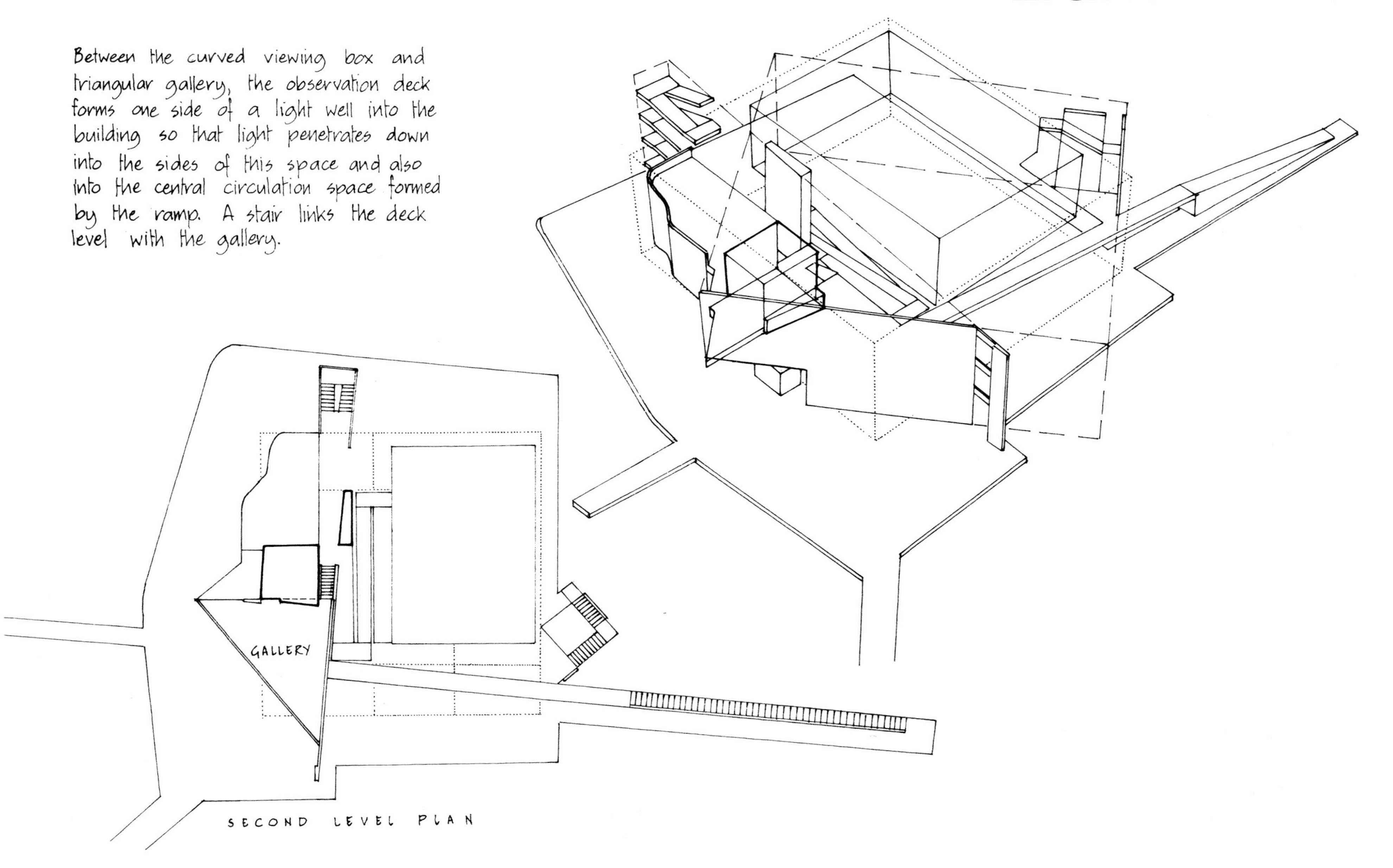

WEST FACADE

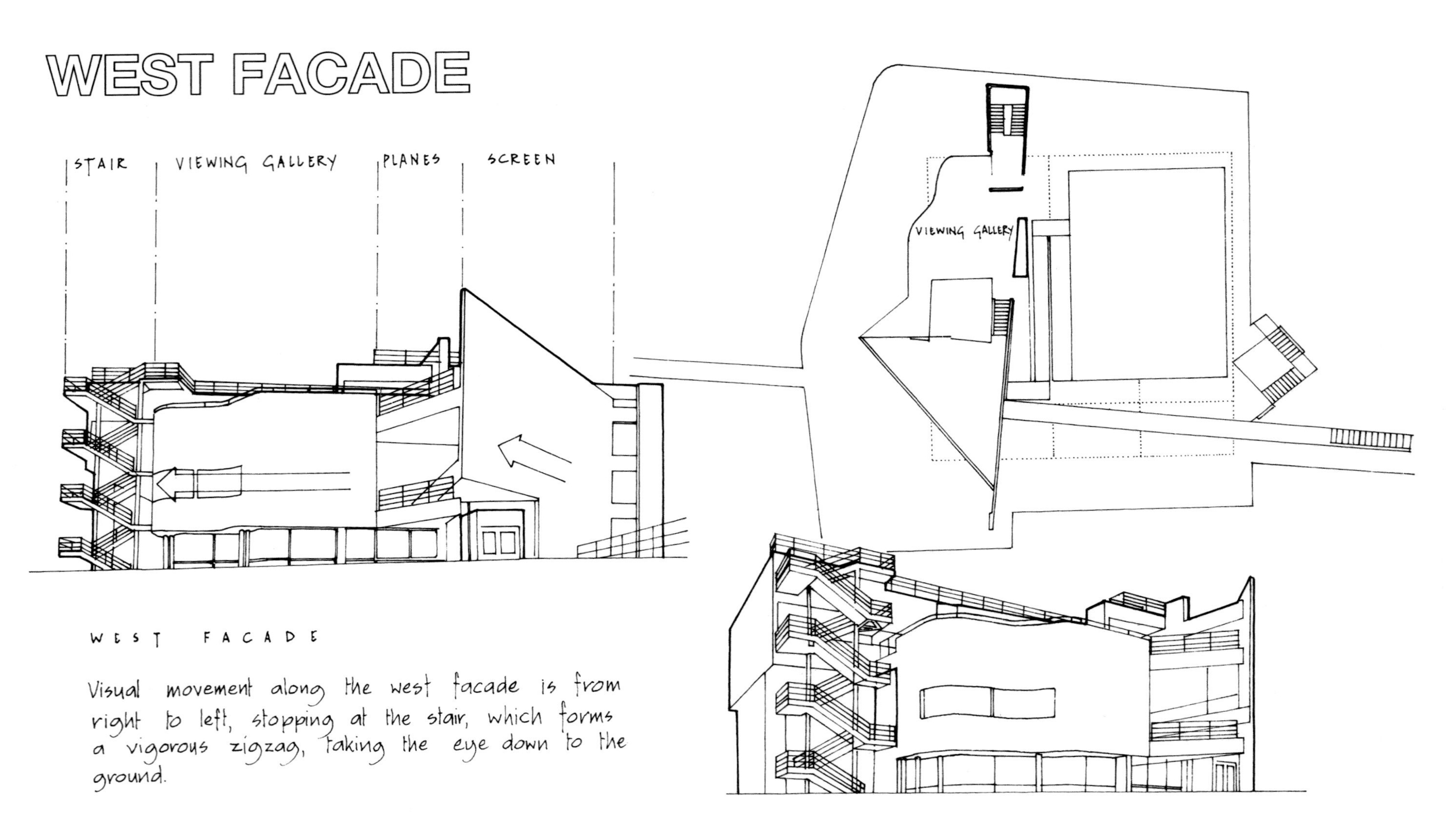

WEST FACADE

Visual movement along the west facade is from right to left, stopping at the stair, which forms a vigorous zigzag, taking the eye down to the ground.

The composition integrates four major elements: the screen, which is a vertical plane; the hovering horizontal planes; the curved viewing box and the stair. The entry box also provides an important visual incident.

The stair pierces the viewing gallery at its northern end where the gallery extends to give access to the auditorium.

SOUTH FACADE

On the south side of the building, a screen is placed on the main grid. This is joined back to the auditorium in the form of a projection box at high level. Below this, the screen is open except for slender vertical supports and horizontal ties back into the main structure.

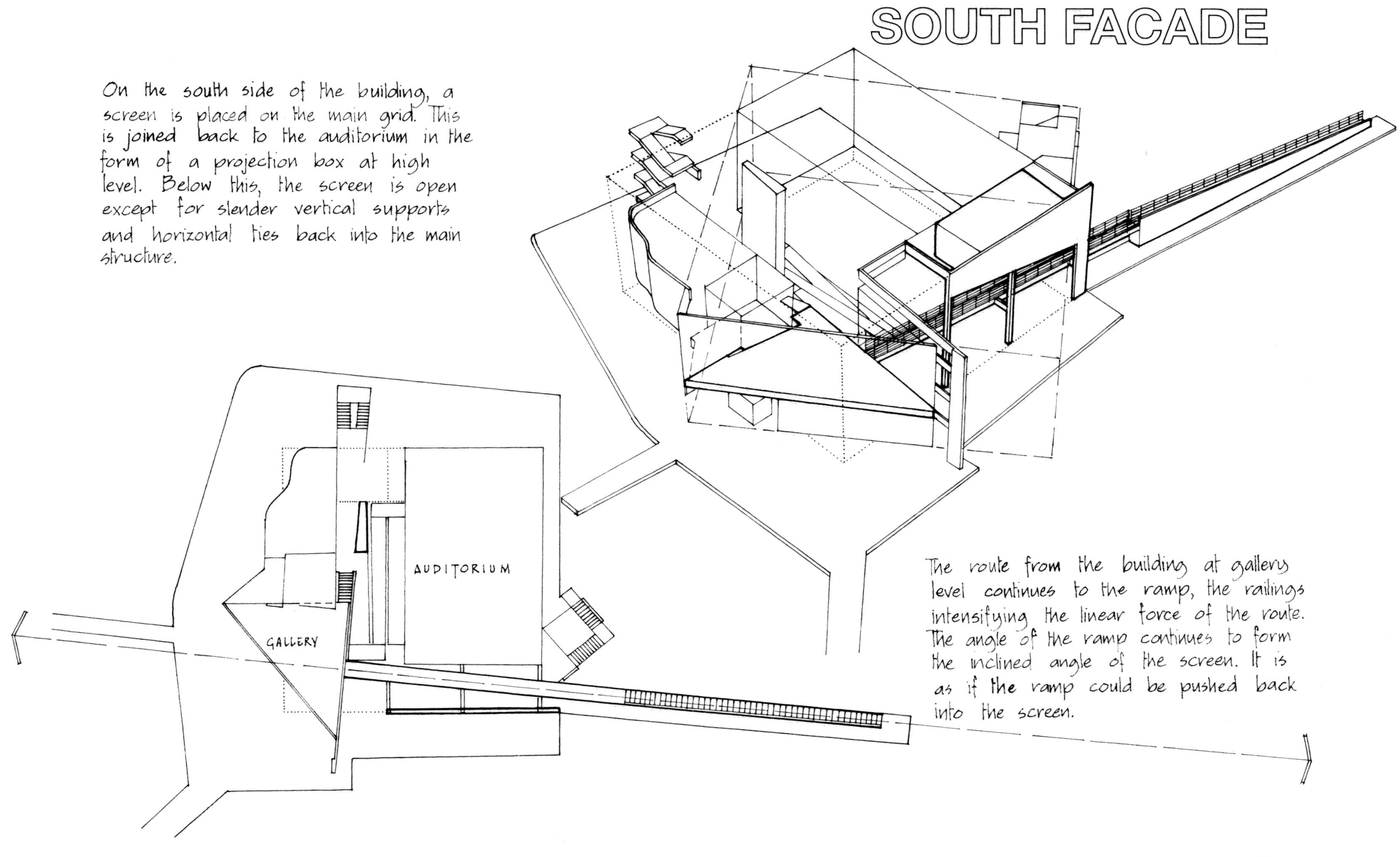

The route from the building at gallery level continues to the ramp, the railings intensifying the linear force of the route. The angle of the ramp continues to form the inclined angle of the screen. It is as if the ramp could be pushed back into the screen.

PENETRATION TO SOUTH

At an upper level, a conference room forms a space leading across a bridge to an observation deck. This is situated on the roof of the curved observation box. From the conference room, a stair descends onto the route out of the building, sliding alongside the main linear route in support of it.

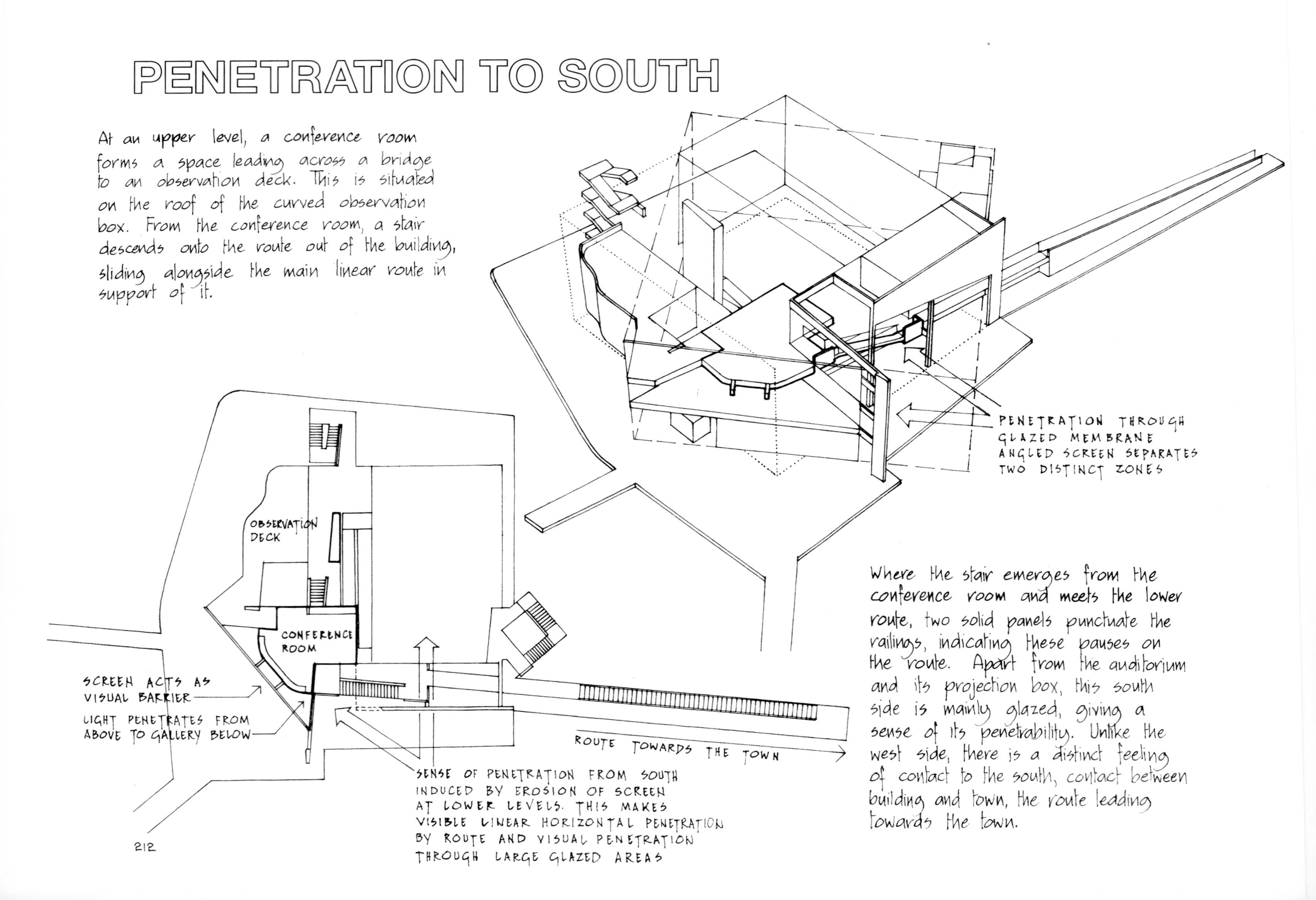

Where the stair emerges from the conference room and meets the lower route, two solid panels punctuate the railings, indicating these pauses on the route. Apart from the auditorium and its projection box, this south side is mainly glazed, giving a sense of its penetrability. Unlike the west side, there is a distinct feeling of contact to the south, contact between building and town, the route leading towards the town.

ROUTE FRAMED

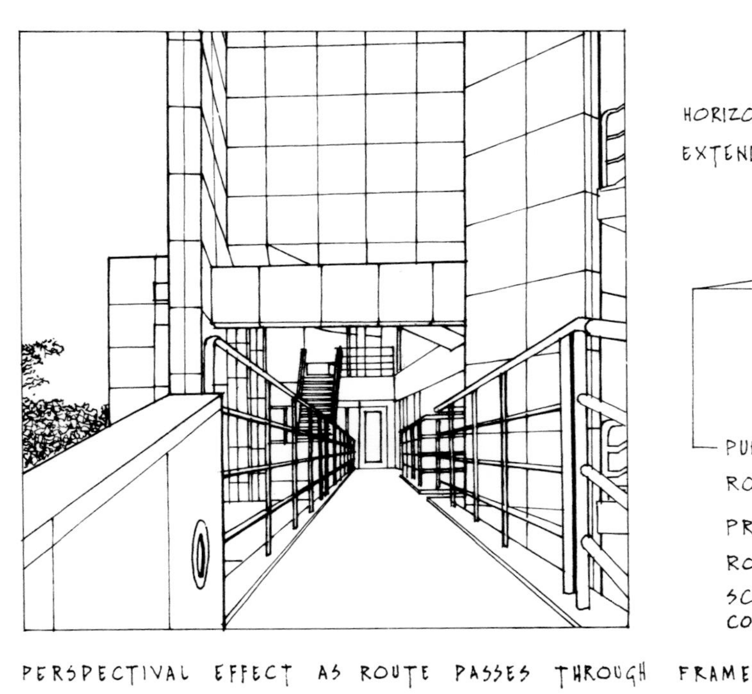

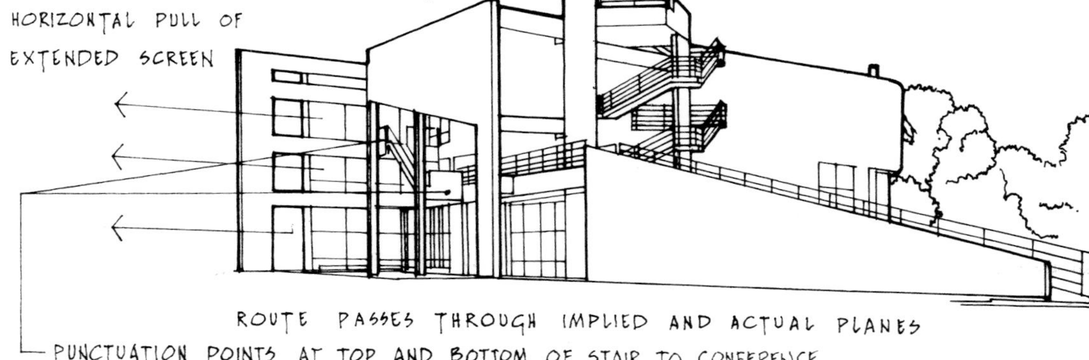

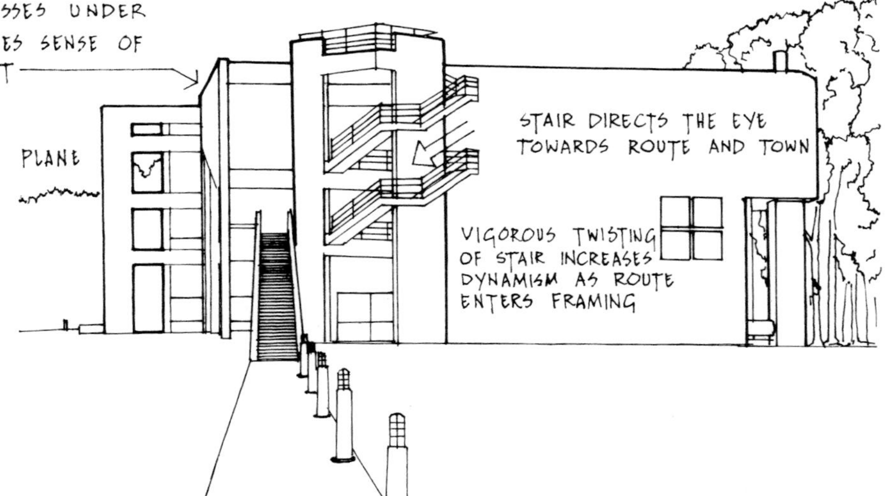

The route to and from the building is framed by vertical and horizontal beams. The route passes through implied and actual planes, sliding behind the outer screen and thrusting through the planes. The framing contributes towards a perspectival effect along the route.

TRANSFORMATION OF BOX

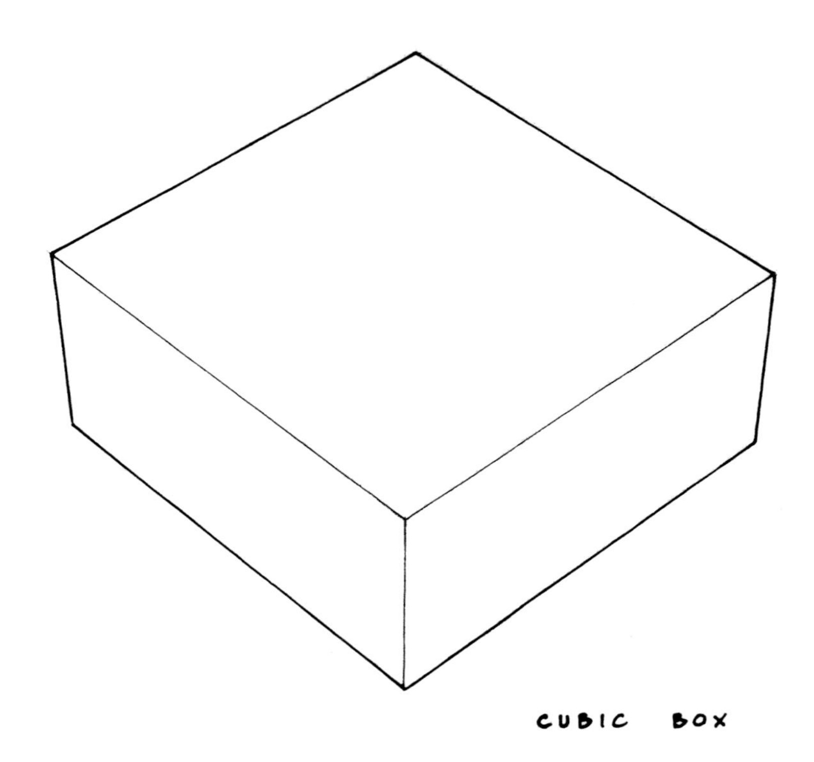

CUBIC BOX

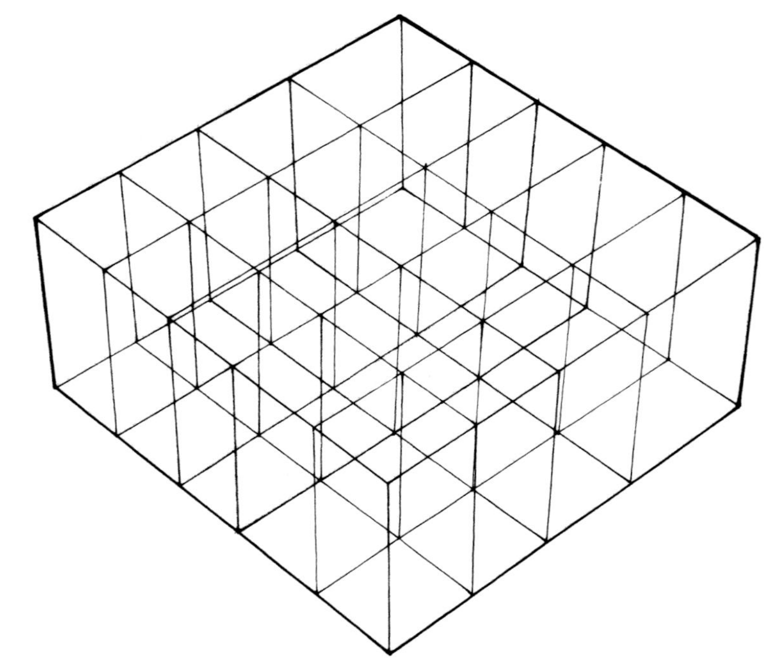

ORTHOGONAL GRID

If we summarize the development of the analysis, the initial box dissolves into planes and solids about two grids. Then along the new grid Meier pushes his linear route through, emerging from the building in the form of a ramp. Finally, a square is imposed on the cubic form allowing the formation of the front screen and square stair.

PLANES AND SOLIDS

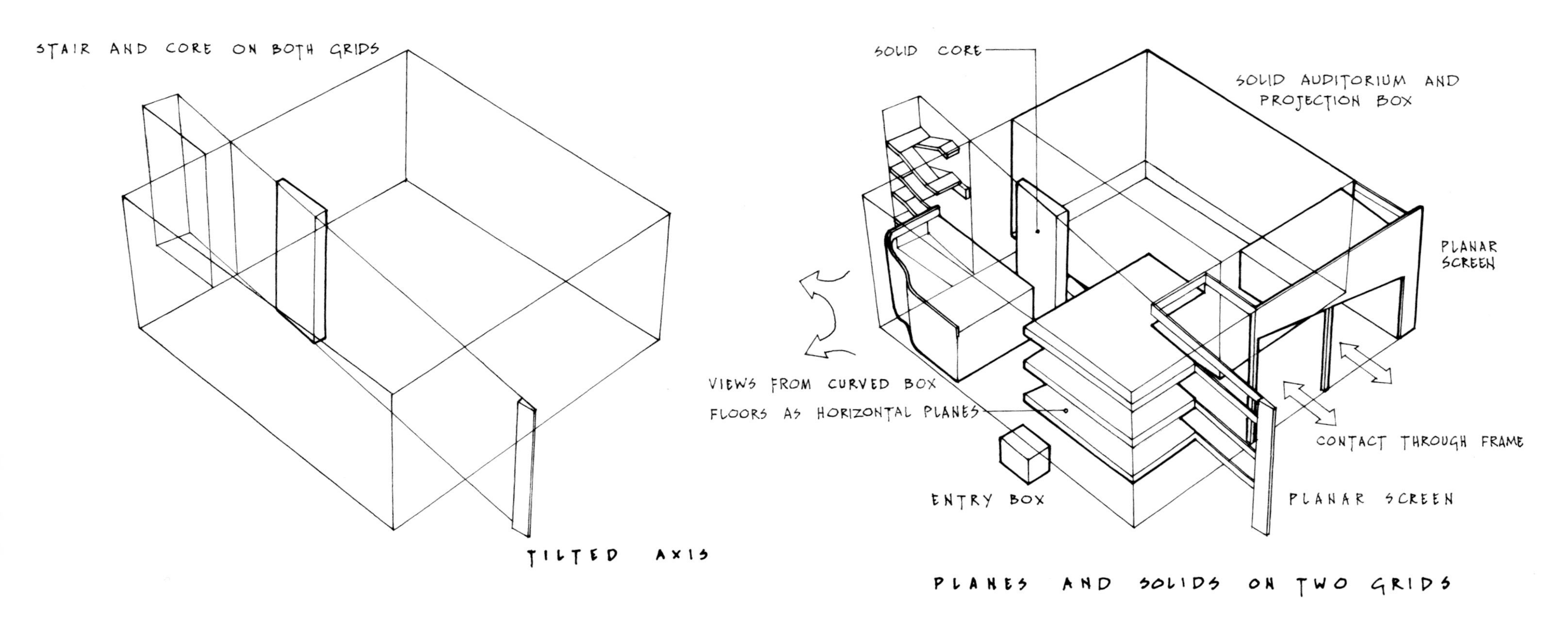

PLANES AND SOLIDS ON TWO GRIDS

SQUARE IMPOSED

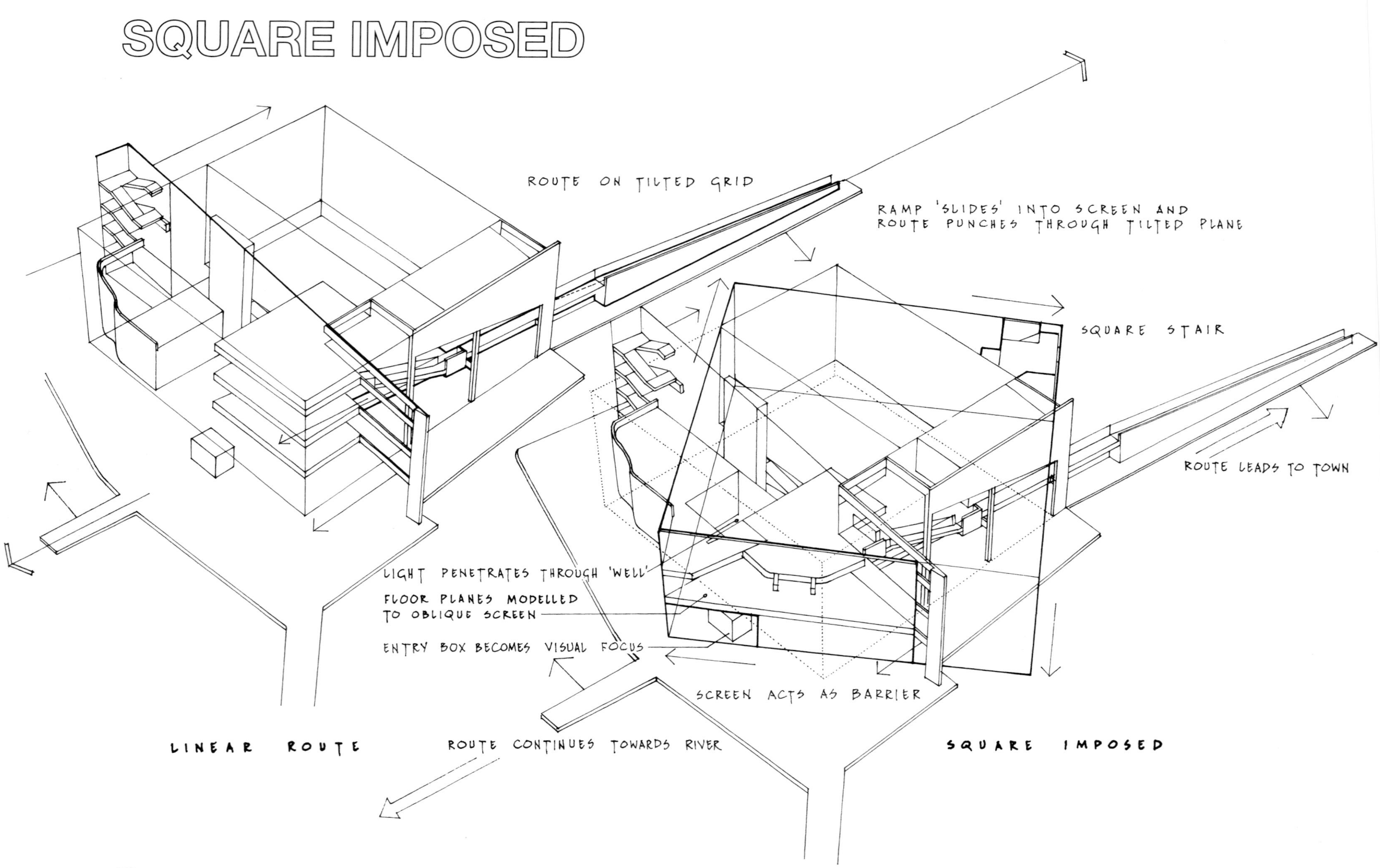

CURVED ADDITION

To complete the form, an addition is placed on the rear of the building. It is curved in response to the natural setting, the soft pastoral quality of the cornfield.

This is added onto the cubic mass, and the angle of the extremity is determined by the stair which is on the second grid. This addition locks the stair into the whole.

A square window concludes the composition and makes a very strong design statement. This square punctuation seems to emphasize the solidity of the mass to the rear. As with the two sets of stairs and oblique screen on the approach route, the window draws attention to one of the corners by pulling the eye toward it. This window lights the auditorium and forms part of a movement sequence inside. The support for the overhang also contains the boiler flue.

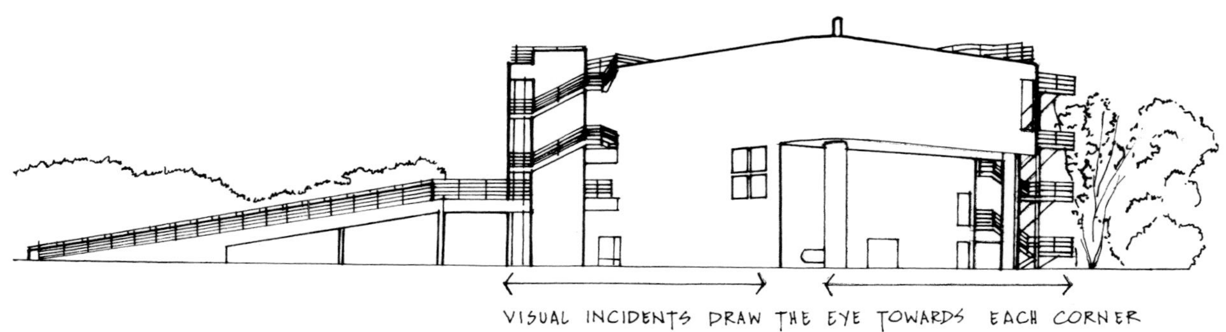

VISUAL INCIDENTS DRAW THE EYE TOWARDS EACH CORNER

VIEW FROM NORTH EAST

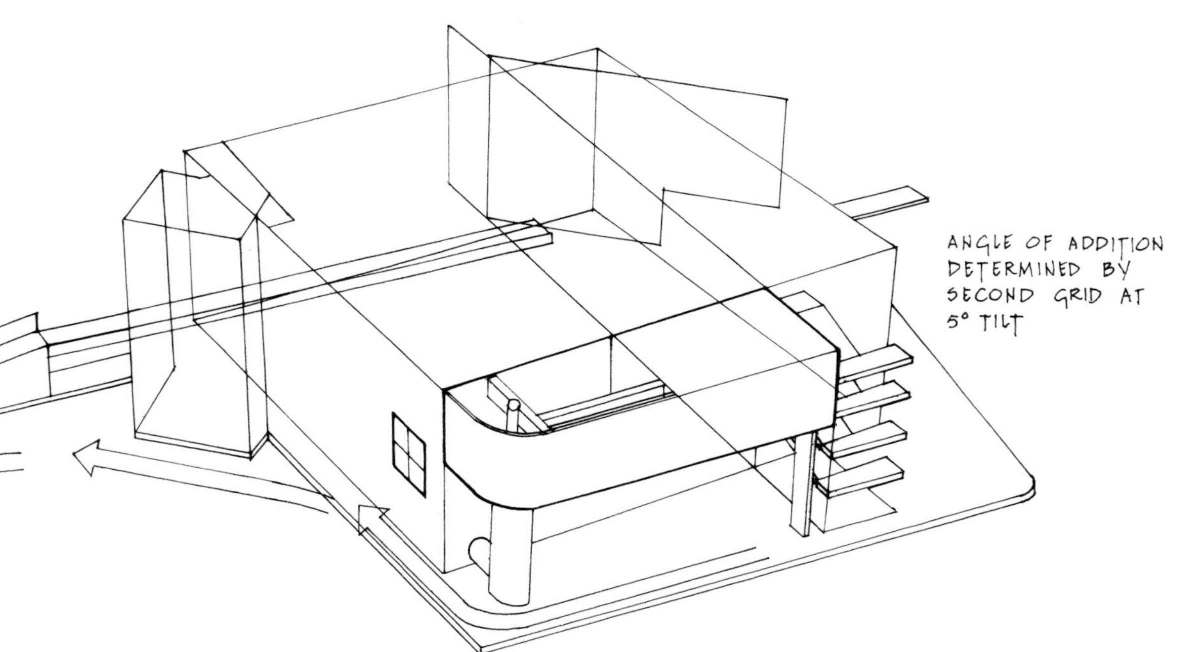

ANGLE OF ADDITION DETERMINED BY SECOND GRID AT 5° TILT

A comparison can be made between Meier's north elevation and the east facade of Le Corbusier's chapel at Ronchamp.[1] In each case the upper volume forms a spatial 'curtain' which can be likened to the proscenium arch in a theatre.

THE EYE IS LED PAST THE CURVE, BELOW IT, AS THE LOWER VOLUME IS CUT AWAY. THE STAIR TO THE WEST STOPS THE SPACE AT THE RIVER SIDE WHILST THE TURNED SQUARE STAIR DIVERTS THE EYE TOWARDS THE RAMP.

1 see G.H. Baker, Le Corbusier: An analysis of form, (Second edition 1989). Van Nostrand Reinhold (International) Co. Ltd, London, p. 256.

GROUND LEVEL

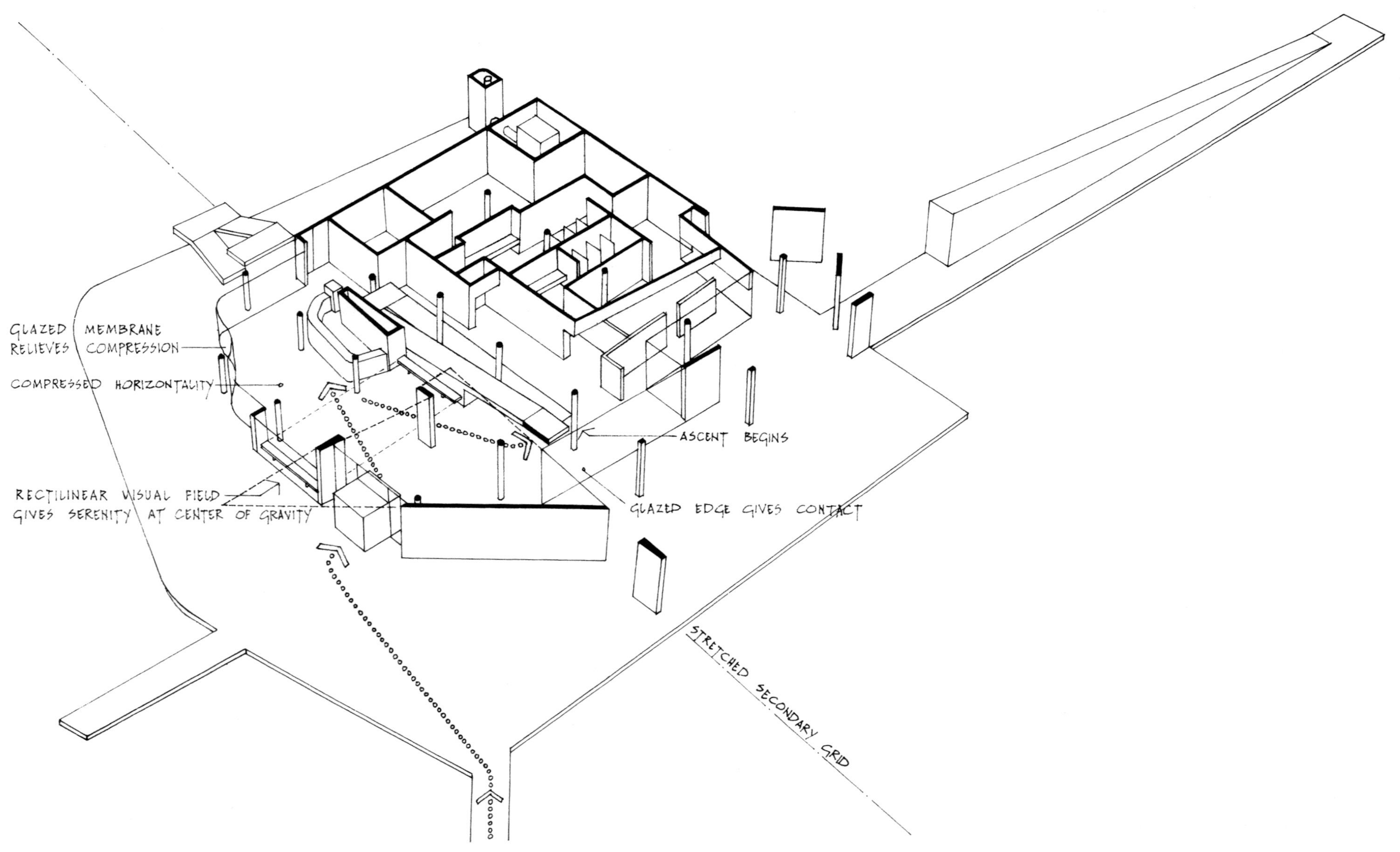

On entry, the eye is drawn to the information counter. The space to the left of entry is kept low with a feeling of compression which begins on movement through the entry box. The low scale is preserved by the entry desk whose high counter top has the effect of making the ceiling seem lower. The sense of horizontal compression is relieved by the glazed curved membrane at the edge of the space and by a higher ceiling to the right of entry in the triangular section.

Two low bench seats reinforce the feeling of compressed horizontality between the floor and ceiling. Being directly opposite each other, they form a rectilinear visual field which has a stabilizing role, being at the centre of gravity in the composition. The serenity which they provide helps to prepare for the vigorous animation of the movement sequence.

From the information counter, movement is under the ramp projection above and adjacent to the base of the ramp. The ramp, which leads to the floor above the main entry space, draws the eye by its sculptural form. The ramp reinforces the feeling of stretching imposed by the second grid and sets in motion the spatial sequence from the low horizontal entry space in a gradual ascent through a central vertical shaft which is toplit above the ramp. The space is stretched out along the oblique plane of the secondary grid. The core and counter observe this grid as does the final ascent of the ramp and eastern side of the external stair.

The orthogonal grid is stated by the way the columns are disposed and the overlaid square is expressed through the screen adjacent to entry. The space is animated by the tension between the primary grid and the stretched secondary grid.

SECOND LEVEL

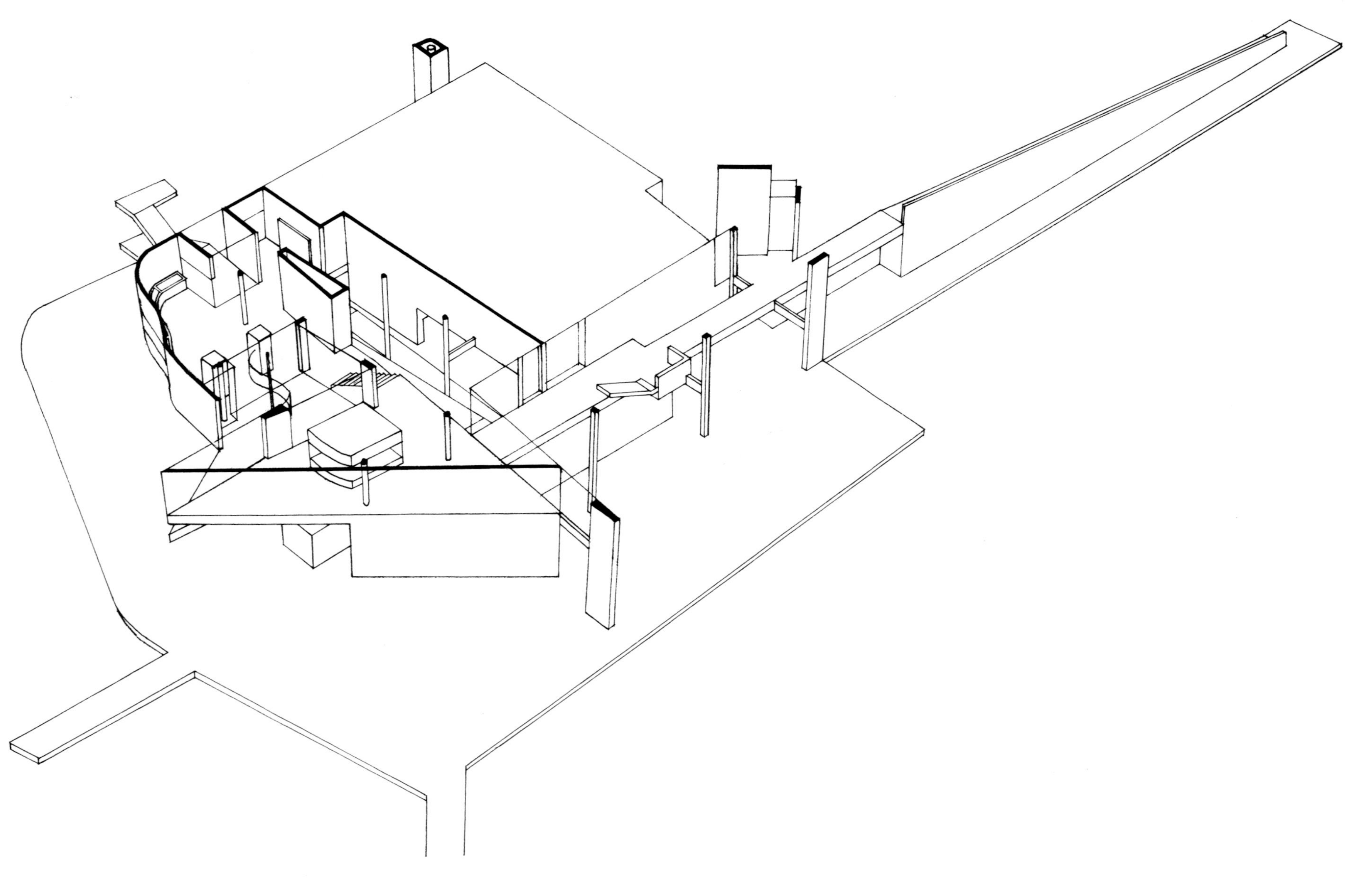

At the second level, the spatial compression is reversed with the low ceiling to the triangular gallery now behind the screen. The gallery to the curved viewing box, being at a lower level, has a higher ceiling. Between the two is the light well.

The visual dynamism consists of the combined interaction of spiraling stair and the swirling outer wall of the viewing box (supported by the swirling curved container for exhibits) these being set against the stretched angled wall into which the triangular gallery adds further dynamism. As on the entry level, triangle and curved box are set against each other dramatically.

Behind the stretched, angled, wall the triangular gallery contains the model of New Harmony. This has a curved end which becomes part of the ceiling above. Light is fed down in the gap between the cutaway and the external oblique screen.

THIRD LEVEL

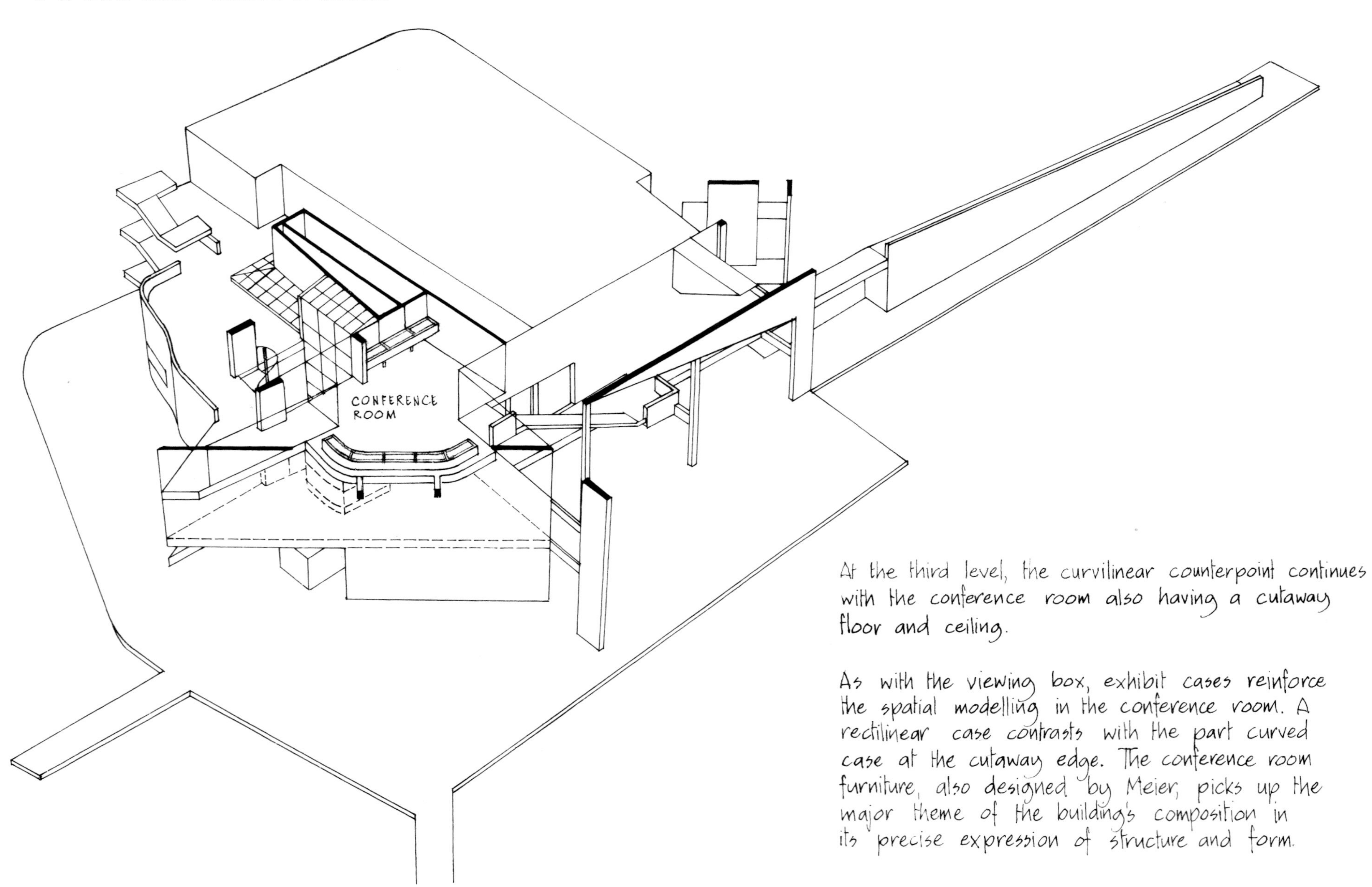

At the third level, the curvilinear counterpoint continues with the conference room also having a cutaway floor and ceiling.

As with the viewing box, exhibit cases reinforce the spatial modelling in the conference room. A rectilinear case contrasts with the part curved case at the cutaway edge. The conference room furniture, also designed by Meier, picks up the major theme of the building's composition in its precise expression of structure and form.

CASCADE AROUND CORE

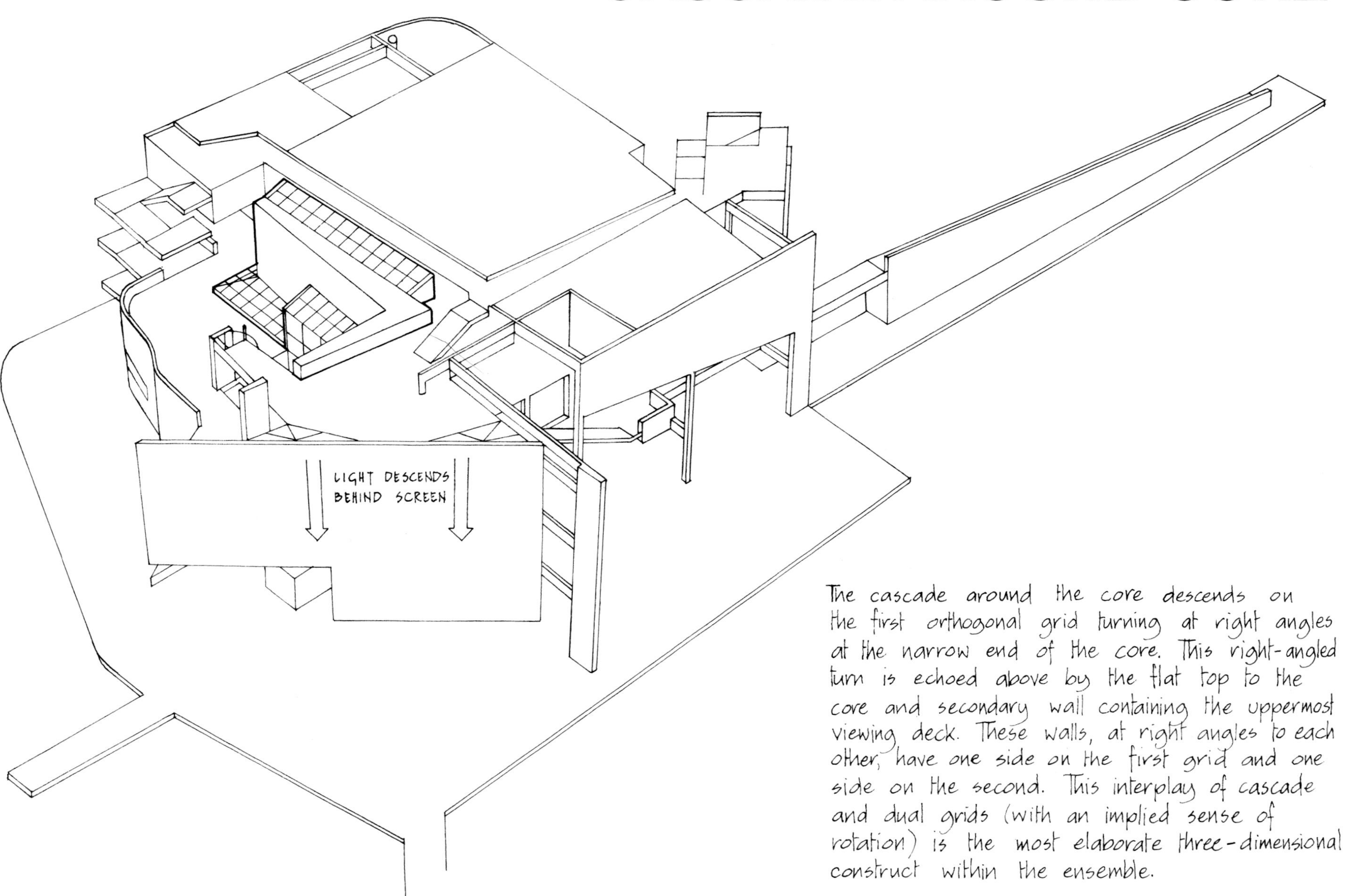

The cascade around the core descends on the first orthogonal grid turning at right angles at the narrow end of the core. This right-angled turn is echoed above by the flat top to the core and secondary wall containing the uppermost viewing deck. These walls, at right angles to each other, have one side on the first grid and one side on the second. This interplay of cascade and dual grids (with an implied sense of rotation) is the most elaborate three-dimensional construct within the ensemble.

VISUAL INTERLOCK

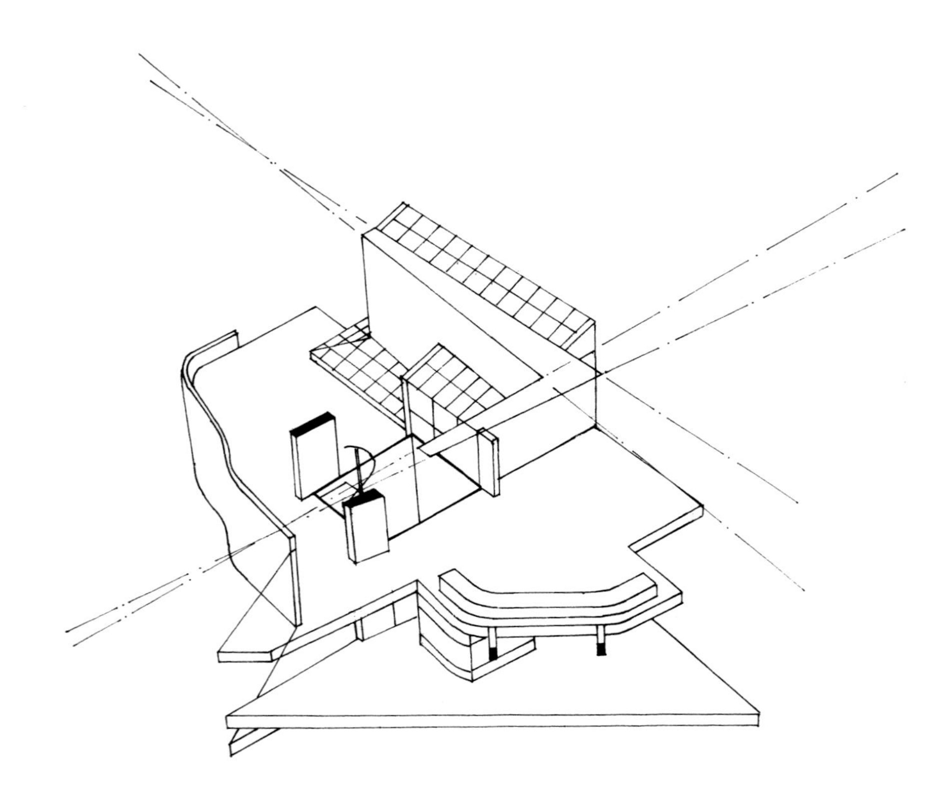

The climax in the three-dimensional modelling of these elements occurs in the way Meier crashes together the curved viewing box and the cutaway layers in the triangular section behind the screen.

They slot together about the light well, which is also part of the exciting cascade of rooflights and the corkscrew of the spiral stair.

Vertical space, cascading glass, sloping ramp and hovering planes are all locked together in a way that is determined by the function of each element.

ELEMENTS LOCK TOGETHER ABOUT THE LIGHT WELL FULLY EXPLOITING THE DUAL GRID SYSTEM

MOVEMENT SEQUENCE

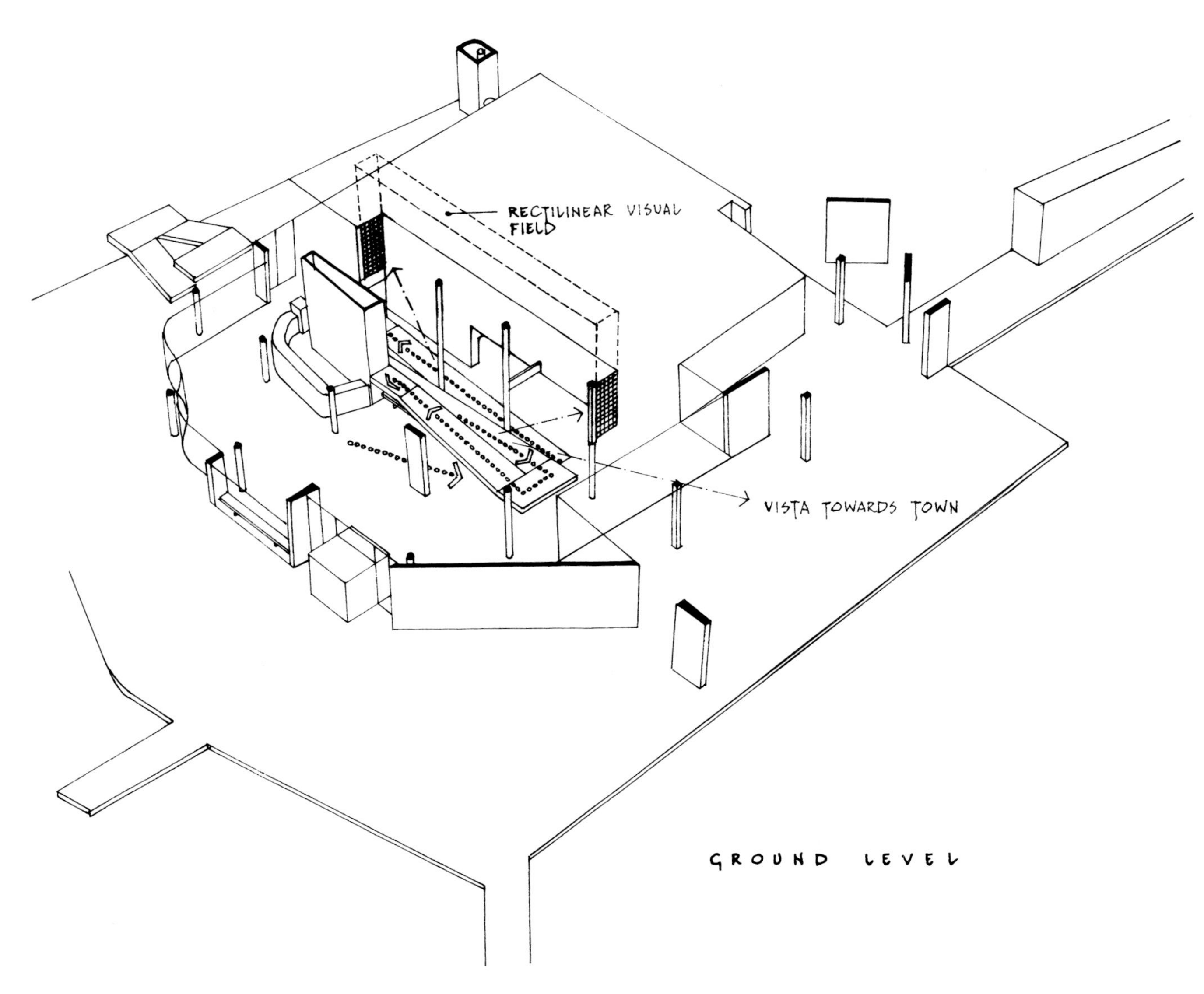

From the ground level entry space, the visitor is drawn towards the ramp by its own overhang, then moving upward at the side of the core on the first orthogonal grid.

On moving along this first part of the ramp, the eye focuses on a panel of glass bricks. These are repeated at the opposite end to form an implied rectilinear visual field.

After the first landing, we are moving away from the core, with vistas into the town. Finally, after one last turn, we are moving along the new imposed grid and the ramp is stopped by the core. Its oblique alignment on plan links it visually with the core.

MOVEMENT SEQUENCE 2

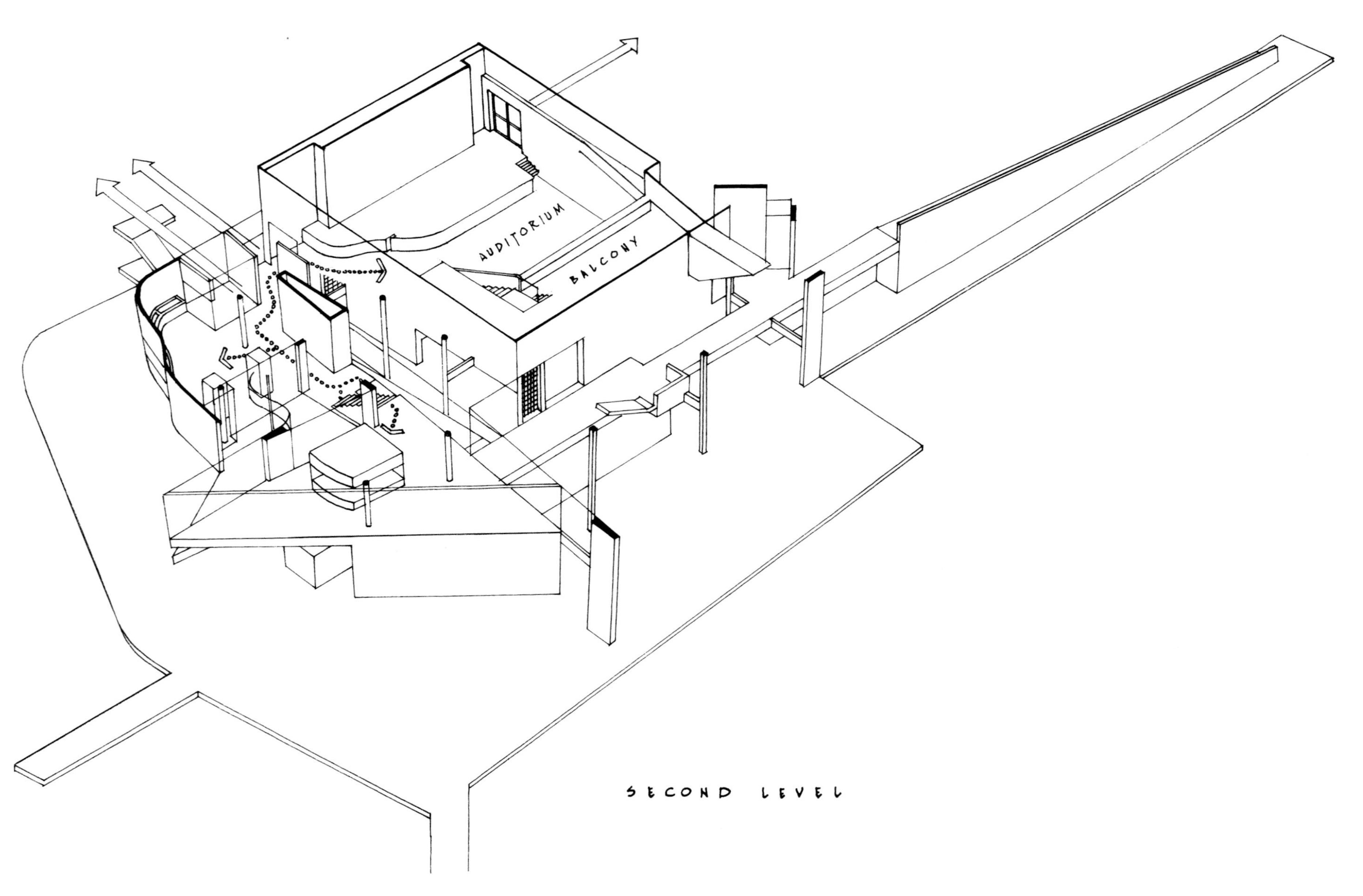

At the top of the ramp the visitor moves past the core towards either the curved viewing box, the triangular gallery, or more directly towards the auditorium.

Visitors start their introduction to New Harmony by seeing a film in the auditorium and on this direct route, movement is drawn by a view through a window directly ahead, then past a pivot door with a further view out; finally there is a right turn into the auditorium where a square window gives the last view out as visitors file to their seats.

This conclusion to the route, arrival in a contained box, is an appropriate termination of the movement sequence, psychologically representing arrival in a darkened enclosed space, in contrast to the openness of the route itself.

This final movement is directed by the curved stage edge, yet another counterpoint in the series of curves. Incised into this curve is a niche which marks out the orthogonal grid, the end of the stairs up to the stage and the start of the stairs to the gallery.

AUDITORIUM

AUDITORIUM

The auditorium is a sculpted rectilinear box in which the overhanging balcony becomes a device which keys in the stair ascending to it. The side gallery is incised into the adjacent side of the box.

The balcony edge extends in a very subtle gesture obliquely on the second grid along the longer side of the box at higher level. The major oblique in the box is the sloping floor with its regular rhythm of seats and the major shape in the box is that of the curved stage.

Only two colours are used to articulate these elements. A plain white is used for the walls, screen and main part of the ceiling, with a dark grey 'carpet' extending over the stage, seats and stairs.

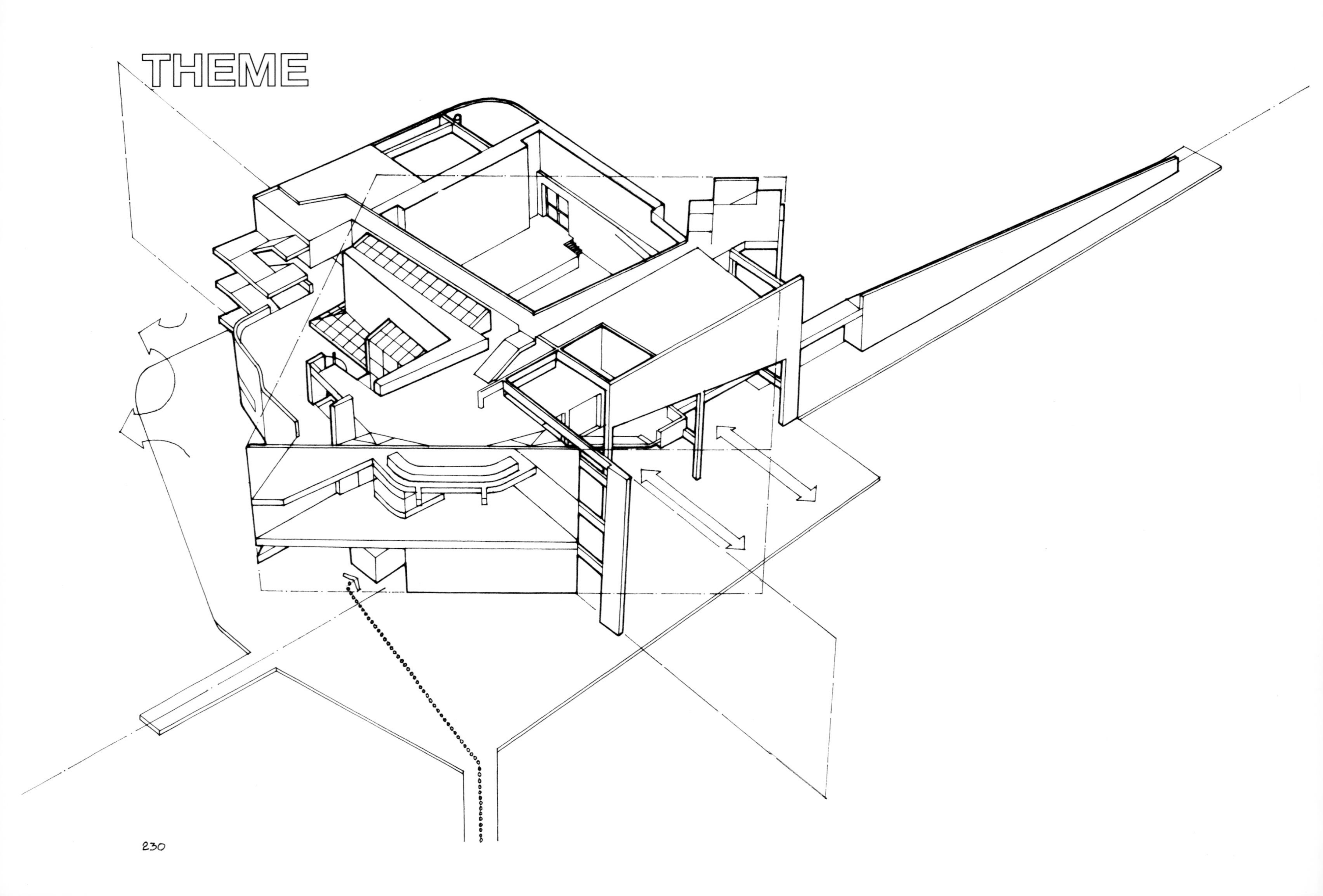
THEME

The design theme for the Atheneum is concerned with the exploitation of the possibilities afforded by imposing a slight shift to an orthogonal grid. The dynamic thrust of the main imposed tilted plane sets up a tension within the cubic box which is strongly reinforced by having placed against it a series of horizontal triangular planes held by the oblique vertical plane which delineates a third geometry, that of the imposed square.

The main route is a particularly dynamic furtherence of the tilted grid, its linear force puncturing the planes of the orthogonal grid before meeting the main oblique plane.

Functional elements such as the curved viewing box, ramp, auditorium and entry box are deployed in accordance with their precise role and are treated accordingly. The curve of the viewing box responds to the river. The ramp is placed centrally to give access to the various levels. Deep back lighting is provided by the light well and by the rooflight cascade over the ramp. Further deep lighting occurs behind the oblique screen. Stairs reinforce both the main oblique thrust and superimposed implied square.

Individually and in their totality, forms, spaces, routes, views and light have a symbolic as well as a practical role. They demonstrate indirectly and abstractly those ideals with which Meier links the building with New Harmony's rich and complex past. He does not speak to us with obvious and banal references. Instead, he uses allegory and metaphor in the way the elements are organized and the way the building is sited so that we are made aware of the river on which the town was founded, the sense of order and harmony inherent in Rapp's vision, and the intellectual utopian commitment of Robert Owen.

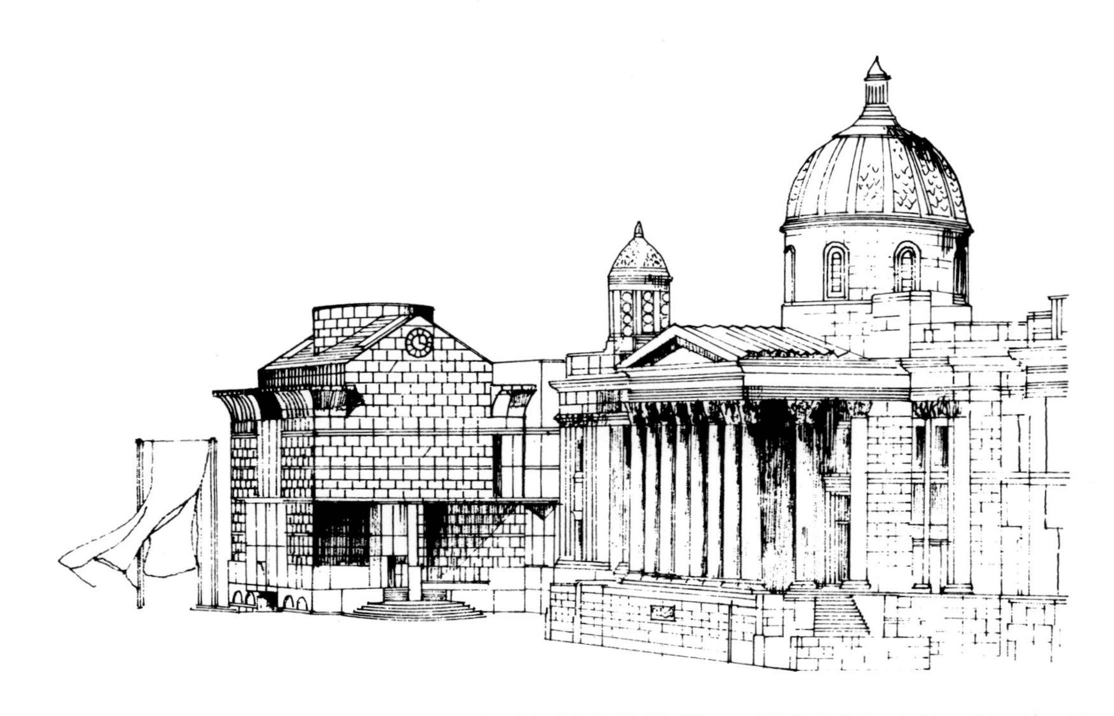

JAMES STIRLING
EXTENSION TO
THE NATIONAL GALLERY, LONDON
competition entry

JAMES STIRLING

The work of James Stirling is characterized by its diversity and an eclecticism which can be traced back to his wide-ranging architectural interests as a student at the University of Liverpool.

As the architect explains, his interests 'oscillated backwards and forwards between the antique and the just arrived Modern Movement,'[1] and like Meier, Stirling acknowledges a debt to his teacher Colin Rowe. A fascination for English Baroque architects such as Archer, Vanburgh and Hawksmoor can be contrasted with an interest in the Constructivists and Le Corbusier. English Victorian architecture, Frank Lloyd Wright's concrete block houses and Johnson Wax building are other sources, as are English castles, French chateaux, Bavarian Rococo, Venetian palazzi and English country houses.

First in partnership with James Gowan, followed by a long association and partnership with Michael Wilford, Stirling quickly acquired an international reputation with a series of important buildings in the fifties and sixties. This has continued, with each decade reflecting current preoccupations. The Ham Common Housing pays homage to Le Corbusier's Maisons Jaoul; Leicester Engineering, Cambridge History and the Florey Building show an interest in a glazed skin and hard planar components; St Andrews University

[1] Taken from 'James Stirling: Architectural Aims and Influences,' an address given at the ceremony for the presentation of the Royal Gold Medal by the Royal Institute of British Architects, R.I.B.A Journal, September 1980, pp. 36, 37.

Residential Expansion is articulated in pre-cast concrete, whilst 'high tech' prefabrication is in evidence at the Olivetti Training School at Hazelmere.

In the seventies and eighties, opportunities presented by competition-winning designs for buildings in strongly contextural situations in Europe and the United States have seen a change towards a greater attention given to massing and surface treatment. Again this reflects the general architectural shift away from abstract functional modernism towards a broader architectural canvas.

In these later works, as with the late work of Le Corbusier, Stirling has evolved an architectural language drawing on the breadth and depth of his interests. Again, as with Le Corbusier, the opportunities presented have coincided with already present skills in articulation together with a greater understanding of the role of architecture and particularly the effect of mass, space, surface, light and colour on the human psyche. The Staatsgalerie in Stuttgart, for example, makes reference to old and new, with 'Egyptian cornices, Romanesque windows, Constructivist canopies, ramps and flowing forms – a union of elements from past and present.'[2]

The unsuccessful competition submission by the Stirling Wilford partnership for the Extension to London's

[2] Ibid., p. 37.

National Gallery has been chosen to conclude the present study because the intended project aptly exemplifies the main argument put forward in this book. This has been to demonstrate that great architecture depends on an understanding of the role of architecture with reference to examples from both past and present; on a concern for a sensitive response to programmatic requirements in terms of the Genius Loci and prevailing culture; and also to show how the many layers of richness of architectural concepts can be revealed by diagrammatic analysis.

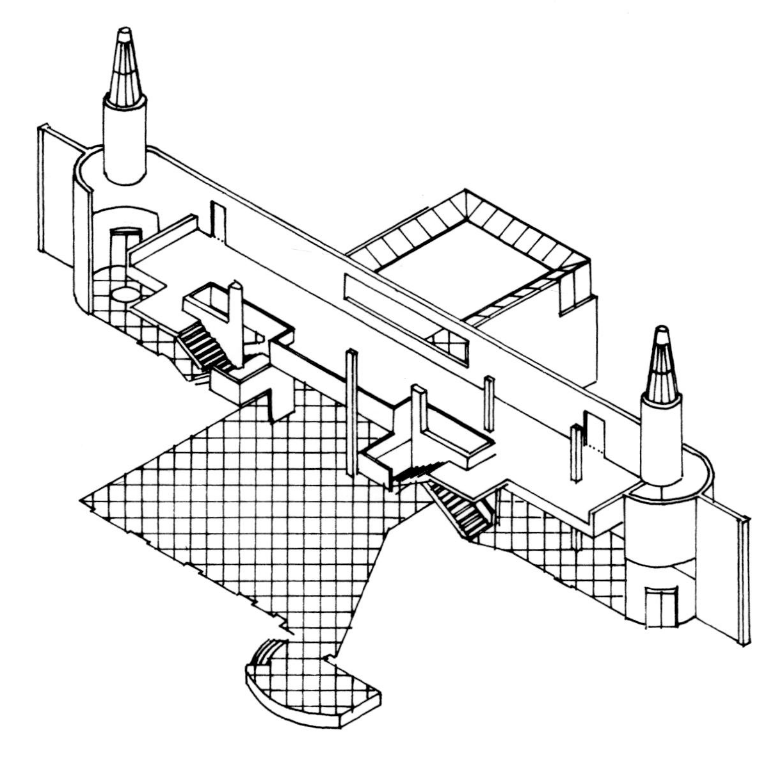

RICE UNIVERSITY 1979-81

SITE FORCES

As part of the triangle linked by the Mall, Whitehall and Birdcage Walk, and containing Buckingham Palace, Westminster Abbey and the Palace of Westminster, Trafalgar Square has considerable cultural significance. The presence of the National Gallery facing the Square adds an authority that becomes possible when a major art collection and the commemoration of a significant historical event combine in a key location.

Although flanked to east and west by substantial building masses, the square dissolves on its southern side, and the cultural forces are expressed through the media of the square and Gallery facade, which, despite the traffic flow and fragmented nature of the rest of the Square, act as a convincing symbolic ensemble. This is due to the way square and facade are locked together by symmetry and by the simple combination of monument, fountains and Wilkins' long facade, which acts as an urbane low-key backcloth, gaining in impact by its dominant position above the Square. Wilkins' use of the classical language with its distinctive hierarchy of elements, establishes the identity of the Gallery in a manner appropriate to the majority of its paintings, which were composed to a similar representational compositional code.

The key elements are the horizontal plane of the Gallery facade, punctuated by the central portico, set against the contained space of the square with its fountains, and the vertical feature provided by Nelson's column.

TRAFALGAR SQUARE

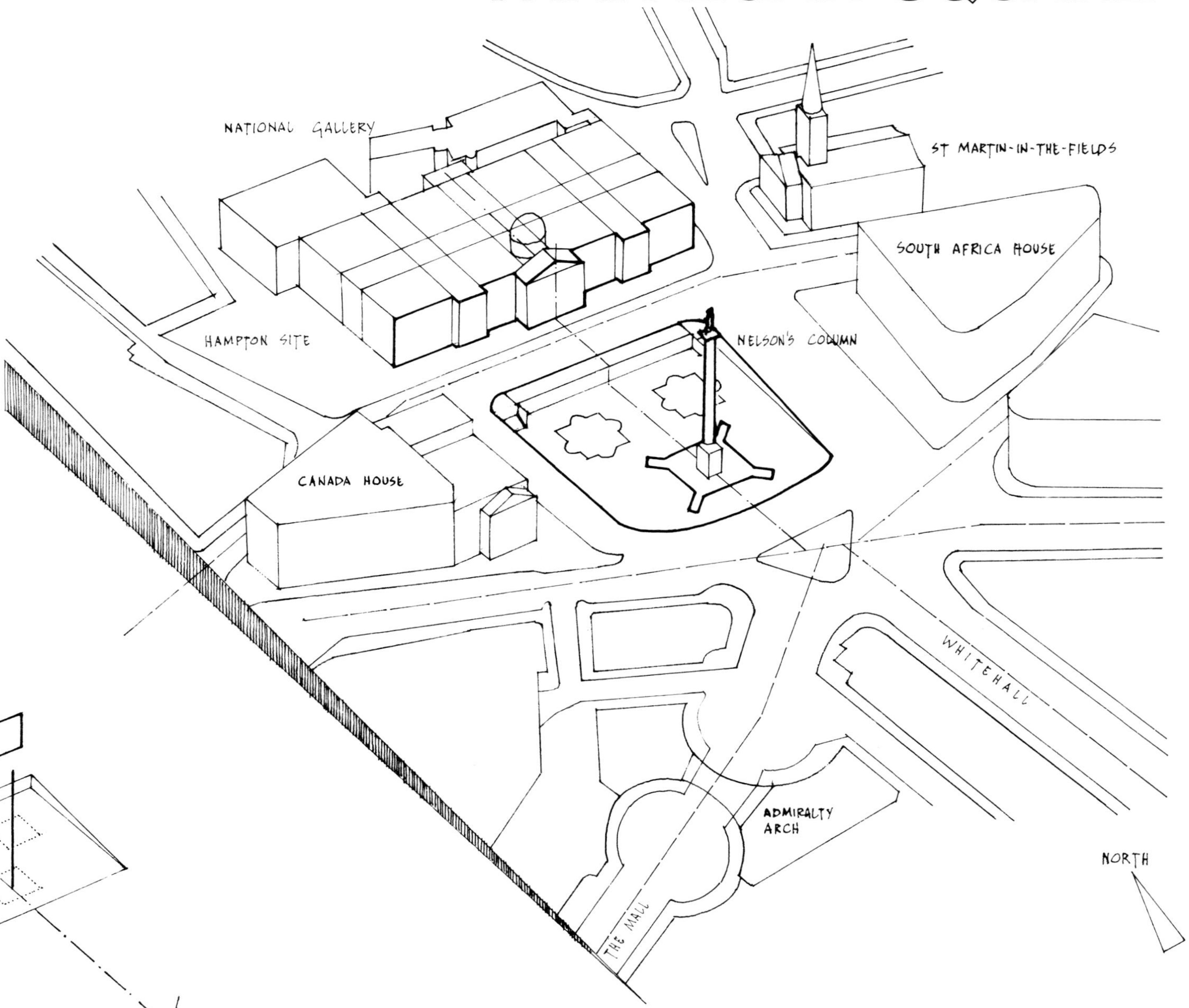

NATIONAL GALLERY
ST MARTIN-IN-THE-FIELDS
SOUTH AFRICA HOUSE
HAMPTON SITE
NELSON'S COLUMN
CANADA HOUSE
WHITEHALL
ADMIRALTY ARCH
THE MALL
NORTH

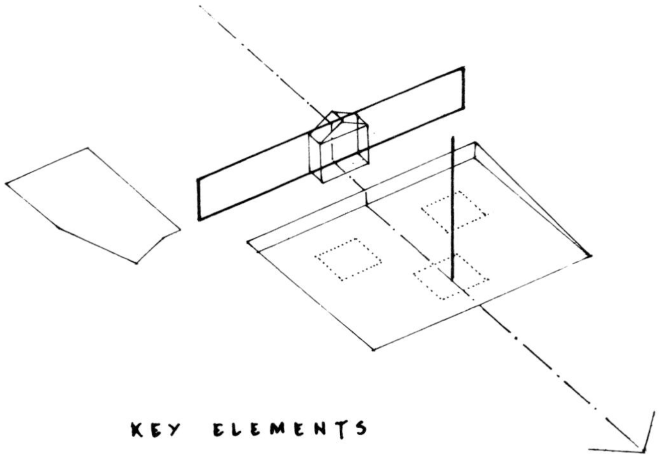

KEY ELEMENTS

NATIONAL GALLERY AND HAMPTON SITE

The principal facade of the National Gallery may be read as a plane with a rhythm of forward projecting pavilions. The three central pavilions express the main internal gallery circulation, whilst the central thrust of the entry portico defines the main lateral axis.

The dominant internal longitudinal axis, which also defines an important circulation route, is parallel to the external longitudinal axis which runs along the north side of the square. This internal axis provides a link opportunity to the proposed extension on the Hampton site, which is slightly wedge-shaped, diminishing at its southeastern corner, and there is a possible route through the site linking Trafalgar and Leicester Squares. (The route to Leicester Square ensures that Trafalgar Square forms part of the entertainment network of central London, giving a sense of one kind of node leading to another).

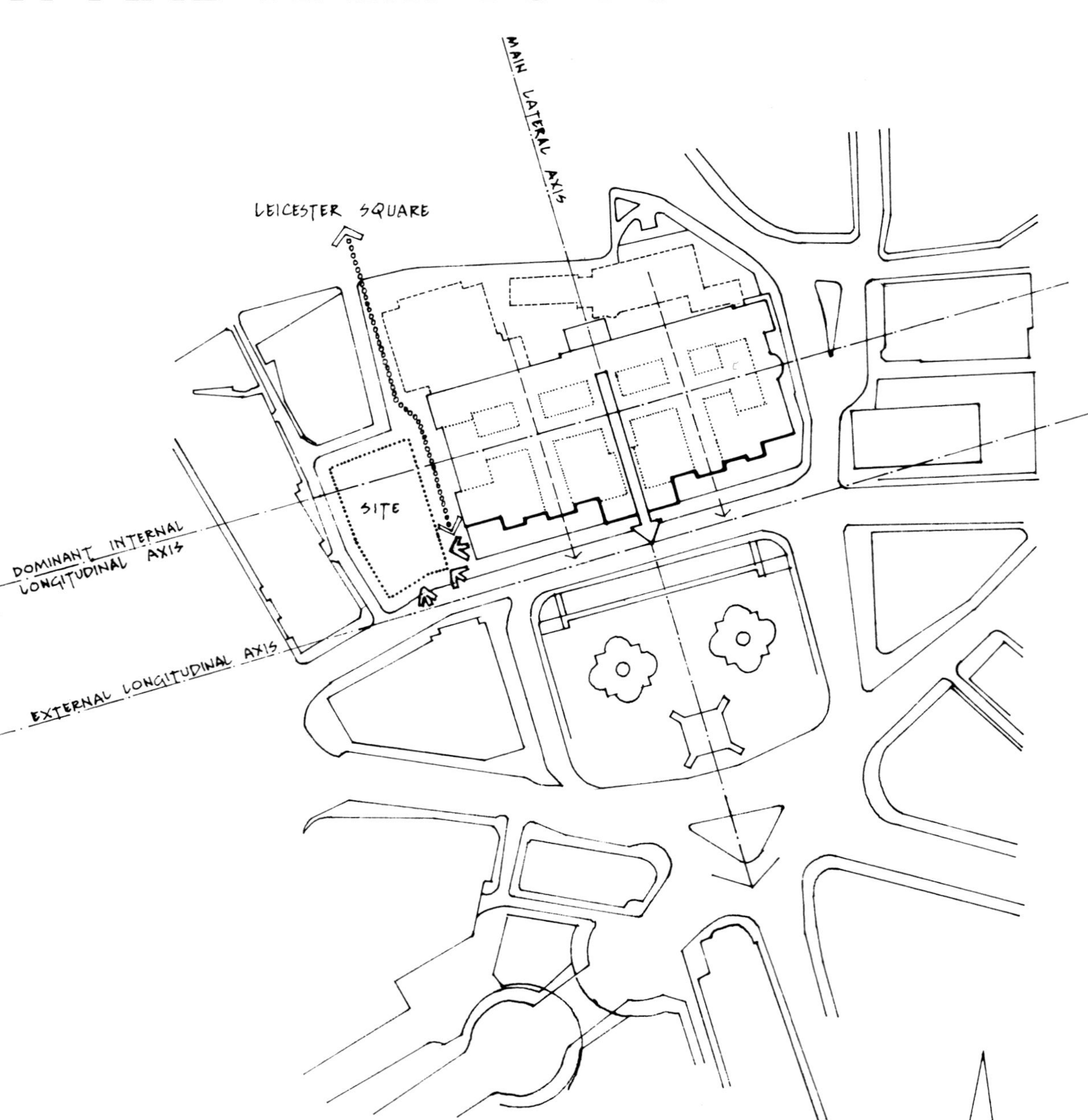

HAMPTON SITE

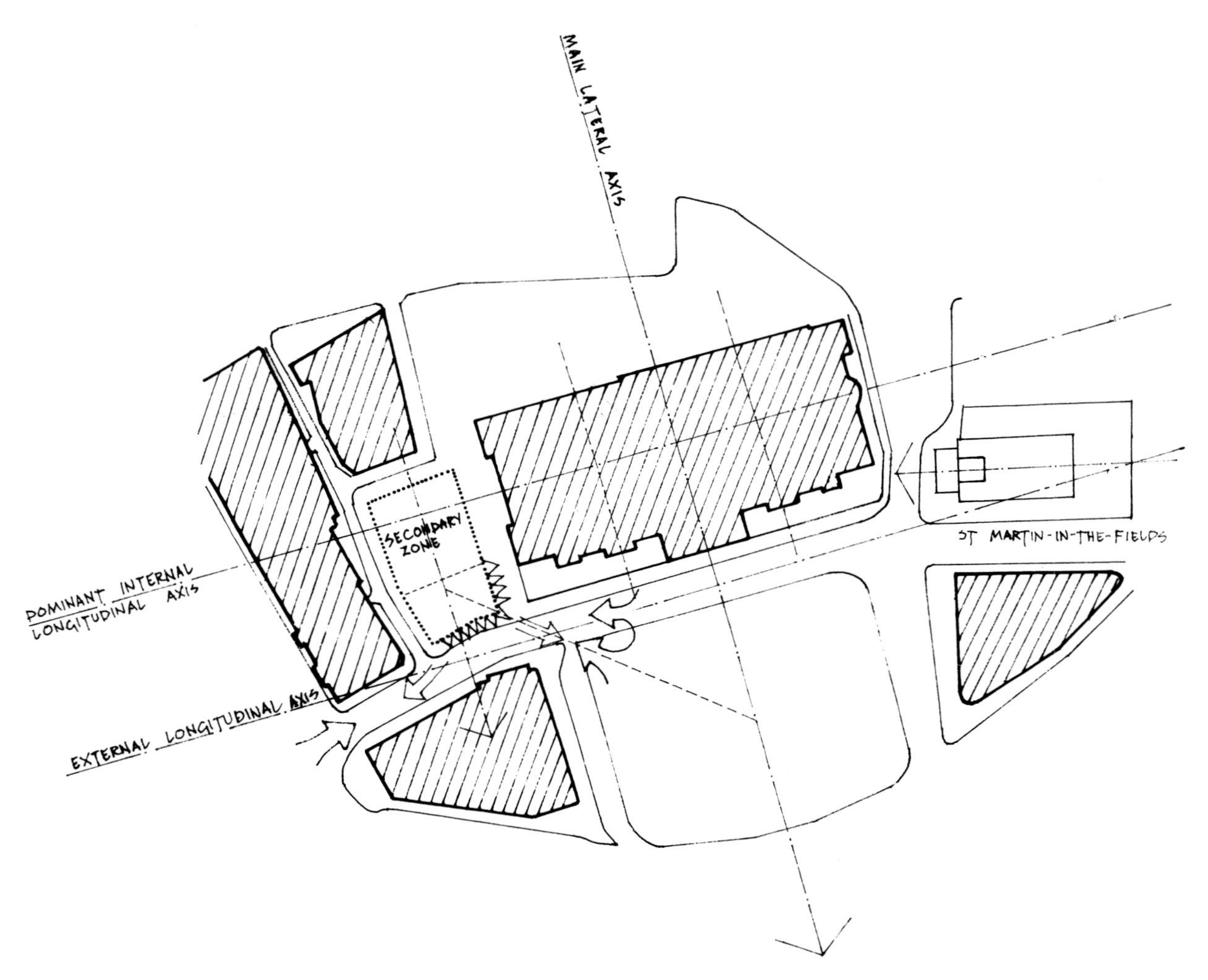

Although the extension site forms a potential stop to one end of the main Gallery facade, and can in this sense be compared to St. Martin-in-the-Fields, the two situations are quite different. Whereas the latter is in a relatively exposed position with its main longitudinal axis pointing towards the Gallery, the former is more enclosed and its main axis runs laterally at right angles to the longitudinal axis of the Gallery.

The site's location creates a link potential between it and Trafalgar Square, inducing a diagonal condition at the southeastern corner of the site. Because it is the access zone, visible from Trafalgar Square, this edge of the site offers the greatest potential for development. There is a secondary zone to the rear.

NATIONAL GALLERY

The Gallery may be read as a horizontal slab with a front and a back. This horizontality is furthered by the layering in which the plinth establishes a base, with a cornice defining the elevational 'canvas.'

An intermediate horizontal band separates the two rows of windows (the upper being blind) which animate the facade. Conforming to classical design principles, the elemental disposition is hierarchical, with clearly defined axes controlling the main gallery organization.

HORIZONTAL SLAB

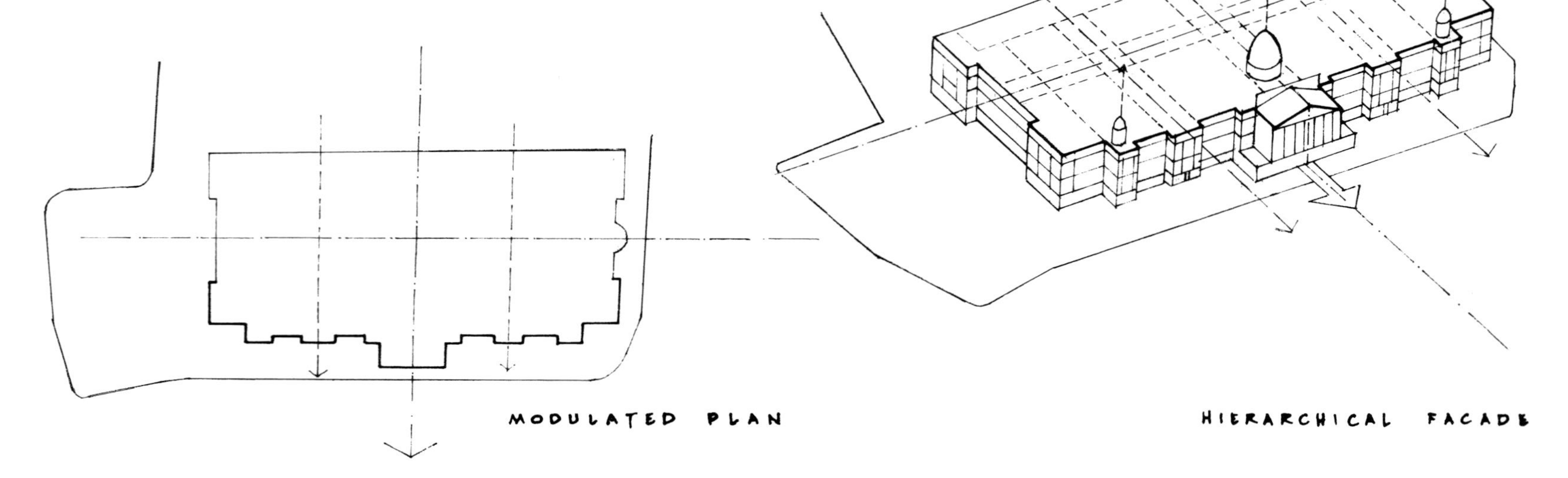

Because of the length of the facade, the external profile of the plan is carefully modulated so that the main axes of the gallery arrangement receive external expression. This occurs in the pavilion-like projections identified by columns, and at entry by a pedimented portico with a dome immediately to the rear.

Care is given to stopping the facade at each end with first a projection surmounted by a dome, followed by a setback where the actual corner occurs. The twin domes at each end have a base which ensures a distinctly vertical thrust.

The surface treatment is low-key with a concern for balance between verticals and horizontals. Although the facade is predominantly horizontal the clusters of columns give localized vertical readings so that when viewed obliquely the facade emphasis becomes vertical.

The use of stone has several consequences for the National Gallery. The Gallery has a mass rather than a planar reading. In combination with the classical language, the use of stone gives the Gallery monumentality, authority and dignity. The sculpting of the mass with pilasters, cornice and columns gives considerable surface richness with the play of light and shadow.

THE EXTENSION

The generic form is linear in acknowledgement of the linear site axis, a static slab alongside the National Gallery. A pavilion projects forward, reduced in width because the site diminishes at this point.

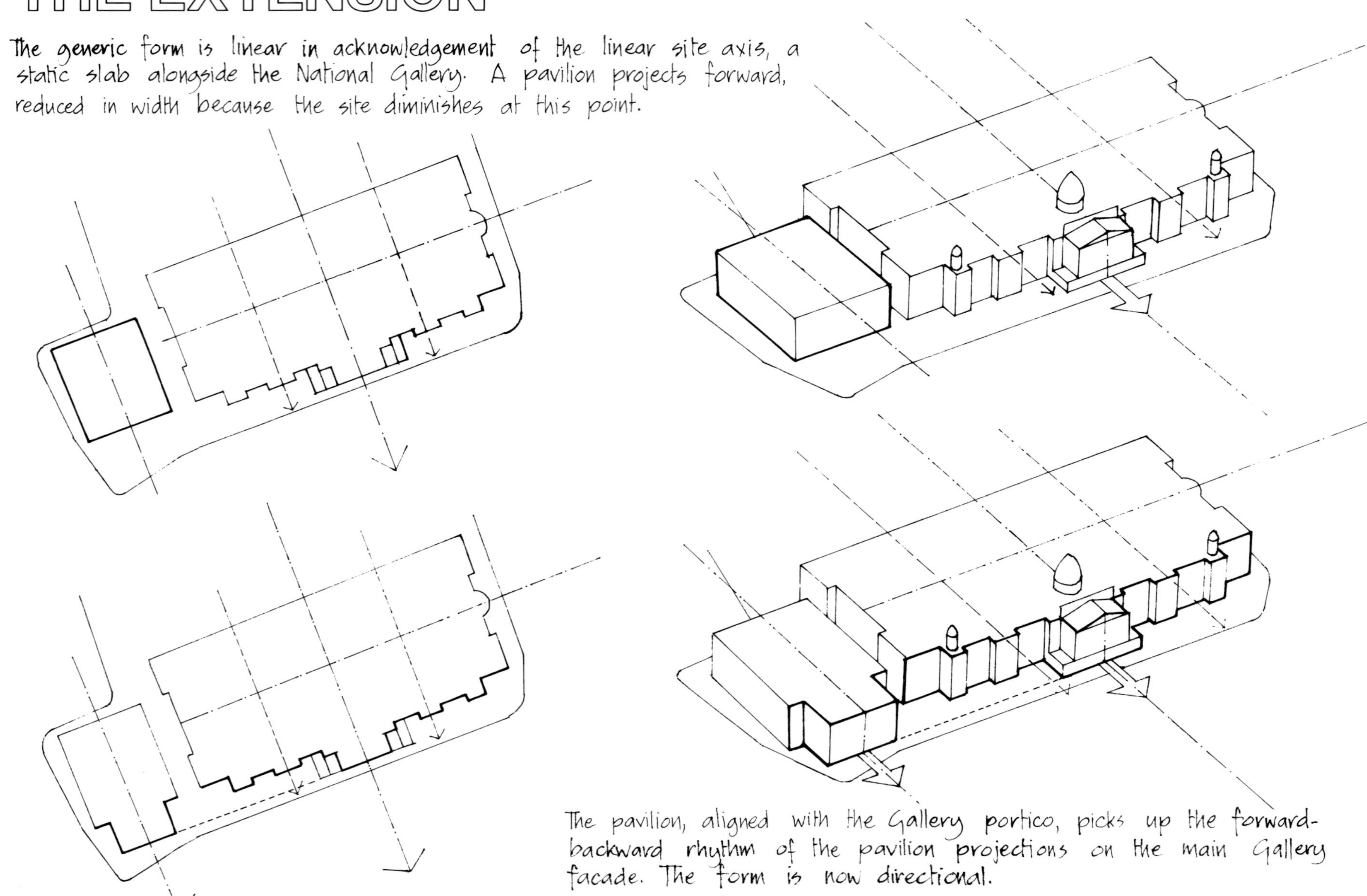

The pavilion, aligned with the Gallery portico, picks up the forward-backward rhythm of the pavilion projections on the main Gallery facade. The form is now directional.

The remainder of the form is echeloned in support of the forward thrust, each setback being aligned with a gallery setback.

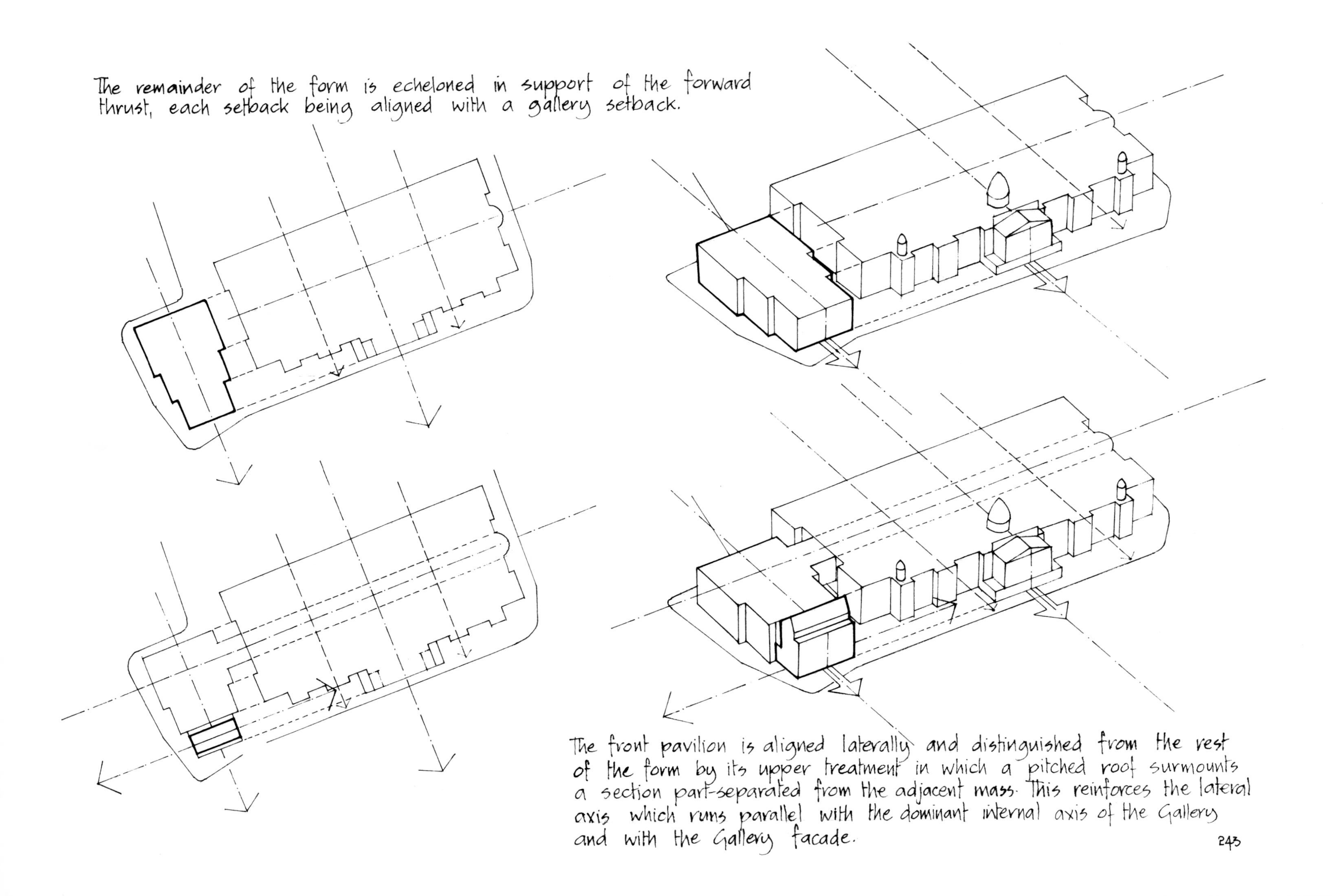

The front pavilion is aligned laterally and distinguished from the rest of the form by its upper treatment in which a pitched roof surmounts a section part-separated from the adjacent mass. This reinforces the lateral axis which runs parallel with the dominant internal axis of the Gallery and with the Gallery facade.

THEME

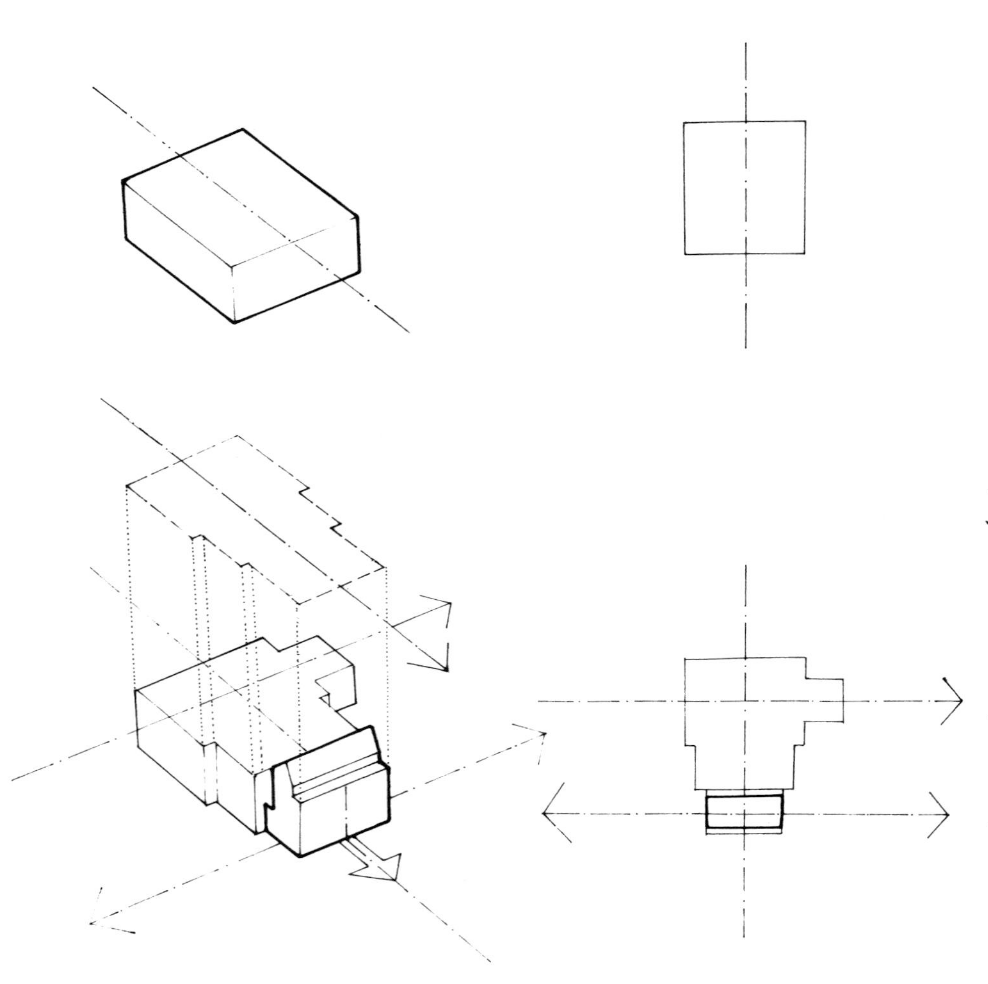

By separating the forwardmost projection of the echeloned mass, Stirling and Wilford recognize zonal differences in the site and establish a powerful contrast with the rest of the form which nevertheless remains part of the echelon system. This transforms a formerly static mass into a dynamic configuration, establishing the theme of the work, which is to exploit the opportunity afforded by a contextual situation to animate and dramatize one part of the form in contrast with the rest.

This dynamism is induced by the axial shift, and by the contrast of the vertical linearity of the forward pavilion when compared with the horizontal, slab-like remainder; opportunities for animation are provided by entry and by identification of the role of the building, particularly in relation to the existing Gallery.

The relationship between the pavilion and the rest of the extension affords a further opportunity to reconcile two geometric configurations, the symmetrical directional organization of the whole and the lateral thrust and part independence of the pavilion itself.

The theme is also concerned with the 'two worlds' encompassed by the programme, the Neo-classical world of the National Gallery and the twentieth-century world of the extension. This semantically rich opportunity is realized through the structure, materials and architectural language used in the extension.

PAVILIONS

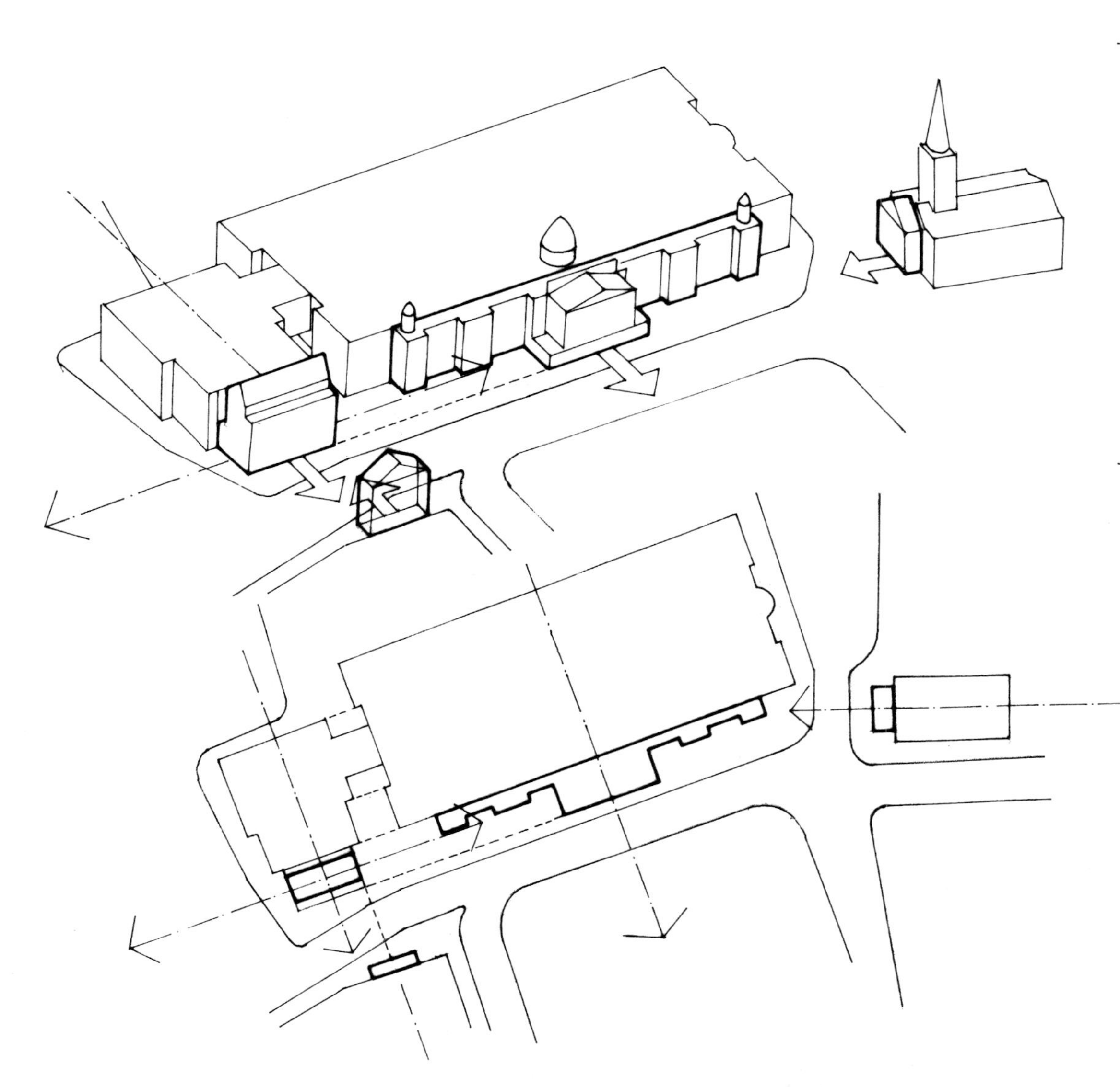

The idea of the portico as a pavilion defining entrances is a major device employed by the Neo-classical buildings around Trafalgar Square.

Immediately opposite the site is the portico to Canada House whilst the portico of St. Martin-in-the-Fields provides a similar incident, this time acting as a stop to the east end of the Gallery facade.

The pavilion to Stirling and Wilford's extension stops the west end of the Gallery whilst being aligned so that the eastern end of the pavilion is placed on the centre of the portico opposite.

THE PAVILION

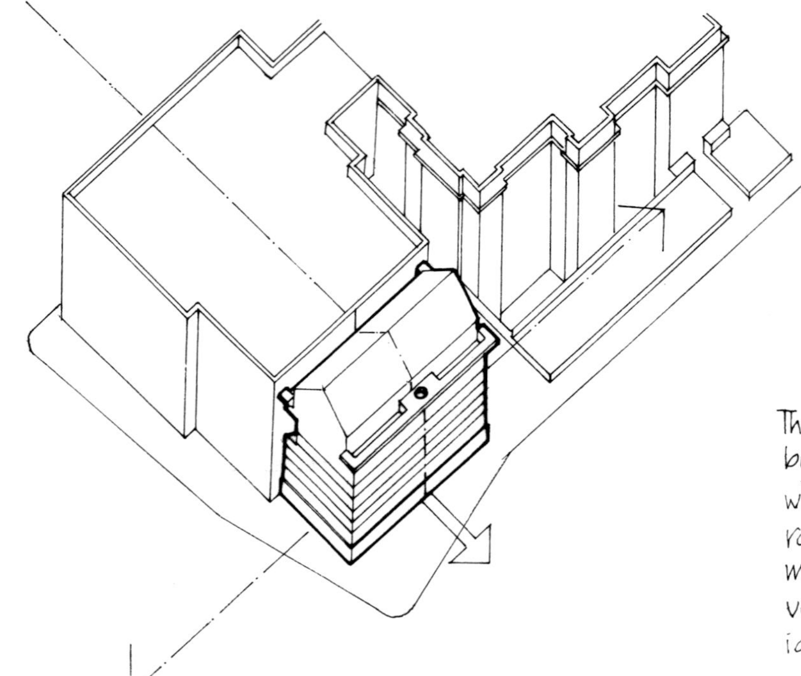

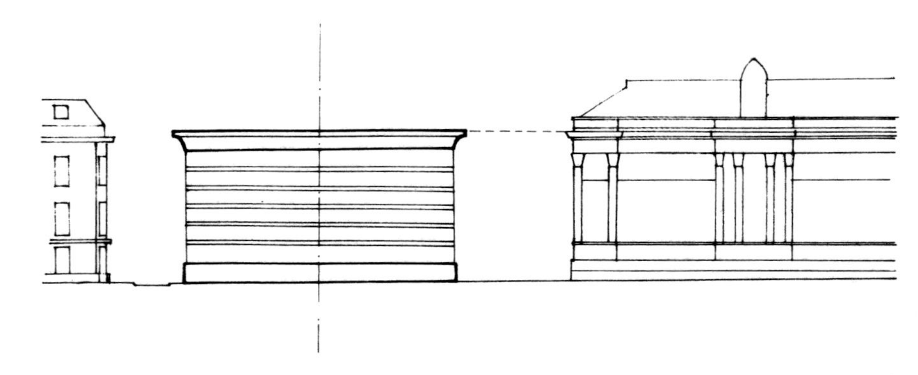

The lateral axis established by the alignment of the pavilion is reinforced by horizontal indentations in the facades, by a plinth and cornice which echo these features of the National Gallery, and by the pitched roof, which defines the axis. Although this linear emphasis echoes the main horizontal layering of the Gallery, it contrasts with the localized vertical reading at the south west corner, establishing a separate identity for the extension pavilion.

This separate identity creates a problem at the point of junction with the main configuration, particularly where the cornice meets the adjacent mass. This is resolved by attaching the cornice to the mass by two 'brackets,' one at either end. This is reflected on the south side by indentations in the cornice so that when seen from above, it appears to have a flat top which joins the mass at either end and also at the centre.

The horizontal indentations in the Portland stone facade give it a 'mass' reading similar to that of a Renaissance palazzo (as the architects describe it). This is carried through with the provision of a base (plinth), middle and top (cornice) as with the National Gallery.

ENTRY

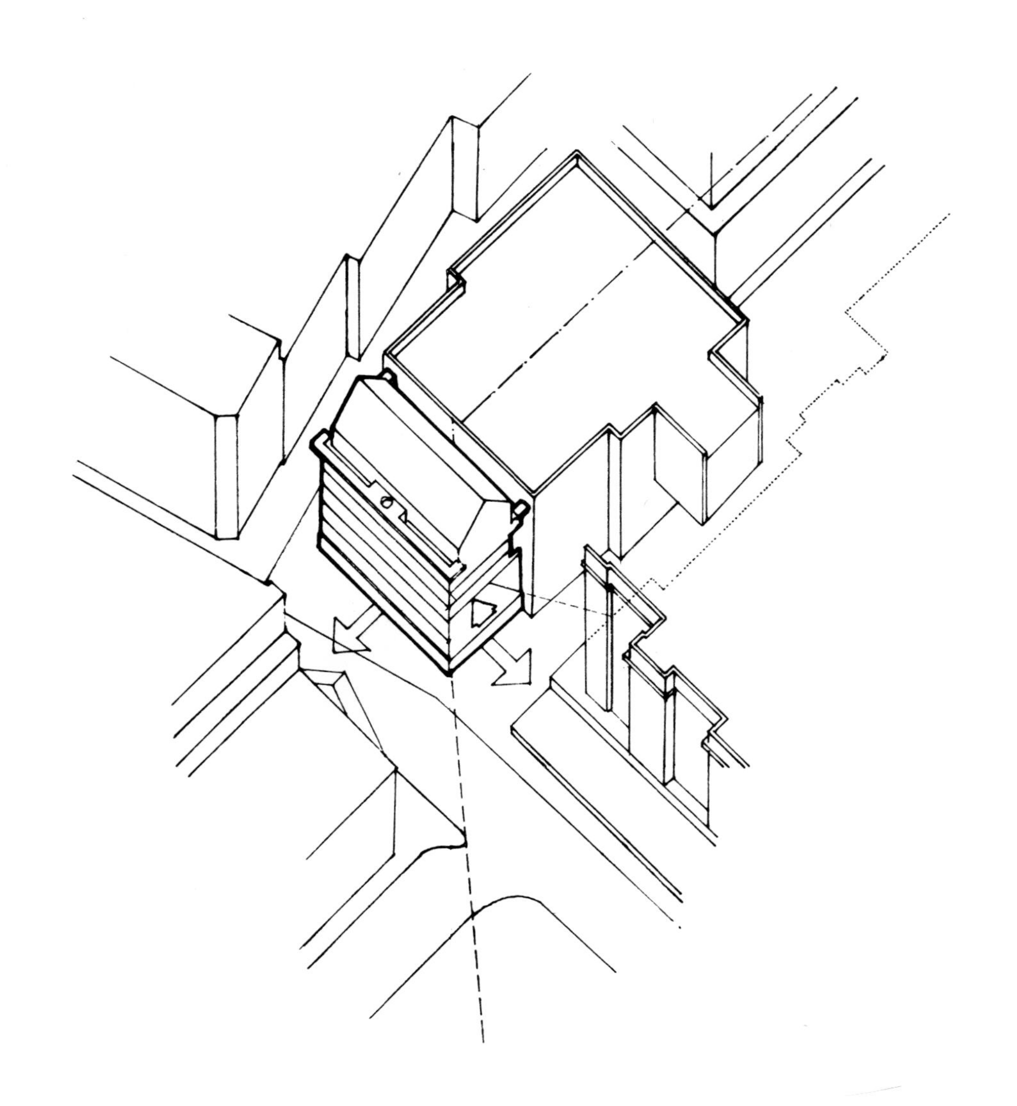

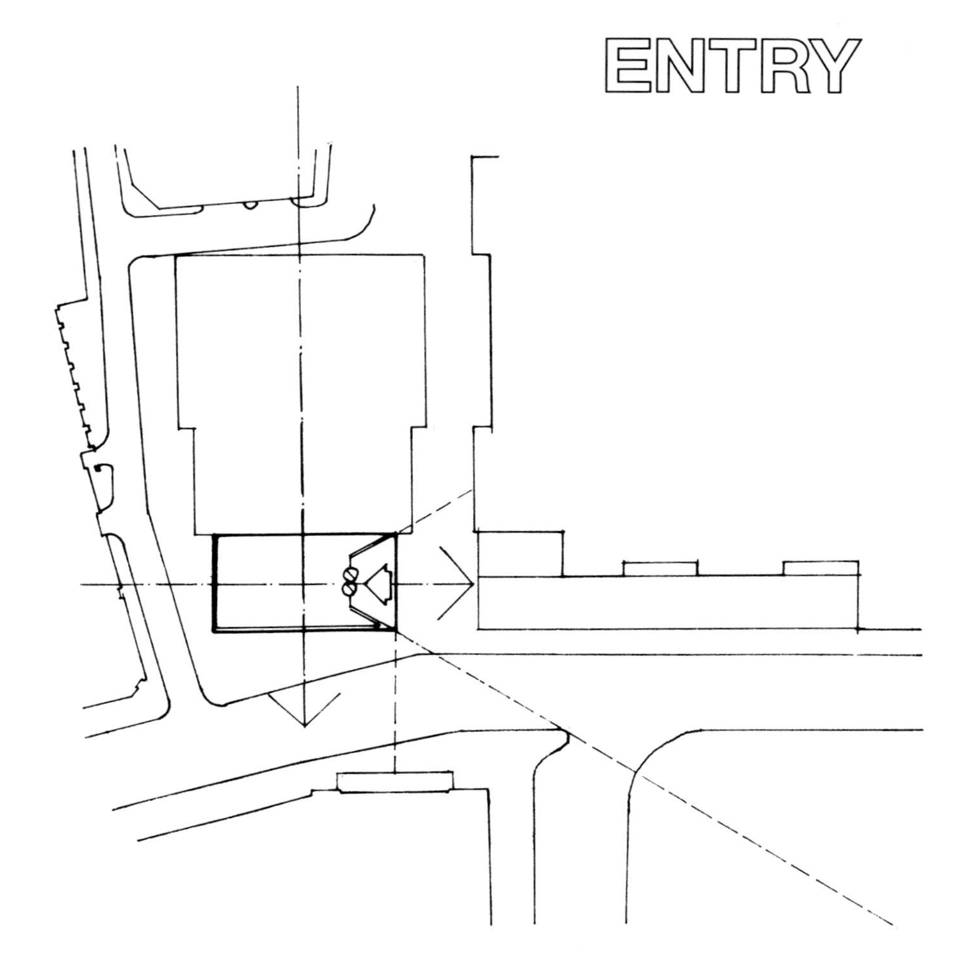

The forward pavilion may be read as a linear box, which becomes directional with the wedge-shaped opening in the lower part of the end facing the National Gallery. This erosion of the mass establishes a link with the space fronting the Gallery and (on oblique) with Trafalgar Square.

CANOPIES

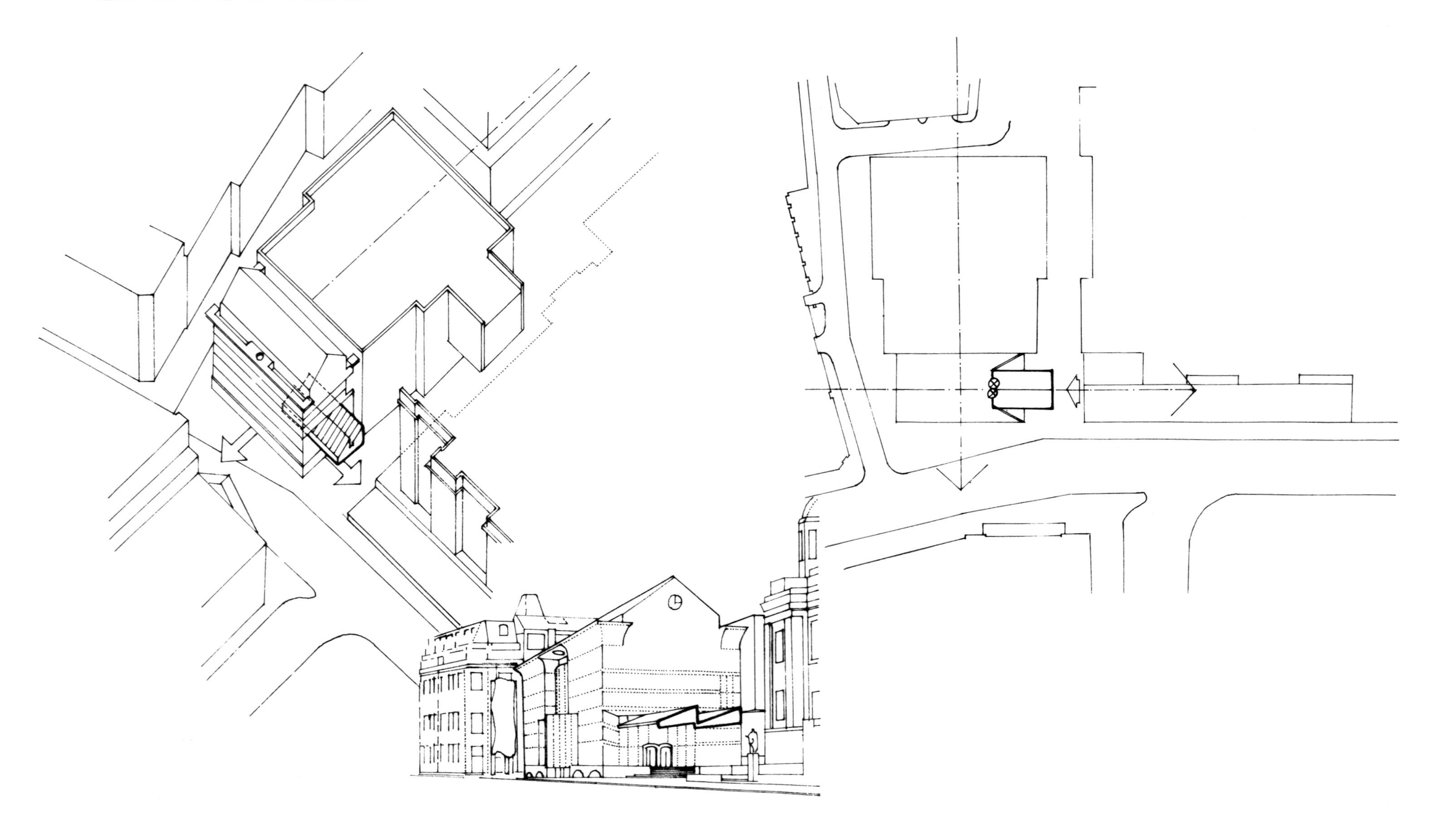

If the wedge-shaped opening invites entry and expresses a link with Trafalgar Square, further definition of entry is added by twin translucent projecting canopies.

These exert a linear rhythm, the more forceful because two obliques are placed alongside each other. Their shape, position, length and translucent quality suggest that they are sliding through the box rather like those swords used by magicians who 'pierce' a lady in a box several times.

The canopy exerts further directional thrust, reinforcing the linear axis and the link with the space fronting the Gallery.

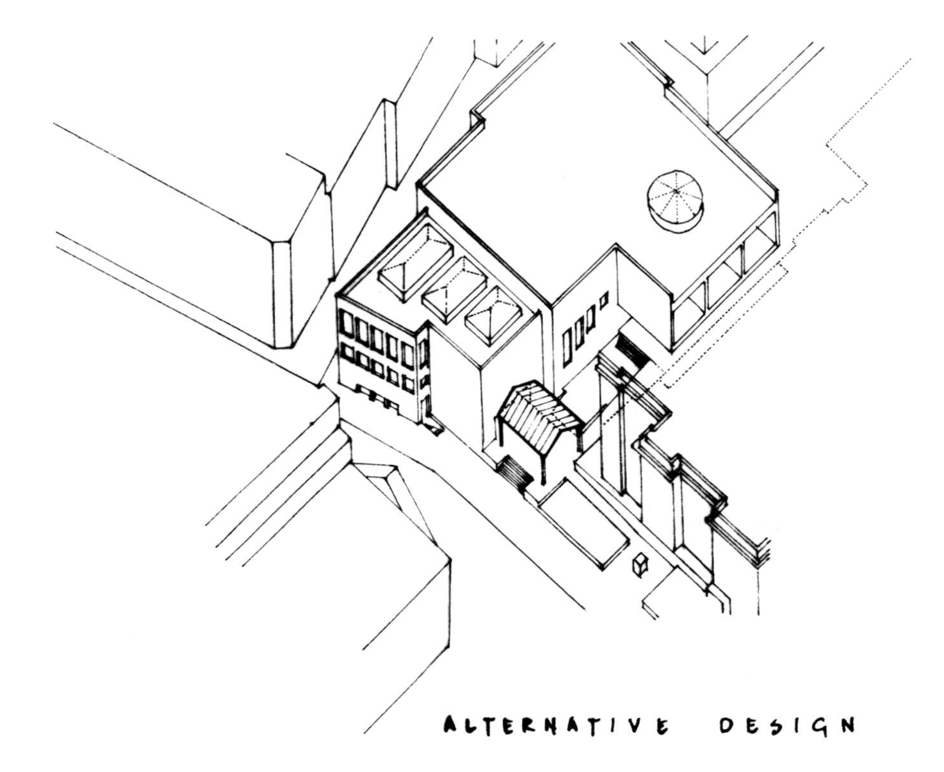

ALTERNATIVE DESIGN

In an alternative design submission (scheme C), Stirling and Wilford proposed a forward pavilion with an angled projection which picks up the alignment of Pall Mall East as it enters Trafalgar Square. Compared with the preferred solution, this results in a restless distortion of the forward mass, which, despite its echelon, fails to lock satisfactorily into the rest of the configuration.

For this design the canopy is a simple pitched roof, giving a serenity necessary to alleviate conflicts caused by the pavilion which it fronts.

CIRCULAR STAGE

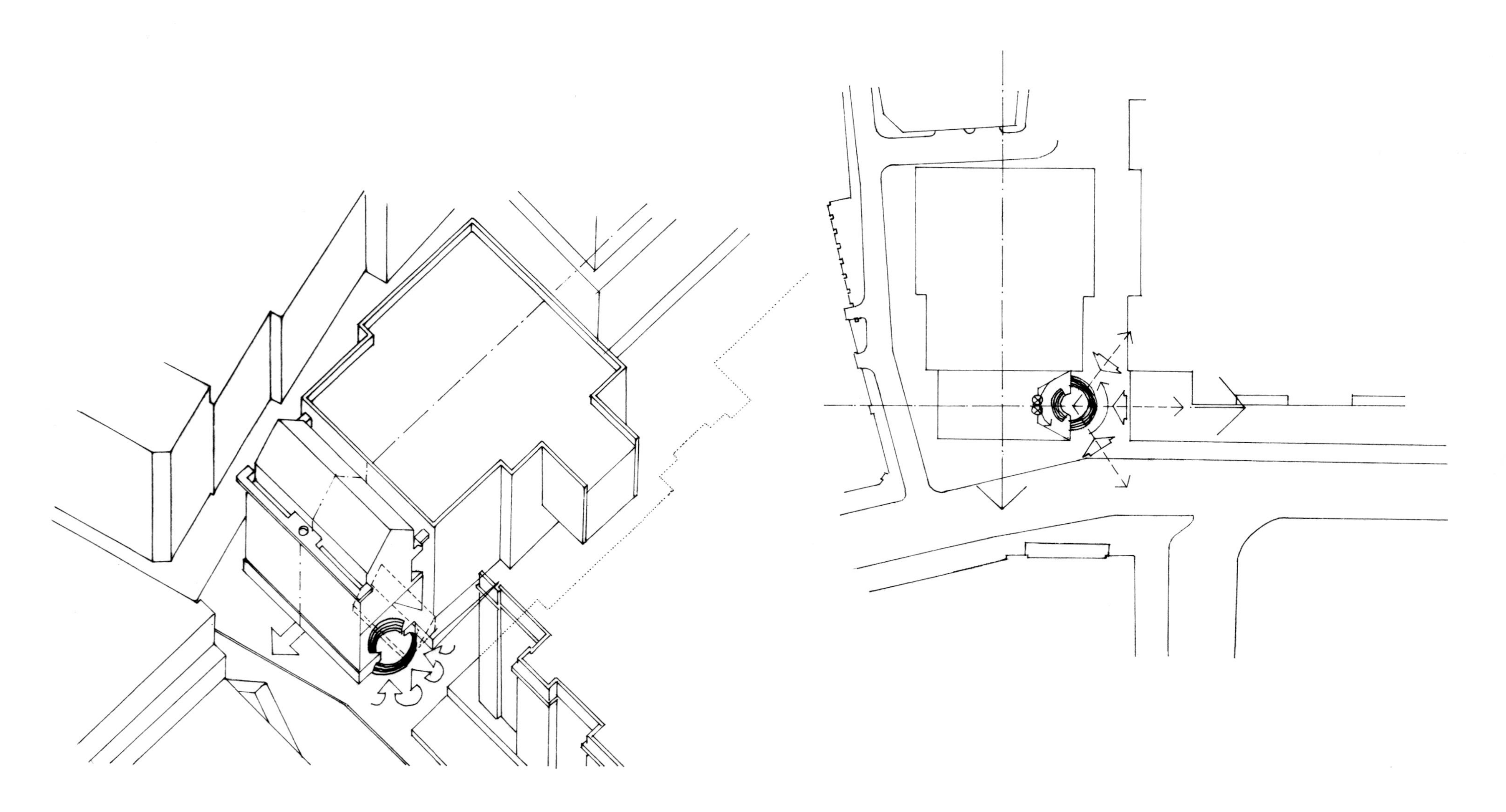

By opening up the box at one end, an inside/outside space is created. This opportunity is furthered by the circular place (described by the architects as a 'stage') which creates a kind of proscenium opening with a circular revolving stage.

This entire device, the wedge-shaped opening in the box and circular stage set into the podium, is a focus which pinpoints entry decisively, being supported by the translucent canopy above. The richness of the solution is compounded by the range of forms used and by their interacting energy components, which comprise: the dramatic and powerful opening into the box; the wedge-shaped 'embrace' of the sides; the stability/movement of the circular stage, itself given an added dimension by being half into and half out of the podium; and finally, in sharp contrast to the rest, the poised elevated thrust of the canopy, gaining in impact by being translucent, by having a double rhythm and containing twin obliques.

SOUTH FACADE

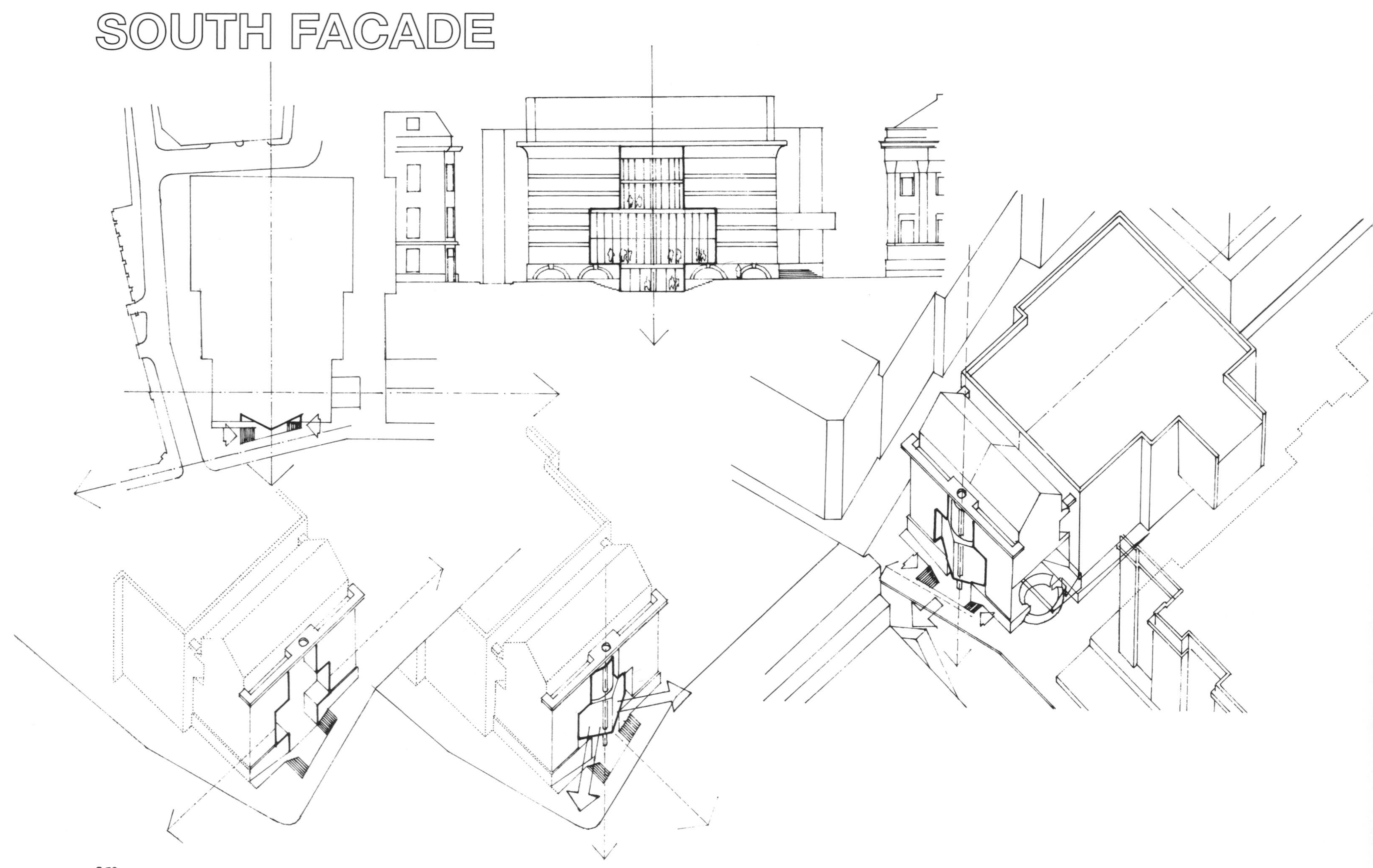

The south facade facing Pall Mall East has its mass reading broken through a double piercing by glazed bays which give views from the building along Pall Mall East and towards Trafalgar Square. It is as if the mass has been pulled sideways centrally. Delineating the dominant internal axis of the configuration, an oblique pointed form thrusts outwards, being surmounted by a more serene curved bay. This erosion also disrupts the cornice, now seen centrally as a slender plane, this being made explicit by the hole which reveals its depth.

The force of this disruption continues downwards, piercing the ground plane and podium in the form of an entry point at a lower level. This is reached by stairs, the outer boundary of which is set at an oblique angle, taking up the external direction of the pavement and of Pall Mall East.

As with the entry facade, elements are compressed together between plinth and cornice. The impact of these forms is increased by the fact that they are transparent (in contrast to the solidity of the mass which they pierce), and by the way their vertical rhythm of glazing bars contrasts with the horizontality of the facade indentations. In furtherence of this vertical/horizontal contrast a downward thrust is also in operation with the presence of a central column which pierces the floors behind the glass, becoming external where it penetrates the baseline at plinth level. Although this column does not coincide vertically with the circular hole in the cornice, the one externalizes the other, the circular hole alluding to the idea of vertical penetration made manifest by the column.

The final directional thrust is at pavement level, where the oblique frame to the stairs giving entry to the shop completes the 'display' whereby a series of primary forms comprising transparent curved and oblique membranes in the vertical plane are juxtaposed against an oblique erosion of the ground plane in such a way as to animate and to an extent dramatize the ensemble.[1]

Four semi-circular windows are located in the plinth, giving light to the shop, this symmetrical deployment increasing the sense of monumentality, whilst the rhythm of curves gives a serene base, countering the dynamism of the punctured mass above. In this sense these windows belong first to the plinth or base, and also to the horizontal mode of the facade plane, their distinctive shape identifying their special function.

[1] This is similar to a familiar tactic in Le Corbusier's work whereby several contrasting forms are compressed together to dramatize a composition for a particular reason. See my analysis of the Monastery of La Tourette, Le Corbusier: An Analysis of Form. (Second Edition 1989) Van Nostrand Reinhold (International) Co. Ltd., London, pp. 267-98.

DESIGN PRINCIPLES

WINDOWS IN THE PLINTH

The windows, in common with several other major elements in the design, perform several roles. These may be defined in terms of the way the theme of the work is interpreted by four constituents of the design strategy :

1. To ensure that every element observes the geometric properties of the configuration as a whole (this being an echeloned symmetrical mass with a directional thrust).
2. To ensure that every element in the design serves its particular function with a shape appropriate in usage and meaning.
3. To ensure that elements conform to what has been perceived as the overall function of the extension within its context and (more specifically) to the theme of the design. (To animate and dramati e one part of the form in contrast with the rest in terms of the 'two worlds' of the program).
4. To ensure that elements observe a correct relationship to their own particular part of the design, this to take account of the geometric characteristics and properties of each specific part of the design.

If we take these in turn in respect of the windows in the plinth :

1. The position of the windows supports the overall symmetry of the form
2. Their shape identifies a particular function, (that of lighting a space below ground level as opposed to giving a view out).
3. Their treatment (with keystones) has classical overtones which allude to the image of the building as a palazzo, this being part of the general perception of the relationship between the extension and the National Gallery.
4. Their semi-circular shape ensures a serene rhythm which supports the passive role of the plinth as the base and foundation of the composition.

MODERN AND POST-MODERN

Although the pierced cornice has Post Modern overtones in its ambiguous series of readings (solid from below, indentations from above), as does the explosion out of the box by twin transparent forms, the integrity of the Modern Movement functional credo is retained. This is evident in the way each device signifies a multi-faceted specific function (the upper fenestration gives a view out whilst recognizing internal differences of use – the curved bay signifies galleries whilst the oblique bay signifies the more animated movement at entry level). Similarly, the presence of a column which pierces each floor behind glass before emerging below the base plane of the pavement has both a Modern and Post-Modern flavour: Modern in the way a structural member behind glass shows the freedom given by twentieth century technology, Post-Modern in the device contradicts the mass reading of the 'palazzo.'

CONFRONTATION AND CORRESPONDENCE

The entire scenario of the extension thus sets out to confront its National Gallery neighbour with several propositions. First it is an independent adjunct, a point made by the architects who explain this in terms of its horizontality when compared to the nearest corner of the National Gallery: second it is linked to its neighbour not only physically, but also by its shape and alignment – the pavilion is symmetrical, it projects forward like the portico to the National Gallery and the mass reading and palazzo image correspond to these features of the National Gallery; third, in contradiction to these correspondencies, the extension sets out to challenge its neighbour. Whereas the National Gallery is straightforward, uncomplicated, honorable and true, the south elevation of the extension is complex, has several layers of meaning, and is by comparison an intellectual puzzle which speaks through metaphor and allusion of present-day attitudes to history, art and technology.

PRIMARY FACADE

The design poses a problem as to which facade (entry to the east or the Pall Mall facade) should be primary. As expressed, the primary reading is held by the entry facade by virtue of its verticality and by the implied pediment provided by the gable end to the pitched roof: as the architects explain, the facade gains additional force by being read as 'a face... looking sideways towards the National Gallery, beyond St. Martins-in-the-Fields, and obliquely into the square.'[2]

This tactic relates to the architects' description of the forward pavilion as 'the head on a body where the rest of the anatomy does not have the same density of external features.'[3]

The distinctive presence of a small clock face confirms the symmetry of the gable and increases the sense of 'personality' which, when combined with the 'ears' of the cornice, makes this a friendly and 'approachable' facade.

[2] Taken from the architects' comments in their explanatory article, Architectural Design, 56 1/2 1986, p. 70.
This 'face' is similar to that used by Stirling and Wilford in the Fogg Museum at Harvard University, see Architectural Review, July 1986, pp 26-33.

[3] Ibid p. 71

WEST FACADE

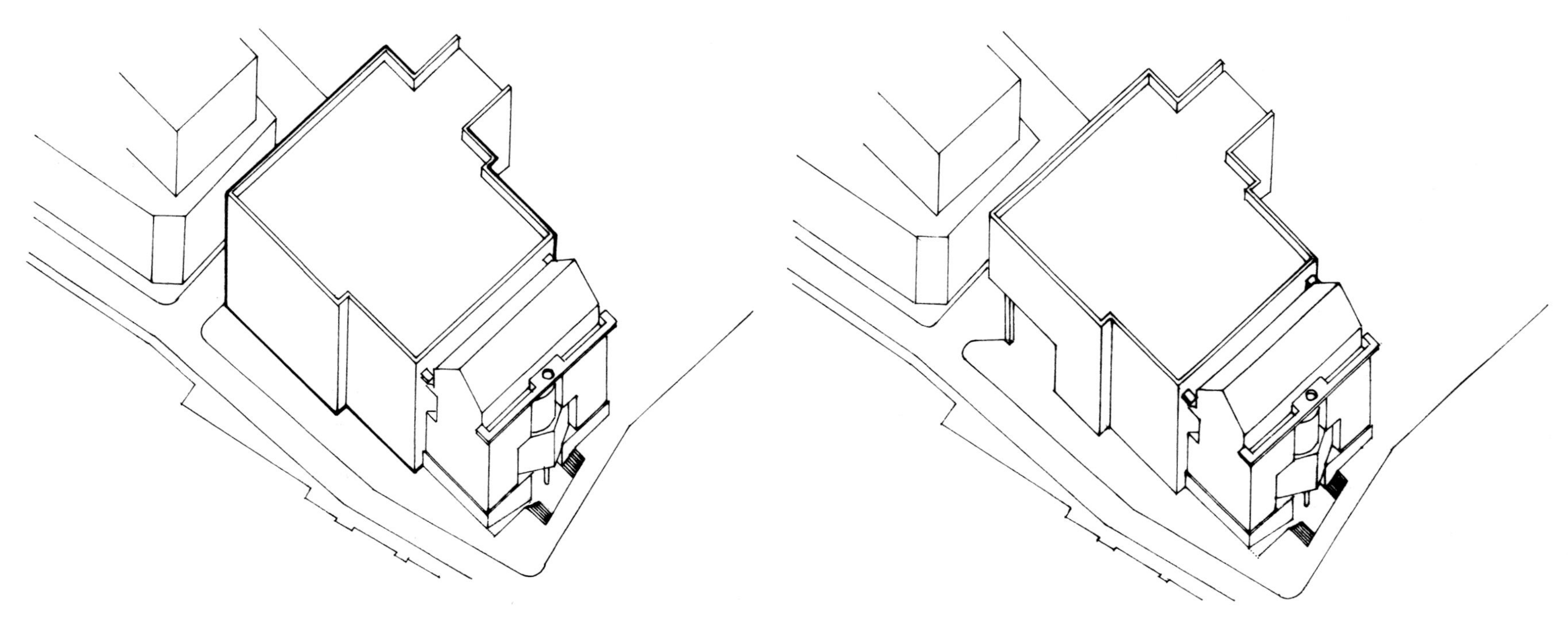

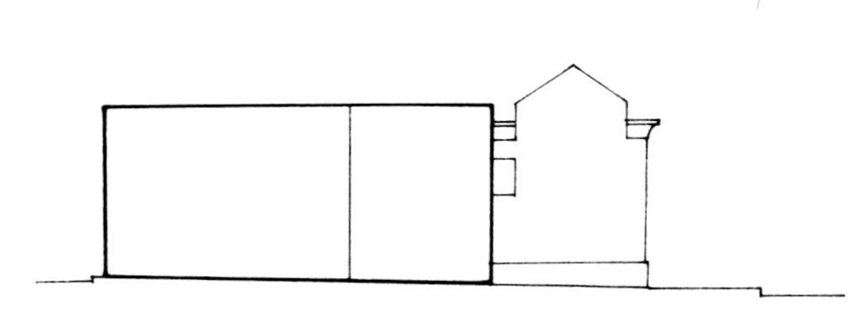

The generic slab has a ground-hugging boxiness that remains with the echelon transformation. Moves to diminish this are put in operation by breaking the rear mass at mid-point with a decisive erosion in the north-west corner to allow vehicle access under the form

DISTORTION

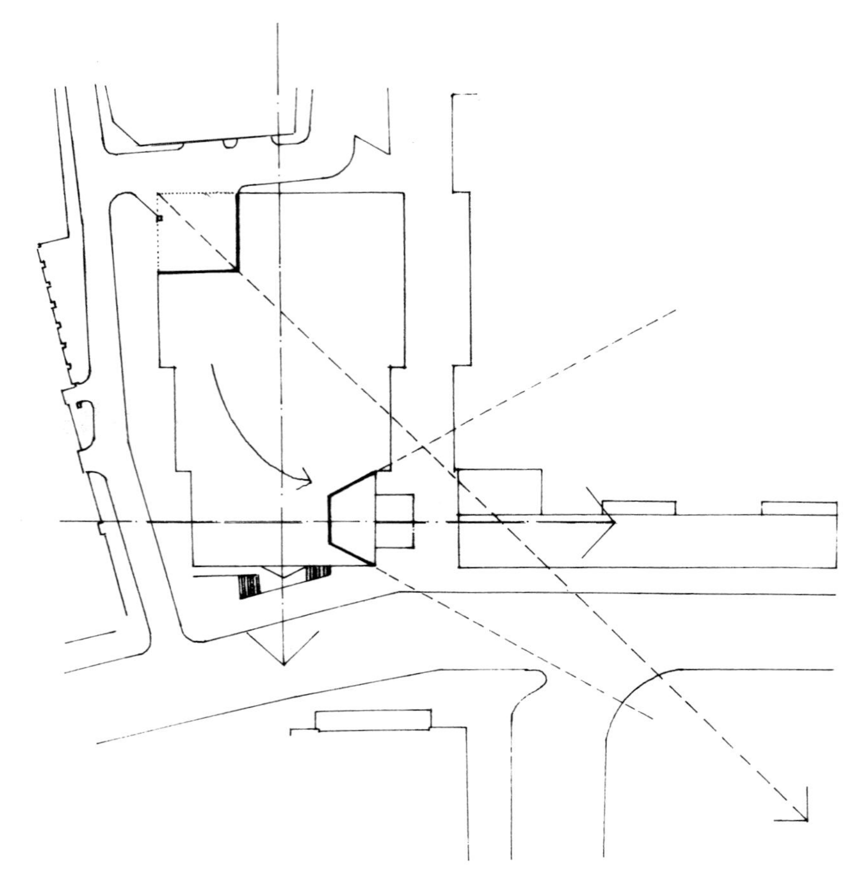

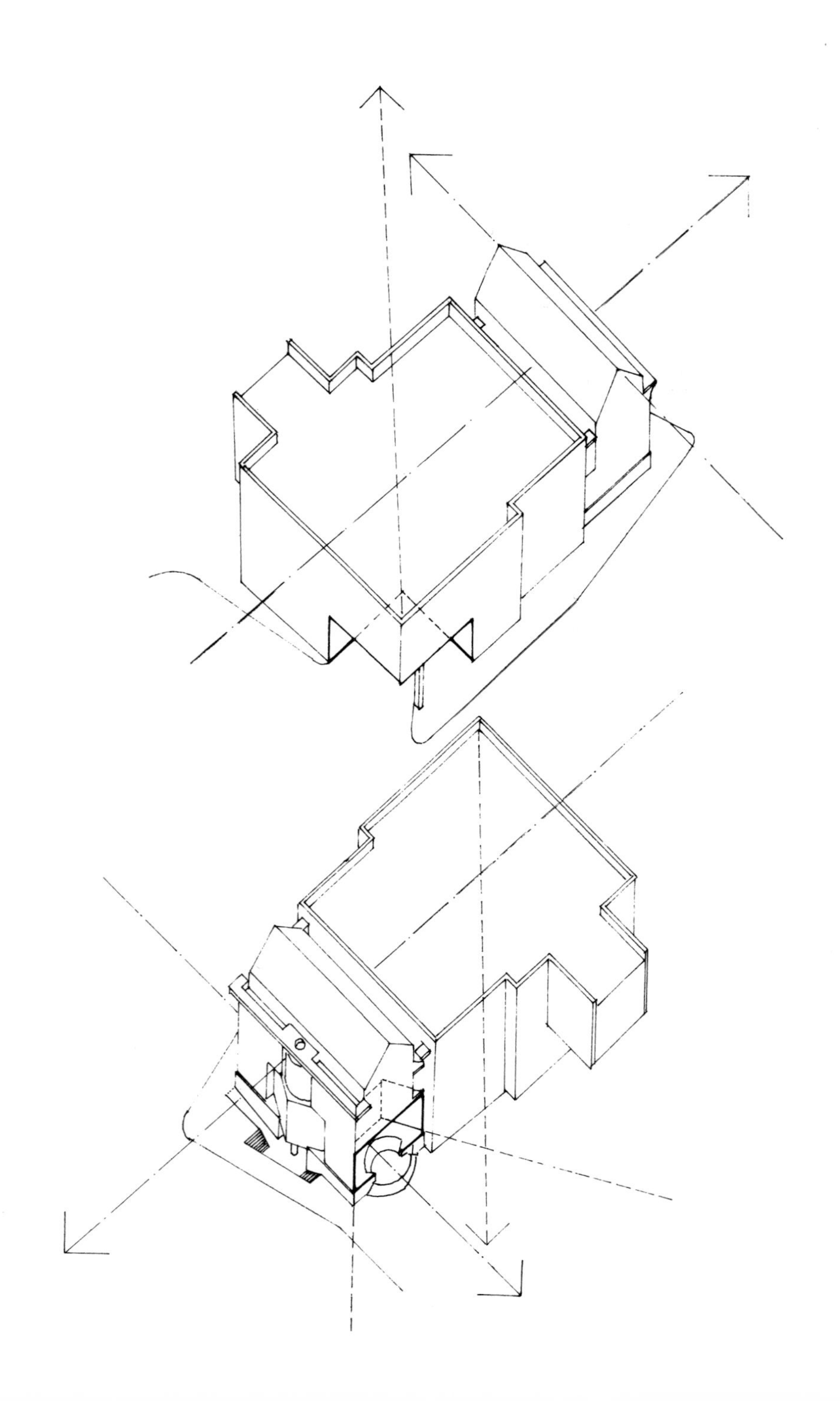

This device has several consequencies. It confirms the 'back' reading of this part of the ensemble: raising the mass creates the impression that the rear boxes are no longer ground hugging; it also significantly erodes a corner, which, although secondary to any reading towards Pall Mall or the square, can be read as opposite to these in importance or potential. The erosion also sets in motion an oblique, which, if carried through, continues towards Trafalgar Square.

The symmetrical echelon form is thus distorted by this turning motion. It is securely held by many other devices, particularly by the central thrust of the longitudinal axis, but there is pressure exerted on the form in a particular direction, i.e. towards the entry point where it faces Gallery and square, this being the main zone of the configuration.

MASS OR PLANES

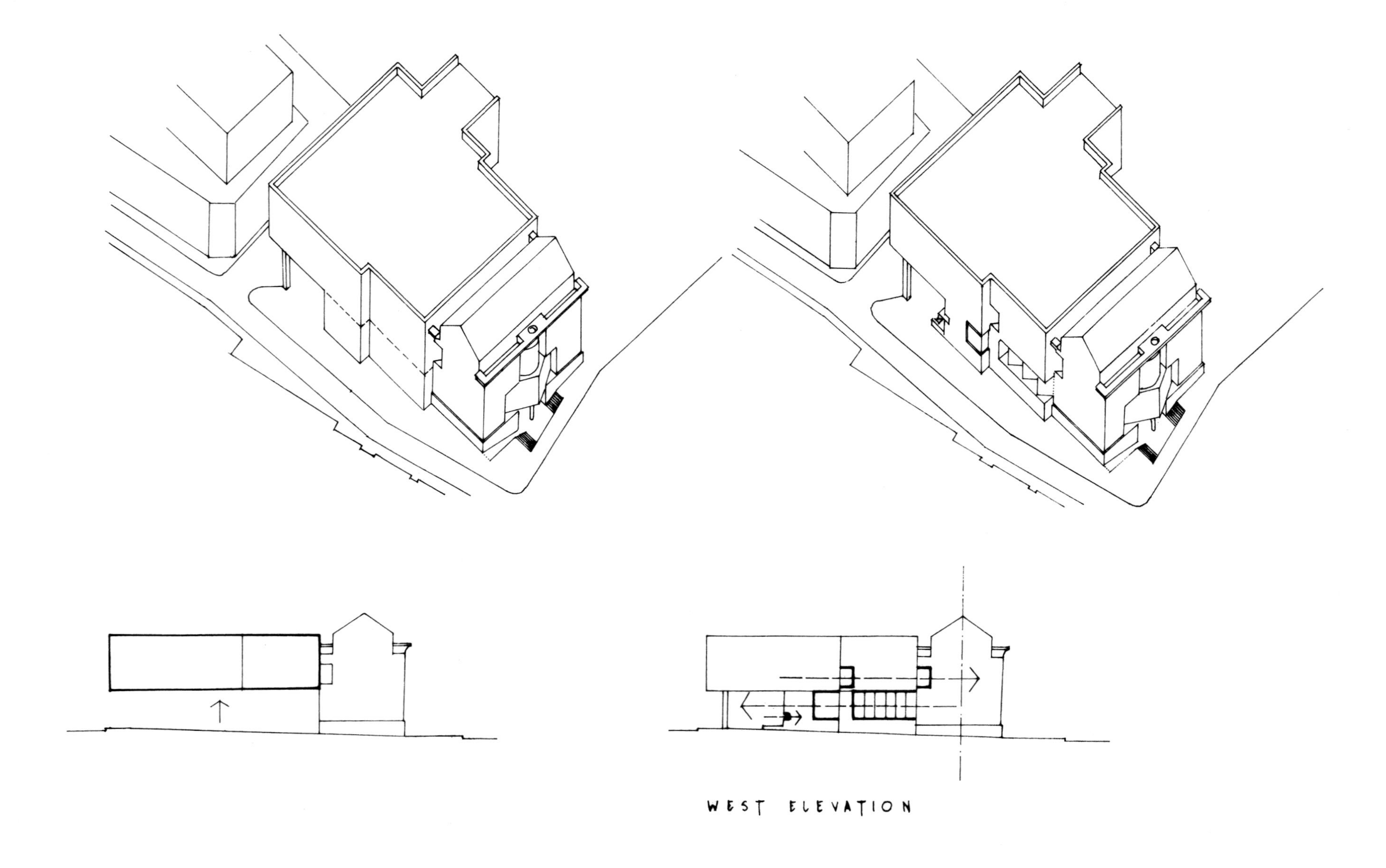

This elevated section sets in being an implied continuity in the separation of upper from lower, expressed in the west elevation by fenestration incisions. These incisions affect the mass reading, particularly at the lower (entry) level where the mass dissolves into a series of planes.

This dichotomy, between a mass or planar reading for the rear of the configuration, is affected by the way the edge of the mass is raised above the flat roof to give a distinct skin or planar reading. This is furthered by the way the incisions push and pull in different directions suggesting both separation and linkage between the two boxes. This movement is stopped by the forward pavilion, although the incision immediately below the cornice bracket attaching it to the rear has its own forward thrust.

The result of these devices is that the elevation loses its mass reading and becomes taut and planar, although it is also part of a series of boxes, which by implication could all slide into each other.

SLIDING BOXES

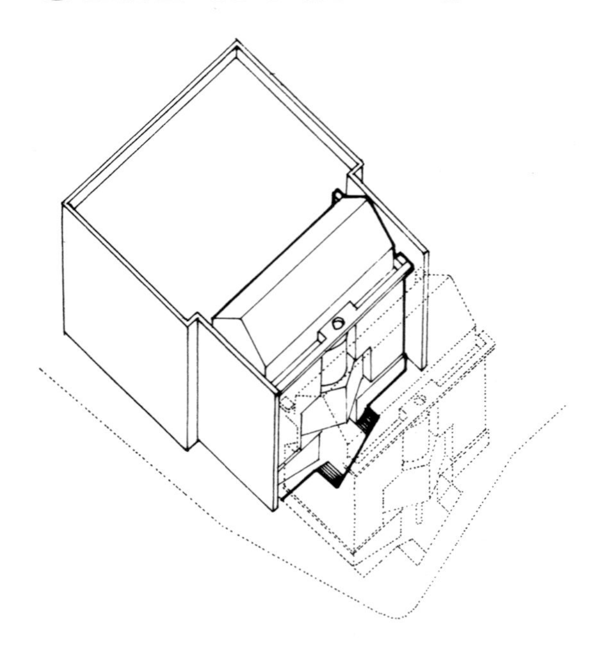

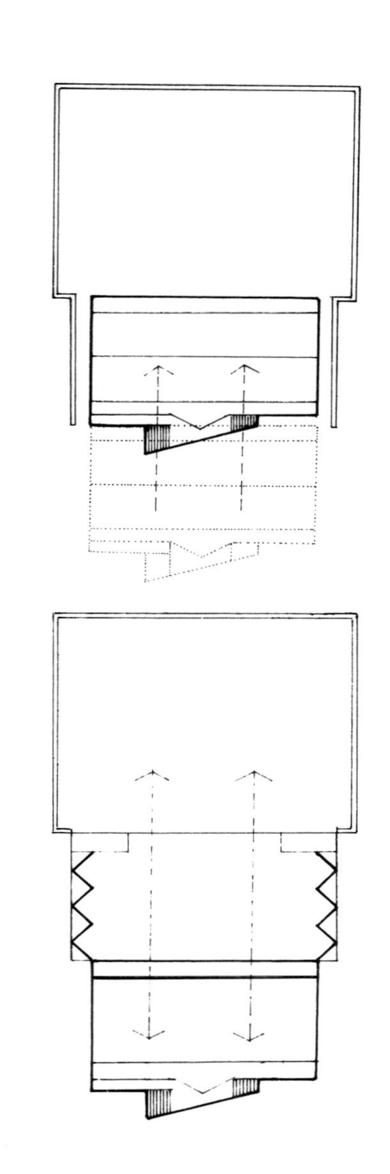

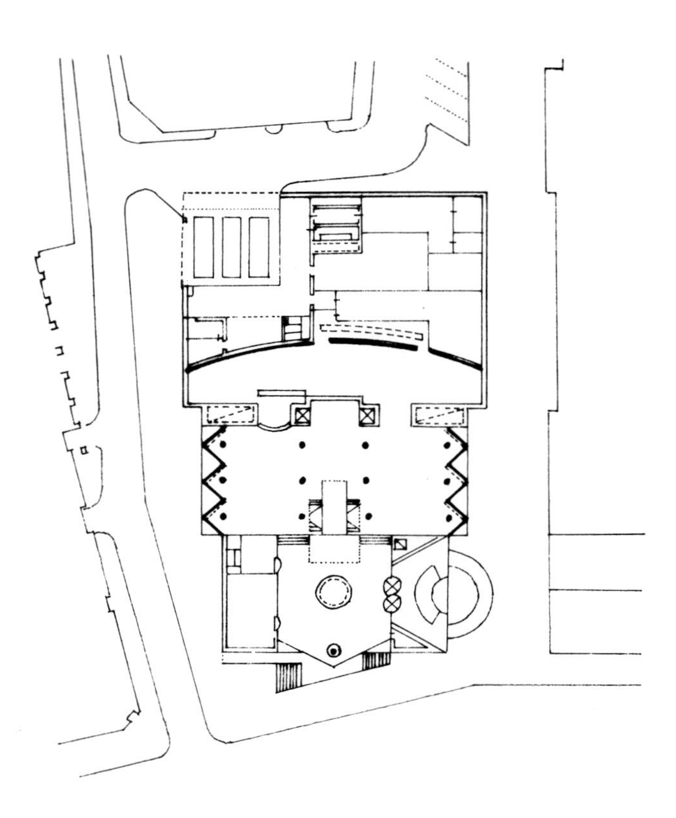

The echelon form may be read as three boxes, each capable of sliding into the one behind. As if in acknowledgement of this possibility the centre box has its edge in the form of a zig-zag at entry level, this 'concertina' allowing the forward pavilion to slide back into the main slab.

This sliding is held by the rows of columns in the foyer which pin the box in position. The columns continue down to the baseline below pavement level, their symmetry and shape signifying on the one hand circulation zones and on the other the structural principle of the building, which is to have a reinforced concrete frame and floor slabs with certain loads transmitted through columns.

The regular columnar rhythm of the foyer gives it a 'hypostyle hall' reading which combines order and formality with structural logic. Within a series of multivalent boxes the columns stabilize literally and metaphorically.

MOVEMENT AND STRUCTURE

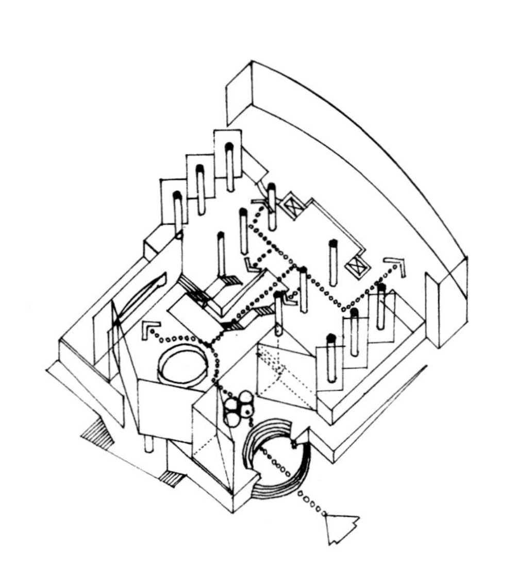

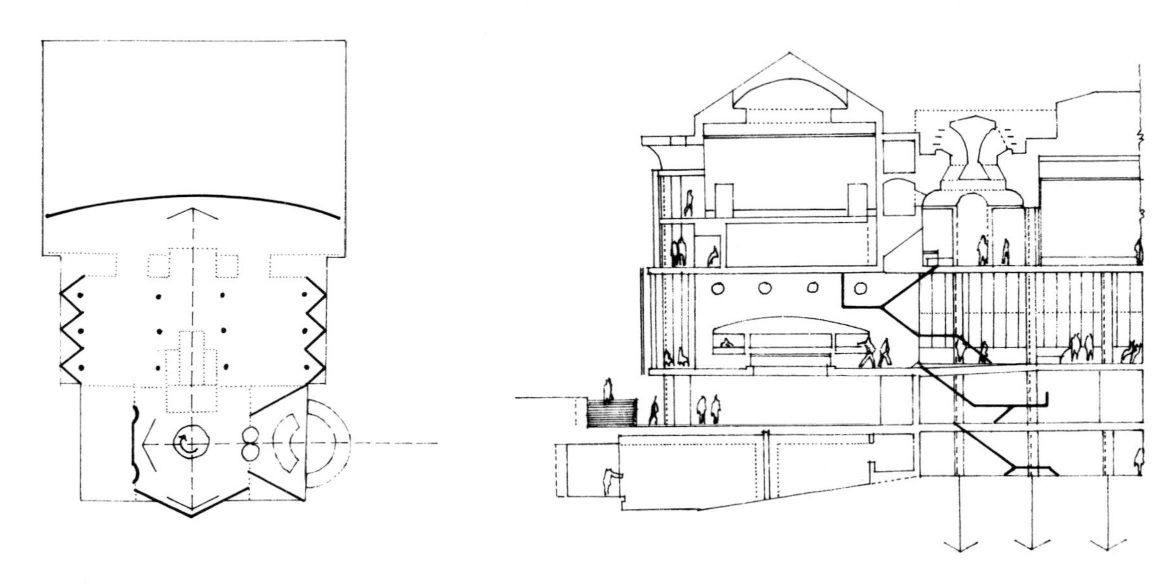

The movement progression from entry goes into a lobby towards a circular opening where the transverse and longitudinal axes meet. This sets in motion movement north along the axis into the transitional foyer zone leading towards the restaurant. From here movement dog-legs back again to the galleries above. The 'elasticity' of this zone signifies that it is a preparatory area at the centre of gravity of the configuration without a decisive directional or functional role. It mediates between back and front and, because of the stair location, between entry and gallery levels.

The stair is a major element, the main focal device of this spatial sequence, its central location and shape affirming the axis and its three dimensional and monumental presence identifying the movement route. By thrusting forward or back dependent on the main direction to be followed the stair becomes a vector of movement having considerable although muted energy. By its function it signifies not only its use but the predominant directional thrust of the building along the linear axis. The precise position of the stair enables it to move from box to box as appropriate, furthering the notion of interaction between the boxes. The movement axes create vistas which are appropriately terminated, the first by the cloaks, curved (in elevation); the second by the curve (in plan) of the restaurant wall. The finality of this restaurant wall signifies the end of movement and of the main circulation zone.

GALLERIES

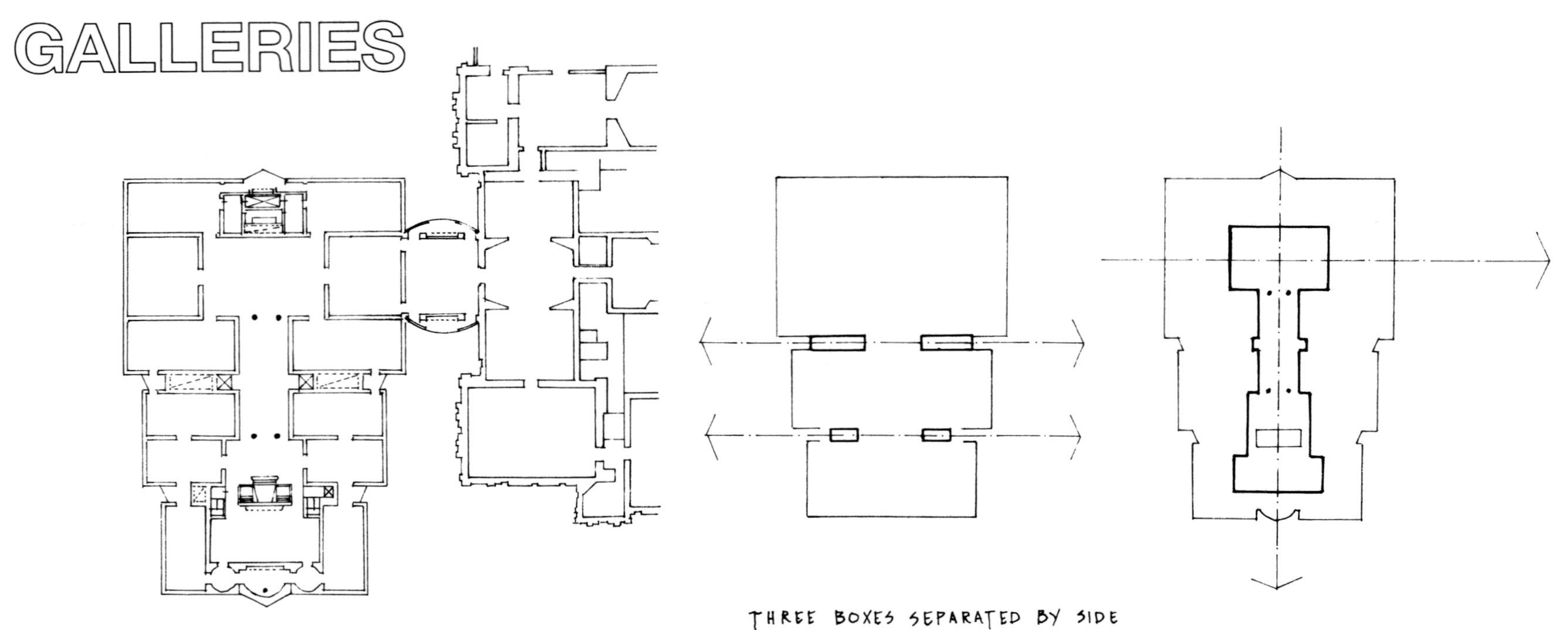

PLAN AT GALLERY LEVEL   NATIONAL GALLERY   THREE BOXES SEPARATED BY SIDE WINDOWS DUCTS AND LIFTS   CIRCULATION CORE

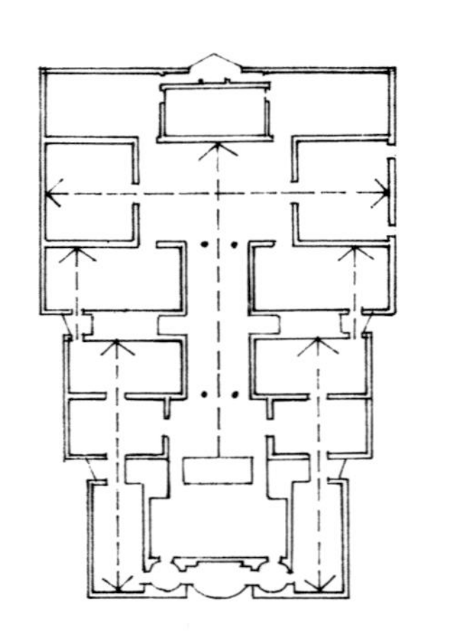

VISTAS IN GALLERIES

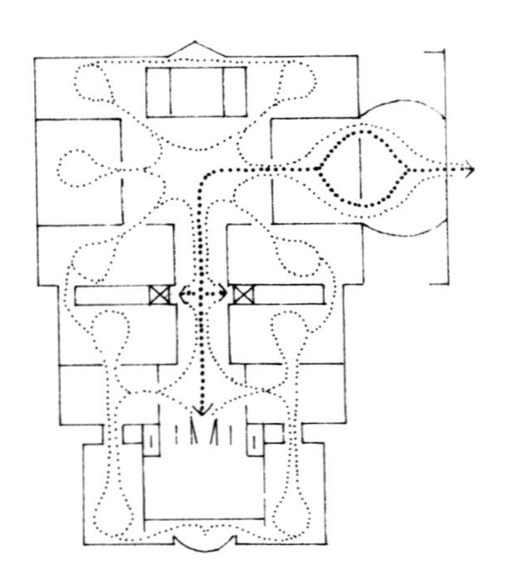

CIRCULATION ROUTES

Above, the gallery level takes over the upper section. This floor is bi-laterally symmetrical, being controlled by the dominant linear axis. This ensures a harmonious and serene disposition of gallèries with a series of vistas arranged on the linear axis.

The form is self-contained with each of the three boxes 'separated' by side windows, ducts and lifts. This containment excludes the link, placed as a separate element on the transverse axis (dominant longitudinal axis of the National Gallery). The separate reading of the link is furthered by the curved exterior, which signifies that this is a special independent zone, neither Gallery nor extension.

The exterior curve in the form of a bay signifies a calm and restful zone. Throughout the design the various zones have a shape intended to signify their use, as for example the rest zone of the circle at entry, the inward movement identified by canopy and wedge shape, the holding areas in the lobby and foyer, followed by the calm, contemplative dignity of the galleries, whose vistas encourage movement in a slow and reflective manner.

The configuration has a circulation core around which the galleries are placed. The shape of the core contrasts with the outer echelon in having its major zone to the north, reversing the general directional thrust of the pavilion. This 'holding' zone is, however, at a centre of gravity between extension and National Gallery, its size warranted by its location and role. Columns define the major spaces and reinforce the general bi-lateral symmetry and identify circulation zones.

LOWER LEVELS

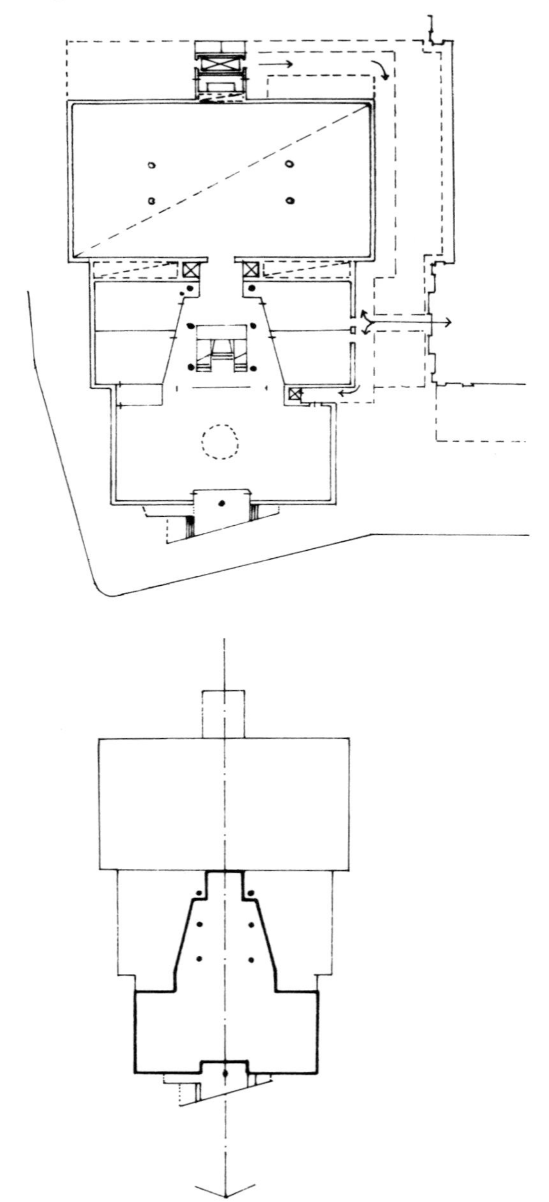

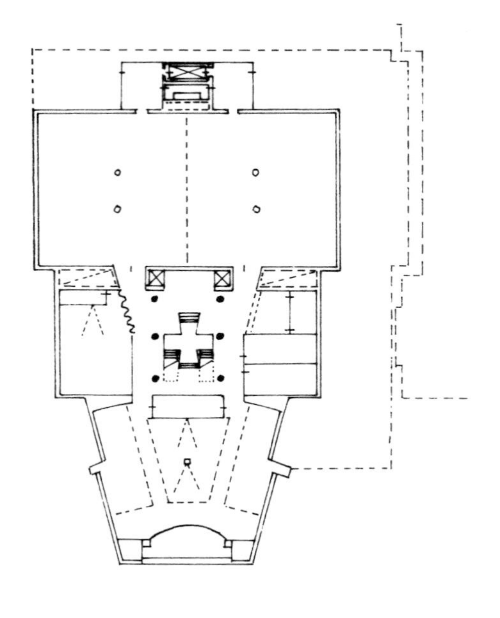

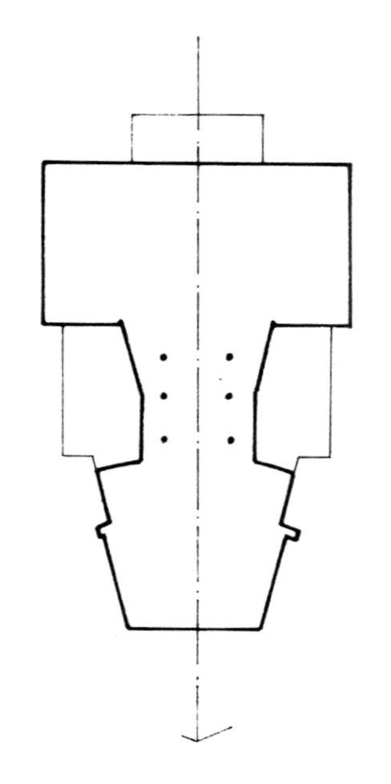

At shop level the three boxes are clearly defined with a wedge picking up the special quality of the central circulation zone, whilst at the lower level the fan shape of the auditorium gives a further interpretation of the echelon idea, the squeezing of the fan maintaining the forward thrust. At each level columns signify circulation zones.

SECTION

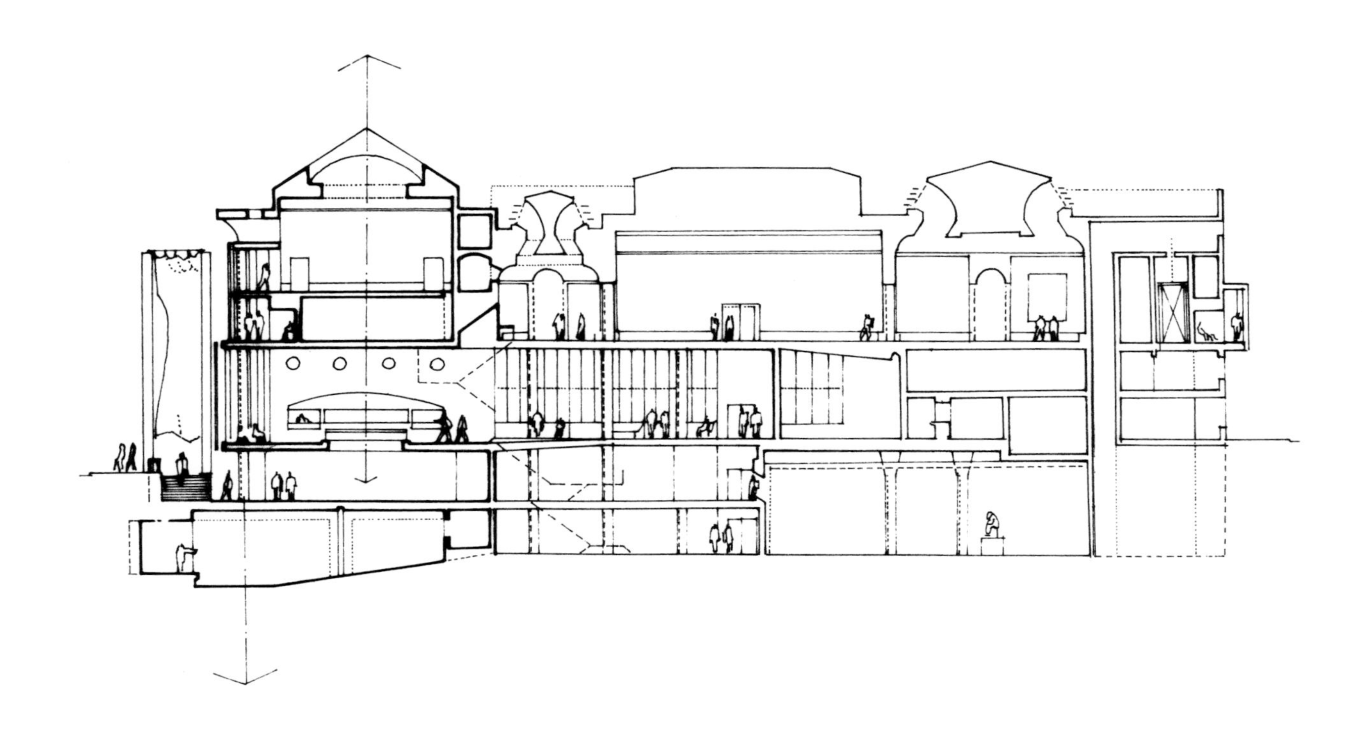

As seen in section, the forward pavilion has a vertical force, which is expressed externally by the ridge of the pitched roof and internally by the piling up of spaces (boardroom and information stacked at the top), with the circular opening in the entry lobby looking down to the shop. The column behind the glazed projections embodies the vertical emphasis within the pavilion.

LIGHTING

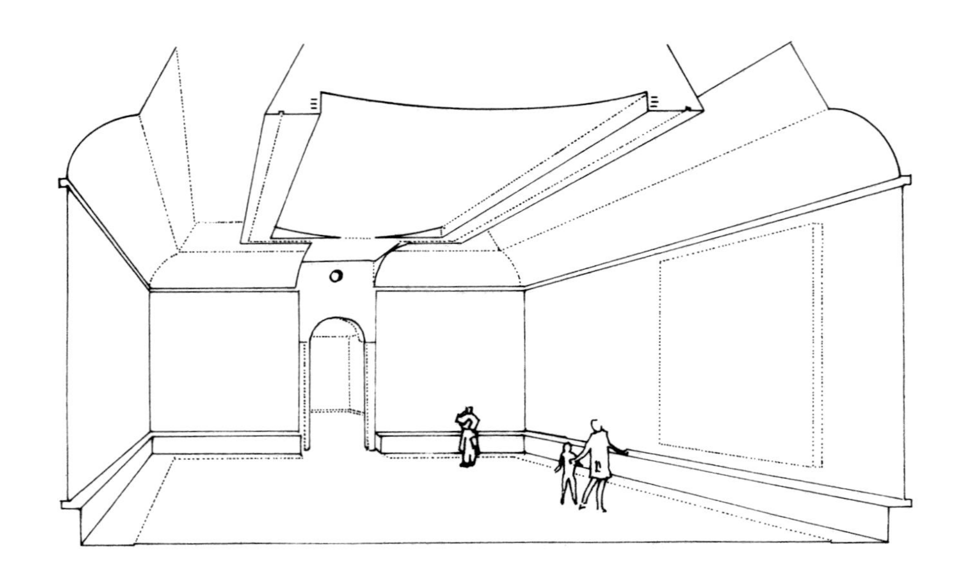

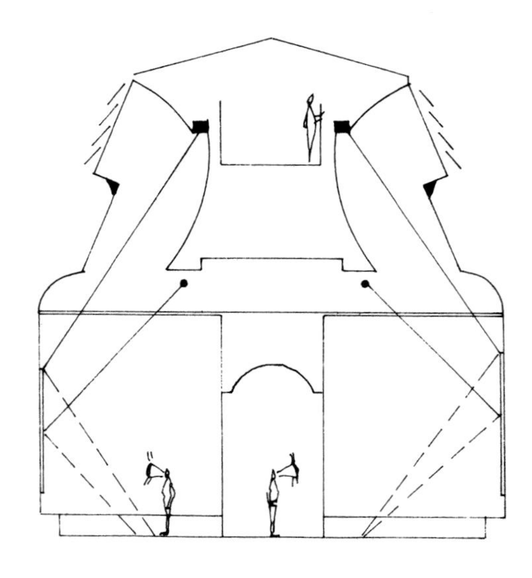

The lighting section for the galleries uses curves to give appropriate lighting and when combined with the use of curves inside the galleries, serves to give three-dimensional enrichment in a graceful manner, reinforcing the idea of dignity inherent in the gallery layout. The section also accommodates space for maintenance.

ROUTE AND BANNER

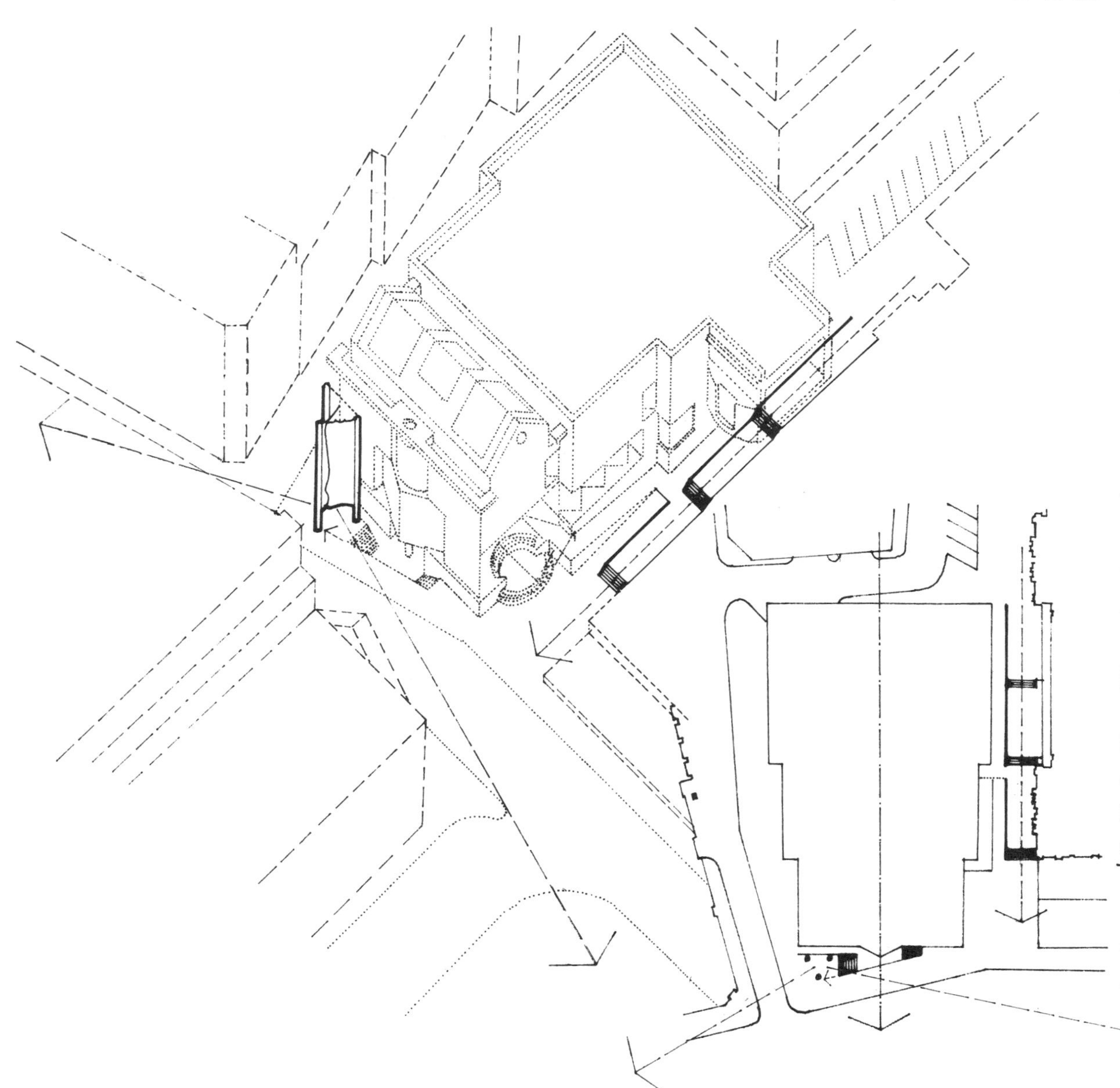

If the theme of the work is to exploit the configurational opportunities provided by the laterally thrusting forward pavilion within an overall linear echelon, the route under the link alongside the National Gallery ensures the primacy of the linear reading. Placed alongside the vigorous articulation of the masses this route is a calm, regular, absolutely straight movement vector whose slow pace does not diminish the significance of its role. Its serenity, cascading horizontality and strength of purpose gives it a vital position of contrast within the ensemble. In this, it echoes the dignity of the whole composition and particularly the gallery level of the extension, being similarly calm and yet assertive in a very low key manner.

The horizontal linearity and flat permanency of the route under the link alongside the National Gallery contrasts with the vertical fragility and transience of the banner at the southwest corner. But, as with the route, functional purpose is exploited to enhance the totality. The vitality of this triangular feature gives a visual link that is multi-directional and also by its 'scaffolding' and 'blowing in the wind' formation, contrasts effectively with the solidity of the extension. This addition is a far more satisfactory response to the wedge-shaped corner than the distortion of the forward mass as seen in Scheme C.

The banner strengthens a corner which is exposed by the wedge shape at this part of the site, its triangular shape on plan extending the play of obliques in the design established by the roof pitch, the projecting glazed membrane at entry, the edge to the stairs down to the shop at pavement level and by the wedge shaped walls at entry.

DEVELOPED DESIGN

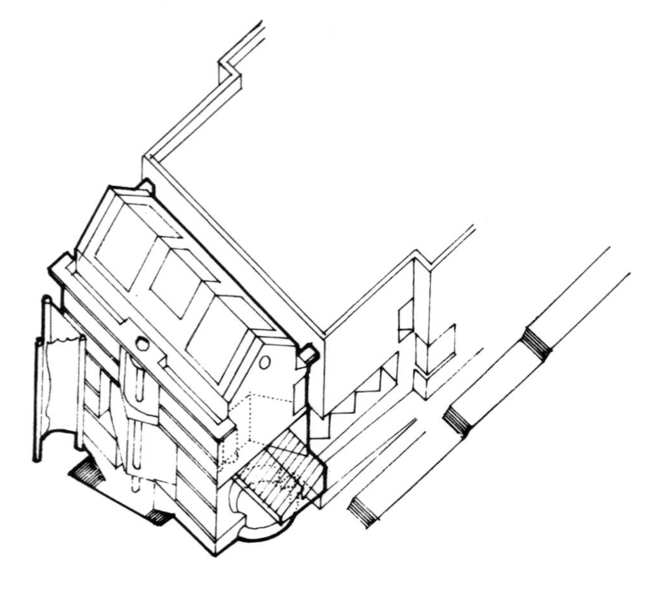

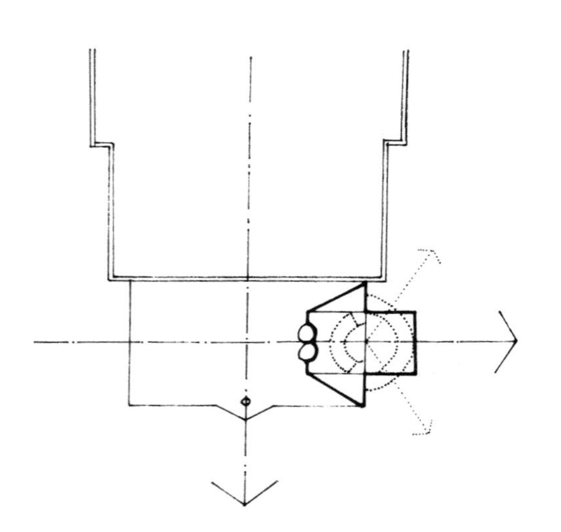

INITIAL DESIGN

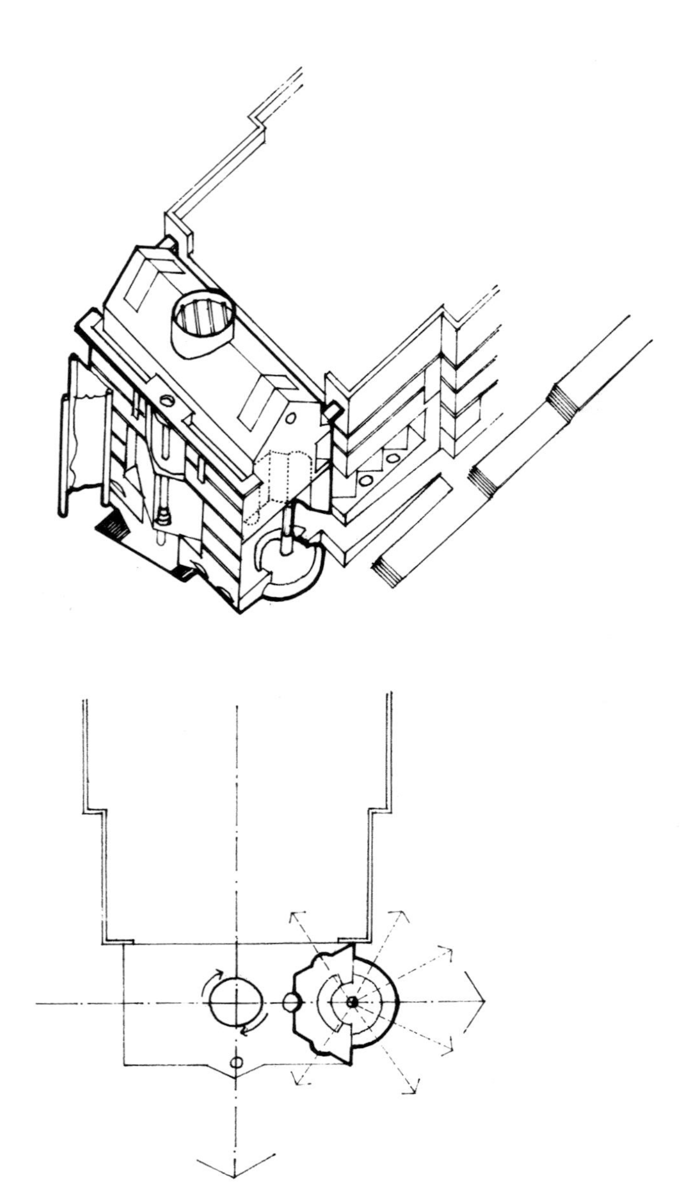

DEVELOPED DESIGN

MASS EXPLODES

There are two main changes to the design as first submitted. First and most significant is the addition of the central drum to the pavilion. This is intended to give additional weight so that the extension may more happily balance with its opposite number, St. Martin-in-the-fields.

Second, the entrance configuration is no longer wedge-shaped with canopies. Instead, the circular 'stage' has been reinforced by curves which now extend into the walls at each side of entry, and the centre is marked by a single column.

This use of the circle, in the form of a cylinder in the centre of the pavilion and reinforcement of the circular 'stage', has several consequences which materially affect the design. The central cylinder reduces the linearity of the pavilion, giving it a pronounced centroidality which, when coupled with the stone cladding to drum and pitched roof, increases the sense of mass.

The way the drum pierces the obliques of the roof with its potential to revolve strongly reinforces the central piercing of the south facade by the glazed membranes.

Just as the mass is pulled out to accommodate this, so too does the mass now explode through the roof, so that, as on the facade, the internal is externalized - the drum lights the boardroom and signifies its importance, the membranes also express internal roles and the upper curved bay and drum 'communicate' with each other.

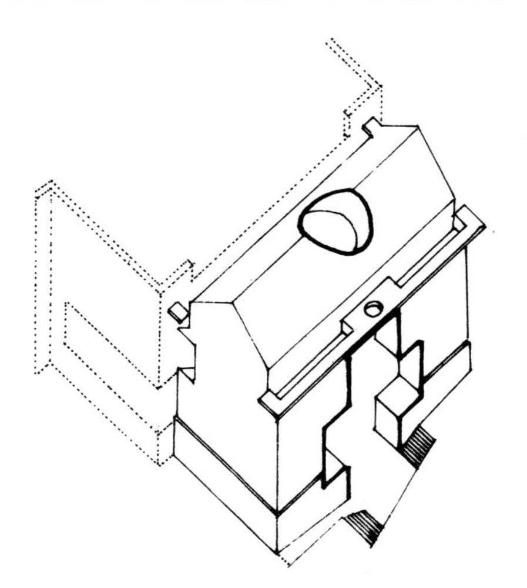

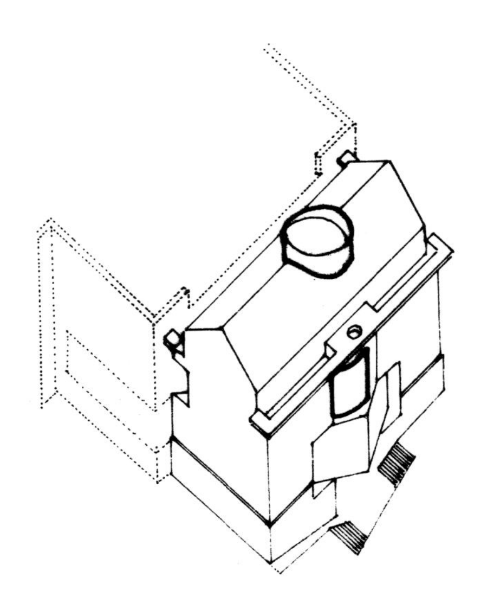

PAVILLION TO PALAZZO

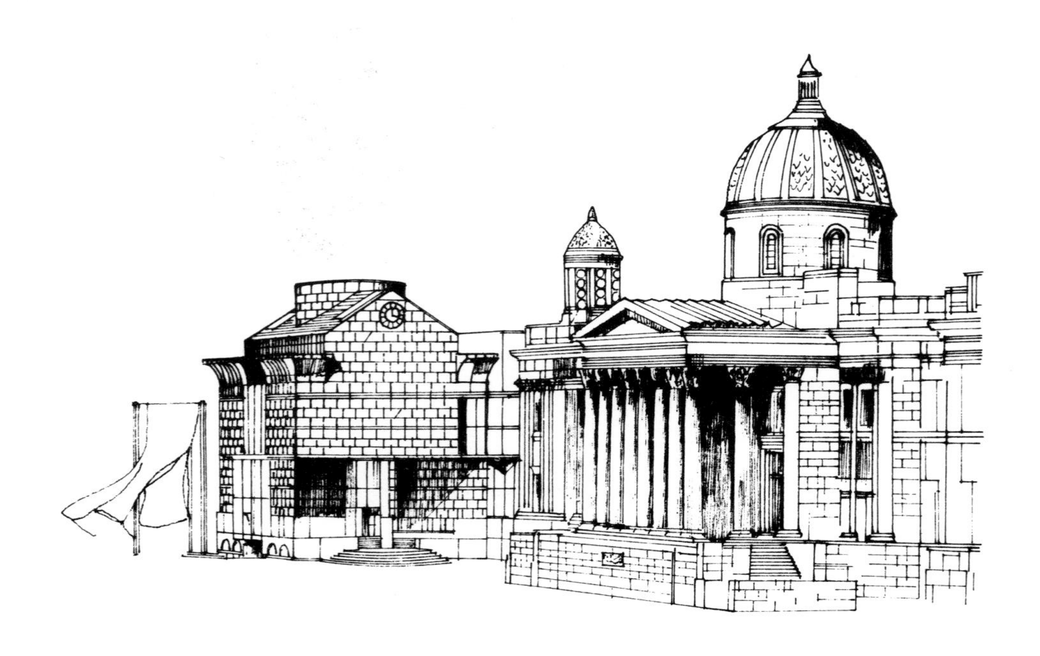

Although the mass is pierced so vigorously, it is strong enough to resist, and its stability is not threatened in any way, so that, on the contrary, the central addition adds power as does the juxtaposition of drum and portico on the National Gallery.

Despite the absence of a dome, the drum to the extension establishes a resonance with the National Gallery, the contradiction of the absent dome furthering the series of allusions already operating in the pavilion.

The change in character from the earlier proposal is a dramatic exploitation of the focal point where lateral and longitudinal axes meet, increasing both the monumentality and sense of historical association. The plugging of this focus changes the image decisively from pavilion to palazzo — always the architects' intention, but now confirmed.

SEATON DELAVEL NORTHUMBERLAND

The total cladding of stone with the rich surface pattern of joints and heavy cornice has a sense of compact power reminiscent of Vanbrugh's Seaton Delavel, similarly a piled up sculpted mass with considerable theatrical content, being similarly animated and full of incident.

There is also a similarity with Mastro Jacopo's S Maria dei Miracoli at Brescia, in which the drum is placed behind the plane of the main facade, itself symmetrical and with a central forward thrust developed flamboyantly at cornice level with a series of semi-circular arches. The composition is held by the twin doorways at either side and by the strength of the central elements including the drum, the potency of this configuration being due to the close juxtaposition of drum and facade plane (each contrasting elements) with the stability of the drum permitting liberties on the facade.

S MARIA DEI MIRACOLI BRESCIA

STAATSGALERIE, STUTTGART

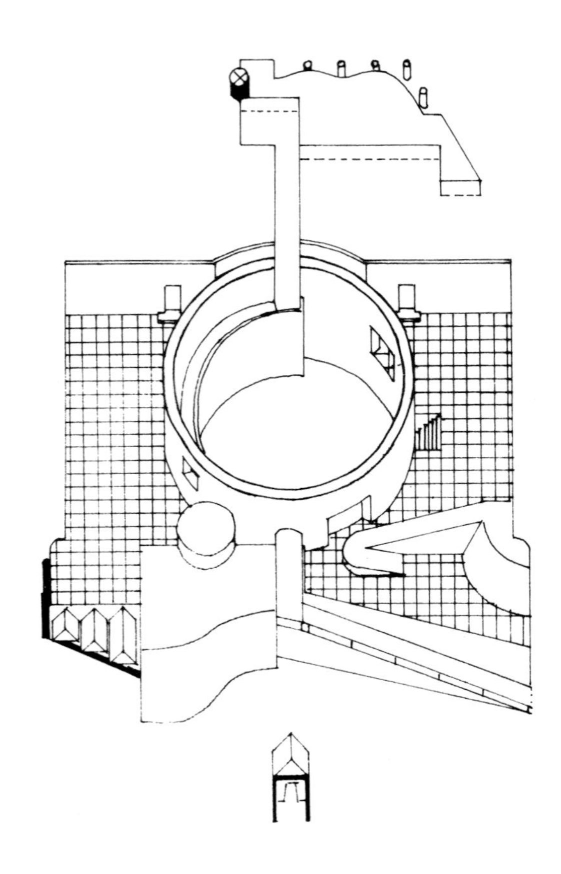

STAATSGALERIE STUTTGART

This is not dissimilar to the way the central drum of the Staatsgalerie at Stuttgart allows Stirling and Wilford to manipulate the forms immediately in front of it. The potential of a drum to 'turn' gives the form in all these examples of its usage a double reading; it is both static and dynamic, stable and yet mobile.

DRUMS AND VISTA

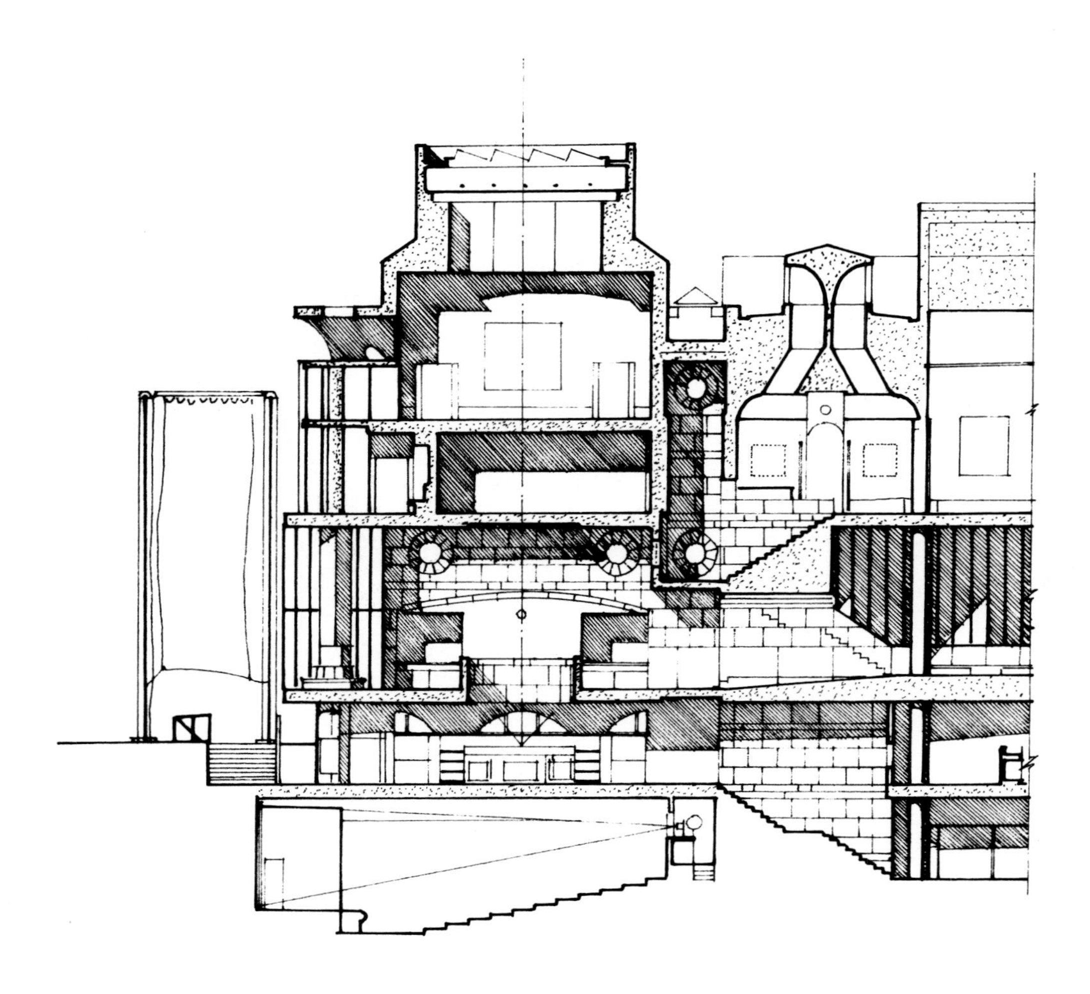

LONGITUDINAL SECTION

DRUMS

The cylindrical penetration of the mass at roof level continues with the cylindrical drum of the hole looking down from entry level to the counter of the shop, this stopping the downward thrust.

VISTA

On gaining entry, the vista is stopped with greater moment by the treatment of the facing wall containing the cloaks. This becomes unambiguously bi-laterally symmetrical with the positioning of the twin rectilinear counter openings below the curve, and with circular openings above each.

SCULPTED FORMS AND SPACES

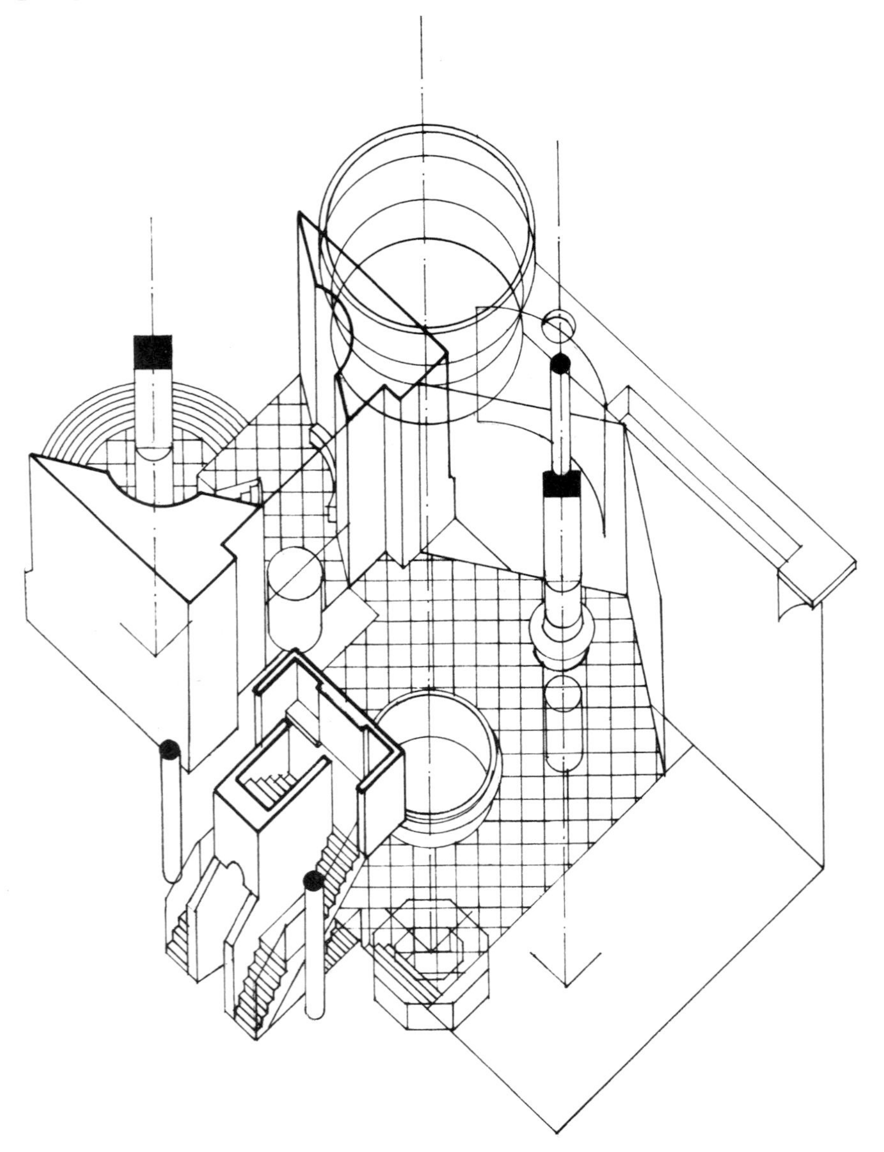

This weighty penetration of the mass by cylindrical voids is echoed and contrasted by the piercing of the floors by the forward central column behind the glazed membranes. This seizes the opportunity present in the submitted Scheme A, but extends the idea into several further dimensions.

At the top the column is now directly below the hole in the cornice, and is slender and cylindrical. It changes at entry level to become square in plan, but turned so that the four edges of the square are most apparent; this sits on a cylindrical base up to plinth level comprising a drum surrounded by seats and concludes at shop level with a sturdy stone-clad cylinder.

The turned square column slots into the diagonal floor pattern at entry level which, along with the circular drum, signifies a holding zone. The metamorphosis of the column, changing to respond to each activity zone – simple elegant cylinder/tranquil galleries – turned square and 'rotating' seats/active entry zone – sturdy, structurally 'functional' cylinder/below ground, holding everything up – is typical of the design philosophy in which the potential of each element is exploited as a demonstration of sculptural and evocative virtuosity.

ENTRY

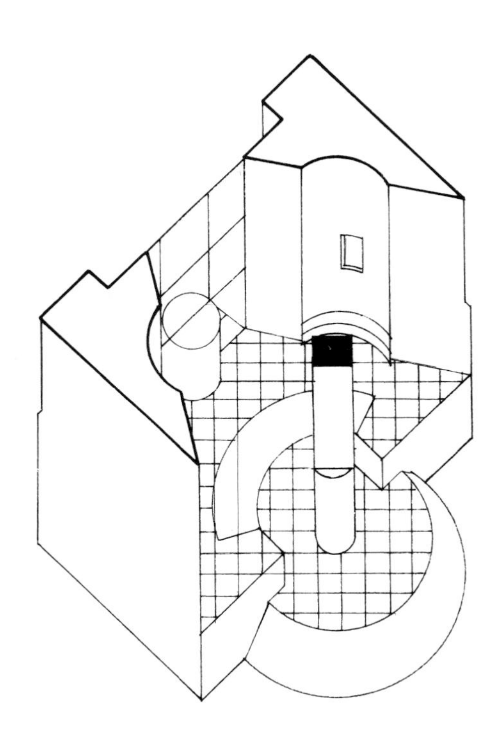

A similar development occurs at the entry point where a column acts as a central focus for the circular 'stage'. This also changes from having a cylindrical base to having a turned square plan above, which in combination with the revolving/static 'stage' has both rotational and stable readings.

The isolation of the column and its multifaceted profile remains consistent with the way the extension seeks to mediate between the two worlds of the program. In all the nearby Neo-classical buildings, the column is eloquently expressive. The porticos by Smirke Wilkins and Gibbs each speak symbolically of entry by reference to Greek and Roman, using base, fluting and capitals to make their point. Within their rectilinear portico format they each enframe views outwards.

Similarly, within a circular format, Stirling and Wilford's column makes its own statement of entry and is consistent to its circular geometric frame, in its singularity perhaps referring to another column in Trafalgar Square.

The central location of a single column also delineates the axis of the palazzo in a way which necessitates not two but one cylindrical entry point, with a consequent funnelling of movement into a potential bottleneck.

Niches on the side walls amplify the curvilinear theme and inset windows reinforce the bi-lateral symmetry. The cylindrical base is up to plinth level, the turned square column locking into the diagonal floor plan of the initial holding zone.

WEST ELEVATION

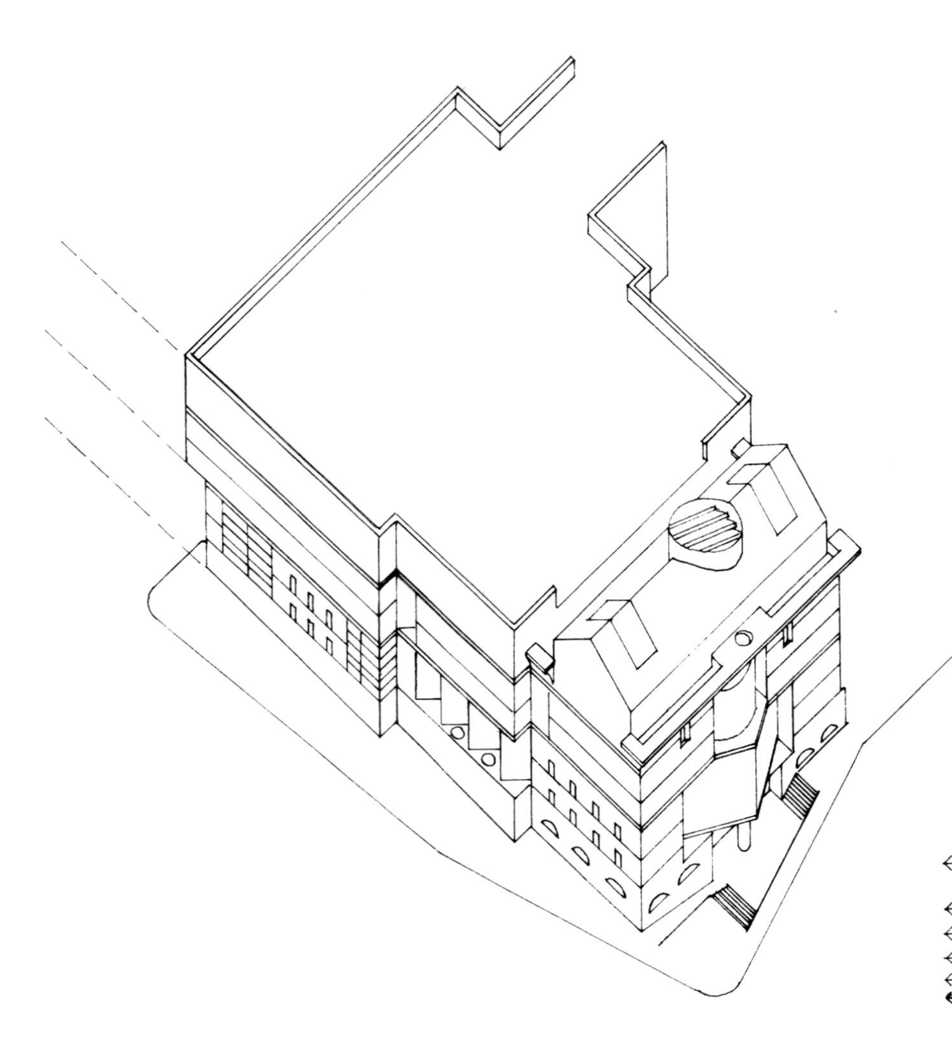

The palazzo now forms part of a more homogeneous whole by virtue of a continuation of the incised courses along the rest of the configuration, although the rear boxes are not stone-clad. The pulling/pushing movement has gone as the design has become more static and monumental. The Modern Movement functional overtones recede as the ensemble concentrates instead on harmony and 'commodity'

Yet there are echoes of Modernism with the horizontal stretched windows in the rear box, which contrast with the insistent vertical rhythm of three pairs of inset windows. The symmetry of this group slows down the prevailing horizontality and increases the mass reading. Similarly four pairs of windows set up a symmetrical rhythm on the palazzo, this being supported by the three semi-circular basement windows. These devices encourage an independent reading of the palazzo. As in the first submission the elevation can be divided into a calm upper and an animated lower zone, the latter now containing a considerable variety of fenestration.

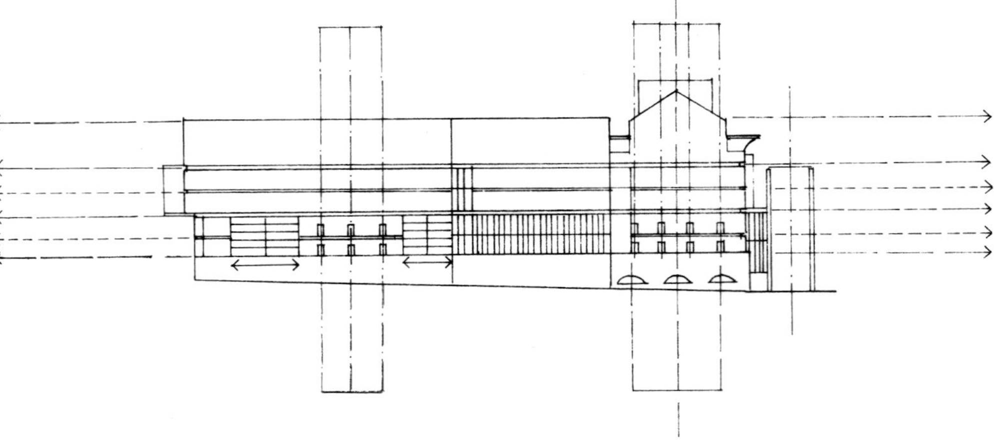

SOUTH ELEVATION

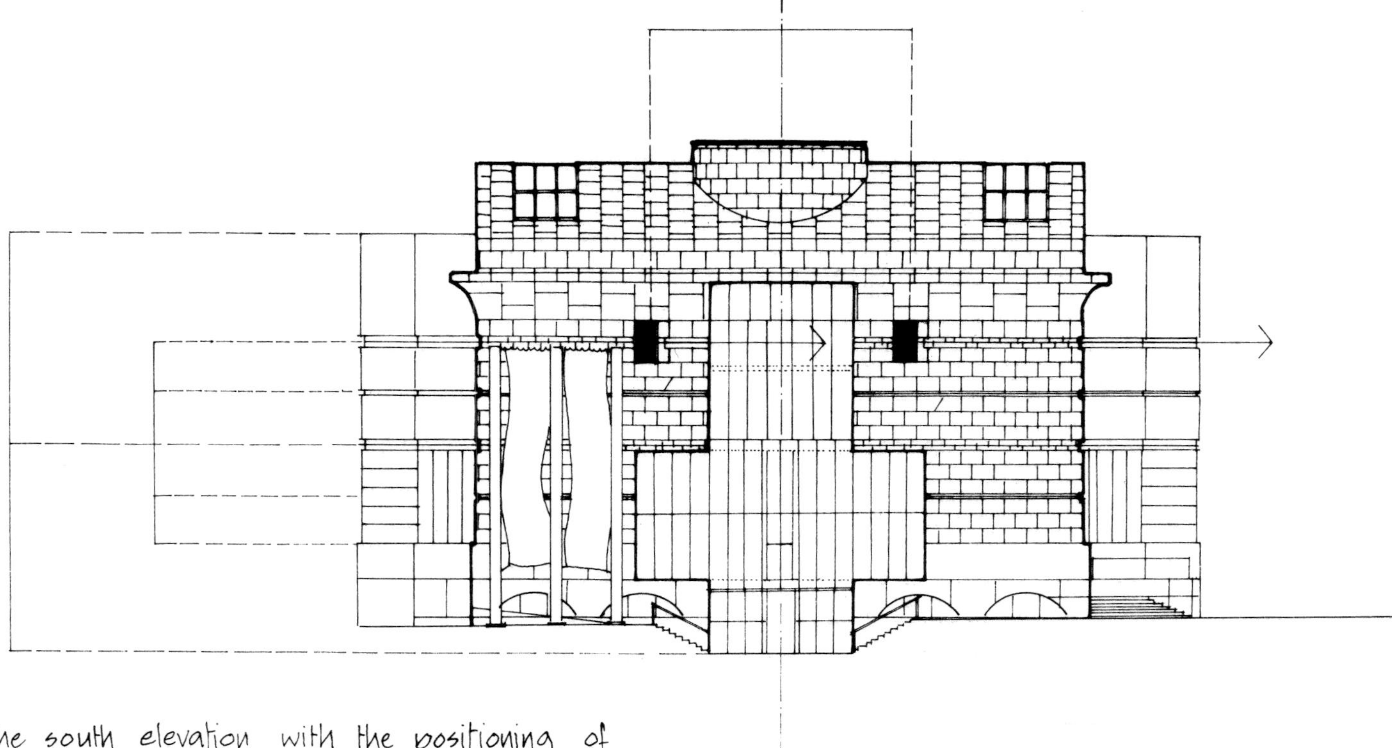

Something similar happens on the south elevation with the positioning of twin rectilinear windows on each side of the central gallery bay. These light the boardroom suite and also by their alignment point towards Trafalgar Square. As with any small opening in a mass they increase rather than diminish the mass statement.

The arcuated basement windows are more subdued than in the first submission and now without keystones, their curvilinear rhythm enriching the plinth, now raised to match that of the National Gallery. The external profile of the building increases the sense of plasticity and when combined with the surface treatment enriches the form.

DESIGN STRATEGY

In any important city centre location, the greatest architectural problem lies in the external image which a building presents. By comparison, the interior is easy; modern architecture has won many advantages over Neo-classical in the organization of circulation and space, the provision of effective lighting and the elimination of pretentiousness and monotony. But the outside remains a problem; the Modern Movement and its successors have not yet convincingly managed to emulate the architecture of previous periods in giving an appropriate cultural identity for major works in historic locations.

Stirling and Wilford have attacked this problem, chiselling out a plan profile for their extension which picks up the outline of the National Gallery, pushing a pavilion forward which fulfils a similar role to the portico of its neighbour whilst managing to project a friendly face towards Trafalgar Square as inviting in its message as its portico but without its overblown cultural implications. The pavilion also stops Wilkins' long facade at its west end in a similar manner to the way St Martin-in-the Fields stops the east end.

A favorite device in London's Neo-classical buildings is the use of deeply recessed coursework in stone. This gives scale, increases the impression of mass and, as part of the classical language, has an inbuilt authority which gives that sense of importance so appropriate in a capital city. This is not copied but is alluded to in the Stirling Wilford extension in a way which sets up a similar mass reading but, by the wide separation of the courses, establishes an undisputed contemporary identity for the building.

This is typical of the design strategy in which, throughout, Stirling and Wilford play a subtle game of cross-reference between the extension and its neighbour, and thereby between past and present, reinforcing key items in the National Gallery such as the need to provide serene and dignified galleries, but enhancing the external modelling by its bag of twentieth-century tricks which include penetration of the box, exploitation of contrasts between mass and plane, geometrical transformations and distortions, a pediment in a kind of metamorphosis, not to mention a series of allusions and metaphors, some direct, some indirect, to its neighbour, to art and to creativity.

But all this is done within a framework of formality; plans and sections exhibit strict geometrical control, observing those correct principles of classical architecture which insist on the establishment of a carefully controlled movement sequence based on the vista and modulated by an observance of axes and by a studied disposition of elements.

In their more recent work the **Stirling Wilford** partnership in common with the **Post-Modern** movement has been exploring the possibilities of mass and surface with the intention of communicating with a wider audience. Their approach has reversed several Modern Movement canons as the late twentieth-century mood swings towards a more romantic range of expression.

Where the Moderns gave structure an almost moral role central to the logic of the program, this now changes so that columns, for example, express a multitude of meanings. Where symmetry was usually avoided it is now exploited. Often entrances were played down, now they can be celebrated. Where the Modernists used geometry as an overriding discipline, this is now sublimated to serve rather than control. From the harsh Constructivist geometry of Stirling's early works and the inherent hostility apparent in the search for consistency in a pure but limited design sense, the expressive range now extends towards form and surface seen psychologically as friendly or serene and having a capacity to endure.

Stirling and Wilford now part company from Post-Modern clichés in the seriousness with which they draw from source. Their statements are not platitudinous, but instead seek as did the Victorians, to use history in an appropriate way, mixing traditional forms such as the drum with late twentieth-century geometrical freedom.

Colin St. John Wilson has argued that architecture is born of use, and that it invents forms that 'celebrate a way of life', insisting that the message of the work must be recognizable in an intelligent way. The integrity of the Stirling Wilford proposal resides in the way the geometrical organization and modelling of the form respond to the precise needs of the building in both a functional and symbolic sense. The galleries are tranquil receptacles for works of art; the circulation has a subdued grandeur which is consistent with the syntax of the general arrangement in which forms and spaces convincingly explain themselves. The design, like that of the National Gallery, is rather low-key but with a dynamism and freshness of spirit which seek to provide a civilized and unpretentious ambience for the viewing experience.

POST SCRIPTUM

My favourite architect or designer is, I suspect, the same as most peoples... 'Anon.' He – (seldom I fear 'she') – is historically the designer/builder of fishing boats and hay-barns, lock-keeper's cottages and farm gates, terrace housing, harbour walls, tiny village churches, warehouses, Welsh village chapels and huts for permanent-way inspectors – each one a product of necessity and of contemporary technology and not one is pretentious, wilful or witty'...

Why were they so good? First they sprang from the necessity to fulfil a simple need. Secondly, they were built often by people on the spot from the few skills and materials locally available – brick, stone and timber. They lasted well and aged gracefully. Thirdly, they obeyed Ruskin's precept – (though few had heard of him) that art is craft and if you begin your work by seeking 'beauty' in inverted commas it will almost certainly evade you.[1]

These observations by Sir Hugh Casson highlight the way architecture is born of necessity, and remind us that the symbolic messages conveyed by such devices as pitched roofs, chimneys or bay windows have conviction because they work so well.

But this architecture of anonymous craftsmen, informed by realities of cost, site and climate, itself may draw on the imaginative creativity of High Art. When Andrea Palladio evolved his Renaissance formula for good building, using the orders, temple pediments and principles drawn from Vitruvius via Serlio, he offered an architectural language that satisfied a broad spectrum of public needs.

[1] Sir Hugh Casson, 'In praise of the house that Anon. built.' The Weekend Guardian, December 24-25 1988

POST SCRIPTUM

As interpreted by Inigo Jones in what became known as the Georgian style, this architecture of good sense and good proportions, with legible communicative motifs in the form of windows and doorways became a large part of the city of London and was exported to the colonies.

The style could be practised on many levels, being concerned with those essential human requirements of humble use and social status. The versatility of the language was properly democratic in allowing a modest or grand expression dependent on income and circumstances. This architecture of expediency and imagination possessed enormous authority in its capacity to encompass practical and symbolic social needs with a surprising range of emotional content ranging from simple charm to elegant pomposity.

Such ordinary dwellings as the Georgian house characterize the idea of fellowship in the community with a certain conformity of design. But as Norberg-Schulz suggests, this is only an indirect expression of fellowship and ideas such as that of community must find expression in monumental architecture, that is, in solutions which manifest those values which are basic to the cultural milieu.[1]

Only special buildings can do this, and it is this monumental architecture in towns and cities, the town halls, churches, libraries and so on, that convincingly demonstrate that an organised community exists. These major public buildings symbolize the collective ideals of a culture and it may be as Norberg Schulz suggests, that it is because they are more complicated than ordinary dwellings, that they are able to transcend purely practical limitations and express the abstract ideals of society. It would not be possible, for example to express an idea such as that of

[1] C. Norberg Schulz, Existence, Space and Architecture, London, 1971, p. 155.

parliamentary democracy other than by a building of some substance not only in scale but also in 'content.' This is the preserve of the architect and the challenge he must face when designing any public building.

In this book I have attempted to identify those issues with which architecture is concerned in a discussion which has ranged from cultural symbolism to the inherent energy in design. An analytical technique has been outlined showing how it is possible to unravel the complexities of a city fabric or major work of architecture. In so doing I have tried to show how particular design strategies have been formulated to enable architects to address problems in terms of their purpose, their siting and their cultural role.

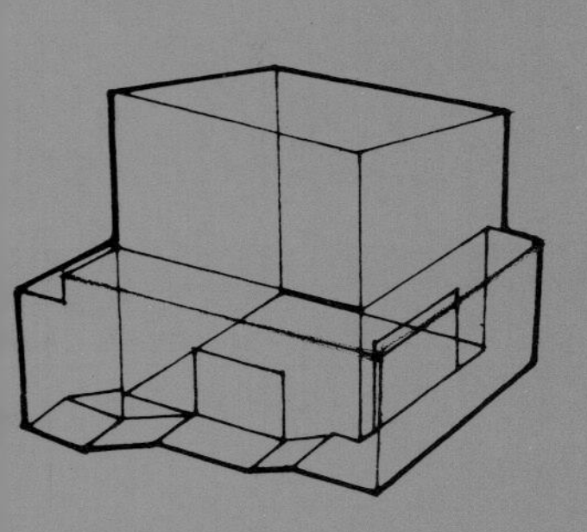

Modern architecture has become extremely complex, and its study has been made more difficult by the changes in fashion, the proliferation of competing styles and related design aesthetics.

Geoffrey Baker, author of an acclaimed review of the architecture of Le Corbusier, develops in this book a methodology for design analysis that reveals the underlying organisation of buildings.

Part One of the book explains the nature and role of architecture by reference to the work of contemporary theorists. This background establishes the importance of key design issues in a wide-ranging discussion extending from geometry to symbolism. Part Two demonstrates the methodology through a series of analyses which cover cities and individual architectural works of modern masters such as Aalto, Meier and Stirling.

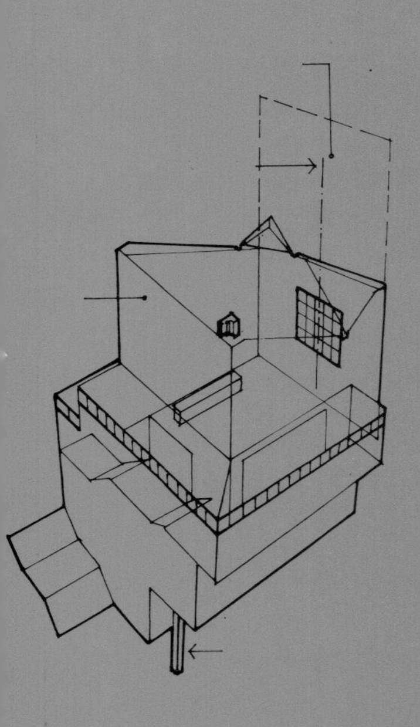

Throughout the book the author's use of three dimensional diagrams and detailed illustrations makes his message clear and accessible. Architectural students will find this an invaluable aid to their understanding of the most sophisticated and complex works of architecture.

The author trained as an architect at Manchester University. Since 1964 he has taught architectural design, history and theory at the University of Newcastle-upon-Tyne and in 1976 was appointed Reader to the School of Architecture and Interior Design, Brighton Polytechnic where he has directed research into design strategies and techniques. His publications include monographs on Frank Lloyd Wright and Le Corbusier and articles specializing in the analysis of works by leading contemporary architects. He has served as a visiting professor and programme director to the University of Arkansas School of Architecture, has been a visiting professor to Queen's University Belfast and acted as a visiting critic at the University of Sheffield. He has lectured extensively in Britain, the United States, Australia and the Far East and is currently teaching analysis and design at Tulane University, New Orleans.

Van Nostrand
Reinhold
(International)
11 New Fetter Lane
London EC4P 4EE

ISBN 0-7476-0041-4

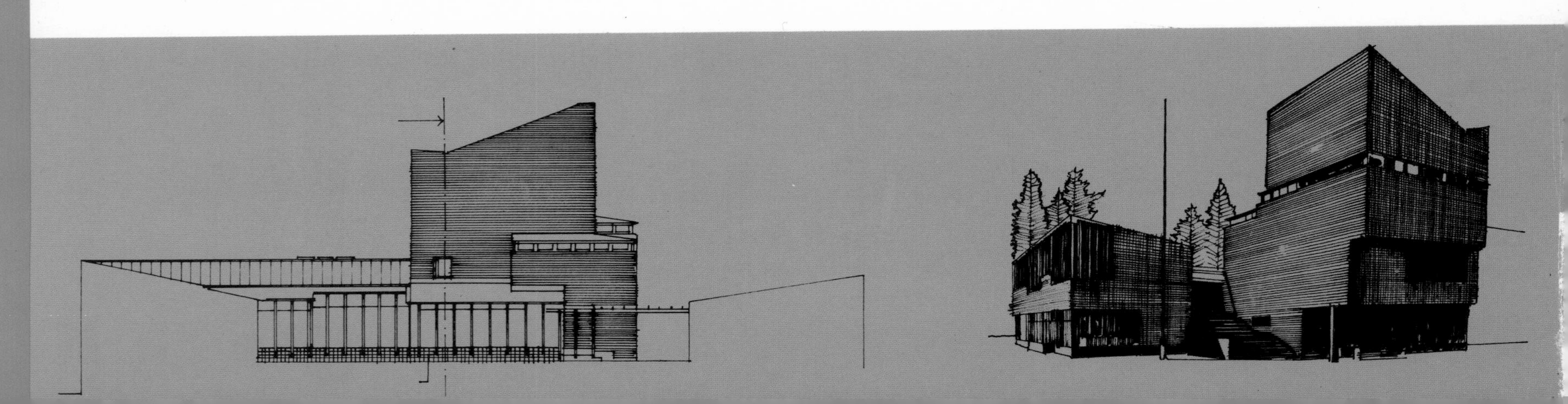